INTERPERSONAL
BEHAVIOR

INTERPERSONAL BEHAVIOR

HARRY C. TRIANDIS
University of Illinois at Urbana-Champaign

BROOKS/COLE PUBLISHING COMPANY
Monterey, California
A Division of Wadsworth Publishing Company, Inc.

ISBN: 0-8185-0188-X
L.C. Catalog Card No.: 76-14005
Printed in the United States of America

10 9 8 7 6 5 4 3 2 1

Production Editor: *Valerie Daigen*
Interior & Cover Design: *John Edeen*
Illustrations: *Charley Watkins*

This book is dedicated to W. W. Lambert, T. A. Ryan, and W. F. Whyte of Cornell University, who started me wondering about the determinants of behavioral intentions a quarter of a century ago, and to the many colleagues and students at the University of Illinois who helped me think through the puzzle. These include in particular John Adamopoulos, Icek Ajzen, Dave Brinberg, Gerald Clore, Andy Davidson, Don Dulany, Fred Fiedler, Marty Fishbein, Uriel Foa, Ivan Steiner, and Ledyard Tucker.

PREFACE

In this book I have sought to achieve two goals: to summarize the literature on interpersonal behavior, so that students of social psychology can have convenient access to it, and to present a particular theoretical framework that is useful in the study of interpersonal behavior. My hope is that this framework will prove productive in redirecting the field of social psychology by showing how cross-cultural and experimental data can be interwoven to increase our understanding of social behavior.

This text is particularly suitable for undergraduate courses concerned with social behavior, such as courses in social perception, social motivation, social learning, interpersonal behavior, and social-behavior change. It will also be useful for courses in introductory social psychology, if it is used together with texts that cover attitudes, group behavior, and other subfields of social psychology. The graduate student and the professional in behavioral science will find the book helpful when reviewing the field, when thinking about new hypotheses, or when preparing research proposals.

My theoretical framework is a conscious wedding of recent behaviorist formulations and cognitive psychology. To explain social behavior, I use the concepts *habit* and *behavioral intentions,* which have been widely used by learning theorists on the one hand and cognitive psychologists on the other. The framework allows us to specify the conditions under which one or the other of these factors will control behavior. For instance, I see behavioral intentions as determined by (1) social cognitions, such as roles, norms, the self-concept, and interpersonal agreements, (2) the emotions that are attached to the thoughts associated with a behavior, and (3) the value of the perceived consequences of the behavior.

The essence of my argument is that, for new, still unlearned social behaviors, the cognitive psychologist has the best answers; that is, the *behavioral intention* component prevails in the determination of behavior. But, once the behavior has taken place many times and has been rewarded or punished, the behavior becomes automatic, and we can understand it best by looking at the frequency of rewards, the amount of time between the behavior and the reward, and so on; in other words, the *habit* component is more relevant. Since most social behavior is not overlearned, the self-monitoring mechanisms are more important than the Skinnerian mechanisms, although this is not true for certain social behaviors, such as touching, looking at, smiling at, and getting close to another.

As I looked at the theoretical battles in the psychological literature, I was often impressed by the fact that the battles were not real confrontations but simply examples of people talking past each other. Most often it is not the case that one theoretical framework is right and another wrong but rather that, for some social behaviors, under particular conditions, one theory predicts behavior better than another, while, for other behaviors or other circumstances, another theory can be verified. When some phenomenon emerges that one theory had not predicted, clever theorists manage to stretch their theory to fit the phenomenon. Such stretching is necessary when the theory is incomplete. It is my hope that the framework presented in this book is complete and sufficiently flexible to account for most social behavior. The view that I propose challenges the generality of behaviorist and cognitive explanations but unifies the field by specifying some of the conditions under which one or the other of the explanations is likely to be applicable.

The book begins by introducing the theoretical framework and goes on to show how the framework can unify our understanding of studies of helping, aggression, conformity, and intimate behavior. I then discuss the antecedents of attribution, of interpersonal attraction, and of action. A chapter is devoted to showing how interpersonal relationships can be changed. In Chapter 9, I examine some of the ideas presented in the previous chapters in terms of their implications for a number of specific social situations, including the employment interview, supervisor-subordinate relations, and marital relations. Chapter 10 offers a summary and conclusion and points to the limitations of the theoretical approach; it also includes a discussion of hoped-for future research.

The writing of this book was facilitated by a Guggenheim Fellowship (1972–73), which gave me the time to read widely and to think through many of these problems. My appointment at the University of Illinois' Center for Advanced Study during that same period was much appreciated. Many colleagues and students at the University of Illinois made helpful comments concerning the theoretical framework as it was developing. Students of an advanced seminar on interpersonal behavior—in particular, John Adamopoulos—made useful comments concerning drafts of the manuscript. My secretaries, Mrs. Alfreda Mitchell and Mrs. Carolyn Foster, were most helpful in typing and retyping the many drafts.

Special thanks are due to Marilynn B. Brewer, University of California, Santa Barbara; Donn Byrne, Purdue University; Uriel G. Foa, Temple University; Norman Miller, University of Southern California; and Lawrence S. Wrightsman, George Peabody College for Teachers, who provided careful reviews of an earlier draft and many suggestions that improved it. Finally, my wife, Pola, was most helpful in editing the whole manuscript and making sure that my inclination to write for my academic colleagues was kept under control and a clarity of exposition suitable for students maintained.

Harry C. Triandis

CONTENTS

INTERPERSONAL
BEHAVIOR

1

INTRODUCTION

1. A job applicant enters the room to be interviewed by a member of a company's personnel department. The interviewer politely asks him to sit down. The applicant sits on the edge of his chair. He is nervous. He plays with his fingers; he shifts positions on his chair. The interviewer asks questions calmly. In the course of the interview, she asks "Why did you leave your previous job?" The job applicant answers "I couldn't get along with the supervisor; no one could." The interview goes on, and later the job applicant finds that he was not hired.

This is an example of one of the billions of social encounters that take place each day. The job applicant said something that was interpreted by the interviewer. He said it because he knew that the interviewer would ask for a recommendation from his previous employer, and, by saying it the way he did, he hoped to influence the weight given to that recommendation. But the interviewer seemed to find elements in the interview that would explain to her satisfaction why the job applicant did not get along with people. She decided to reject him.

2. The boss asks "When will you finish the report?" The employee answers "When do you think I should finish it?" Here, the boss has asked the employee to decide with him when a particular job should be completed, but the employee has refused to participate. She expects the boss to tell her when she should finish the job.

3. A student, who has worked very hard, asks the teacher "Why did I get only a B?" The teacher replies "You did very well, but not as well as some of the others." The student in this case used an absolute standard, the teacher a relative standard, about grades.

4. The tourist smiles at the native, who smiles back. To the delight of both, they discover that they have a language in common, and they exchange

quite a few views. Then the native asks "How much do you make per month?" The tourist feels cold anger at such intimacy, such inappropriate behavior.

5. The husband often stays at the office, not coming home for dinner. When he comes home, he and his wife often argue. The wife is considering a divorce.

These are five brief glimpses into chains of interpersonal behavior that are quite different from one another, yet have something in common. In this book, I will show how we can make sense out of the innumerable social encounters that take place each day by recognizing some patterns that they have in common.

In science, events that are distinct but have many elements in common are treated as though they were identical. In short, experience is categorized. Different categories are different with respect to particular qualities, which are called *dimensions,* or *variables.* Variables are often related to each other in systematic or even lawful ways. A theory arises when a network of relationships or laws is developed. From the theory, predictions of future events are made. When these predictions are confirmed, the theory is supported.

To apply this reasoning to the study of interpersonal behavior, a theorist can start with samples of social encounters. Encounters that have much in common are classified similarly. In measuring some of the characteristics or attributes of the social behaviors that take place in these encounters, the theorist will soon find that the attributes are related to each other in systematic ways.

Look at the five examples I gave. In each of them, two people were involved. One person did or said something. That person perceived what he or she did or said to have particular causes. The other person also perceived some causes of this behavior, but the causes perceived by one were different from the causes perceived by the other. The result was that interpersonal behavior did not occur smoothly.

Let's look at the five examples more carefully. In the first, the job applicant saw his behavior as reasonable, given that prospective employers usually ask previous employers for letters of recommendation. He felt that, if he mentioned that he did not get along with his former boss *and* that no one else did either, a reasonable interviewer would either not ask the previous boss for a recommendation or would give very little weight to it. The interviewer saw a different cause for this behavior. She saw the job applicant as naïve in telling the truth about his previous job. The interviewer also noted that the applicant was nervous, and she inferred that the applicant made other people nervous and it was no wonder his boss couldn't get along with him. The interviewer therefore decided against recommending the applicant for the job. Note that the two perceived causes of the applicant's verbal behavior were totally different from each other.

Again, in the second example, the perceived causes were different. The boss saw himself asking the employee to participate in the decision about when the job should be completed. The employee refused to do that and expected the boss to tell her when to finish the job. The idea of participation didn't even enter the employee's mind.

In the third example, the student saw the teacher's behavior (giving her a B) as inappropriate, given her conception that the "proper" cause of the behavior should have been how hard the student had worked. She knew she had worked very hard. The teacher saw the behavior as appropriate, given his conception of grades as indicators of performance relative to the rest of the class.

In the fourth example, the native's behavior was seen as inappropriate by the tourist. The native saw his behavior as due to natural curiosity about people from other lands. The discrepancy occurred because, in the tourist's culture, there are *norms* (agreements among people about proper behavior) that specify that people are not supposed to ask each other about their income; in the native's culture, such norms did not exist. The tourist assumed that norms that are important in his culture would be operating all over the world, and he was upset to discover otherwise.

In the last example, the husband sees his behavior (working and not coming home for dinner) as consistent with his self-image as a go-getting, highly promising young executive. His wife interprets the same behavior as rejection. Again, each person attributes a different cause to the behavior. The husband sees his self-image and role definition as important; the wife sees the husband's lack of love for her as the cause.

Using a Model to Make Sense of Complex Phenomena

Interpersonal behavior is obviously very complex. In any interpersonal encounter, the behavior is determined by the participants' conceptions of what is appropriate, since they have been taught that some behaviors are correct and others are not. But their behavior is also determined by what other people pressure them to do, how much they enjoy or dislike this behavior, what consequences they see connected with the behavior, and how much they value these consequences. In addition, what persons do in an encounter feeds on the behavior that has just taken place. These previous behaviors are interpreted according to what are assumed to be the causes of these behaviors. The total social setting and some aspects of the personalities of the actors may also modify the course of interpersonal relations.

In order to understand the determinants of interpersonal behavior, we must examine in greater detail what causes behavior *in general*. The model that is presented in the next section is a broad conceptual framework designed to permit understanding of what determines behavior. To understand this model, you must realize that we start with the behavior itself and work backward, looking at more and more remote determinants of behavior. After the model is presented, you will see why and how different types of behavior take place in different types of situations.

The model I have developed has several functions. First, it guides data collection. It tells researchers the important variables that they should study. This is particularly helpful when cognitions and other psychological states are being related to behavior, because the number of types of human cognitions is immense. In fact, social scientists have used a very large number of concepts to explain and describe predispositions toward action. Among these are associations, attitudes, beliefs, concepts, evaluations, expectations, memories, opinions, percepts, role perceptions, stereotypes, and values. Campbell (1963) has pointed out that there are 80 concepts of this sort in wide use in the social sciences. Which of these 80 concepts have maximum utility? I explored this question in detail (Triandis, Vassiliou, Vassiliou, Tanaka, & Shanmugam, 1972) and made the first suggestions that resulted in the proposed model.

Second, the model can help us see why in some studies particular measures of concepts are related to other measures, while in other studies they are not.

This attribute of the model is particularly evident in the case of the investigation of the so-called relationship between attitudes and behavior. The model to be presented has very definite implications for understanding under what conditions there will be a close relationship between attitudes and behavior.

Third, it allows us to summarize many studies within a single framework. This summary helps us to remember the studies—because they are clustered—and helps in the development of new research by revealing which parts of the framework we don't know enough about.

Fourth, the model suggests how to describe similarities and differences in the way people think about social behavior. This guide is particularly helpful in cross-cultural studies in which we want to focus on contact between people from two cultures. Related to this purpose is the fact that, to do a good job of describing such cognitions, we must have a set of variables that are applicable to all cultures and measurable in any culture. If we find a good way to describe similarities and differences in cognition about social behavior, we will also be able to learn how to index these similarities and differences and then relate the indexes to the effectiveness of interpersonal relationships.

Despite all their attributes, however, models are never final products. They are ever-changing vehicles for research and synthesis. As more and more information becomes available, we reshape our models and keep changing them, making finer and finer distinctions and accepting more conditions until some new integration of the elements of the model can provide a more elegant way of conceptualizing a field of science.

A MODEL OF INTERPERSONAL BEHAVIOR

Theoretical Concepts

Acts. An *act* is a socially defined pattern of muscle movements. Specific acts, such as hitting someone, taking off one's hat, or spitting in somebody's face are too brief, subject to too many influences, and too numerous to constitute the appropriate primitive terms of good theory. Such acts do not have meaning in themselves. They acquire meaning only from the contexts in which they occur.

Acts differ in a number of ways, such as in duration, intensity, frequency, probability of occurence, and so on. Each of these attributes can be used as a dependent variable when testing the model, and the expectation is that results will be different for each dependent variable. For example, Farina, Chapnick, Chapnick, and Misiti (1972) showed that politically radical subjects administered intense shocks to conservatives, but the correlation of intensity and duration was $-.56$. On the other hand, conservative subjects administered shocks that were both relatively intense and of long duration (r of .49) to radicals. Berkowitz (1969) has also found different patterns of results, in laboratory studies of aggression, for the duration and intensity dependent variables.

The frequency of an act is in part a function of how natural the act is for the particular organism. For example, pigeons do a lot of pecking. It is not necessary to reward the pecking behavior of a pigeon in order to make the pigeon peck. Behaviors that are natural for a particular animal may have different determinants from behaviors that occur infrequently and for which the animal is not prepared (Seligman, 1970).

Goals and Intentions. Acts are typically organized into patterns that reflect particular *goals* and *intentions*. A *goal* is an outcome of a sequence of specific acts. Individuals can report goals when asked "What are you trying to do?" or "What do you hope to get?" A *behavioral intention* is a cognitive antecedent of an act. Answers to the two questions above may yield information about either goals or intentions. Intentions are of two kinds: specific and general.

Acts correspond to *specific intentions.* A man who wants to reach his mother on the phone lifts the receiver, listens for the dial tone, dials, and so on. This pattern of acts is organized, sequential, and specific to his goal. Any specific intention may be a manifestation of a number of different *general intentions.* For example, the general intention "to show concern" may be expressed in the specific intention "to call mother." Or, the general intention "to obtain help" might be expressed by the same specific intention. General intentions are sufficiently few in number to permit an adequate scientific analysis.

As an illustration of the way behavioral intentions can be measured, here are the instructions that I used in a study of the behavioral intentions of Blacks and Whites toward several types of people (Triandis, 1976).

BEHAVIORAL INTENTIONS
Instructions

We are interested in finding out how people act with other people. In order to do this, we have made a list of different kinds of people and a list of a number of things you might do with each one. A different type of person is specified at the top of each page, and below are the things you might do with him (or her). Beside each item is a space. We would like you to write a number from 0–9 in this space, depending on your chances of doing each thing with (or to) the type of person named. You should follow this rule in answering:

Write 0 in the space if you would *never do* that thing with that person.

Write 1 in the space if you would *seldom do* that thing with that person.

Write 2 in the space if you would *rarely do* that thing with that person.

Write 3 in the space if you would *sometimes do* that thing with that person.

Write 4 in the space if you would *maybe not do* that thing with that person, but aren't quite sure.

Write 5 in the space if you would *maybe do* that thing with that person, but aren't quite sure.

Write 6 in the space if you would do that thing with that person *more often than not.*

Write 7 in the space if you would *usually do* that thing with that person.

Write 8 in the space if you would *almost always do* that thing with that person.

Write 9 in the space if you would *always do* that thing with that person.

This example will show more clearly how the rule works.

Gas Station Attendant:

pay him for gas <u>9</u>

ask him about a noise in your car <u>3</u>

tell him your personal problems <u>0</u>

ask him to check your oil <u>6</u>

You know that you must pay for products, either with cash or a credit card, so 9 for *always* goes in the first space. If your car has a strange noise that you can't figure out, you might *sometimes* ask the gas station attendant for help, so a 3 goes in the next space. Unless the station attendant were also a good friend, you would not tell him your problems, so a 0 goes there. If you are a careful driver, you would want to know about your oil, so *more often than not* you would have it checked.

Read each thing mentioned and decide what number belongs in the space next to it. The rule will be printed on each page to help you. Remember to write a number in *each* space. You can work quickly, but don't be careless, because your *true* opinions are very important. The types of persons and the things you might do with (or to) them have been suggested by many different people and are not our opinions in any way. We are interested in your ideas, because you are the expert on how you feel and believe.

Thank you very much for your cooperation.

Note: Because both men and women are answering this questionnaire, some items will seem silly, like asking if you (if you are a man) would marry or date another man. Don't leave these items blank. Instead, write a 0 (for "never") in the space. Thank you.

BLACK POLICEMEN

Never do: 0	May do: 5
Seldom do: 1	More often than not do: 6
Rarely do: 2	Usually do: 7
Sometimes do: 3	Almost always do: 8
Maybe not do: 4	Always do: 9

Criticize ____	Be sincere with ____
Go out with ____	Beat up ____
Respect ____	Ignore ____

Eat lunch with ___	Call names ___
Listen to ___	Do as he says ___
Help ___	Treat as a brother ___
Stay away from ___	Have coffee with ___
Trust ___	Ask direction ___
Ask for advice ___	Talk about
Be friends with ___	race problems with ___

Norms. Norms are beliefs that certain behaviors are correct, appropriate, or desirable and other behaviors are incorrect, inappropriate, immoral, or undesirable. The Ten Commandments specify norms of social behavior that are subscribed to by a whole social group. Other groups have very different norms about the same behaviors. For example, the Ten Commandments assume a monogamous marriage, but many societies practice polygyny (one husband, many wives), and some societies practice polyandry (one wife, many husbands). Similarly, theft is a meaningless concept in societies in which all property is owned communally.

Some norms are very weak, while other norms are extremely strong. Some norms apply to all, while other norms apply only to certain people or to certain situations. The consequences of breaking a norm are also quite diverse. In our society, extramarital sexual relations are less severely punished now than was the case 100 years ago, but still they are more severely punished than behaviors that break other norms. Also, in some societies, breaking a norm brings little in the way of punishments or public condemnation. In other societies, punishment is prompt and severe, and a person may be ostracized or even killed.

Roles. Roles are sets of behaviors that are considered appropriate for persons holding particular positions in a group. Behaviors associated with the positions of father, son, leader, salesperson, and so on are examples of role behaviors. For example, in many traditional societies it is part of the role of the parents to find spouses for their children. Parents who tell their children to find their own spouses might well be considered "crazy," and children who refuse to marry the person indicated by their parents may well be considered "bad". That this is obviously not the case in the U.S. shows that roles are defined differently in different societies. It should also be clear that, over time, different roles in traditional societies are shaped so that they become consistent, and "role conflict" is avoided. In modern societies, roles keep changing, and people often belong to several different groups, which may make conflicting demands on them. When this happens, people are often in role conflict, and there are studies that show that high levels of role conflict are associated with high frequencies of peptic ulcers, hospital visits, and so on. Thus, while it may seem highly desirable that we no longer have the rigid roles of traditional societies, we should not forget that some of the freedom from such social pressures has been purchased at a cost.

Self-image. This term refers to a person's ideas about who he or she is. These ideas include the person's self-esteem—or sense of how valuable he or she is—as well as ideas about what behaviors are correct, appropriate, or desirable. Many times we think: "I am the kind of person who does that." This is a self-attribution that is related to behavior. For example, a man who thinks of himself as honest is more likely to act honestly than one who does not have such a thought.

Affect. Affect toward a behavior refers to the emotions a person feels at the thought of the behavior. These emotions might be positive (pleasant) or negative (unpleasant) and strong or weak. A behavior may become associated with pleasant stimulation or with disgust, anxiety, or distress.

Perceived Consequences. The term *perceived consequences* refers to the subjective probability—the person's bet—that certain consequences will follow a behavior. For example, a person might think: "If I finish college, I'll get a good job." The behavior is to finish college; the consequence is to get a good job. Obviously, the connection between the two is not always strong; also, perceived consequences and actual consequences may differ.

Value of the Consequences. This term refers to how good or bad one would feel if a particular consequence actually happened. For example, getting a good job, in the previous example, might be something wonderful for a poor kid and something relatively boring for the offspring of a millionaire. We don't react to all good outcomes with equal enthusiasm, nor do we get equally upset when we encounter different calamities.

Relations among the Concepts

The concepts that I have just presented and defined are related to each other and to the probability that a particular act will take place in ways that I will specify below.

Determinants of the Probability of an Act. The probability of an act (P_a) depends on three major factors: (1) the strength of the habit of emitting the act, which is indexed by the number of times the act has already occured in the history of the organism, (2) the behavioral intention to emit the act, and (3) the presence or absence of conditions that facilitate performance of the act. We can express these ideas as follows:

$$P_a = (w_H \cdot H + w_I \cdot I) \cdot F. \qquad \text{Equation 1}$$

P_a is the probability of an act and will vary from 0 to 1. "0" indicates certainty that the act will not take place; "1" indicates certainty that it will. If $P_a = .5$, there is a 50–50 chance that the act will occur.

H is the habit to act and is measured by the number of times the act has already been performed by the person.

I is the intention to act.

F refers to facilitating conditions, such as the ability of the person to carry out the act, the person's arousal to carry out the act (for example, a hungry person is more likely than one who is satiated to eat when food is around), and the person's knowledge.

The w_H and w_I symbols refer to the weights of the habit and intention components. These weights can be determined by a statistical procedure that is called *multiple regression analysis.* The basic idea behind this analysis is to take into account the correlations among the variables under consideration. If, to simplify the situation, we fix the *F* at a constant value, then the weights are given by the following expressions:

$$w_H = \frac{r_{PH} - r_{PI} \cdot r_{HI}}{1 - r_{HI}^2}. \qquad w_I = \frac{r_{PI} - r_{PH} \cdot r_{HI}}{1 - r_{HI}^2}.$$

In other words, the weights depend on the correlations among the P_a, *H*, and *I* variables and express the extent to which you can predict P_a if you know *H* and *I*.

Imagine a social situation in which 100 people acted in a certain way. Let's say that some of these 100 had acted in this way many times, some had acted in this way a few times, and some had never acted this way. This "habit," then, rank-orders the individuals. If our observations of who acted and who did not act rank-order the individuals in about the same way, then there is a high correlation between P_a and *H*; that is, r_{PH} is relatively high. Suppose that we also ask these 100 people if they intended to behave in the specified way. Some say they did, some that they were uncertain, and still others say that they did not intend to do so. Again, we can rank-order the 100 people. Suppose we find that this ranking is also reasonably consistent with the way the people behaved, but not very consistent with their habits; that is, r_{PI} is high, and r_{HI} is low. In that case, we can predict the probability of an act from habits and intentions very well, and each term makes an independent contribution to the prediction.

The point of this analysis is that, if we find acts that we predict mostly from habit, and other acts that we predict mostly from intentions, or if we find social situations or particular individuals whose behaviors are best predicted from one or another of these terms, we can begin specifying the *parameters* that need to be considered in order to improve our predictions of social behavior. A *parameter* is a variable that modifies a relationship. For example, suppose we find that, for certain behaviors, such as how far a person sits from another, how frequently the person looks at the other, and so on, the habit component is very important, while, for the prediction of the kinds of moves a person makes in chess, the intention component is important. Then we can formulate a parameter, distinguishing "unexamined" (habitual) from "carefully examined" (intentional) behavior.

Equation 1 can be rewritten as follows:

$$P_a = w_{HF}H \cdot F + w_{IF}I \cdot F.$$

The first part of this equation has much in common with a very famous equation proposed by Hull (1943), one of the major behavior theorists. He suggested that

$$_sE_R = f(_sH_R) \cdot f(D),$$

where $_sE_R$ is the reaction potential (a concept comparable to P_a), $_sH_R$ is the habit strength associating a given stimulus with a given response, and D is drive. Hull thought that habit strength can be indexed by many observations, such as the probability of the correct response, the amplitude of the correct response (getting "more" or "less" of the response), the latency of the response (time before the correct response is made), and the resistance of the response to extinction (well-learned responses will persist even when the organism is not rewarded for making them). Hull thought that habit strength depended on, among other factors, the number of reinforcements (rewards) associated with the behavior, the amount of reinforcement, and the length of the interval between the act and the reinforcement (the longer the interval, the less the increase in habit strength). Drive was measured by the number of hours of deprivation of the organism, as, for example, when a rat is not given food.

Hull's theory is very complex; what I presented above is an oversimplification, but it serves to point out a formal similarity to my model. As mentioned earlier, F includes the organism's action-specific arousal, which is similar to Hull's D, drive. So the HF product of my formulation is parallel to the HD product of the Hullian formulation. However, there are also differences; I measure H by the number of times the behavior has previously occurred, while Hull measures it by the number of times the behavior has been reinforced. Many other theorists have proposed formulae in this area, but limitations of space preclude presentation and discussion of these theories here.

The second part of my formulation, the IF product, has something in common with cognitive theories, such as those proposed by Tolman. This will be particularly clear after I present the equation that relates some of the variables already discussed to behavioral intentions. Before doing this, however, there are a few more observations to be made about the first equation.

Equation 1 states that the act potential is higher the greater the "habit," which can be indexed by the frequency of occurrence of the act in the previous history of the organism. Such a "habit" may be strong for several reasons. The act may occur naturally for the particular animal, in the sense that pecking is a frequent response for a pigeon; or the animal may have received large and/or frequent reinforcement in the past for emitting this act or developed the expectation that acting in this way would lead to reinforcement. For our purposes, the causes of high H are not important. It is sufficient to know that the organism has frequently emitted this act in the past. We might obtain the best measurement of H by counting the number of times, in the life of the organism, that the act has appeared. Since obtaining this information for humans is often impractical, we may have to settle for a self-report of how frequently the subject has done something. Thus, we might ask "Did you ever spit in somebody's face?" If the subject says "Yes," we might ask "How many times in your life do you think you have done this?"

Equation 1 also indicates that the act potential is proportional to the behavioral intention (I) corresponding to the act. Finally, the sum of the habit and behavioral-intention terms must be multiplied by the person's ability to carry out the act: $F(w_H H + w_I I)$. That is, if a man is gagged, he may not be able to spit in anybody's face, no matter how frequently he has done it in the past or how high his level of behavioral intentions might be.

The two weights reflect the extent to which the act is overlearned or automatic versus deliberate, requiring thought and planning. (The more deliberate, the larger the w_I.) The w_H value is also a function of the social situation and may reflect individual differences. The more the social situation resembles situations in which the act has occurred in the past, the larger the w_H. Some individuals may be more "creatures of habit" than others, so we might predict their behavior better using a larger w_H. The w_I also depends on the social situation and on individual differences (personality). When the social situation is novel and the behavior has not yet become "automatic," the w_I value will be larger than in a familiar situation. Some individuals intentionally try new behavior patterns, thus suppressing the relative size of w_H in relation to w_I.

When the subject is highly aroused, as in situations of uncertainty, novelty, threat, social facilitation (being observed by an audience), or anxiety, w_H becomes much larger than w_I. As stated earlier, behaviors that are overlearned have a large w_H value. Arousal increases w_H further, so that, for overlearned behaviors, arousal leads to improved performance. Novel behaviors have nonsignificant w_H values, and, when arousal increases the w_H value, there is interference with the novel behavior, hence a deterioration in performance. This is consistent with Zajonc's (1965) analysis of social facilitation, as well as with observations of panic behavior. In the latter case, typically, people "do not think" but behave according to overlearned patterns, which may be counterproductive.

The way w_H and w_I may vary from moment to moment is illustrated by my experience with a Japanese psychologist whom I had met during a previous stay in Japan. While crossing the street on the way to the hotel where an international congress was to take place, I recognized her and began a conversation. But we soon stopped walking. Analysis of the circumstances suggested the reason. This woman, in the proper Japanese manner, was in the habit of walking behind men; I, in the proper Western manner, was in the habit of walking next to or slightly behind a woman. Result: a clash of habits, which resulted in a standstill. At once my behavioral intentions took hold of my habitual walking behavior. I walked slightly ahead, and progress was normal—until my attention was diverted and the well-established habits "unintentionally" again controlled my behavior. Again we came to a standstill. Again my behavioral intentions took hold of the behavior, and again we made normal progress toward the hotel.

Here, then, you have an example of the changing relative influence of behavioral intentions and habits, which could best be described by a complex mathematical model, showing feedback loops and a switch from habits to behavioral intentions after every stop. Much behavior may well be under similar influences, and its mathematical description may require such a complex set of considerations.

It should be clear to the reader that Equation 1 is dynamic, in the sense that the relative weights for habit and intention may vary from moment to moment. When we study a particular behavior, we capture the weights at a particular point in time. It is like a photograph of a person who is moving. Over time, as particular situations recur, we move from a large w_I to a large w_H, which means that we move from a small emphasis on habit to a small emphasis on intention.

The Determinants of Behavioral Intentions. The determinants of behavioral intentions may be expressed in a simple equation:

$$I = w_S(S) + w_A(A) + w_C(C), \qquad \text{Equation 2}$$

where I is as in Equation 1, S is social factors, A is the affect attached to the behavior itself, C is the value of the perceived consequences of the behavior, and w's are weights, as discussed earlier.

(1) *Social factors* (*S*) are the norms, roles, and general behavioral intentions that derive from the relationship between our subject and other people. Also included are the "contractual arrangements" made by our subject with other people and the subject's conceptions of behavior consistent with his or her self-concept.

Rules of behavior such as one finds in etiquette books (for example, Post, 1965) determine some of the variance of behavior in many social situations. Such rules concern introductions, greetings and farewells, names and titles, behavior in public places, formal entertainment, showers, cocktail parties, overnight guests, special events (such as a new baby, graduation, debuts, engagements, weddings, funerals), and many other social situations. Behavior on certain ceremonial occasions, such as an audience with a king or pope, is almost entirely determined by such rules. Careful observation and analysis of such rules, as in Goffman (1963), can provide generalizations about behavior in different kinds of settings.

Contractual arrangements are often very specific. An agreement between *P* and *O* to meet at 8:00 P.M. is an example of such an arrangement. Such arrangements can become goals that guide a chain of behavioral intentions, such as to walk to the car, enter, start the ignition, and so on, that are all done a few minutes before 8 P.M. Kanfer and his associates (Karoly & Kanfer, 1974; Kanfer, Cox, Greiner, & Karoly, 1974; Kanfer & Grimm, 1975) have provided much evidence on the importance of such contracts. For example, if an experimenter and a subject agree that the subject should keep his hand in an ice bucket, the subject keeps it in the water much longer than if there is no such agreement.

Another aspect of the *S* component concerns self-monitoring. *Self-monitoring* (Snyder, 1974) is self-observation and self-control guided by situational cues to social appropriateness. People often decide what kind of "line" to use in presenting themselves to others. They then make sure that their behavior sticks closely to what is required by the particular "line" they have adopted. According to Snyder, people may monitor their self-presentation of expressive behavior for several quite different reasons, including (1) to accurately communicate their true emotional state by means of an intensified expressive presentation, (2) to communicate an arbitrary emotional state that need not be congruent with actual emotional experience, (3) to adaptively conceal an inappropriate emotional state and appear unresponsive and unexpressive, (4) to adaptively conceal an inappropriate emotional state and appear to be experiencing an appropriate one, or (5) to appear to be experiencing some emotion when they are actually experiencing nothing but when nonresponse is inappropriate. Snyder found that there are individual differences in the amount of self-monitoring, and he developed a scale that measures these differences. Individuals high in self-monitoring are good at learning what is socially appropriate in new situations, have good control of their emotional expressions, and can effectively use these abilities to create the impressions that they want. Theater actors scored higher and hospitalized ward patients scored lower than university students on measures of self-monitoring.

The *self-concept* consists of self-attributed traits and behavior patterns. If a woman considers herself "kind," she is more likely to use behavioral intentions consistent with this self-concept than if she thought of herself as "aloof." Eisen (1972) found that boys who possess self-esteem behave honestly. Certain behaviors are felt to be more consistent with a person's self-concept than others. For example, the behavior "typing an article" is more consistent with my self-conception than the behavior "hitting somebody." Self-conceptions, then, facilitate or inhibit particular behavioral intentions. If one thinks of oneself as "the kind of person who drives a fast car," one will be interested in buying a car having "fast" as an attribute. Usually, we think of ourselves in certain ways because friends, parents, or other important humans have acted in ways that suggest that we are one thing rather than another. This means that our self-concept is strongly influenced by what others think of us (or at least by what we think others think of us!), communicated by the way others act toward us. Memory of past behavior is another determinant of the self-concept.

The conceptions that people have about the kinds of traits they possess are important. Bem (1974) has identified a set of traits, called *male-valued*, that both males and females consider desirable for males and another set of traits, called *female-valued,* commonly considered desirable for females. Individuals who saw themselves as possessing *both* male-valued and female-valued traits were called *androgynous.* Bem (1975) showed that those high in androgyny behaved more flexibly in two situations that required very different kinds of responses. Specifically, in a conformity-type situation, the androgynous individuals, both male and female, showed more independence and resisted attempts by the experimenter to make them conform; in a situation calling for playfulness with a kitten, androgynous individuals played more. Spence, Helmreich, and Stapp (1974) provided further support for the concept of androgyny, which they view as a positive trait, by showing that those high in androgyny, as measured by a different scale developed by them, had higher self-esteem than those lower in adrogyny.

I have described, so far, several kinds of social factors that enter the social component: norms, roles, social contracts, self-monitoring, and the self-concept. Exactly how these are combined is still unclear. My guess is that each of them is added to the others to determine the strength of the social component. However, other possibilities need to be compared, empirically, with this simple additive conception. Fishbein (1967b), for instance, has adapted from Dulany (1968) the idea that a person might be differentially willing to yield to pressure exerted by others. He asks people what various others—such as their parents or friends—want them to do and whether or not they want to comply with this request. This he calls the "motivation to comply" measure. He then multiplies the extent to which the subject sees a significant other as wanting him or her to do something by the subject's motivation to comply. Similarly, Acock and DeFleur (1972) suggest that the strengths of norms, roles, and so on, might be multiplied. If we represent these strengths with $S_1, S_2, \ldots S_n$, this would imply that $S = S_1 \cdot S_2 \ldots S_n$.

Further research is needed before we'll know how best to combine the information about the social component.

(2) Cues associated with any behavior, including special cues such as the cognitive representation of the behavior as a behavioral intention, become associated with certain pleasant or unpleasant outcomes. Thus, a particular configuration of emotions becomes activated at the thought of the behavior. This is the affect (A) associated with the behavior.

One explanation for this association of emotion and behavior is that the thought of the behavior, which is like a conditioned stimulus, becomes associated with the emotions attached to pleasant or unpleasant events, which act like unconditioned stimuli. Frequent temporal contiguity between conditioned and unconditioned stimuli results in what Pavlov studied under the label of classical conditioning, which you undoubtedly learned about in your introductory psychology course. Such conditioning can be one of the determinants of action, but apparently, for relatively novel behaviors, only people who are *aware* of the rules connecting stimuli, actions, and outcomes respond lawfully. On the other hand, for behavior that has taken place *several times* under the influence of intentions, habits might "take over," and then we would see the behavior under the control of "unconscious processes" (that is, the subjects would not be able to give an account of why they behaved the way they did). So it is possible, in the case of an old and well-established behavior, for the behavior to occur without the subject being able to give an account of the reason he or she acted, although careful investigation of the history of the subject might discover a classical-conditioning link between the behavior and pleasant events or avoidance of unpleasant events. Similar sorts of "unconscious" processes might be noted for older, well-established behaviors that were originally established because the behavior was strongly linked with affect.

(3) Behavior can also become linked to consequences. The greater the frequency of contiguity of behavior and outcome, the stronger the connection between behavior and perceived consequences.

The *value* of the perceived consequences, C, depends on the sum of the products of the subjective probability that a particular consequence will follow a behavior (P_c) and the value of (or affect attached to) that consequence (V_c). Thus, following the decision theorists, as well as Peak (1955), Rosenberg (1956), and Fishbein (1963), I propose that:

$$C = \sum_{i=1}^{n} P_{c_i} V_{c_i}. \qquad\qquad \text{Equation 3}$$

where n is the number of consequences that a subject perceives as likely to follow a particular behavior.

It should be clear that, the greater the frequency of contiguity of an act and an outcome, the larger the P_c terms. The larger the value of the outcome V_{c_i}, the larger the C value.[1,2]

Much of human behavior is goal directed. The consequences in Equation 3 often include goals that have particular values. The value of the goal is symbolized V_g. *Plans* are sequences of behavior (B) having the characteristics

$$B_1 \rightarrow B_2 \rightarrow B_3 \rightarrow \ \ldots \ \rightarrow B_n \rightarrow G.$$

$$P_{B_{1G}} < P_{B_{2G}} < \ \ldots \ < P_{B_{nG}}.$$

Thus, the C component of behavior B_n is $P_{B_{nG}} \cdot V_G$. If it is certain that B_n will lead to the goal, then the C component is simply the value of the goal, V_G. Behaviors that are further from the goal will have smaller C components and hence will be less likely to occur than behaviors near the goal. As long as the organism attends to the goal, the C component will be activated; however, behavior may not take place if the A or S components are larger than the C component. For example, although a behavior may be perceived to lead to a goal of high value, a person may experience much negative affect concerning this behavior and/or much pressure from peers not to do it. In such a case, the person may not undertake it. As a more specific example, a supervisor who knows that firing an employee would raise his profits but finds the act of firing extremely distasteful, and/or is under social pressure not to do so, may not fire this employee after all. It all depends on the relative size of the weights of Equation 2.

Self-Reports of the S, A, and C Components. When subjects are asked to account for their behavior, they are likely to give explanations invoking social influence ("he made me do it"), hedonism ("I love to do it"), or the consequences of the behavior ("I did it to get something").

It is interesting that Collins, Martin, Ashmore, and Ross (1973) found four kinds of factors that people use to explain their own behavior. The three most important factors correspond to the S, A, and C components. The first

[1]Several theorists have used concepts of expectancy similar to the P_c term of my model. For example, Rotter (1954), Bolles (1972), Estes (1972), and Irwin (1971) have used concepts that are rather similar to P_c. Although most of the evidence presented by these writers comes from the animal laboratory, it seems consistent with my arguments.

[2]A number of personality variables might be reflected in particular relationships between the variables of Equation 3. Thus, if a person sees valuable outcomes as occurring infrequently, the correlation between V_{c_i} and P_c values will be negative. For very optimistic individuals, however, the correlation may be positive. Steiner (1970) has provided a very interesting analysis of the relationships among components of this equation. He considers the costs of a behavior separately, as negative outcomes. Some individuals may see a positive correlation between such costs and the value of outcomes (for example, hard work leads to wealth); that is, they relate some negative aspects of the consequences of the behavior to valuable outcomes.

factor, which they labeled *other-direction*, is indicated by a self-report of strong use of the equivalent of the S component of the model. The three test items that best define this factor are (1) "I live too much by other people's standards," (2) "In order to get along and be liked, I tend to be what people expect me to be rather than anything else," and (3) "I guess I put on a show to impress people. I know I'm not the person I pretend to be." The second factor suggests a strong C component. Here are some of the items: (1) "I am basically good at following through with my plans," (2) "I have my own code of behavior and I follow it to the letter," and (3) "All one's behavior should be directed toward a certain small number of definite personal goals." The third factor suggests the A component. The subjects agreed with the statement, "I can only argue for ideas to which I am strongly committed."

To illustrate how the components of the model might be measured, I offer the following example. Suppose you are interested in predicting whether a White female medical student might date a Black medical student.

Habits

You might observe whether she has dated similar men. Or you might ask the subject "How many times have you dated a Black medical student?"

Behavioral Intentions

Ask the subject to rate the likelihood of dating on the following scale:

A 25-year-old Black medical student whose father is an unskilled laborer

would ____ ____ ____ ____ ____ ____ ____ ____ ____ would not
                                      date

Role Perceptions

Medical student/Medical student
            (female)   (male)

should ____ ____ ____ ____ ____ ____ ____ ____ ____ should not
                                      date

Norms

Do you believe that your *parents* would approve or disapprove of your dating a 25-year-old Black medical student whose father is an unskilled laborer?

would strongly approve ___ ___ ___ would strongly disapprove

Do you believe that your *friends* would approve or disapprove of your dating . . .

Self-Concept

Are you the kind of person who would date a 25-year-old Black medical student whose father is an unskilled laborer?

definitely yes ___ ___ ___ ___ ___ ___ ___ ___ definitely no

Do you feel that you have a moral obligation to date a 25-year-old Black medical . . .

Affect toward the Act

Dating a 25-year-old Black medical student whose father is an unskilled laborer would be

delightful ___ ___ ___ ___ ___ ___ ___ ___ ___ disgusting
dull ___ ___ ___ ___ ___ ___ ___ ___ ___ exciting
enjoyable ___ ___ ___ ___ ___ ___ ___ ___ ___ nauseating

Perceived Consequences

If I date a 25-year-old Black medical student whose father is an unskilled laborer, the chances are that I will be invited to dinner at his parents' house.

Chances: ___ ___ ___ ___ ___ ___ ___ ___ ___ ___ ___
         0   1   2   3   4   5   6   7   8   9   10
               out of 10

Value of Consequences

Being invited to dinner at the house of the parents of a 25-year-old Black medical student whose father is an unskilled laborer would be

good ___ ___ ___ ___ ___ ___ ___ ___ ___ bad
pleasant ___ ___ ___ ___ ___ ___ ___ ___ ___ unpleasant
disagreeable ___ ___ ___ ___ ___ ___ ___ ___ ___ agreeable

Some Limitations of the Model

The capacity of the model to predict behavior is limited by certain conditions. I have reviewed evidence suggesting that, when the components of the model (habits, norms, affect, and so on) are consistent, behavior can be predicted very well; when they are inconsistent, it is less easy to predict behavior (Triandis, 1971). For example, if a person lives in a culture in which smoking is disapproved of, and he or she does not like smoking, we can be almost sure that that person will not smoke. But, if one or the other of these two factors favors smoking, we can be less sure. In the first case, the behavior is *overdetermined* by the predictors. In the second case, the predictors are in conflict, and, if our measurements are not good enough, error in prediction is more likely. Another way to think about this is to consider the error of measurement. In the first case, the error of measurement is small; hence, the reliability of prediction is good. In the second, it is larger; hence, the prediction is less reliable. The same point has been made by Norman (1975), who studied cognitive-affective consistency and predicted the volunteering behavior of subjects. He found good correlations between A- and C-type measures and behavior for consistent but not for inconsistent subjects.

If the perceived consequences of behavior are related to the actual consequences only some of the time, or not at all, then the P_c values will be very low, and the C component will not predict behavior. In some environments, there is more confusion than lawfulness; in such cases, there is no reason to expect that the C component will predict behavior.

The more certain subjects are about their attitudes (Sample & Warland, 1973), the more ego involved they are in their attitudes (Sherif, Kelly, Rodgers, Sarup, & Tittler, 1973), and the more specific the measurement of their attitudes (Weigel, Vernon, & Tognacci, 1974), the better the prediction of behavior. In other words, if you are sure of your behavioral intentions, or the measurement of these intentions is highly specific (for example, you are asked "Are you going to vote tomorrow morning for X or for Y?"), or if you feel committed to your position, then the prediction of your behavior will be good. To be even more specific, a member of an extreme political party is likely to vote for a candidate who holds the same political ideology, while a more moderate voter might see both good and bad attributes in his or her favorite candidate and might therefore be uncertain about how to vote. The prediction of the behavior of the extremist is better than the prediction of the behavior of the moderate.

Strategy for Using the Model in Future Research

The model should not be considered a precise way of describing the information processing that takes place in the heads of people. Rather, it should be seen as a quick and imprecise way of organizing a lot of information in order to make more precise theoretical statements possible.

It is extremely difficult to distinguish empirically a model that uses linear regression, such as the one presented here, from thousands of other models that can be generated from permutations and combinations of the major variables included in the model. To distinguish among models, one needs to have extremely "good" (error-free) data. This is only possible, at the present time, when the same subject is carefully trained, over a long period of time under highly controlled laboratory conditions, to give highly reliable answers. This approach characterizes the work of Anderson (1972a), which will be discussed in detail later. It has the serious limitation that only limited social phenomena can be investigated, because most social phenomena change their character when they are brought into the laboratory. The present model was specifically developed to be robust—usable in different cultures and in both field and laboratory settings. As you will see later, it has been used in ghettos in the United States, in other cultures, such as Mexico, and in a variety of other settings with success. The very nature of data that have much error in them—the only kind that can be collected in such field settings—precludes comparisons among models. In other words, mine is not offered as a model to be tested but as one to organize information. Note, also, that its linear, simple character makes the fewest possible assumptions about the interrelationships of the determinants of behavior.

If the model is not to be tested, how is it to be used? It should be used as a framework for data collection. The criterion of a good model, in this case, is that it accounts for more of the variance of observations than do other models. In addition, when we find that the weights for one kind of behavior are very different from the weights for another kind of behavior, we learn what to look for in developing typologies of behavior. The same analysis can be done for the development of typologies of situations or persons. As one uses the model over and over again, one learns that some of the variables predict very little of the variance of behavior and can therefore be dropped. In some situations, the model predicts little of the variance of behavior, indicating that there are other variables, not now included in the model, that must be added to improve prediction. As we work with data, we are perfectly justified in combining them in different ways, studying empirically whether some combinations work better than others. If we find consistent improvements in prediction for certain combinations of variables (say, when we multiply rather than add variables), then we are justified in modifying the model—always keeping in mind, however, that these changes may not be conclusive, since they may be due to characteristics of the particular data that suggested them.

Many highly sophisticated statistical approaches—such as path analysis, which allows one to detect the direction of causal influences from data for two or more periods of time—can also be used to modify the model.

However, the single most important function of the model is to guide investigations of typologies of behaviors, settings, and people. Such typologies can be developed in a number of ways. One approach is a statistical technique called factor analysis. While there is no need to understand the details, it's a good idea to grasp the purpose of this analysis.

Imagine that 100 people have been tested on two variables and their scores ranked for each variable. The more similar these two rankings, the higher the rank-order correlation between the two variables. When we talk about a correlation between two variables, we mean that whatever is being measured by one test rank-orders the people similarly to whatever is being measured by the other.

Now suppose we have ten variables and a matrix of correlations in which every variable is correlated with every other variable. This matrix may have some pattern. That is, some variables may correlate highly among themselves but not correlate with any of the other variables. In this situation, the variables form a *factor*. For example, suppose you present various films to a sample of people and ask them to rate them on various scales, such as *good, loud, strong, pleasant,* and *beautiful.* Suppose you note that the scales *good, pleasant,* and *beautiful* correlate among themselves, and *loud* and *strong* correlate, but the first set does not correlate with the second. This would suggest that there are two factors. You might call the first factor *evaluation*, since the rating scales evaluate the films, and the second factor *potency*, since the scales have something to do with power. Evaluation and potency are now factors. When we say that a variable has high loadings on a factor, we mean that it correlates very highly with other variables that constitute the factor.

In short, factor analysis is a method that extracts from data patterns of consistency in responses. In our example, people who viewed a film as good tended also to view it as beautiful; those who viewed it as bad tended to view it as ugly, and so on. By looking at the patterns of correlation among the variables, we can extract patterns of consistency. In this case, the consistency is among ratings of films.

This method can also be used to find consistency in all sorts of variables. For example, suppose you have a lot of information about the way 100 people have rated films on a lot of scales. You can correlate the people instead of the scales. This will give you information about similarities and differences among people. Let's say that Jones and Brown gave very similar responses that differed from the responses of others; they form a factor. Or, instead of correlating people, you can correlate films. For example, you might look at whether there is a similarity in the way various films have been rated. If two films have been rated the same way by most people, then the two films form a factor.

All of this tells us that factor analysis is a very flexible way to discover typologies among any entities that we wish to study. We can get typologies of people, or typologies of behavior, or typologies of settings. Assuming that we do get such typologies, should we incorporate the dimensions suggested by the typologies into our theories? It depends on whether the typologies help us predict what we want to predict. If we use factor analysis and find that there are certain types of people, certain types of settings, and certain types of behaviors, we will certainly want to take this information into account when we construct our theory about people's behavior in different settings, provided this information improves our predictions. To find out whether it does, we can use the model. We separate the data by type of person, setting, and behavior and compute the weights for each equation of the model for every combination of these types. If the weights are very different across these computations, we conclude that the typologies do help us and must be incorporated in the theory. Then we try to develop independent ways of assessing to which particular kind of typology certain types of people, certain types of behaviors, and certain kinds of settings belong. In short, in addition to factor analysis, other methods of discovering types are used. When convergence among methods is obtained, we have a theory relating characteristics of persons, settings, and behaviors. From this theory we make predictions about new situations, new behaviors, and new samples of persons. Then we can test the theory by predicting the behavior of these persons in those situations, and, if our prediction is good, we know that our theory has merit.

For example, suppose we find that White people who were raised by very severe parents tend to exclude Blacks from intimate relationships. Here we have a typology of persons (how they were raised), a type of behavior (exclusion of Blacks), and a particular setting (intimate relationships). The next step is to set up an experimental situation involving an intimate relationship and predict that certain people will exclude a Black confederate from that situation while others will not. If our observation confirms the prediction, we will have shown the utility of the particular typologies.

Most of the work outlined above remains to be done. However, there is already enough such work in the published literature to suggest that the approach outlined here is likely to help in the development of a general theory of social behavior. To review this literature, we need to examine studies that suggest a typology of social behavior and studies that suggest different weights for the components of the model across types of social behavior.

KINDS OF INTERPERSONAL BEHAVIOR

Remember the tense interview that was described in the beginning of the chapter? In this social situation, we find all of the elements of interpersonal behavior. First, the interviewer made *attributions*. She judged the interviewee as not too intelligent, rather unkind, a bit too independent, and so on. Second, the interviewer felt very little attraction toward the interviewee.

Other people were seen as more attractive. Such responses are called *affective*, since they involve emotion. Third, the interviewer acted in certain ways, such as asking questions. This behavior we call *overt*. Overt behavior can be of two kinds: verbal or nonverbal.

We need to distinguish among attributive, affective, and overt behaviors, because they do not necessarily follow the same laws. As we shall see in later chapters, there are theories that account for the way humans make attributions; other theories, such as a theory that relates interpersonal similarity to attraction, account for interpersonal liking. Still other theories account for the different types of overt social behavior, such as the types shown in Table 1.1 (page 26). In the present chapter, I will focus particularly on overt behavior, but, to keep the presentation complete, I have to say a word about the other two types.

Attributive behaviors concern ideas that a person P has about the causes of the behavior of another person O. For example, P may think that O has some personality attribute (for example, intelligence, kindness, dependence) that is the cause of O's behavior. Stereotyping is a special case of such attribution. If P attributes characteristics to O's membership groups, he or she is stereotyping. Sometimes the stereotypes are accurate, in the sense that a carefully done study has found that a particular group does indeed have a characteristic. Such relatively accurate stereotypes are called *sociotypes*. For example, the attribution "Northern Blacks are Democrats" is correct and, therefore, a sociotype, in the sense that over 90 percent of Northern Blacks have voted for Democratic candidates in the elections held in the last 30 years (Campbell, 1968). However, the attribution "Blacks are musical" is incorrect. There is no evidence supporting this attribution. The evidence suggests that there are many Black musicians because historically there has been less discrimination in the musical world than in other walks of life; talent has been considered more important than race. Most stereotypes are grossly inaccurate.

Affective behaviors are emotional reactions to others, such as feelings of attraction or disgust. When a person P is presented with derogatory statements with respect to O and an experimenter records a strong galvanic skin response (GSR), we can infer that P is not neutral about O. Experiments done by Cooper (1959) show that derogatory statements presented together with the names of liked groups, or complimentary statements presented with the names of disliked groups, produce large GSR changes. When a person rates another on a like/dislike or a good/bad scale, we obtain measures of affect toward the other.

Overt behavior is behavior we see. Such behavior can be verbal or nonverbal. For example, when a person rejects another, the behavior may be *scolding* (verbal) or *hitting* (nonverbal). Some nonverbal behavior is quite subtle. Although it can be observed by careful investigators, it may escape the attention of those who are not prepared to see it. What is broadly called *proxemic* behavior (Argyle & Kendon, 1967; Hall, 1959, 1966; Watson, 1970) falls in this category. Such behavior includes the decision of a person to sit near another, the probability that one person will touch another, the amount of eye contact, the level of sound generated by the encounter, and so on. It is not *what* is said but *how* it is said that is included under proxemic behavior.

The relative importance of the components of the model does vary, depending on the kind of social behavior being analyzed. For example, proxemic behaviors are under the control of habits. Only under special conditions, as in the example with the Japanese psychologist, does proxemic behavior come under intentional control.

Most social behavior, until it becomes routinized, is under the control of intentions. However, the weights of the social, affective, and consequences factors that determine the intentions may differ, depending on the situation and the behavior. For example, suppose a politician attends a picnic sponsored by a particular ethnic group. The norms in such a case call for the politician to voice highly complimentary attributions about the ethnic group. These attributions may or may not be believed, but the point is that they are appropriate in that setting, and they may get the politician some votes. Thus, the social and the consequence components will combine to determine the attributions that the politician will make. It is even possible that the politician dislikes making such attributions, because he really dislikes the particular ethnic group. However, unless the weight of the affective component is much greater than the combined weights of the social and consequences components, the positive attributions are likely to be made.

In order to understand the variables that change the weights of the components of the model, we need to have a typology of social behaviors. This typology is presented in the next section. Evidence from different types of investigations suggests that interpersonal behaviors differ in ways that can be systematically described. Furthermore, different types of interpersonal behavior appear to be under the control of specifiable combinations of determinants.

A Typology of Social Behaviors

The typology that is presented below was developed empirically from factor analyses of the behavioral intentions of individuals responding to a large number of hypothetical social situations (Triandis, 1964; Triandis, Vassiliou, & Nassiakou, 1968; Triandis, Vassiliou, Vassiliou, Tanaka, & Shanmugam, 1972). It was then found to be consistent with other kinds of empirical studies and also with theoretical statements concerning the major dimensions of interpersonal behavior. The major dimensions appear to be four:

1. *Associative* versus *dissociative* behaviors—for example, *gossip with* versus *quarrel with.*
2. *Superordinate* versus *coordinate* versus *subordinate* behaviors—for example, *appoint, discuss with,* and *obey.*
3. *Intimate* versus *informal* versus *formal* behaviors—for example, *pet, advise,* and *appoint.*
4. *Overt action* versus *feeling* versus *attribution*—for example, *ask for help, admire,* and *say he is admirable.*

Table 1.1 presents a typology with 36 kinds of social behavior and one example of each kind.[3]

Table 1.1   A Typology of Social Behaviors

	Dissociative		Associative		
	Overt Action	*Feeling*	*Overt Action*	*Feeling*	
Superordinate	Scold	Reject	Pet	Feel nurturant	*Intimate*
	Castigate	Dislike	Advise	Like	*Informal*
	Denounce	Feel indignant toward	Appoint	Support	*Formal*
Coordinate	Quarrel	Hate	Marry	Love	*Intimate*
	Dispute	Not trust	Gossip	Enjoy	*Informal*
	Fight	Be enemy of	Discuss	Feel embarrassed	*Formal*
Subordinate	Hide from	Envy	Fall in love	Idolize	*Intimate*
	Avoid	Feel disgust	Ask help	Admire	*Informal*
	Be blackmailed	Fear	Obey	Respect	*Formal*

[3]Several theorists use the association and superordination dimensions, although they often give them different names. Thus, Foa (1961) discusses the giving and taking away of love or status and Leary (1957) discusses interpersonal behavior in terms of dominance versus submission and hate versus love. Schaefer (1965) analyzes mother-child behavior in terms of warm/cold and autonomous/controlling mothers, Mehrabian (1970) analyzes social behavior according to evaluation, potency, and responsiveness, Lorr and his associates (for example, Lorr & McNair, 1965; Lorr & Suziedelis, 1969) use dominance and affection, LaForge and Suczek (1955) use love/hate and dominance/submission, Stogdill and Coons (1957) use consideration and initiating structure to describe the behavior of leaders as they are perceived by their subordinates, and Brown (1965) uses solidarity and dominance to explain the choice of formal or informal forms of address in languages that make that distinction. Schlosberg (1954), Triandis and Lambert (1958), and Osgood (1966) have used similar dimensions to describe the perception of emotion.

Review of Empirical Studies

How do we know about the varieties of social behavior that exist? Three basic approaches are open to us in studying interpersonal behavior:

1. direct observation of the behavior,
2. reports by persons who know our subjects, describing their typical behavior, and
3. self-reports, or self-rating of traits.

All of these methods have been used, and they converge to produce a remarkably consistent picture. Whether one observes animals or humans, college students or mothers interacting with their children, or whether one asks people about how others have behaved or how they themselves would behave, one gets a set of dimensions that correspond to the four dimensions mentioned earlier.

Let's look at these dimensions in greater detail.

Association: behaviors such as helping, supporting, taking care of, and so on are characteristic of this pole of the dimension.
Dissociation: behaviors such as avoiding, fighting with, hitting, and so on.
Superordination: behaviors such as criticizing, ordering, checking on.
Subordination: behaviors such as obeying, agreeing, asking for help.
Intimacy: behaviors such as kissing, petting, hitting.
Formality: behaviors such as sending a written invitation, praying.

Different researchers who have studied interpersonal behavior have found the same dimensions, although often they have given them different names. This happens because researchers try to appear more original than they really are but also because they want the name they use to be the best descriptor of the dimension. Obviously, slight variations in the dimension will be observed because different studies use different settings. Also, in some settings, some dimensions will simply not emerge. For example, if we observe mothers interacting with their children, it's unlikely that we'll get an intimacy/formality dimension, because most of the behaviors are intimate. It is only when there is enough variation on a given dimension in a given study that the dimension will emerge.

Let's review some relevant studies, beginning with those using direct observation. Mason (1964) reports studies that show that animals, including primates, engage in associative behaviors. For example, they groom each other and help each other. Of course, it's well known that animals fight, often for territory or for sexual advantage. In addition, dominance hierarchies, known as pecking orders, develop in many species, such as birds and primates. These behaviors correspond to the association/dissociation and superordination/subordination dimensions of the typology.

Bales (1950) observed the behavior of students in problem-solving groups. He used a system for categorizing behavior that took into account who started an interaction, whom it was directed to, and what its content was. His analysis suggested the emergence of two kinds of leaders: (1) an expressive leader, who kept the group going and mediated when tensions developed among the members (associative behavior) and (2) an instrumental leader, who helped the group reach its goal of solving the problem. The instrumental leader answered questions and structured the interaction so the group could solve the problem, acting largely in a superordinate way, while the other members of the group acted largely in a subordinate way.

Longabaugh (1966) reported the early phases of analyses of the behavior of children in six cultures. The completed analyses were reported only recently (Whiting & Whiting, 1975). The data once again suggest dimensions such as association, superordination, and intimacy.

Mehrabian (1971) observed the behavior of students during the first few minutes of an encounter. He obtained many measures, including measures of proxemic behavior. Again, the dimensions had much in common with my dimensions.

Norman (1969) asked subjects to report the behavior of some of their friends and examined similarities in the factor structure (after a factor analysis) of self-ratings and peer ratings. Again, the dimensions that were extracted had much in common with my dimensions.

In another self-report study (Triandis, 1964), I presented complex stimulus persons—for example, a Black 28-year-old female physician—to subjects, who were asked to indicate whether they would or would not behave in certain ways toward such persons. A factor analysis of the correlations among the judgments yielded five factors: *respect* (I would admire the ideas of, I would vote for, I would admire the character of), *marital acceptance* (I would marry, I would date, I would kiss), *friendship acceptance* (I would play with, I would eat with, I would gossip with), *social distance* (I would exclude from my neighborhood, I would exclude from my club), and *superordination* (I would criticize, I would order). Careful examination of the results of several studies using similar methodologies (Triandis, Vassiliou, Vassiliou, Tanaka, & Shanmugam, 1972) suggested that *respect* and *friendship acceptance* are related to the association factor, *marital acceptance* to the intimacy factor, *social distance* to dissociation, and *superordination* to the superordination factor of my present typology.

In addition to studying behavior itself, researchers have measured people's *conceptions* of social behavior and again come up with dimensions resembling those we're now considering.

In a review of the evidence concerning the way people conceptualize behavior, Benjamin (1974) uses associative/dissociative and initiating/reacting dimensions, which correspond to my associative and superordinate dimensions. She presents a chart showing different kinds of social behavior and their complements. If an actor acts in a certain way, the complement represents a likely reaction. For example, *dominate* has the complement *submit, injure* has the complement *do not touch me, exclude* has the complement *compete,* and *kiss* had the complement *accept.* Benjamin also introduces the idea of an antidote. An antidote is the behavior that would neutralize the actor's action. For example, *defy* has the antidote *reasoned persuasion,* and *cooperate* has the antidote *exploit, trust* has the antidote *reject,* and *obey routines* has the antidote *encourage divergence.* She shows how her chart can be used to find the complement or the antidote of a particular behavior. Benjamin's model collapses the intimacy and association dimensions and does not consider explicitly the covert/overt dimension. Nevertheless, it is interesting because of the complement and antidote ideas.

An example of a study of the way people conceptualize social behavior is a study I undertook with Vassiliou and Nassiakou (1968). In this study, 100 role pairs, such as father/son, male/female, and prostitute/client, were judged by samples of Americans and Greeks on a set of 60 scales defined by interpersonal behaviors. Subjects were asked to judge the appropriateness of the behavior for the particular role relationship. A typical item was:

Male/Female

would ____ ____ ____ ____ ____ ____ ____ ____ ____ would not

let go first through a door

The subject judged whether the actor (male) is likely, in the subject's culture, to act (let go first) in relation to the target (female).

The study involved 6000 such items. The correlations among the scales were subjected to factor analysis. Four factors emerged: *association/dissociation* (help, reward, advise, be eager to see, versus grow impatient with, be indignant with, argue with, fear, be prejudiced against), *superordination/subordination* (command, advise, treat as a subordinate, versus ask for help, apologize to, obey), *intimacy* (kiss, cuddle, love, marry, pet), and *hostility* (throw rocks at, fight with, exploit, cheat). These four factors emerged in both the American and the Greek data. Additional factors obtained from the American data were *contempt, tutoring, kinship acceptance, high intensity, envy,* and *work acceptance.* The Greek data yielded a factor that included the behaviors "adore the same God with," "be saddened by attitude of," and "desire good attitude of," suggesting a cluster of behaviors appropriate for one to engage in with people who are similar to one. We named the factor *ingroup concern for consensus.* Note, then, some of the flavor of the similarities and differences in the perception of social behavior across cultures.

It is clear that the factors obtained in this study are not identical to the four dimensions we have been discussing in this chapter. One should keep in mind, however, that, in any empirical study, one gets some results that are accidental, due to the sampling of people, stimuli (in this case, roles), and so on. It is only when we look at many studies, with many kinds of subjects and stimuli, that we can obtain some idea of a stable structure. Further studies of this kind (for example, Triandis, Vassiliou, Vassiliou, Tanaka, & Shanmugam, 1972) suggest that the four dimensions we're considering are likely to be universal. Any specific empirical study will fit these dimensions to some extent, but not perfectly. For example, consider, in Figure 1.1, how the universal dimensions we are discussing here might relate to the factors extracted in the specific Triandis et al. (1968) study. Since the superordination and intimacy dimensions correspond well enough, I have simplified the presentation by ignoring them here. Note that the empirically extracted association/dissociation dimension tends to be similar to the postulated dimension, except for the difference in the "flavor," with the association pole including more overt than covert behaviors and the dissociation pole including more covert than overt behaviors. The empirically extracted hostility factor is a mixture of overt and dissociative behaviors. Such a factor can emerge when the sampling of behaviors is not well balanced. It is likely that, in the empirical study, we did not include enough covert behaviors that were

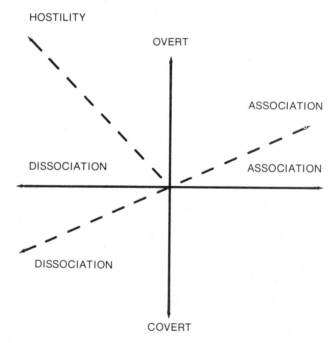

Figure 1.1   Relationship between postulated universal dimensions of social behavior (solid lines) and empirically extracted dimensions (broken lines) from the Triandis, Vassiliou, and Nassiakou (1968) study.

Table 1.2 A Classification of Studies of Social Behavior

	Direct Observation	*Peer Rating*	*Self-Rating*
Attribution	Leary (1957)	LaForge & Suczek (1955)	Lorr & McNair (1965)
Affect	Schlosberg (1954) Triandis & Lambert (1958)*		Osgood (1966)
Overt Behavior (human)	Bales (1950) Carter (1954) Mehrabian (1970) Schaefer (1959) Hall (1959, 1966)* Watson (1970)*	Stogdill & Coons (1957)	Schutz (1958) Triandis (1964) Triandis, Vassiliou, Vassiliou, Tanaka, & Shanmugam (1972)*
	Brown (1965)*	Brown (1965)	Brown (1965)*
(animal)	Mason (1964)		

*A cross-cultural study

associative or neutral on the association/dissociation dimension. One can think of association/dissociation and overt/covert as basic ingredients that can combine in an infinite number of ways; one of the more probable combinations is dissociation and overt acts, which produces hostility.

This example should give you some of the flavor of the way one proceeds in such studies. You should be very much aware of sampling errors present in empirical results. Many replications, using many different samples, are required before a stable pattern can emerge. Once the stable pattern becomes apparent, it can be used as a basis for theoretical work.

What I have tried to make clear in this section is that many methodologies and many kinds of observations done in many different cultures yield similar results, suggesting that the four dimensions I am positing are of universal significance. Table 1.2 gives the authors and dates of studies that offer supporting evidence, ordered according to the methodology used and the kind of behavior investigated.

What Are the Determinants of This Typology?

The typology I am presenting reflects the fact that there are different kinds of social relationships. The reasons for differences in social behavior are many.

Accounting for the fact that some behavior is associative and some dissociative is the fact that people may or may not have similar goals. When they have similar goals, as when they all want to extinguish a fire, their relationship has been called *promotive*, but, when they have opposite goals, as when a salesman bargains with a customer, their relationship is said to be *contrient* (Deutsch, 1949). The difference between promotive and contrient social situations is very large. In promotive situations, associative behaviors are very likely, while in contrient situations dissociative behaviors are likely. Since humans live in environments where resources are finite and limited, it is to be expected that contrient interdependence is likely to characterize interaction rather frequently.

Second, humans have differential access to resources. Some have a lot of money or a lot of status; others have little money or little status. Some have much information; others have little, and so on. Such inequalities in access to resources is bound to lead to difference in social behavior. The superordination/subordination dimension reflects that.

Third, the relationship between two humans is guided by biological and cultural constraints. When people belong to the same family, for instance, nature and culture generally dictate that intimate behaviors are appropriate. The length of a relationship is also a factor in determining behavior: when two persons meet for the first time, they are more likely to use formal behaviors than when they have a well-established relationship. Factors such as this account for some of the diversity along the intimate/informal/formal continuum.

Fourth, behavior may occur overtly or mentally. We all have fantasies, and there are certain things we refrain from doing, because we are afraid of the consequences. Thus, much of a person's social behavior is limited to the mind, and only some of it is overt and manifest for all to see.

Differences in the Weights of Components That Determine Behavior

Differences Due to the Type of Behavior. It should be clear, from what has been discussed already, that the components of the model will have different weights, depending on the type of behavior being predicted. For example, for fantasy behaviors, the social component should have a zero weight, since there are few norms about what one may or may not fantasize (although the Ten Commandments do include one such proscription). Also, the consequences of one fantasy as opposed to another are likely to be of no importance. Thus, in determining fantasies, the affective component will have a large and the other components zero weights.

The social component is more important in the case of intimate than in the case of formal behaviors (Triandis & Davis, 1965; Goldstein & Davis, 1972). For example, parents pressure their children much more when their children are considering dating or kissing than when their children are considering sending a written invitation to a slumber party to someone. It is very probable that the affective component will be relevant for both associative and dissociative behaviors. The affective component will also be relevant for intimate behaviors, but not so much for formal ones. The consequences component will have relevance for most social behaviors that have consequences. Again, formal behaviors have few consequences if they are appropriate, but they have serious consequences if they are inappropriate. For example, during a state visit, behavior that is correct and according to protocol will not improve the relationship between a visiting dignitary and the host, but incorrect behavior could certainly have adverse effects.

Differences Due to the Type of Situation. The weights of the three coefficients of Equation 2 must also reflect situational factors, if the equation is to be useful for prediction. Certain social settings evoke relatively large w_S coefficients. For example, in most religious establishments, there is a detailed specification of the norms, roles, and contractual expectations. A person may do what is expected of him or her by a church because of social pressure or out of fear of the strong negative consequences for behaviors that are inconsistent with these norms. In this case, we would expect relatively large w_S and w_c coefficients but relatively small w_A coefficients. Also, most church settings tend to favor formal rather than intimate behavior.

On the other hand, at a party the w_A coefficients may be the largest, while in a battle the w_C coefficients may be the largest. When the norms, roles, and social arrangements have a large weight, the *behavior setting* (Barker, 1968) is a very important determinant of the behavior. Wicker (1972) has examined a number of theoretical perspectives that may account for the consistency between behavior and social environment and has shown that the behavior setting needs to be considered.

The *behavior setting* is the basic concept used by ecological psychology. To explain this concept, I propose to focus on behavior in the classroom. The classroom is a behavior setting. We note that the behavior setting has both place (the particular location of the classroom) and time (the particular time the class is meeting) coordinates; it is composed of physical entities (chairs, walls, paper), appropriate behaviors (lecturing, listening, notetaking), and other processes (such as air circulation). What is in the setting can easily be distinguished from what is outside of it, there are several structural features (for example, all chairs face the blackboard), and it exists independently of any particular person's perception of it.

The point is that the behavior setting increases the probability of certain behaviors (in our example, say notetaking) and decreases the probability of other behaviors (say, kissing). For this reason, the w_S that is due to a setting will be different depending on the type of behavior being predicted.[4]

Much social behavior is under the influence of rules (Harré, 1974). Harré argues that a playwright's control of actors' behavior is a good model of social action because so much human social behavior is under the influence of etiquette, rules of the game, rituals, and ceremonies. Harré has proposed the systematic study of such rules as the principal way for social scientists to make progress. This view seems a bit extreme, since it is surely true that not all social behavior can be explained by such rules. However, it must be conceded that much social behavior is under their influence, and it is clear that for such behavior the importance of the S component is very great. Again, then, we conclude that the weight to be given to the S component depends on the behavior *and* the setting.

Differences Due to the Type of Individual. Individual differences can be noted in the relative sizes of the components that determine behavior. There is a type of person who tends to do the "right thing" (high w_S). The compulsive type in Freudian theory is such a person. There is also the impulsive type, who does not do what is expected of him or her, or what maximizes good consequences, but rather does what is most pleasant during a brief moment of time. This person's behavior has strong affective determinants. Finally, the calculating, rational, and intellectual type behaves in ways that could best be predicted using large w_c values.[5]

A Comment on the Distinctions among Components

Some theorists do not make the distinction between affect (A) and the value of consequences (C). For example, Fishbein (1967b) assumes that one is an index of the other. However, this is likely to be the case only some of the

[4]Barker also discussed four kinds of "circuits" that pattern behavior in settings: (1) goal circuits, (2) program circuits, (3) deviation-countering circuits, and (4) vetoing circuits. The goal circuit includes people's perception of goals within the setting, ways to achieve goals, and satisfaction derived by their achievement. Program circuits concern the program of the setting. For example, a syllabus provides a program of readings, examinations, and so on related to a course. Deviation-countering circuits are actions that bring people who are not operating as expected within the setting "into line." Vetoing circuits are like deviation-countering circuits except that they eliminate rather than alter an element of the situation. For example, if the teacher expels a pupil from the classroom, rather than simply giving the student a poor grade, a vetoing circuit has been used. See Price (1975) for a good discussion of behavior-setting theory.

[5]It is easy to find names for different types of behavior where the elements of the model are consistent or inconsistent with the behavior. For example, when the S, A, C components are consistent and agree with the behavior, the behavior might be called *integrated.* When there is agreement between the behavior and the S component only, we might call the behavior *ritualistic.* When there is agreement between the behavior and the A component only, we might call it *hedonistic.* When there is agreement between the behavior and the C component only, we might call it *superrationalistic.* When there is agreement between the behavior and the A and C components, but the behavior is contrary to the S component, we have a *rebellion.* If the components agree among themselves, but there is no evidence of the behavior, we might suspect *inability.* If all components are inconsistent among themselves and with behavior, we might suspect some form of mental illness.

time. Many human behaviors are very unpleasant, although they are perceived as having very good consequences. For example, many behaviors that
go under the label "duty" are in themselves unpleasant but are conceived by
individuals as having desirable consequences. Other human behaviors are
very pleasant but lead to undesirable consequences. For example, many may
find that engaging in extramarital activities is intrinsically very enjoyable but
that the consequences are disastrous.

The C component develops when the person acquires information from
others (for example, that going to New York is likely to increase the chances
of seeing a good play) or directly (for example, observing well-off physicians
and concluding that having an M.D. means being well-off). The utility of the
distinction between affect (A) and information (C) can be seen in the diagram
adapted from Clore and Byrne (1974). Figure 1.2 shows a classification of
stimuli that have positive or negative information (consequences) and positive or negative affect.

The execution of an enemy spy may involve positive information, such
as that the person will no longer spy or that the enemy will be discouraged

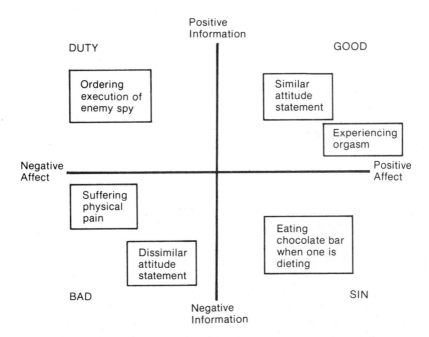

Figure 1.2 A schematic representation of the informational and affective components of evaluative stimuli. Adapted from "A Reinforcement-Affect Model of Attraction," by G. L. Clore and D. Bryne. In T.
L. Huston (Ed.), *Foundation of Interpersonal Attraction.* Copyright 1974
by Academic Press, Inc. Reprinted by permission.

from spying, but it may be associated with intensive negative affect. Many duties have positive consequences associated with unpleasant emotions. When a person makes a statement that reveals attitudes similar to the listener's, this suggests other positive consequences and is affectively positive for the listener. Orgasm and suffering pain are strongly emotional behaviors but often do not have remote consequences. Eating chocolate when one is dieting is very pleasant but has disastrous consequences. Many sins have this characteristic: the behavior itself is very enjoyable, and the consequences are most disagreeable.

The distinction between S and C is also worth discussing. Of course, the norms and roles we perceive as relevant to a particular behavior determine a class of consequences. If we break a norm, we may be punished by the social group to which we belong. However, not all norm breaking has clearly defined consequences. Often we internalize norms, so that they become parts of our values, and the consequences of breaking them may be self-inflicted. At other times, we can see that the probability of a particular consequence is really remote, although the norms are very clear. Furthermore, not all consequences are social in character. Some, if not most, are consequences we experience because of the way the physical environment is structured.

Whether a determinant of behavior should be grouped under the S, A, or C component is sometimes unclear. The rule is that, when the determinant is a social consequence, a perceived social pressure, or a moral concept, it is placed under S. When it is an emotion it is placed under A. And when it is anything else, under C. Some theorists have argued that all one needs is the C component. The reason I make the distinction between S, A, and C and do not deal with all determinants under the C component is that the weights given to S and A may be quite different from the weights given to the C component by some people, for some behaviors, or in some situations.

FEEDBACK

It should be clear that an act has consequences that modify many of the components of the model. Obviously, if the consequences are pleasant or unpleasant, this will change the affect associated with the behavior and the perceived probabilities of the consequences that have occurred, as well as the value of these consequences.

There is considerable evidence that behavior causes attitudes to change. For example, a study by Bruvold (1973) assessed beliefs, attitude, and behavior with reference to water reclaimed from domestic sewage. The water was to supply a public golf course, a recreational park, or a swimming pool. Usage of the three facilities by a sample of people from the community was determined by a series of structured questions. Beliefs about the water were assessed with open-ended questions. Attitude toward the water was assessed through a 26-item scale, focusing on affective statements about the use of reclaimed water. People generally have negative feelings about reclaimed water, but those who use it change their attitudes. Bruvold found that beliefs and behavior determined attitudes (multiple correlation R of .4).

Cognitive-dissonance theorists (Festinger, 1957) have examined the case in which a person does something (for example, smokes), while the cognition of doing it ("I smoke") is inconsistent with some of his or her beliefs (for example, that smoking causes lung cancer). This inconsistency is uncomfortable. One way to reduce the discomfort is to change the beliefs and attitudes and make them consistent with the behavior that has occurred (believing, for example, that there is no *good* evidence that smoking causes cancer). This is presumably what was observed by Bruvold. People who used the reclaimed water may have changed their beliefs and attitudes about the water in order to relieve the discomfort of cognitive dissonance.

SUMMARY

The major points of this chapter can be summarized as follows:

1. Interpersonal behavior is a function of behavioral intentions and habits.

2. The determinants of the probability of an act are the strength of the habit to emit the act, the behavioral intention to emit the act, and the individual's ability to emit the act.

3. The relative weights of the determinants of behavior are ever changing. A novel behavior tends to be determined more by intentions than by habit. Over time, the behavior comes more under the control of habits.

4. Behavioral intentions are a function of social factors, affect, and the value to the actor of the perceived consequences of the behavior.

5. Social influences include norms, roles, social contracts, the social situation, and the person's self-concept.

6. The more frequent the association of the behavior with pleasant events, the more positive the affect associated with the behavior.

7. The value of the perceived consequences of a behavior is a function of the subjective probability that a particular consequence will follow the behavior and the affect attached to that consequence.

8. Social behaviors differ in the degree to which they are (a) associative versus dissociative, (b) superordinate versus subordinate, (c) intimate versus formal, and (d) overt versus covert.

9. The greater the promotive goal interdependence between two individuals, the more likely it is that interpersonal behaviors between them will be associative.

10. The more resources people have under their control, the more superordinate their behavior is likely to be.

11. The greater the length of a social relationship, the more intimate the behaviors that occur in this relationship are likely to be.

12. The stronger the perceived connection between a behavior and positive consequences, the more likely is an overt expression of the behavior.

13. The relative importance of the social, affective, and consequence influences on behavior depends on the type of behavior, the type of social setting, and the type of person who is behaving.

14. The consequences of an act serve as feedback, modifying the components that determine behavior. Thus, behavior can change attitudes.

2

INTERACTION

In the previous chapter, we examined the determinants of particular social behaviors, such as *helping*, *fighting*, *criticizing*, and *obeying*. In the present chapter, we will examine sequences of such behaviors. When P acts and O reacts, this is called an *interaction*. This chapter is concerned with interactions. First we'll examine how we determine whether interactions are going to take place at all.

INTERACTION POTENTIAL

When two persons are in physical proximity, they may or may not interact. The *interaction potential* of their relationship is the probability that interaction will take place.

The interaction potential of a relationship depends on several factors. In general, when people belong to the same family, have a long acquaintance, or are in situations of common fate (where what happens to one will also happen to the other), they are more likely to interact than if these conditions don't hold. Interaction by a given pair is more probable when there are very few other people in a social setting than when there are many others, and it is more likely to take place in private than in public settings.

For example, people who know each other or who know that they belong to the same tribe, village, or race, and who meet in a strange place or under unusual circumstances—say, in a stuck elevator—are much more likely to interact in this situation than are people who do not know each other or who belong to different tribes. When two people meet in a private home, they are more likely to interact, even if they have not been introduced, than if they meet in a public space, such as the university library. However, if there are many people in the room, the interaction potential is reduced. This reduction is particularly the case if one of them knows one of the other people in the room, in which case interaction between acquaintances might take place and the unknown person might be excluded from the interaction.

The interaction potential of a relationship depends also on how attracted P and O are to each other. Attraction is dependent on the similarity of P and O. Similarity in status, beliefs, or other attributes are differentially important in different settings.

The interaction potential increases when the relationship is rewarding. The greater the rewards received from the interaction, and the fewer the costs, the more likely it is that interaction will take place again in the future. For example, when a person finds it particularly enjoyable to be with another, interaction potential increases; on the other hand, when a person annoys, makes unreasonable demands of, or embarrasses the other, the interaction potential decreases. One way of thinking about such changes in interaction potential is to think of the resources that are exchanged in an interaction. Different types of social interaction are characterized by different exchanges of resources. The typology of social behavior you learned about in the previous chapter can be shown to involve different kinds of exchanges of resources.

TYPES OF INTERACTIONS

Interactions can be conceived as exchanges of *resources*. The typology of social behavior presented in Chapter 1 can be restated in a form that is useful when we discuss interactions. Associative behaviors are characterized by P's *giving O* a resource. Dissociative behaviors are characterized by P's *taking away* or *depriving O* of a resource.

Resources differ in kind. Foa and Foa (1974) have identified six kinds of resources and arranged them in a circular structure, as shown in Figure 2.1. The six kinds of resources are (1) money, (2) goods (for example, a present), (3) services (for example, a physician checking the health of a patient), (4) love, (5) status (for example, giving admiration or respect), and (6) information.

The reason these resources form a circular structure is that they differ on two dimensions at the same time: particularism/universalism and concreteness/abstractness. Particularistic resources are exchanged in private settings and are generally considered intimate behaviors. They are called particularistic because it makes a great difference who the particular person is whom the actor interacts with. A lover exchanges love with a particular person; people who are close to important public figures are accorded status when they appear with them on a podium. In terms of interaction, then, in-

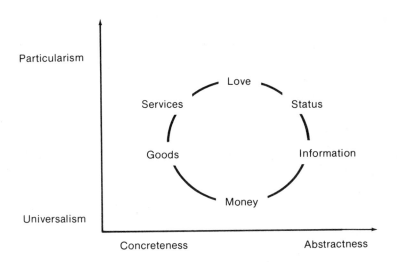

Figure 2.1 Diagram of Foa's theory of interpersonal exchanges.

timacy is the *exchange* of *particularistic resources*. In contrast, one can exchange money with anyone, and, in fact, many financial transactions, from cashing checks to buying and selling stocks and bonds, are quite anonymous. This *exchange* of *universalistic resources* constitutes formal behavior. Thus, one of the ways resources differ is in particularism; the other is in level of abstractness. It is obvious that the resources along the right side of the circle are more abstract and those along the left more concrete than the resources in the middle.

So far, we have identified associative and intimate interactions. We also need to consider, in regard to *interactions*, the superordination/subordination dimension of the typology presented in the previous chapter.

Persons who have more resources than others are in a position to act in a superordinate way. Persons who seek resources from others generally act in a subordinate way. For example, if *P* has a lot of status, *P* can criticize, order people about, and give advice (even when not asked), in ways that would not be likely to happen if *P* had no status. Other people are likely to react to *P* in a subordinate way—by obeying, asking for advice, and so on. Those who obey hope to be given status from the association with and approval of *P*.

One aspect of superordination that is particularly interesting is that superordinate people tend to be the ones who start interaction. Typically, when the boss comes to a conference room, people wait for him or her to start the ball rolling. This is called *initiation of interaction*. There is a dependable phenomenon: people get quite upset when a low-status person initiates interaction with them. For example, if a secretary tells a boss that he/she must do something, the secretary must be sure to phrase it in a way that is not too demanding—otherwise, the boss will be annoyed. Whyte (1948) has discussed extensively the concept of a person initiating interaction for another. Interactions initiated by a high-status person are usually accepted by low-status persons; however, when a low-status person initiates interaction for a high-status person, the interaction may be unacceptable. Whyte (1948) tells the story of the nonresponsiveness of cooks in a Chicago restaurant to the orders brought to them by waitresses. In the restaurant hierarchy, cooks have very high status, and waitresses have low status. The waitresses were under pressure from the customers and yet could not get the cooks to respond. The reason: low-status persons were initiating interaction for high-status persons. The result was that the waitresses broke down and cried. The consultant to this restaurant suggested that a high-status person be introduced into the social system to receive the orders and give them to the cooks. When this "dispatcher" was placed in the social system, the problem of the crying waitresses disappeared. The explanation, of course, is that the cooks were willing to accept initiation of interaction from the dispatcher, since he had more status than the cooks.

To summarize, then, the three main dimensions of the typology of the previous chapter can be restated as follows: Association is *giving* a resource; dissociation is *taking away* or denying a resource. Superordination happens when a person has a lot of one or more resources and *initiates* interaction; subordination is seeking resources or *accepting* the other person's initiation of interaction. Intimacy is *exchanging* a *particularistic resource*; formality is *exchanging* a *universalistic resource*. Of course, corresponding to each action there are feelings, so that the action may be overt or covert.

Foa and Foa (1974) argue that, when a person acts by giving a particular resource, the "natural" reaction for the receiver of this resource is to return a resource of the same kind. Thus, the most natural reaction to receiving love is to give love, to receiving status is to give status, and so on. For example, when P compliments O, O is likely to compliment P. However, if the most natural reaction is not feasible, then reactions that involve adjacent resources (for example, for love, giving status or services; for money, giving goods or information) are most appropriate. Reactions that involve a resource that is far removed on the circle shown in Figure 2.1 (for example, giving money in return for love) are least appropriate. Reciprocity in kind is less frequent the less particularistic the resource (Foa & Foa, 1974). So, money is more likely to be exchanged for goods, services, or information than for money.

Foa and Foa (1974) review a number of studies showing that people do act so as to give resources similar in kind to the resources they receive from others. Furthermore, when a resource is taken away, the reaction is retaliation involving a similar resource. Retaliation will not necessarily wipe out all of the resentment that comes from having a resource taken away, but the residual resentment is greater when a person can retaliate only with a very different resource than when retaliation involves the same resource. Donnenwerth and Foa (1974) discovered that, the farther away on the circle the resources available for retaliation are from the resources in which the loss was incurred, the greater the intensity of the retaliation behavior and the greater the residual hostility.

In an experiment, Donnenwerth and Foa arranged for subjects to be exposed to one of six types of resource loss and allowed to retaliate only by taking away money or love. They found that, when the subjects had experienced loss of love and could retaliate by taking away love, the intensity of the retaliation was smaller than when they could retaliate by taking away money (27.0 units versus 28.2 units of retaliation). When they had experienced loss of money but could retaliate only by taking away love, they did so with greater intensity (38.2 units) than when they could retaliate by taking away money (16.7 units). Measures of the amount of hostility that was left over showed a similar pattern of outcomes.

In other words, the retaliation that follows the formula "an eye for an eye" is likely to involve less intensity than the retaliation by which the person is forced to use very different resources. This might explain some events noted in international relations. For example, when a small nation is humiliated by a big power's sinking one of its ships, the small nation would be satisfied if it could sink one of the ships of the big nation in return. However, since it cannot do so, the reaction increases hatred of the great power far out of proportion to the incident. The inability to retaliate in kind increases the intensity of retaliation.

Lorr, Suziedelis, and Kinnane (1969) did a study that provides us with another chance to test Foa's notions—this time with a rather different method of collecting data. They asked subjects how they believed they would react to the behavior of another. The study involved four types of behavior: *control* (denying status, in Foa's system), *hostility* (denying both status and love), *support* (giving love), and *dependence* (giving status and love). Here are some of the specific behaviors that were used as examples of each type of behavior:

Control:	Tells me all about his accomplishments.
	Attempts to make decisions for me.
Hostility:	Laughs at things that are important to me.
	Avoids talking to me.
Support:	Goes out of his way to please me.
	Praises me to others.
Dependence:	Asks my advice.
	Comes to me for sympathy.

The subjects indicated how they react when another behaves as described above. Specifically, in response to the *control* behaviors, their reactions were:

Type of Reaction	*Example*
Hostility (denying status and love):	Get angry and tell him off.
or	
Sufferance (denying love):	Get annoyed but keep quiet.
or	
Compliance (neutrality of love and giving status):	Go along with it.
or	
Ignoring (denying love and status):	Laugh and ignore it.
In response to *hostility:*	
Hostility (denying love and status):	Get annoyed and tell him off.
or	
Ignoring (denying love and status):	Just ignore it.
or	
Sufferance (denying love):	Get annoyed but do not say anything.
or	
Negotiation (neutrality and denying status):	Ask what is wrong.
In response to *supportiveness:*	
Acceptance (giving love):	Show my appreciation.
or	
Suspicion (neutrality and denying love):	Find out why he is being nice.
or	
Rejection (denying status and love):	Wish he would not be so personal.
In response to *help-seeking:*	
Rebuff (denying status):	Take over and tell him what to do.
or	
Support (denying status and giving love):	Encourage him to be more positive.
or	
Noninvolvement (denying status and love):	Let him work it out for himself.

The study by Lorr and his associates is thus an independent study of interpersonal exchanges. To what extent does it conform with Foa's predictions? If we look at the summaries of data shown above, the prediction of reactions similar in kind to the original action is confirmed in 15 of 18 examples. This is relatively strong support for Foa's position.

In other words, we have seen that interactions follow certain laws. We are now ready to ask what laws govern the relationship between interactions and rewards and costs. As we saw earlier, interaction potential increases as the interactions become more rewarding and decreases as the interactions become more costly. We need to specify the relationship between the various kinds of interactions described in this section and rewards versus costs.

REWARDS AND COSTS

When *P* receives a resource from *O,* this will be called a *reward*. If *P* has a resource taken away, or is denied a resource, this will be called a *cost*. When the resource is particularistic, the reward or cost is particularly high. Frequently, loss of love or status is more costly than loss of money.

When the relationship between *P* and *O* is such that each receives more rewards than costs, it is likely that the interaction potential will increase. Thibaut and Kelley (1959) have outlined a theory in which rewards and costs are the determinants of interpersonal behavior.

Whether a behavior is rewarding or costly depends on four classes of variables: (1) the behavior itself, (2) the perceived causes of the behavior, (3) the expectations of the perceiver, and (4) the needs of the recipient.

The importance of the first class is obvious. If *P* loves *O*, or if *P* gives status to *O*, or if *P* gives money to *O*, such behavior is rewarding to *O*. In contrast, if *P* denies love (that is, hates *O*), or if *P* denies status (for example, ridicules *O*), or if *P* takes money away from *O*, then the behavior is costly to *O*.

However, *O*'s perception of *P*'s behavior, and vice versa, is not only a function of what is actually taking place but also a function of the perceived causes of this behavior. In a later chapter, when I discuss attribution theory, we'll explore this matter in detail. Here I will give only some brief examples. Consider the situation of *P*'s giving *O* some money. If *O* sees this as a bribe, then the behavior will not be rewarding; in fact, it might be costly. Or imagine that *P* gives *O* some status—for example, a compliment—but *O* sees *P* as trying to manipulate him or her. Again, the situation can hardly be called rewarding for *O*. It is clear that the subjective *meaning* of the behavior is crucial: *O* does not react to the actual behavior but to his or her perception of the behavior—including the perception of its causes.

The causes of *P*'s behavior as perceived by *O* can be analyzed using all the elements of the model of social behavior outlined in the previous chapter. Suppose that *P* does something very nice for *O*. First, *O* might see *P*'s behavior as accidental. In such a case *O* might give it a neutral meaning. Second, *P*'s behavior might be felt to be under the influence of facilitating conditions. For example, if *P* is a multimillionaire who makes a $10 gift to *O*, *O* is not likely to be as impressed with the gift as would be the case if the gift represented 50% of *P*'s savings (Maslach, Tashiro, & Gergen, 1972). In short, the ease of making the gift is relevant. Third, the behavior might be seen as a consequence of social factors. For example, if everybody is complimenting *O*, then *P*'s compliments will have less value for *O*, since they will appear as a consequence of *P*'s wanting to do what everybody else is doing. The behavior might also be seen as a consequence of *P*'s role. For example, say *P* invites *O* to dinner. If *O* sees this as part of *P*'s role (say, *P* is the manager of the factory in which *O* works) rather than as a consequence of *O*'s attractiveness to *P*, then *O* will be less impressed by the invitation. Fourth, the behavior might be seen as giving *P* great pleasure. For example, *O* might know that *P* enjoys giving compliments and gives compliments all the time to all sorts of people. In that case, *P*'s compliment will not be very rewarding. Fifth, *O* might see *P*'s behavior as having consequences that will benefit *P*. For example, *O* might see that *P*'s compliment might make him do something that is particularly rewarding to *P*. In such a case, *O* might again feel manipulated and not find *P*'s compliment very rewarding.

In other words, if we think back over the various components of the model, *P*'s behavior might be explained by *O* in a number of ways. It might be seen as due to social factors, such as norms or roles, to *P*'s feelings about the behavior, to *P*'s perceived consequences and the value of these consequences, to facilitating conditions, or to an accident. In none of these cases is *P* going to get much credit from *O* for having behaved in a rewarding way, because *O* does not see that *P*'s behavior has much to do with *O*'s characteristics. On the other hand, if *O* feels *P*'s behavior to be the result of *O*'s charm, attractiveness, intelligence, or whatever, *O* will find *P*'s behavior much more rewarding.

Conversely, if *P* does something that is very costly to *O*, this behavior may also not have a great impact on the relationship, depending on how *O* perceives the causes of *P*'s behavior. Again, if the behavior is seen as accidental (say, *P* kicked *O* by mistake) it will have a small impact, and a mere "I'm sorry" is likely to restore the good relationship. If *P* acted because norms or roles required it (say, the boss was seen as required by his or her role to warn the employees that they would lose their jobs because of bad business conditions), the impact of this for the interpersonal-relationship behavior would be relatively small. If *P* was seen as hating to do the costly act, or as doing it in spite of the fact that it would have bad consequences for him or her, again, the interpersonal impact would be small. On the other hand, if *P*'s act is seen as a consequence of one of *O*'s characteristics, the impact will be greater.

The third factor concerns the expectations of *O* concerning *P*'s behavior. Given the particular social situation, *O* is likely to expect *P* to behave in certain ways. For example, *P* might be a person of high status, and *O* might expect *P* to initiate interaction. If *P* does behave as expected, the situation is rewarding; but, if *P* behaves in unexpected ways, the situation might be costly. For example, if *O* expects a reward, and *P* takes away a resource (for example, if *O* expects *P*'s thanks and instead is scolded), or if *O* expects one resource and receives another (for example, *O* expects to be paid for some work and instead receives only a compliment), then the interaction is costly.

Expectations in particular social situations depend on the definition of the situation. If the situation is one in which there is promotive interdependence, such as common goals, *O* is likely to expect *P*'s interactions to be rewarding. If the situation is competitive, *O* might expect *P*'s interactions to be costly. If *P* has many resources, *O* might expect *P* to initiate action, while, if *O*'s resources are greater than *P*'s, the expectation is likely to be that *O* will be the initiator.

The fourth factor concerns the needs of the recipient. If the resource that is being offered satisfies those needs directly, it is more valuable than if it does so indirectly. For example, a student who has been rejected by a girlfriend/boyfriend will be much more rewarded by expressions of *love* from another girlfriend/boyfriend than by an offer of *money* from someone.

Norms Governing Expectations of Interaction

Expectations come from norms found in human societies. According to Gouldner (1960), in most cultures a person expects to be helped by people whom he or she has helped; in short, there is a norm of *reciprocity*. As a minimum, one expects that people who have been helped will not act in costly ways.

The appropriateness of a behavior in response to another's behavior is generally governed by norms such as reciprocity. Specifically, there is a tendency to respond to the giving of a resource with the giving of a resource and to the taking away of a resource with the taking away of a resource. Of course, there are ideologies (for example, turning the other cheek) that specify a different norm. But these are not nearly so widely adhered to as the norm of reciprocity.

As mentioned earlier, Foa and Foa (1974) present much evidence that people feel that the most appropriate response to the giving of a particular resource is the returning of a resource of the same kind. This kind of exchange reflects a norm that can be found in many human societies. Many other kinds of norms can be found, and among the most interesting are those that concern *equity* versus *equality*.

Suppose that a team consisting of three players wins a prize. Suppose further that one of the players is superb, while the other two are average. How should they divide the prize? One norm would say equally; that is the norm of equality. Another norm would say according to ability; that is the norm of equity.

The principle of equity (Adams, 1965) can be stated as the equality of the ratios of inputs to outputs of P and O. In short, $I_p/O_p = I_o/O_o$. In the example above, the superb player should get more of the money. If we represent the best player's contribution to winning the prize by I_p, the other two members' combined contribution by I_o, the amount of money received by the superb player by O_p, and the money received by the others by O_o, then the equity equation tells how the money should be divided.

$$O_p = \frac{I_p}{I_o} O_o.$$

For example, a person who has more education, is more attractive, has more expertise or is more influential than another person with whom he or she is collaborating might expect to receive more rewards as the result of the collaboration than the other person. In a later section, I will discuss some reformulations of the equity principle (Walster, Berscheid, & Walster, 1973) and examine evidence of the way it operates.

The operation of the equity principle can make an exchange appear inappropriate. For example, suppose a U.S. Supreme Court Justice meets a law student in an elevator and smiles at him. The equity principle would require that the law student respond with a behavior that is much more valuable than a mere smile. He might, for example, tell the justice that his recent court decision was admirable. If he just smiles back, the behavior might be seen as inadequate.

There are circumstances when people will use the norm of equality instead of the norm of equity. For example, at a dinner party, people usually get equal shares of the food, rather than portions proportional to their status. In general, when the outputs involve the same resource as the inputs, equity is the principle that operates most strongly; when the outputs involve a very different resource, equality may be the principle, particularly if it is ideologically imposed (as, for example, in the socialist countries).

In general, the principle of reciprocity is relevant to direct interpersonal relationships; the principles of equity and equality prevail in situations where there is interdependence within a social system.

In examining the effects of exchanges in restoring equity—as, for instance, when a person receives a favor that he or she did not expect—it is desirable to think of the *kind* and *amount* of the resource that is exchanged. Foa and Foa (1974) review literature that suggests that, the more appropriate the resource that is being given, the smaller the amount needed to be given in return in order to restore equity. In our example, if one can return the favor, equity is restored; but if one is forced to give money in exchange, a good deal of money might be required to restore the equity. Furthermore, the appropriateness of the resource depends on the needs of the recipient. If a person has lost status by being rejected from participation in some important activity, what he or she needs to be given most is status. If, instead, somebody gives the person money, the amount given must be a great deal in order to make up for the loss of status.

Because of the importance of reciprocity in social exchanges, when we receive a resource, we feel obliged to give back a resource. As a consequence, when we receive a resource and are unable to reciprocate, we feel embarrassed. For this reason, interpersonal attraction depends on both the extent to which one person can provide resources that the other needs and the extent to which resources can be reciprocated. A very high-status individual may not be an ideal partner because he or she may need too little of what we might be able to give. When such a person makes a mistake, he or she becomes more attractive because we are now able to give something (sympathy). Such factors explain, in part, the failure of U.S. foreign-aid programs. When the U.S. gives aid to India, for instance, India finds that it doesn't have enough to give back. The reaction is one of frustration, resentment, and devaluation of the significance of the aid. Gergen (1969) reports an experiment that showed that people are most attracted to a gift giver under conditions of maximum reciprocity and least attracted when they have (a) no obligation to return the gift or (b) an obligation to return the gift with interest and also to do a favor.

Reactions to Inappropriate Actions

If *P* does something that is considered inappropriate and is aware of the inappropriateness, he or she will feel guilty or ashamed. Self-punishment is a likely response to this situation. Self-punishment can take many forms. For example, *P* might engage in behaviors that are costly to him or her and rewarding to other people. In general, rewarding another can increase the actor's self-esteem, since the mere fact of being able to reward the other is indicative of the actor's having resources to spare.

When people receive more rewards than they consider appropriate, they are also likely to feel embarrassed. When they receive less than they expect, they are likely to feel cheated. Thus, deviation from expectation, or from the level of reward that a person considers appropriate, is likely to lead to dissatisfaction (Baron, 1966). When people receive resources greater than what is called for by their definition of the situation, they are likely to restore balance by giving a resource. People who lack the resources to reciprocate feel resentful of those who have given them a resource (Gergen, 1969).

When a person of high inputs gives a resource to a person with low inputs, *in a situation that calls for equity,* the low-inputs person may be particularly resentful, since he or she is required to reciprocate with more rewards than he or she has received. The person may not have so many resources and may therefore feel embarrassed. The giver might also feel embarrassed when it becomes clear that the receiver is unable to reciprocate. For example, if the Supreme Court Justice were to praise to the sky our mere law student, the law student would be embarrassed, since it would be almost impossible for him to return the compliment. The most likely reaction of the law student would be to say something that would reduce his own status, thus reducing the intensity of the compliment.

Guilt, shame, embarrassment, and other negative feelings result in reductions in the interaction potential. In short, when O behaves inappropriately, P experiences a cost. Costs reduce the interaction potential. In contrast, rewards increase the interaction potential.

INTERPERSONAL ATTRACTION
AND INTERACTION

The more attractive O is to P, the more likely P is to interact with O. Hence, interaction potential is a function of interpersonal attraction.

Interaction potential is obviously greatly facilitated by propinquity. The nearer P and O are to each other, the more likely they are to have a relationship high in interaction potential. For example, when we look at the friendship patterns in suburbs (Whyte, 1956), we note that people become friends and interact much more with people who are located near them than with people who are located far from them. Only when they get together for a specific purpose, such as to play chess or to eat a gourmet meal, are they likely to choose friends who are not their direct neighbors.

The direction of causality in the propinquity/attraction relationship has been a matter of dispute. One can argue that propinquity leads to attraction or that attraction leads to propinquity. My theoretical analysis suggests that people like those who reward them and that, if the other is similar and near, the relationship will be rewarding.

It is much easier to interact with someone who is near than with someone who is far. If there is no interaction, the other's similarity or difference has no effect on the interaction potential. However, if there is interaction, the other's similarity or difference becomes crucial. The more similar others are to us, the more likely they are to agree with our views, and agreement is itself rewarding. Furthermore, our own understanding of the world is imperfect, and we are not sure of our own position on a lot of issues. When we find others who share our positions, particularly on confusing issues, we feel more confident of our views, and this is also rewarding. Much evidence consistent with these ideas was presented in a classic study by Festinger, Schachter, and Back (1950). When proximity and physical features of the environment increased the probability of interaction, the results were higher rates of interaction and interpersonal attraction. Thus, at least when people are similar to start with, propinquity is the cause of attraction.

This can be seen well in a study done with 44 Maryland state police trainees (Segal, 1974). One can guess that people who decide to become police officers have much in common. In this particular case, all subjects were white, male, and between the ages of 21 and 30; they were largely of blue-collar backgrounds, Protestant, and married. They were assigned to rooms and to seats in the classroom on the basis of the alphabetical order of their last names. Therefore, the closer two trainees were in alphabetical order, the more likely they were to room near each other and to be near each other in training sessions. When the trainees were asked for the names of their three closest friends on the force, 45% of the choices were trainees adjacent to the choosers on the alphabetical list. The correlation between the chooser's place in alphabetical order and the men he chose as his friends was .92—a correlation that can occur by chance fewer than once in a thousand times. Proximity clearly occurs prior to friendship, since people acquire names long before they go to police school.

When a person evaluates another positively, he or she is likely to be evaluated by the other positively; negative O's are evaluated negatively by P. However, the amount of liking reported depends on whether the evaluator is trying to be accurate about his or her emotions or to please another (Lowe & Goldstein, 1970). Both liking and disliking are greater when O tries to be accurate than when O tries to please.

PROXIMAL VERSUS DISTAL ANTECEDENTS OF INTERACTION

Most of the variables that I've presented so far in my discussion as antecedents of interaction are directly and closely related to interaction. However, if we are to obtain a broad view of determinants of interaction, we should look at an enlarged theoretical framework. The work of Jessor and Jessor (1973) is particularly helpful in this respect. They argue that it is possible and useful to order the environments that determine interaction along a proximal/distal dimension. Expectations of others, evaluations of others, social approval, and so on are proximal variables. The most distal variables include climate, race, culture, and social structure. Between these two extremes there are variables of intermediate proximity to the effects we wish to study. Thus, a variable such as "normative conflict" is intermediate in proximity; it emerges from the cultural and social environment, which may provide conflicting norms with respect to a particular interaction.

Thus, to understand social interaction, we might look at a broad set of variables. The expectation is that the proximal variables will be the best to explain interaction. However, the distal variables will act *through* them and *can* be used to explain interaction—but they will not show as powerful relationships as proximal variables do. Thus, knowing that P and O are of a different race will not be nearly so helpful as knowing the kinds of interactions that have just taken place between them, the kinds of expectations they have about interaction, and other proximal variables.

INTERIM SUMMARY

People exchange resources, which differ in particularism. The more particularistic resources are exchanged in intimate rather than formal settings. When a person gives a resource, he or she acts associatively; when a person takes away a resource, he or she acts dissociatively. When P has more resources than O, and initiates action for O, P is acting in a superordinate manner. Thus, the basic dimensions of human interaction are giving versus taking resources, initiating or not initiating the exchange, and the extent of particularism of the resource being exchanged. Situations can differ in interaction potential. The greater the familiarity, the sense of a common fate, and the attraction between P and O, the more likely is interaction between them. Propinquity increases interaction potential.

In general, receiving resources is rewarding and having resources taken away is punishing (costly). Particularistic exchanges are more rewarding than universalistic ones. Initiating interaction is more rewarding than passively accepting another's initiatives. People act so as to maximize rewards and minimize costs. Interaction is rewarding or costly not just on the basis of what actually is exchanged but also on the basis of what is perceived as the cause of the exchange. The expectations that P and O have about interactions determine how satisfied they will be with them. The more O behaves according to P's expectations of how O is to behave, the more P will be satisfied with O's behavior and will find it rewarding.

People develop norms concerning interaction. Reciprocity, equity, and equality are three kinds of norms. When O behaves in ways that are inappropriate according to the norms, P feels angry, guilty, or ashamed.

GENERALIZED EQUITY THEORY

Some of the propositions listed in the interim summary have been placed within the framework of a generalized equity theory by Walster, Berscheid, and Walster (1973). Walster and her associates (1973) list the following propositions:

I. Individuals will try to maximize their outcomes (where outcomes are rewards minus costs).

II.A. Groups can maximize collective rewards by evolving accepted systems for "equitably" apportioning rewards and costs among members. Thus, members will evolve such systems of equity and will attempt to induce members to accept and adhere to these systems.

II.B. Groups will generally reward members who treat others equitably and generally punish (increase costs for) members who treat others inequitably.

III. When individuals find themselves participating in inequitable relationships, they become distressed. The more inequitable the relationship, the more distressed individuals feel.

IV. Individuals who discover they are in an inequitable relationship attempt to eliminate their distress by restoring equity. The greater the inequity that exists, the more distress they feel and the harder they try to restore equity.

Walster and her associates discuss the number of applications of this generalized equity theory. The most interesting applications, for interpersonal behavior, are those that concern (a) exploitative relationships, (b) helping relationships, and (c) intimate relationships.

Exploitation involves O's commission of an act that causes P to obtain outcomes that fall short of O's outcomes. When people know that they have received high outcomes at someone else's expense, they feel distressed. The label may be "guilt," "fear of retaliation," "dissonance," "empathy," or "conditioned anxiety," but the point is that they feel distressed. The source of the distress can be fear of retaliation and/or threatened self-esteem. Many people are socialized to feel anxious when they behave unfairly. However, there are many ways to decrease this distress. One can, for example, balance some of the harm by giving to the other a resource—that is, by *compensating* the victim. For instance, a child who eats the last piece of cake may offer part of his or her ice cream to those who were cheated. Another way to deal with this distress is to change one's attitude. For example, one might convince oneself that some people *deserve* to get less, because they are less good. Triandis and Triandis (1960) hypothesized that some of the White prejudice toward Blacks was exactly this kind of reduction of distress. Whites knew they were cheating Blacks—economically, politically, socially; the cognition "Blacks are inferior" is consistent with this behavior, since it justifies it. Walster and her associates review other studies that show that people often derogate a victim, minimize the victim's suffering, deny responsibility for the exploitative act, or distort the perception of reality in some other way. In general, when the harm-doer uses compensation, he or she does not use derogation or justification, and vice versa. Thus, compensation and justification are mutually exclusive techniques. Walster and her associates argue that, the more adequate and the less costly is a technique to reduce inequity, the more likely is the harm-doer to adopt that technique. An "adequate" compensation is one that can exactly balance the harm done. Both insufficient and excessive compensations are inadequate.

To restore complete equity in a relationship, O will need, if he or she has harmed P, to conceive of justifications that adequately excuse the harm and are plausible to O, to the victim, and to others. A justification that requires little distortion of reality is more credible than one that requires a great deal of distortion. A justification that no one believes does not restore equity. The more contact O has (or anticipates having) with P the less likely O is to use justification for the harm-doing. That last point is supported by the fact that, the more contact between P and O, the more information each has about the other, so that any cognitive distortions of reality may be contradicted by facts. Furthermore, much contact between P and O means that O will have trouble maintaining the justification in the face of further contradictions in the future.

The equity-restoring technique that will be adopted by the exploiter will tend to be the least costly technique. If the victim retaliates—or forgives—the exploiter will often not need to do anything more to restore equity. An apology is another way of restoring equity.

We turn now to Walster's discussion of helping relationships. If O helps P, the relationship becomes inequitable because now P is "indebted" to O. P can restore balance by giving O something valuable or by justifying the help. If P has the ability to repay, he or she will probably use compensation as the technique of restoring equity; if P does not have the ability to repay, he or she will probably use justification. Individuals are more likely to accept gifts that can be reciprocated than gifts that cannot be repaid.

Finally, Walster and her associates examine intimate relationships. The main proposition is that individuals' romantic choices are influenced by considerations of equity. People tend to choose and prefer partners of approximately their own "social worth." However, there is an upward bias in one's choices. Individuals persist in trying to form relations with partners who they feel are somewhat more desirable than themselves. Intimate relationships are influenced in part by equity and in part by fantasy.

There are two essential aspects to equity theory. First, people compare their worth (inputs) with the rewards (outputs) they obtain from social interaction. Second, they compare the ratios of their inputs and outputs with the ratios of the inputs and outputs of others. Which others? Those others who are in the same physical situation, who are perceived as similar, and who are attractive or prestigeful.

Walster and her associates have given us a generalized equity theory that incorporates many of the propositions we presented in the summary of the argument to this point. They show how people restore equity by compensating for or justifying exploitation. It should be recognized that equity theory is a cognitive consistency theory. There is a good deal of evidence (Abelson et al., 1968) supportive of the proposition that people seek some forms of consistency and avoid some forms of inconsistency among their cognitions and between their behaviors and their cognitions.

A QUICK REVIEW OF CONSISTENCY THEORIES

One of the most important areas of research in social psychology concerns the phenomenon that people try to maintain some sort of balance among their cognitions. The idea is that inconsistency among cognitive elements is unpleasant and that subjects have a natural tendency to change their cognitions to make them consistent. For example, if P likes O and X, but O dislikes X, and P knows that O dislikes X, P has cognitions that are incompatible: "I like O, but O dislikes X, and I like X." The inconsistency can be removed by the person's changing his or her attitude, either toward O or toward X. Let's take as an example the second case. Now the cognitions are "I like O, O dislikes X, and I dislike X." Of course, things are more complicated. One might also (a) stop thinking about it, (b) bolster one of the cognitions (I like O in spite of the fact that he/she does not like X), (c) differentiate one of the cognitions (O does not like to talk with X, but he does like to play golf with him), or (d) transcend the inconsistency (people such as O generally don't like X). Many more permutations have been found, which cannot be reviewed here (for a more adequate review, see Triandis, 1971, pp. 68–84).

The crucial point of cognitive-consistency theories is that people are uncomfortable when they hold inconsistent ideas and that they'll do something about changing their ideas to make them consistent. The ideas can be of many kinds. They may be beliefs, such as "The federal government is spending too much money," affect, such as "I like the President of the U.S.," and behavioral intentions, such as "I intend to vote against the President of the U.S." There is much evidence that people hold consistent beliefs, affect, and behavioral intentions. Also, when people have behaved in a certain way, they tend to develop beliefs, affect, and behavioral intentions that are consistent and justify their behavior.

One of the most important aspects of consistency theory, for our purposes, is its implication for the relationship between attitude toward the other and attitude toward the behaviors one engages in with respect to the other.

Attitude toward Behavior and toward the Other

The model in Chapter 1 examines the determinants of behavior and includes the affect attached to the behavior as one of the determinants of behavior. Common-sense thinking about interpersonal behavior tells us that people do nice things to those they like and nasty things to those they dislike. If we place this in the framework we've been using, P will reward O if he or she likes O; P will increase O's costs if he or she dislikes O.

People may act to give another a resource because they like the other. However, O may not perceive this action as a reward. P and O may use different causes as explanations of the behavior, or the behavior may cause the relationship to become inequitable. For example, if P gives O some money, which O perceives as a bribe, P's action is not rewarding to O. Or if P gives a present to O that O is unable to repay with a suitable present or other favor, inequity results, and, again, O does not feel rewarded. So, although in general "nice" behavior on the part of P is likely to be rewarding to O, this is not always the case.

To the extent that P and O are aware of the possibility of discrepancies in the interpretation of behavior and of the problem of inequity, they may act to avoid such misinterpretations and to maintain or restore equity. Such actions may not be entirely consistent with their interpersonal attraction, so interpersonal attraction may not always be a good predictor of action. For example, P and O may dislike each other and yet exchange compliments. It's a good idea to keep such complexities in mind when analyzing interpersonal relationships.

In the previous section, we examined different types of interactions and discussed sequences of actions and interactions and some of the determinants of such sequences. In order for social psychologists to study interactions, they must have ways of measuring them. The kinds of methods that were developed for the measurement of interactions clarify further the meaning of the concept of interaction. We turn now to an examination of the measurement of interaction.

MEASURING INTERACTION

Over the years, a number of systems have been developed to measure interaction. Probably the best known is that of Bales (1950), which is shown in Table 2.1. Category 1 involves what the Foas would call giving love and status, while Category 12 involves taking away love and status. The A categories are generally rewarding, while the D categories are costly to those receiving the interaction. The B categories involve giving resources and the C asking for resources.

This system was developed to classify the interactions of problem-solving groups. The usual experimental situation involved several Harvard students who got together to discuss and solve some problem. Obviously, in such situations some of the exchanges postulated by Foa were not likely to

Table 2.1 A System of Categories of Interactions

A. 1.	Shows solidarity, raises other's status, gives help, reward.
A. 2.	Shows tension release, jokes, laughs, shows satisfaction.
A. 3.	Agrees, shows passive acceptance, understands, concurs, complies.
B. 4.	Gives suggestion, direction, implying autonomy for other.
B. 5.	Gives opinion, evaluation, analysis, expresses feeling, wish.
B. 6.	Gives orientation, information, repeats, clarifies, confirms.
C. 7.	Asks for orientation, information, repetition, confirmation.
C. 8.	Asks for opinion, evaluation, analysis, expression of feeling.
C. 9.	Asks for suggestion, direction, possible ways of action.
D.10.	Disagrees, shows passive rejection, formality, withholds help.
D.11.	Shows tension, asks for help, withdraws out of field.
D.12.	Shows antagonism, deflates other's status, defends or asserts self.

take place. For example, in this kind of setting students were very unlikely to give each other a back rub (a service), or a present (goods), or money. The very fact that the setting involved exchanges of ideas limited the interactions to the more abstract aspects of Foa's circle.

The same kind of limitation is likely to be faced in any experimental setting. It is simply too costly to examine all possible types of interpersonal behaviors in the laboratory. Thus, a general system of observation of interactions has not yet been developed, although we can imagine how Foa's conceptualization might be used in different settings.

The Bales system is useful because it forces the observer to classify everything that happens. What the observer sees is a variety of specific acts—most of them verbal but quite a few nonverbal. The verbal can be classified quite easily. For example, when a person says to the other: "I think your idea is stupid; I have a much better one," it is easy to classify the interaction as Category 12. There are many nonverbal behaviors that are less clearly classifiable.

Many other systems have been developed for the study of interaction in particular settings. For example, there are systems for the study of the interaction of teachers and pupils in the classroom. Generally, these systems break down the Bales categories even more finely, distinguishing behaviors that their developers think are particularly important in the classroom.

NONVERBAL BEHAVIOR

There are two general types of nonverbal behavior: *proxemics* are spatial factors, such as how far people sit from each other, whether they touch each other, and how frequently they have eye contact; *paralinguistic* factors are voice qualities.

People speak with the rest of their bodies almost as much as with their mouths. Gestures, eye contact, grimaces, touching, blinking, and many emotional expressions are used in interaction. A fast-developing field of social psychology is the study of proxemic behavior, paralinguistics (Mehrabian, 1972), and nonverbal communication, including silent messages (Mehrabian, 1971).

Mehrabian and Ksionzky (1972) studied the first two minutes of interaction between strangers. They found evidence that different kinds of nonverbal behaviors "go together" to form factors. Table 2.2 shows six factors of social behavior. Note that *affiliative* behavior is indexed by such elements as talking a lot, looking at the other a lot, saying positive things, and making a lot of gestures. *Responsiveness* is reflected by a lot of loud vocal activity. *Relaxation* is indexed by leaning and by few rocking or foot and leg movements. *Ingratiation* involves a pleasant voice, few negative statements, and the asking of many questions. *Distress* includes walking about, playing with objects, and placing one's arms in asymmetrical positions. Finally, *intimacy* is reflected in sitting close to and with shoulder away from the other and looking around.

Earlier work by Mehrabian (1970) had found three dimensions of nonverbal behavior, which he labeled *evaluation, potency,* and *responsiveness.* Evaluation is like giving love, potency is a status dimension, and responsiveness is an activation or activity dimension. Positive evaluation is denoted by sitting closer to another, leaning forward, making eye contact, and directly facing the other. Increases in potency or status are denoted by greater degrees of postural relaxation. Increases in responsiveness are marked by greater facial activity, changes in speech intonation, and faster speech. Mehrabian (1971) also found, in experimental situations, that one can manipulate these dimensions and that each dimension has specific correlates. For example, the dimension positive affect is related to the number of statements made per minute. Avoidance behavior can be elicited in human subjects by simply having someone stare at them (Ellsworth, Carlsmith, & Henson, 1972).

Continuing this line of work, Mehrabian and Ksionzky (1972) manipulated the extent to which *P* received positive or negative reinforcements from *O* and anticipated cooperation or competition with *O*. They developed a composite index for each variable. For example, affiliative behavior was indexed by the total number of statements, percent duration of eye contact, positive verbal content, head nods per minute, hand and arm gestures per minute, and pleasantness of facial expressions.

They found more affiliative behavior among those who had a high affiliative tendency (a personality variable obtained by questionnaire), who

Table 2.2 Nonverbal Factors of Social Behavior

	Loading Direction on Factor
Factor I: Affiliative Behavior	
Total number of statements per minute	(+)
Number of declarative statements per minute	(+)
Percent duration of eye contact with confederate	(+)
Percent duration of subject's speech	(+)
Percent duration of confederate's speech	(+)
Positive verbal content	(+)
Head nods per minute	(+)
Hand and arm gestures per minute	(+)
Pleasantness of facial expressions	(+)
Factor II: Responsiveness	
Vocal activity	(+)
Speech rate	(+)
Speech volume	(+)
Factor III: Relaxation	
Rocking movements per minute	(−)
Leg and foot movements per minute	(−)
Body lean	(+)
Factor IV: Ingratiation	
Pleasantness of vocal expressions	(+)
Negative verbal content	(−)
Verbal reinforcers given per minute	(+)
Number of questions per minute	(+)
Self-manipulations per minute	(+)
Factor V: Distress	
Percent duration of walking	(+)
Object manipulations per minute	(+)
Arm position asymmetry	(+)
Factor VI: Intimacy	
Shoulder orientation away from confederate	(+)
Distance from confederate	(−)
Head turns per minute (looking around)	(+)

From "Categories of Social Behavior," by A. Mehrabian and S. Ksionzky, *Comparative Group Studies,* 1972, *3,* 425–436, as adapted from *Nonverbal Communication,* by A. Mehrabian. Reprinted by permission of the publisher, Sage Publications, Inc.

expected cooperation, or who had anticipated *competition* but received both a lot of rewards and a lot of costs; there was little affiliative behavior among those who had anticipated *cooperation* but received a lot of both rewards *and* costs. Affiliative behavior was low for affiliators who received high costs and high for such people when they received low costs from interaction.

Ekman (1965) suggested that aspects of affective communication that are carried by the head are different from those carried by the body. To understand his experiments, it is necessary to understand Schlosberg's (1954) theory of emotion. According to Schlosberg, emotional expressions differ on three dimensions: pleasant versus unpleasant, attention versus rejection, and tension versus sleep. The emotional labels love and anger, surprise and disgust, and high-intensity emotion and sleep define the poles of these three dimensions.

These dimensions are apparently cultural universals, since Lambert and I (Triandis & Lambert, 1958) and Wolf (cited in Lambert & Lambert, 1973) have shown that the dimensions account for emotional expressions among such diverse groups as Greek and Chinese villagers. Ekman (1965) showed subjects photographs of a person undergoing a stress interview, and the subjects rated the picture on the three Schlosberg dimensions. In some experimental conditions, only the head was shown, in other conditions only the body, and in still others both the head and the body. Ekman showed that subjects made reliable ratings of the emotions of the interviewee. However, the correlations, based on the head cues, were much higher on the pleasant/unpleasant dimension than on the sleep/tension dimension, while, when body cues were shown, the pattern of correlations was reversed. That is, the correlations among ratings on the sleep/tension dimension were large, and the correlations of ratings on the pleasant/unpleasant dimension were insignificant. In short, Ekman developed the theory that the head communicates the *meaning* and the body the *intensity* of the emotion.

Ekman and Friesen (1967) later revised this theory, claiming that the face is an affect display system, while the body shows the person's attempts to deal with affect. Information about the nature of the emotion can be obtained from both head and body, but, since the rate of facial expressions exceeds the rate of body movements, the perception of specific emotions can more frequently be made from head than from body cues. The intensity of emotion can also be obtained from both types of cues. Facial expressions can convey the full range of intensity information, but the most extreme intensities are often not conveyed. Body acts usually convey from moderate- to high-intensity information. One reason for this difference between facial and body expression is that, although social norms prohibit extremes of facial expression, usually there are few normative specifications concerning body movements.

Ekman and Friesen (1972) also distinguished among three kinds of hand movements. *Emblems* are movements that have a definite meaning, such as indicating an unambiguous "sit down," "stop talking," or whatever. Schnapper (1969) has provided pictures of Swazi (an African tribe) gestures, which are quite specific, such as "a drink of water," "beer drunk from a calabash," "milk drunk from a cow's teat," and so on. *Illustrators* are gestures used to augment or contradict what is being said. The authors use a number of other terms to identify various illustrators, such as *batons* (movements that accent or emphasize a particular word or phrase), *ideographs* (movements that sketch the path or direction of thought), *pictographs* (movements that draw a picture in the air of the shape of the referent), and so on. Finally, *adaptors* are movements first learned as part of an effort to satisfy self needs or body needs, to cope with emotions, to maintain interpersonal relationships, or to learn instrumental activities. While emblems and illustrators are emitted intentionally, adaptors are under habit control. These distinctions among hand movements, according to the authors, also apply to facial and leg movements and have relevance for psychopathology (Ekman & Friesen, 1974). By carefully measuring gestural movements, the psychologist can reach useful conclusions concerning the state of psychiatric patients.

Many nonverbal interactions are indicative of interpersonal difficulties. One of the most interesting ideas, in this regard, is the notion of "personal space." By personal space, we mean the amount of space that individuals feel belongs to them. When another (O) comes close to P and enters his or her personal space, P may try to get away from O, may feel uncomfortable with O's "intrusion," and may try to stay as far as possible from O. For example, at a cocktail party, a person with a small personal space may come very close to a person with a large space. Then the latter might try to get away from the former, but the former may "chase" him or her around the floor (Hall, 1959, 1966). All of this can happen without either realizing what is going on. People do not verbalize that they have a small or large personal space, so they cannot understand why they feel uncomfortable when someone else "invades" their personal space. In general, personal space is larger among those who are disturbed, who are in tension, or who have been brought up in areas of the world that are not influenced by Mediterranean cultures. Mediterraneans (Southern Europeans and Arabs) tend to have very small personal spaces. South Americans, influenced by the Iberian cultures (Spanish and Portuguese), also have small personal spaces. Often people who have small personal space also use many gestures, touch a lot, speak loudly, and use a lot of eye contact; gestures and personal space are interrelated.

While the Ekman and Friesen viewpoint about the relevance and importance of gestures is highly persuasive, I should offer some cautions. Evans and Howard (1973), in their review of studies of "personal space," note a lack of consistent findings. There seems to be some evidence that subjects who are distressed need more personal space, but the relationship between abnormalities and personal space is unclear. There is evidence that demographic variables are relevant: females have smaller personal spaces than males, and heterosexual pairs have smaller spaces than same-sexed pairs. Persons of the same age approach each other more closely than do persons of different ages.

There is a good deal of evidence suggesting cultural differences in personal space. Watson (1970) reviewed several studies, starting with the classic books by Hall (1959, 1966). Following Hall, he distinguished high-contact (Arab, Latin American, and Southern European) from noncontact (Asian, Indian-Pakistani, and Northern European) cultures. He showed significant differences in proxemic behavior between these two groups of cultures, represented among the students at the University of Colorado. Careful observations showed differences in orientation of the relationship (where *close* is defined as face-to-face and *far* is defined as facing in opposite directions), in physical closeness (distance when standing next to each other), in touching (holding and caressing versus no contact), in visual contact (focusing directly on the other's eyes versus looking down or gazing into space), and in voice loudness (very loud to very soft). On all these measures, the culturally defined contact group was significantly different from the noncontact group. The correlations among the five measures of proxemic behavior tended to be positive and significant. Watson's analysis suggests that proxemic behavior is under habit control and is learned through imitation.

In general, studies show that threat leads to greater personal distance. Persons who are more friendly use smaller spaces than persons who are less friendly. Hall has suggested that personal space operates similarly to individual distance in animals. Crook (1974) has analyzed primate behavior and related it to the ecology. He shows that, when there is too little food, primates tend to disperse and to form social structures in which several males have no offspring. Dispersion can be obtained through territorial behavior, which includes vigorous group displays and adult males facing each other with tails raised. Aggression usually occurs only when territory is violated.

Evans and Howard (1973) suggest that personal space allows humans to keep stress at acceptable levels and aids animals in the control of intraspecies aggression. Watson's review suggests the same thing. The size of the primates' territory is based on the available food supply. Dispersal not only reduces aggression but also helps reduce mortality through the reduction of the spread of disease. In sum, it appears that the maintenance of a certain amount of personal space is a habitual behavioral pattern that has been reinforced through reduction of aggression and through the maintenance of minimal stress levels.

This section has suggested the multiplicity of measurements that have been used in analyses of interaction, including classifications of verbal statements, gestures, eye contact, the rate of speech, the axis of orientation, distance, and loudness of voice.

SUMMARY

When *P* acts and *O* reacts, an interaction has occurred. The probability that interaction will take place between two people in proximity is called the interaction potential and is affected by numerous factors. Any interaction involves three basic dimensions: giving and receiving resources, initiating and accepting another's initiation of action, and the degree to which the resources involved are particularistic or universal. Interaction can be rewarding or costly, depending on the behavior, the perceived causes of the behavior, the needs of the recipient, and the expectations of the perceiver. There are norms that govern what response a person will make to another. Reciprocity, equity, and equality are such norms, and each corresponds to a particular expectation about behavior. The expectations that each actor has about the behavior of the other are important determinants of interpersonal attraction. If people behave as we expect them to behave, their behavior is rewarding; when others behave in ways that are unexpected, the behavior is punishing. Interpersonal attitudes help to determine what action will take place in an interaction. Propinquity is related to such attitudes; if *O* is both similar to and near to *P*, the relationship will be rewarding. Understanding the determinants of interaction requires that we look at a broad set of variables, some of which are directly related to interaction (proximal variables) and some of which operate through these proximal variables (distal variables). Equity theory is useful in explaining interaction. When a relationship is inequitable, a person may try to compensate the other or to justify the inequity. Measuring interaction is complex and difficult; several methods have been used. Some are classifications of verbal behavior, others of nonverbal behavior. Proxemics and paralinguistics focus on closeness and voice-quality dimensions of interaction, respectively.

3

SOME APPLICATIONS OF THE MODEL

In the previous two chapters, I presented a model that purports to account for the determinants of particular acts and an analysis of different kinds of interpersonal acts. We examined a number of theoretical formulations that may account for interpersonal behavior and specified conditions that affect the probability that interactions will take place.

In this chapter, we will apply these ideas to five kinds of interpersonal behavior. The five kinds of behavior are representative of the major dimensions of behavior discussed in the previous chapters. *Helping* behavior is characterized by associative acts. It usually involves giving a resource—often, a service. In many cases it is an altruistic behavior. *Aggressive* behavior is characterized by dissociative acts. It usually involves taking away a resource. *Conformity* behaviors are characterized by subordination. Usually, the subject accepts the initiation of interaction of someone else. *Interpenetration* behaviors are characterized by intimacy. They usually involve particularistic exchanges. Finally, we'll examine the determinants of inaction—that is, of *covert* behavior.

In the standard social-psychological literature, helping, aggression, conformity, and interpenetration are usual topics. I will review some of this literature to show to what extent the model I presented in Chapter 1 and the theoretical ideas of Chapter 2 can help us create some order in this otherwise chaotic literature.

In the discussion that follows, we will focus mostly on the components of Equation 2—that is, on the social, affective, and cognitive (consequences) determinants of behavior. In addition, we will examine factors that lead to rewards experienced after a behavior has taken place, since such factors are determinants of habits.

HELPING BEHAVIOR

Whether a person *P* will help a person *O,* who is in distress, depends on many factors. These include the norms of *P*'s society concerning help, *P*'s cognitions about his or her moral obligation to help, *P*'s self-esteem, and how *P* perceives the roles of both. In addition, *P*'s perception of how much trouble it will be to help and how unpleasant the required behaviors will be, plus the perceived consequences of helping—including cognitions about whether what *P* does will *really* help *O*—will determine behavioral intentions. Once the behavior has taken place, if it gets reinforced, it can become a habit. The existence of a habit will tend to increase the probability that *P* will help, particularly if *O* is similar to people whom *P* has helped in the past. Finally, if *P* has the knowledge and ability to help (for example, if *O* requires medical attention and *P* is a physician), the probability of giving help is increased. In this section, we will examine some studies that support some of these generalizations. Much of the research in this area was initiated by studies by Latané and Darley (1970), which will be reviewed later.

The Social Component

You will recall that the social component of the model presented in Chapter 1 includes the norms, roles, self-concept, and interpersonal agreements relevant to a particular behavior.

There are large differences among cultures in the norms governing helping. For example, my studies with Vassiliou (Triandis & Vassiliou, 1972) comparing Americans and Greeks, found that norms and roles differ in some important respects in the two societies. Specifically, Greeks have one set of norms for members of their ingroup (family, friends, and other people concerned with a person's welfare) and another set for their outgroup (everybody else). The outgroup consists mostly of other Greeks. Foreigners are placed in a special category—*xenos*—whose members are "checked" for possible inclusion in the ingroup. The support of the new member is then enlisted in whatever the ingroup is doing. The Greeks have a strong norm to help foreigners. This norm is an attempt to give *xenos* the benefit of the doubt until his or her status in the ingroup or outgroup can be determined. Compared with Americans, who do not make such sharp distinctions between ingroup and outgroup (but who make distinctions along racial lines), the Greeks are particularly likely to help a member of their ingroup and less likely to help a member of their outgroup. Feldman (1968) did a study of the percentages of passersby in Boston, Paris, and Athens who refused to help when asked to deliver a letter. The request was made in a subway, and the requester explained that he was waiting for a friend and could not leave but that the delivery of the letter was urgent. Roughly half the passersby in Paris and Boston refused to help; but in Athens over 90% refused to help (since the Greek requester was a member of their outgroup).

In large American cities, people are considered nosy if they get involved in an argument taking place in public. Not so in Greece. One observes, for instance, that in Greek buses, if two people get into an argument, the onlookers will often get involved and take sides. Americans are more likely to look away from such a scene. Again, what we have is a difference in norms.

In addition to norms, roles are important. For example, a supervisor is expected to help an employee who does not understand how to do a job. Parents are supposed to help children, police officers to help citizens in danger, and so on.

Furthermore, the person's self-concept is important. Schwartz (1970, 1973) has summarized a series of studies of helping behavior by concluding that three factors must be present in order for helping to occur. (1) *P* must recognize that *O* is confronted with a situation that has serious consequences for *O,* (2) *P* must be aware that the moral norms call for people in general to help *O,* and (3) *P* must believe that he/she has a personal responsibility to take action. That is, *P*'s self-concept must be consistent with the idea that "people who are like me, when confronted with such situations, take action."

When people are told that it is their job to help, and they accept that it is, the self-attribution becomes a cause for action. The person experiences definite pressures to help. Even children are apt to help other children when they are told that they are in charge and are supposed to take care of things; they help even in situations in which they would normally not get involved (Staub, 1969).

Norms can change. As groups interact, people change their views of what is correct behavior. When a person sees many others act in concert, he or she often believes that the norms have become consistent with such action. This can work both for and against the probability that a person will help another in a public place. For example, if *P* realizes that *O* is in need of help but that there are other people nearer to *O* who are not doing anything, *P* may think that inaction is the norm and therefore do nothing. In contrast, if some people start helping, *P* may jump in and help. The norm is often shaped by what large numbers of people do.

People are more likely to donate to a worthy cause if they are aware that others have contributed than if they have not seen others contribute (Bryan & Test, 1967; Macaulay, 1970; Wheeler & Wagner, 1968). In some studies, a model induced subjects to do something helpful that was rather costly to them. For example, Bryan and Test (1967) staged an incident in which their accomplice apparently helped another confederate fix a flat tire.

Passing motorists were more willing to stop and help a woman driver have-ing the same difficulty after witnessing this event than if they had not seen it.

Affect as a Determinant

It is obvious that people are more likely to help if helping is en-joyable—if it gives them a big kick. However, other emotional factors are also relevant. In general, when a person is in a good mood, or is able to im-agine the emotions experienced by others (empathize), then the person is more likely than otherwise to help. Conversely, other things being equal, when the act of helping is very distasteful, the person is less likely to help than if the act is neutral or pleasant.

A good mood can lead to helping behavior. Berkowitz and Connor (1966) showed that subjects worked harder for a peer who was dependent on them if they had just succeeded on a task than if they had just failed. Other studies (Isen, 1970; Isen & Levin, 1972; Isen, Horn, & Rosenhan, 1973) show similar tendencies for people to be more helpful after they have experienced success than after they have experienced failure. Specifically, in the Isen and Levin study "feeling good" was induced by arranging for subjects to receive cookies while studying in a library or by arranging for them to find a dime in the coin return of a public telephone while making a call. Helping behavior involved the subjects' volunteering to reply to a student's request or spon-taneously helping to pick up papers that were dropped in front of them. It was found that subjects who had been made to feel good were more helpful than subjects who had not been put in a good mood.

When a person cries in distress, others are likely to become emotionally aroused. If they feel distressed and believe that they can help without taking a large risk, they are likely to do so. Examples of empathy arousal in the lab-oratory have been provided by Lazarus, Opton, Nomikos, and Rankin (1965). When subjects watched a safety-education film portraying accidents suffered by wood mill operators, in which the workers lost fingers, they became very upset.

The Perceived Consequences of Helping as Determinants

In many studies, it has been shown that people are not likely to help unless they believe that their actions can indeed benefit others. In other words, people must see high probabilities that their acts will result in sub-stantial help for the other. In studies by Schwartz (1970), for instance, people who were convinced that they alone could be helpful to a young woman in need of bone marrow by agreeing to a transplant were more likely to agree to help than those not so convinced.

In addition, the other person's degree of need is an important variable. The more the other needs help, the more likely it is that a person will provide help. The other's need is here equivalent to the value-of-the-consequence (V_c) term of the third equation of the model (see page 16). Thus, the more a person sees a direct connection between what he or she does and the reduction of the other's need (P_c), and the greater the other's need (V_c), the more likely it is that he or she will help.

A case of nonhelp that attracted national publicity happened in New York City. A woman by the name of Kitty Genovese was attacked by a man in March 1964, as she was returning to her home in Queens. Her screams drove the assailant off at first, but he returned when it became obvious that no one was coming to the woman's aid. Again and again he stabbed her, while no one from the surrounding apartments came to help her. The next day, 38 people admitted to the police that they had heard the screams. Careful investigations of such social situations suggest that many bystanders do not interpret such incidents as emergencies requiring help. Many thought that it was a mere lover's quarrel and none of their business.

Latané and Darley (1970) concluded that, for people to intervene in an emergency, they must first (a) notice the incident, (b) interpret it as an emergency, (c) decide that they have a personal responsibility to act, and (d) believe that they can carry out the required behavior. In short, relevant values must become salient, and people must believe that they can act on these values and achieve the desired consequence. ($P_c V_c$).

Attributions about the Other's Behavior as Determinants

Recall the discussion in Chapter 2 in which we noted that a person's conception of what caused the behavior of another affects the way the person will react to the other's behavior. It was pointed out that, if the other's positive behavior is unintentional—under habit control, in conformity to norms, roles, or social inducements, or especially enjoyable to the actor—the effect of the behavior on the other will be small. In short, if P helps O under duress or unintentionally, P gets little credit, and O is unlikely to return the help.

Several studies are consistent with this argument. Goranson and Berkowitz (1966) found that women who had an opportunity to help a peer who had aided them earlier did so much more vigorously when the helper was seen as having helped of her own free will rather than as having been required to give help. Similarly, Nemeth (1970) found that subjects feel more liking for those who help them if the help is voluntary than if it is required. This means that the attributions made by subjects about the causes of the behavior of the other are important determinants of reciprocal help. When O

helps voluntarily, O's behavior "counts" more than if O is forced to help. Similarly, if O's behavior costs O little, O gets little credit.

Tesser, Gatewood, & Driver (1968) concluded that people feel most gratitude to those who help them intentionally and at a considerable cost to themselves. These findings are also consistent with equity theory. If O helps P in spite of having little money, the I_o/O_o ratio is small, since the inputs are small and the outputs are large. Then, P may feel much gratitude and restore equity by giving much (O_P) in return (compensation); or P may engage in cognitive distortions (justification), so that the I_p/O_p ratio will again be very small.

Helping behavior also depends upon why O needs help—whether because of factors beyond O's control or because of some "inner deficiency" (Schopler & Matthews, 1965; Horowitz, 1968; Berkowitz, 1969). Berkowitz (1975) reports a study by Bryan and Davenport that showed that readers of the *New York Times* were more generous to persons in need of help, during the Christmas season, because of factors beyond those persons' control (for example, they were children) than they were to those needing help because of factors that might be attributed to an inner deficiency (for example, alcoholism).

One's Own Previous Behavior as a Determinant

There is evidence that people will be more likely to help if they have done something that made them feel guilty than if they have not (Freedman, 1970). Feeling guilty causes people to punish themselves or to do "good deeds" that will restore their self-esteem. McMillen and Austin (1971) did a study that supports this interpretation. Students were induced to lie to an experimenter and were later asked to help the experimenter score some questionnaires. The amount of time the student offered to spend helping was a dependent variable. Those who had lied offered to help for longer amounts of time than those who had not lied.

Freedman and Fraser (1966) did two experiments that tested the proposition that, once someone has agreed to a small request, he or she is more likely than someone who has not done so to comply with a larger request. In the first experiment, 156 Palo Alto, California, women were randomly selected from the telephone directory. They were contacted by phone. The small request was to answer some questions, with the information to be included in a magazine of the California Consumers Group. The large request was to cooperate in a survey that would involve five or six men coming to the woman's home for about two hours to enumerate and classify all the household products. These men would have full freedom in the house. The information would again be used for the magazine of the Consumers Group.

Several control groups were run, but for our purposes it is sufficient to know that those who were approached first with the large request complied 22% of the time, while those who were approached first with the small request and then with the large request complied 53% of the time. In another experiment, it was shown that the effect of a small request on compliance with a large request is found even when different people make the two requests. A theoretical explanation for this is that the person's self-concept changes after agreement with the small request. *P* now thinks that he/she is "the kind of person who agrees to help, who cooperates with good causes," and so on. In addition, once a helping behavior has taken place, the habit determinant of helping begins building up, so that the probability that a similar behavior will take place in the future is increased.

Habit As a Determinant of Helping

The probability that a person will help another depends on many factors, one of the most important being whether or not the person has helped similar people in the past and been rewarded for it. Gaertner and Bickman (1971) used the "wrong number" technique to determine the probability that Blacks or Whites would help a person whose voice was clearly that of a White or a Black. The voice claimed that he was calling his mechanic and had reached a wrong number by mistake. He was on the parkway because his car had broken down; he had no more change, and he needed help. Would the subject please call his mechanic? White subjects helped a White 65% of the time and a Black 53% of the time; Black subjects helped a White 67% and a Black 60% of the time. The significant difference ($p < .01$) between the percentages of Whites and Blacks who were helped by Whites could be attributed to racial prejudice; but an equally plausible interpretation is that Whites are in the habit of helping Whites but not Blacks, while Blacks have helping habits that are somewhat more equal in strength because there are relatively more Whites around to help. One can't exclude the possibility, of course, that both racial prejudice and habits determined the observed rates of help. Furthermore, it should be remembered that other factors also contribute to the habit of not helping: urban dwellers tend to have little experience with helping. The impersonality of large cities creates an environment in which people learn to mind their own business. The Kitty Genovese case, mentioned earlier, is one of the classic examples of the city dweller's reluctance to help.

Our behavior is often well routinized—that is, under the control of habits—and events that one might have expected would change our behavior often fail to do so.

In a study by Darley and Batson (1973), students at the Princeton Theological Seminary were asked to give a brief talk about the parable of the

Good Samaritan. While each student walked to the laboratory to tape his talk, he passed by a man slumped in a doorway with his eyes closed. Even though the student was presumably particularly aware of the parable of the Good Samaritan, he was not significantly more likely to help the stranger than a control group of students who were asked to give a talk on another topic. In other words, the behavior of these students was so automatic that cognitive factors, such as the ideas contained in the parable, did not have a chance to change their behavior.

The Other's Actions as a Determinant

If O is particularly helpful to P, then P is more likely than otherwise to help O later. If O initiates interaction inappropriately, P is less likely than otherwise to help. When O pushes too hard or makes unreasonable demands, P is less likely to be cooperative (Willis & Goethals, 1973). In short, if O is reinforcing to P, P will tend to help O.

In general, the more rewarding the behavior of O, the more likely is P to help O; the more costly to P is O's behavior during a previous period of time, the less likely is P to help. However, whether O's behavior will result in changes in P's behavior depends not only on the actual behavior but also on what P expects and on what attributions P makes concerning the causes of O's behavior. As discussed earlier, equity theory would predict that a person who makes a gift is more attractive to the receiver if he or she is poor than if he or she is rich (Maslach, Tashiro, & Gergen, 1972).

Facilitating Conditions

It is more probable that a person will help when it is easy to help than when it is difficult. In large cities, people have definite appointments and move swiftly from one place to another. If somebody needs help, that's his or her problem. In a student research project done at the University of Illinois, we found that the probability that a student will be helped when he appears sick near the steps of the university auditorium is proportional to the time remaining before the performance is to start. At two minutes before the performance, almost no one helps; at twenty minutes before the performance, half the people help. Furthermore, if help is not costly, it is more likely to be rendered than if it is costly. Latané and Darley (1970) sent students into the streets of Manhattan to get data on the percentages of passersby who would heed various requests. They found that 85% gave the time, 73% made change for a quarter, and 34% gave a dime when the money was requested.

Schaps (1972) arranged for experimental accomplices to enter a shoe store when the store was full (high cost) or relatively empty (low cost) and to either pose as normal shoe customers (low dependence) or limp into the store with a shoe that had a broken heel (high dependence). These "customers" proved to be very demanding and asked the salespeople to show them more and more shoes. The number of pairs shown, the time spent serving, and the number of trips to the stockroom to get additional shoes were used as measures of service provided. Service was greater in the low- than in the high-cost condition. In addition, much more service was provided to highly dependent subjects when the store was relatively empty than when it was full. In short, there was the greatest willingness to help the customer find the shoes she wanted when it was easy to do so and when the customer was simultaneously highly dependent.

Differences in Interaction Potential

In Chapter 2, I mentioned that interaction potential (the probability that some interaction will take place) depends on the number of people in a given social situation. It follows that, when people are alone with someone who needs help, they are particularly likely to be helpful; when they are in the presence of many others, they are less likely to help. There is much evidence that this is indeed the case. Most observers of this phenomenon have argued that, when many others are present, there is a lower sense of responsibility for helping. The principle of diffusion of personal responsibility for help follows the observation that people are inclined to let others do unpleasant acts, if they can get away with it. Thus, Latané and Darley (1970) found that, when subjects thought they were in an experiment with others whom they could hear on an intercom system, and one of the others apparently became sick, subjects were much more likely to call the experimenter to give help to the sick fellow student if they thought that they were alone than if they thought that they were in an experiment with several others.

Other experiments show that subjects are more likely to help if they believe that the person who needs help is one of their friends or a person who is similar to them than if the person is a stranger or someone different from them (Stotland, 1969).

Suppose that a person has a chance to do something that will help another. Is he or she likely to work hard so that the other will benefit? As L'Armand and Pepitone (1975) point out in their theoretical analysis, a norm of social responsibility may operate that requires a person to be helpful in such a situation. In addition, if individuals picture themselves as kind, good, and generous, they are more likely to help than if they don't picture themselves this way. Further, if these individuals are aware of a norm of equity, they may want to ensure that the other achieves a "just" reward. And, finally, the individuals may help because the behavior itself is socially desirable and a useful thing to do.

In some cultures, people use the concept of limited good (Foster, 1965). That is, they think that the good in the world is limited, and, if another gets it, then the giver will have less of it. When this view prevails, a person will not be inclined to help another, because helping gives the other some of the good, which puts the helper at a disadvantage. The opposite concept is that of an expanding pie. Good expands: if you help the other, the other will help you, and everybody will have more "good" than if you had not helped. George Foster, a well-known anthropologist, has argued that people in peasant societies use the idea of limited good. Vassiliou and I (Triandis & Vassiliou, 1972a) have found our discussion of a narrow ingroup among traditional Greeks consistent with the viewpoint of limited good. If a member of the outgroup gets ahead, that's bad news. It's better to make sure that the other is "kept down," so that he or she will have less of the total good available, which will leave more good for the ingroup. It's likely that the image of limited good is found in societies in which most good comes from the land. If the other group has more land, then you have less. The relationship is a zero-sum one; that is, whatever you win, the other loses, and whatever the other loses, you win, so that the losses and winnings add up to zero.

It follows that, if a society uses the concept of limited rather than expanding good, people will be less likely to help others, even in situations in which it costs them little to help. Anthropological analyses suggested that India is such a culture, so L'Armand and Pepitone studied whether a male would help another in Philadelphia and in Madras, India.

The procedure involved a game in which the subject wagered coins representing money provided by the experimenter. Each U.S. subject was given $5 and each Indian subject the equivalent in rupees and each was told that he could wager some of the coins on each of nine jars. The jars contained blue and yellow marbles. Each jar held ten marbles, and the proportion of blue marbles varied. There was a label on each jar that showed the proportion of blue marbles. Each time the jar was brought out, the subject had to decide how many coins to wager on that jar. After the coins were wagered on each of the nine jars, the experimenter overturned them. If a blue marble dropped, it was a successful (winning) wager.

Two major experimental conditions will be reviewed here. A self-reward condition was one in which the subject kept the money if he won, or lost the money (to the experimenter) if he made bad wagers. In the other-reward condition, another subject kept the money the subject won. The question, then, was whether the subjects would place good bets so that the other person would win (be helped).

The results show that the subjects in both cultures behaved rationally; that is, they wagered more coins on the jars that had large proportions of blue marbles and fewer coins on the jars that provided unfavorable conditions for winning. The researchers used an index that reflected the extent to which the subjects placed larger bets on the jars that provided favorable odds than on the jars that provided unfavorable odds. This index, called the maximizing index, reflects the extent to which the subjects tried hard to win.

Americans tried hard whether they were working for themselves or for the other. In fact, they tended to work a little harder for the other than for themselves (the maximizing indexes were 65 and 55 for the other- and self-reward conditions, respectively). The Indian subjects did not work as hard for the other as they did for themselves. Their indexes were 50 for the self-reward and 25 for the other-reward condition. Apparently, Indians have a weaker social-responsibility norm, a less help-oriented self-image, or a concept of limited good. The family income of the Indian students was correlated with the maximizing index, suggesting that the wealthier students tended to work for the other more than the poorer students did. This suggests that the quasi-competitiveness suggested by the image of limited good is stronger for the poor than for the wealthy.

Comment. It is important to realize that, in societies such as India or Greece, a person is supposed to do very much for his or her ingroup but has no obligations to outgroup members. Most members of the society are outgroup members. Thus, Indians will work very hard for another who is a member of their own family—much harder, probably, than they will work for themselves. However, when it comes to working for an unknown Indian, as in this experiment, they feel no responsibility and believe that the others should take care of themselves. In America, the other is more likely to be seen as a member of the ingroup, and people do feel responsibility for helping.

This study, then, suggests how norms of responsibility and conceptions about the way "good" is distributed in the world may affect helping behavior.

Individual Differences

The model specifies that whether habits, norms, affect, or consequences are the important determinants of a person's action depends on the type of behavior, the type of situation, and the type of person. In short, there are variations due to the interaction of personality and the situation. The effect of individual differences on helping behavior can be seen in an investigation by Berkowitz and Friedman (1967). Following the suggestion of the German sociologist Georg Simmel that some people might follow a reciprocity principle in their social dealings to a greater extent than others do, Berkowitz and Friedman reasoned that children whose fathers are middle-class entrepreneurs will be more likely to use the reciprocity norm in their social relations than will children of other backgrounds. In an experiment that permitted reciprocity, they showed that this was indeed the case. In short, experience with reciprocal exchanges makes a child particularly sensitive to the reciprocity norm.

Norms and values can be held with differing degrees of strength. London (1970) interviewed Christians who rescued Jews from the Nazis and found that they traced their strong moral beliefs to their identification with a parent who had very strong moral views. Their strong sense of morality overcame their fear of the obvious risks involved in the behavior. In terms of the model, the weight given to the social component (which includes moral obligations) was very large, overcoming the cognitive (P_cV_c) component, which must have included the perception that their acts might lead to very serious negative consequences.

AGGRESSION

The previous section dealt with associative behavior. Now we can look at the other pole of this dimension. A large percentage of aggressive behavior appears to be impulsive. For example, killings are "spontaneous acts of passion" rather than "products of a single determination to kill," according to the analysis of the National Commission on the Causes and Prevention of Violence (Mulvihill & Tumin, 1969). People learn to become aggressive when their aggressive acts are rewarded—that is, when aggression is successful or when they see others get rewarded for aggression. Obviously, a youngster who snatches away an old lady's purse and finds $100 in it will experience a reward. Experiencing many such incidents can build up the habit of taking away resources. Once *P* has learned to act violently toward one class of people, generalization takes place, and *P* may act violently toward other classes of people. Walters and Brown (1963) rewarded children for punching a large plastic doll. These children were more likely than control children to act aggressively toward another youngster in another setting.

Facilitating Conditions

While the previous experience of *P* is important and builds up a habit component, the habit component is multiplied by facilitating conditions to produce, in part, the probability of an act. Facilitating conditions include the state of the actor and any environmental conditions that make the act easy.

Under some conditions, any kind of arousal might increase the probability of aggression. Zillman (1971) suggested that residual excitation, deriving from exposure to *sexual* stimuli, which was interpolated between the provoking of an individual and his or her opportunity to respond aggressively, greatly increased aggressive responses. Zillman, Katcher, and Milavsky (1972) found that, under some conditions, *physical exercise* can provide enough excitation to increase aggressive behavior.

There is evidence that *any* arousal can increase the probability of an aggressive act. Noise (Geen & O'Neal, 1969), pain (Ulrich & Azrin, 1962), frustration (Berkowitz, 1962, 1969), hot and humid weather (Goranson & King 1971), an insult (Buss, 1963; Geen & Berkowitz, 1967), or the removal of an accustomed reward (Azrin, Hutchinson, & Hake, 1966) can increase the probability of aggression. Among the most widely researched hypotheses is the one that posits that frustration (the blocking of ongoing goal-directed activity) is likely to instigate aggression. Ulrich and Favell (1970) had 10-year-old children erect a stack of small rubber bottle stoppers. They were told that another person was working nearby on the same task. This other person could shake the subject's table by pressing a button. The subject also had a button that he or she could press to shake the other's table. The experimenter arranged for vibrations of the table and noted whether the subjects used their button to shake the table of the other person they thought was working nearby. The data indicate that subjects pressed their buttons mostly after a vibration had prevented them from reaching their goal. A vibration that did not have an effect on their job was not taken seriously. Thus, the blocking of progress toward a goal is a crucial factor.

Viewing violence on TV can increase arousal, provide information on how to carry out a crime (for example, how to make explosives), and suggest criminal courses of action. Many crimes have been observed to follow the "form" of criminal episodes viewed on TV a few days prior to the committing of the crime. In a recent case, a helicopter escape of prisoners from a prison courtyard was shown on TV a few days before it actually happened.

Other major facilitative conditions include the availability of weapons, poor security measures, and so on. Feldman (1968) dropped one-dollar and five-dollar bills in the streets of Boston and similar amounts in the streets of Paris and Athens to see whether people would falsely claim the bill. The rates of false claiming were particularly high in Boston, and the subjects, when asked by another experimenter "What is going on here? Does this guy give away money?" indicated that, in their highly competitive environment one grabs what one can. Grabbing is a relatively easy thing to do. If the subjects had had to climb, stretch, go over hurdles, and so on, we might guess that the rate of false claims would have been lower.

The Social Component

Norms are important determinants of aggression, primarily because they inhibit it. In most societies, there is a prohibition of ingroup aggression. However, in some societies, people are allowed to disregard the prohibition under certain conditions. There are circumstances under which "revenge," in the form of aggressive acts, is permitted or even expected. For example, in traditional Greek villages, a brother was supposed to kill a man who had dishonored his sister. If she had consented to the relationship, she was supposed to be killed also. Such killings were consistent with folk norms although against the laws of the state.

Geen (1972) reviewed several studies that suggest that the observation of violence committed by others may lead to aggression. It may be that observed aggressive acts (1) provide modeling cues that shift norms by legitimizing the action, (2) elicit responses previously conditioned to violence, or (3) increase arousal.

Gang members who beat up an "enemy" intruding on their "turf" or assault an innocent victim often gain status and approval from others in their group. Here the norm not only doesn't prohibit aggression but actually encourages it. Violent gangs reward, in various ways, the members who have the greatest fighting skills (Whyte, 1943; Short, 1969).

Parents who use physical punishment act as models of this behavior for their children. The result is that their children become aggressive. The norm of aggression under some conditions and nonaggression under other conditions is often too complicated for a child. If the parent acts aggressively, the child learns to act aggressively toward *his/her* children. Thus, a norm of aggression is transmitted from one generation to another (Bandura & Walters, 1963; Sears, Maccoby, & Levin, 1957). Children of parents who use frequent physical punishment are more aggressive outside the home than children of parents who do not use physical punishment (Eron, Walder, &

Lefkowitz, 1971). In some subcultures, the social norms allow and encourage physical punishment (spare the rod and spoil the child), and, as a result, different rates of aggression are to be expected among subcultures.

Cultural differences in rates of mortality from homicide can be indexed by the number of deaths per 100,000 that are the result of homicide. The U.S. is the most violent of the highly developed countries. The rate of deaths due to homicide in the U.S. is 6.6 per 100,000 for Whites—triple that of Canada, ten times that of Scandinavia, eight times that of Western Europe, and four times that of Japan. The rate among non-Whites is 11 times higher than the rate among Whites, which makes it 115 times higher than the Scandinavian rate! This difference must not be interpreted as all due to differences in norms. Economic inequalities are larger in the U.S. than in Scandinavia. As Jessor, Graves, Hanson, and Jessor (1968) have pointed out, deviations from norms are typical among people who have a low position in the opportunity structure, who are not strongly controlled by norms prohibiting the deviant behavior, and who have access to the means of deviance. In the U.S., non-Whites often are in a very unfavorable position within the opportunity structure; the norms against violence are not as strong as in other countries, and people have easy access to weapons. In most European countries, weapons such as guns are not available or are prohibited. Not only are the norms different, but the facilitating conditions are much more favorable to a high rate of homicide in the U.S. The White/non-White difference probably reflects differences in position in the opportunity structure rather than differences in norms, because there is at least one study that shows that adult Blacks disapprove of one teenage boy punching another even more strongly than do adult Whites (Erlanger, 1974). The lower-class environment is characterized by fierce competition for a few resources. In that setting, strength and fighting prowess, toughness, and the quick drawing of a knife are essential for survival (Miller, Geertz, & Cutter, 1961).

Frequently, norms concerning aggression are contradictory—on the one hand discouraging violence in general and on the other encouraging violence in "self-defense." The situations that call for "self-defense" may be more numerous in the lower than in the middle class. For example, an insult can be defined as self-threatening. Short and Strodtbeck (1965) found evidence of greater acceptance of the need to be a good fighter among lower-class than among middle-class boys. This would suggest that the self-image of lower-class boys is generally more congruent with the thought of acts of violence than is the case with middle-class boys.

The high rates of violence shown on television in the U.S. and Japan contrast sharply with the rates of TV violence in Western and Northern Europe. The high U.S. rates of homicide and aggression, however, reflect several other factors. First, there are numerous studies that imply very strongly that there is a link between television violence and displays of aggression, at least among immature individuals (Bandura, 1972; Liebert, 1971; Lefkowitz, Eron, Walder, & Huesmann, 1971). This evidence has been suppressed, in the U.S., in a most scandalous way (Bogart, 1973). The Surgeon General's Study of Television and Social Behavior was conducted by a commission whose membership was "controlled" by the mass media, since they vetoed the participation of seven distinguished social scientists. The result is that the commission published a weak report (Cisin et al., 1972). Bogart reviews several studies that document the high rates of violence on U.S. television and the effects of this violence on children's fantasies, actions, and later behavior. For example, one study concluded that "a preference for violent television in the third grade is causally related to aggressive behavior ten years later" (Bogart, 1973, p. 505). Incidentally, there is evidence that viewing of violent programs is more frequent among non-Whites than among Whites—a finding consistent with differences in homicide rates.

It is well known that, if a person was previously rewarded for being aggressive, the chances are greater that he or she will attack someone after having an unpleasant experience than if the behavior had not previously been rewarded (Bandura, 1972). Such rewards can be found in some sub-cultures, such as the Black ghetto, with greater frequency than in other settings.

Another major factor is that aggressive attitudes are highly correlated with norms that are very popular in the U.S. Blumenthal (1972) found that norms supportive of retributive justice and self-defense are highly correlated with positive attitudes toward violence. American "westerns" almost always use the themes of retribution or self-defense. A representative sample of American men showed strong tendencies to approve of retribution. Even the biblical "an eye for an eye and a tooth for a tooth," when called "a good rule for living" was *strongly agreed* with by 9% and *agreed with* by another 15% of the men. Other, less extreme retributive statements received agreement from the majority of the respondents. Similarly, self-defense statements, such as "a man has a right to kill a person to defend his house" were agreed with by more than half the sample of men. In short, the norms of action with respect to aggression provide a number of justifications for aggression.

In analyzing the determinants of aggression, a paper by Blumenthal (1972) is particularly worth noting. It begins with the point that violence has been a conspicuous part of American life, with assassinations, riots, student disruption, and violent crime being characteristic particularly of the 1962–1972 period. Historically, there has been much violence in American life. To understand why violence is so typically American (some have said that it's as American as apple pie), Blumenthal developed a model designed to predict attitudes toward violence. To test this model, she surveyed the attitudes of a representative random sample of 1374 American men between the ages of 16 and 64. The interviews were carried out in 1969 and had a final response rate of 80%. Black men were oversampled (303 Blacks were in the sample), so the data could be analyzed separately for that group.

Blumenthal conceives of forces that drive the level of violence that is perceived as justified up or down. These include: (1) basic cultural values that discourage violence, such as "Thou shalt not kill" and the New Testament golden rule, (2) basic cultural values that encourage violence, such as the biblical "an eye for an eye," the glorification of the hard-riding, straight-shooting frontiersman, and the condoning of self-defense, (3) identification with the aggressor, such as feeling a common bond with the persons who started a riot, (4) identification with the victim, such as feeling a common bond with the targets of a riot or, conversely, feeling that the targets of aggression are somehow subhuman and violence against them does not count, and (5) the definition of violent behavior as something other than violence—for instance, thinking of a violent act as "restoring law and order."

To test this model, Blumenthal developed scales to measure under what conditions people think that violence is justified. She presented a scenario—such as a description of hoodlum gangs destroying property and terrifying citizens—and asked subjects what the police should do. The answers that people in her sample could give ranged from "almost always" to "never" in response to specific questions such as "Should the police let it go and not do anything?" and "Should the police shoot to kill?"

The answers she obtained indicate a strong predisposition toward having the police do something. For example, in response to the scenario describing a ghetto riot, 77% answered that the police should never let it go and not do anything, 18% went so far as to say that the police should almost always shoot, 73% thought the police should sometimes shoot, and 80% thought the police should use clubs. This kind of pattern suggests the "activist" orientation that is central to the American value system and also shows a good deal of acceptance of violence. In response to the scenario involving student disturbances, the answers were remarkably similar to those obtained for the scenario of the ghetto riot.

In a more specific test of her model, Blumenthal accounted

for about a third of the variance in attitudes toward violence from the values, identification with the aggressor and the victim, and definitions of violence that she had hypothesized to be related to such attitudes. Specifically, she found much evidence that men justify violence as retribution. For example, 64% of her sample agreed that it is "often necessary to use violence to prevent it," 71% agreed with the statement "people who commit murder deserve capital punishment," and 44% agreed with "violence deserves violence." Of the sample, fully 89% agreed that killing another man was justified in self-defense, and 58% justified a man's killing "to defend his house." Those who had a humanistic orientation—valuing freedom, equality, and human dignity—were less likely than those without such an orientation to agree with statements that justified violence. The majority of the respondents (83%) identified with the police rather than with White student demonstrators or Black protestors. The dictionary definition of violence is "the exertion of physical force so as to injure or abuse," Yet 58% of the sample thought that burning a draft card was violence, 30% viewed the beating of a student by police as *not* violence, and 57% thought that the shooting of looters by police was not violence! In other words, protests were thought of by the men as violence, but violent police action was seen as something else.

Most homicides occur in large cities. In such settings, there is an additional variable, called *deindividuation*, that contributes to high rates of aggression. Zimbardo (1969) argued that deindividuation, or a feeling of anonymity and a consequent lack of concern over social evaluation, allows individuals to act aggressively. The loss of identity can be experienced when a person is submerged in a crowd, disguised, masked, dressed in a uniform, or in darkness. In a controlled laboratory experiment, Zimbardo arranged for female subjects to believe that they were administering shocks to another subject. Aggression was measured by the duration and number of shocks. In one condition, the subjects were deindividuated—no names were used, the experiment took place in the dark, and subjects wore a hood over their heads. These subjects shocked their victims much more than did subjects in other conditions. Watson (1973) examined the Human Relations Area Files (an organized file of most of the world's ethnographic materials) to find in what cultures soldiers are particularly high on aggression (killing, torturing, and mutilating the enemy). Deindividuation was coded when the soldiers of the culture changed their appearance before going into battle—using body or face paint, wearing special garments or masks, and so on. It was found that those societies in which soldiers change their appearance are more aggressive than those societies in which soldiers don't change their appearance. Fraser, Kelem, Diener, & Beamna (1972) observed 1300 children during Halloween, under conditions of either anonymity or group presence. The children were given opportunities to steal extra candy and money when they thought no adults were watching. More stealing was observed in the deindividuated than in the group condition. Industrialized society tends to create more and more settings in which people become deindividuated, and hence there is increasing aggression.

The Affective Component

There are large individual differences in feelings about aggression. The difference between the emotions of pleasure that a sadist might experience at the thought of hurting others and the emotions of disgust and horror that most people feel about hurting others is evidence for tremendous variation. Furthermore, one person might find killing with a rifle quite neutral but be completely horrified at the thought of piercing somebody with a butcher knife. These kinds of emotions are undoubtedly relevant in understanding variations in aggressive behavior. People differ in the extent to which they are able to put themselves in the other's place—an ability that has been called *empathy*. Hogan (1969) developed a scale to measure this tendency. It is a reasonable expectation that people who are high on this trait will be inhibited in hurting others.

The Perceived Consequences of Aggression

The consequences of aggression are greatly dependent on the probability that the state, the police, or others can provide sanctions for it. In the Black ghetto, most crimes are not even reported. Retaliation is widely used, but it may not be effective against a strong opponent. In short, the probability (P_c) that violence will lead to negative consequences can vary from zero to a high value. P's who are not afraid of the punishment that O may inflict on them will be more tempted to aggress than P's who are afraid. Geen and Pigg (1970) found that, when a man is rewarded for physically attacking another, he becomes more likely to have aggressive thoughts than someone who has not been rewarded.

The value of the consequences of aggression may vary. One might imagine a sadist anticipating positive consequences of aggression and most persons anticipating negative consequences.

Individual Differences

The way children are socialized often has consequences for their aggressive tendencies. Child-rearing experts have found two relevant dimensions of parental behavior, which have been named warm/cold and autonomous/controlling. Warm parents do much touching, kissing, petting, supporting, rewarding; cold parents are aloof and stern, punish frequently, and give little support to their children. Autonomous parents are those who support the child's efforts to become independent; controlling parents are those who try to shape the child according to some rigid standard. Different combinations of these two dimensions make up different child-rearing styles. For example, a warm-controlling parent uses an overprotective style. A cold-controlling parent is likely to have a child with an authoritarian personality. In families organized along hierarchical lines, authoritarian tendencies are apparently generated when fathers are aloof and stern and administer much physical punishment.

Cold parents have boys who tend to be aggressive. Bandura and Walters (1959), for instance, compared male teenagers who were in legal difficulties because of their assaultiveness with a matched group of boys. The aggressive boys had a history of parents who were cold and indifferent, in contrast with the background of the normal boys. In general, children reared by cold parents are more aggressive than children reared by warm parents, but those reared by cold-autonomous parents are particularly aggressive. The most law-abiding children are those raised by warm-controlling parents. However, this is not the best child-rearing pattern, if we consider other criteria, such as the child's creativity. The best pattern, according to many experts, is the warm-autonomous because it produces little aggression and relatively high creativity. The cold-controlling pattern results in children who are reasonably law-abiding but who are more aggressive than children reared by warm parents. In fact, the cold-controlling pattern, combined with physical punishment, often leads to an authoritarian personality that appears to be associated with high aggressive tendencies toward low-status targets (Epstein, 1965). It is important to note the distinction about the status of the targets. Authoritarian subjects tend to aggress against low-status targets, while the less authoritarian aggress mostly against high-status targets and do not aggress against equal- or low-status targets (Lipetz & Ossorio, 1967).

As mentioned earlier, an additional factor concerns the extent to which parents are models of aggressive behavior. The more physical punishment used by parents, the more aggressive the child is likely to be (Sears et al., 1957; Eron et al., 1971).

CONFORMITY

The two preceding sections dealt with the determinants of associative and dissociative behavior, respectively; this section will be concerned with superordination/subordination—and, in particular, conformity.

Habits of superordination develop when a person is frequently reinforced for initiating behavior. This typically happens when the person's status or role requires that he or she initiate. The initiation of action proves enjoyable to some people, who are then particularly likely to engage in this behavior. The consequences of initiating action are frequently positive for certain kinds of people, who then become particularly likely to take the lead.

Conformity is the opposite phenomenon. In the case of conformity, a person accepts action that was initiated by others. The well-known experiment by Milgram (1965) is a demonstration of the strength of the forces toward conformity. Recall that the subject was required to give shocks to a person in an adjoining room, who screamed and objected to the shocks. The question was whether the subject would obey the experimenter's instructions to increase the level of shock. Most of the subjects administered what they thought were extreme shocks, in spite of the "victim's" protests. The compliance of the subjects was probably in part dependent on previous reinforcements, in part due to norms requiring compliance with authority figures, and in part due to expectations of punishment for nonconformity.

The history of reinforcement of a person can mold him/her into an independent, a conformist, or a nonconformist. These tendencies are reflected in the habit component of the determinants of action.

The Social Component

In general, the more ambiguous the social situation, the more likely a person is to conform. We conform much more when we have no way to judge objective reality or no way to check the validity of social pressures than when we have a way to check the objective reality or the validity of the social pressures. However, as the well-known studies by Asch have demonstrated, under conditions of uniformity of social opinion, even objective reality may be disregarded. In Asch's studies, subjects were confronted with a discrepancy between their sensations and the apparent judgments of a group of other students (who were confederates of the experimenter) concerning the length of lines. Many subjects, when asked to judge the length of lines, disregarded their sensations and conformed to the judgments of the majority.

When others disagree among themselves, then conformity is reduced. The larger the number of people in apparent agreement, the greater the conformity, up to a certain point, after which further increases in group size do not increase conformity. When the group is cohesive, the members have personal goals consistent with group goals, and, if they depend on the group, they are more likely to conform than if the group were not cohesive.

It is a well-established phenomenon that, in the absence of any standards on how to behave, a group often converges on some sort of intermediate position, which then becomes the "correct" standard. Specifically, Sherif (1936) showed that people placed in a dark room in which there was a small spot of light, when asked to estimate the amount of movement of the light, gave a range of answers, but gradually converged to give similar answers.

In short, when we do not know what is the "correct" behavior, we use the standards that others supply for us. When a worker joins a new work group, he or she typically is told by other workers how much to produce. If the new worker produces too much, he or she is called a "rate buster" and is ridiculed, pressured, or even sabotaged. If the worker produces too little, he or she is called a "chiseler" and is urged to work harder. The group has definite ideas of what is the proper rate of production and provides sanctions for handling deviations from these standards. Festinger (1954) argued that people often cannot find objective standards by which to evaluate an issue. When this happens, they use other people as sources of standards. When a lot of people think the same way, conformity to that opinion is likely.

When O has much power and can reward handsomely or punish severely, people are particularly likely to do what O asks. A distinction can be made between normative social influence and informational social influence, or between compliance and internalization (Kelman, 1958). Acting under normative social influence, or complying, is doing what is demanded by the other, without acceptance of the viewpoint of the other but out of fear of punishment or expectation of reward. Acting under informational social influence, or internalizing, involves acceptance of the views of the other; what the other demands is seen to be consistent with one's values and is internalized.

Societies differ in the kinds of norms they have about conformity. When the ecology is such that hunting and fishing are good ways to get food, people (for example, the Eskimos) tend to be rather independent. Hunting and fishing in the Arctic is typically a job for an individual, and coordination among several people is not particularly helpful. In contrast, in agricultural societies (for example, the Temne of Africa), coordination of effort is very important. For example, irrigation for farming often requires digging a large ditch, which is a job that a single person cannot do. In societies that require cooperation, then, people learn to conform. Berry (1967) tested Eskimo and Temne subjects with a variation of the Asch conformity task. He found, as expected, that the Eskimos were less conforming than the Temnes.

Similar differences have been found among social classes. In general, working-class parents want their children to be obedient, clean, orderly, and respectful; upper-middle-class parents want their children to be creative, original, and independent. In both Italy and the U.S., Kohn (1969) found that working-class children were more conforming than upper-middle-class children. This is consistent with patterns of reward for behaviors in each social class. Working-class people generally get rewarded for doing what they're told. Upper-class people get rewarded for originality and creativity.

National differences in conformity have been found by Milgram (1961) in a study of French and Norwegian university students. Using a modified Asch procedure requiring judgments of the durations of sounds, he found that the Norwegians were more conforming than the French. One possible explanation of this difference can be found in the university systems of these two countries. The French system is extremely competitive, so that persons get rewarded for "beating" their peers. If the peer appears to be wrong in his or her judgments, then so much the better. Norwegians, whose university system is less competitive, have apparently learned to rely on peer views more than the French.

When peers are unanimous, the norm seems much clearer, and hence conformity is much more probable than when they are not unanimous. Total unanimity leads to "groupthink" (Janis, 1972), and people find it difficult to challenge "the obviously correct solution." Eichman explained that he accepted the so-called "final solution" because he saw no one at all who opposed it (Arendt, 1963). As soon as unanimity is broken, the pressure of the norms decreases (Allen & Levine, 1971).

The reference group that a person chooses as his or her source of norms is particularly important in the case of conformity, since it determines which fads, fashions, and other forms of social "contagion" a person is likely to follow.

Low-status persons are frequently forced to conform in situations in which high-status persons can escape from conformity. High-status persons may have acquired "credit" with their group (Hollander, 1958) that makes deviation possible. However, those at the top are often expected to act in ways consistent with group norms, particularly if their job is ceremonial (for example, being the Queen of England). Those at the bottom can't lose much status by not conforming, since they can't lose what they don't have. As a result, in many groups the people who conform most are those in the middle of the status hierarchy—they have much to lose by not conforming and much to gain by conforming.

Affect

Conformity can be enjoyable. If conformity is associated with pleasant events, such as the approval of others or the reduction of tension, it will, of course, acquire a positive value.

A particularly common case is conformity to the behavior of attractive others. Since nonconformity is often seen as a negative behavior, tendencies toward cognitive consistency result in people's conforming to the behavior or attitudes of people they find attractive.

The Perceived Consequences of Conformity

One of the more probable consequences of nonconformity is punishment. Fear of punishment can increase conformity. In addition, conformity may be seen as leading to approval, tension reduction, and other benefits.

Individual Differences

Persons who conform have been found to be younger, less self-confident, less intelligent, less original, less cognitively complex, lower in need for achievement, higher in need for affiliation, more conventional, and more likely to view another as competent and worthy of respect than persons who do not conform (Berg & Bass, 1961). Many studies have shown people with authoritarian personalities to be more conforming, but Steiner and Johnson (1963) caution that, when associates are not unanimous, authoritarians may be nonconformists. In general, when others are in agreement, their actions control the subject's behavior, while, when they are not in agreement, the subject may act according to his or her attitudes and perceptions of reality (Helson, Blake, & Mouton, 1958).

Children raised by parents who reward or punish *without explanation* are likely to become conformists. The reason is that they don't learn what it is that they are supposed to do; they only learn that they are supposed to conform to the wishes of their parents (Harvey, Hunt, & Schroder, 1961). Firstborns are also more likely than later-born children to be conformists. One hypothesis is that inexperienced parents rush to the aid of a firstborn, thus teaching the child to be dependent rather than self-reliant (Schachter, 1959). And dependent people are more likely than independent people to do what others ask them to do (Mehrabian & Ksionsky, 1970), to ask for help, and to seek approval from others.

THE PROCESS OF SOCIAL PENETRATION

The third dimension of interpersonal behavior concerns the intimacy of interaction. Altman and Taylor (1973) have summarized the literature on interpenetration, including many of their own studies. They identify four stages of the interpenetration process: orientation, exploratory affective exchange, full affective exchange, and stable exchange. *Orientation* involves superficial exchanges. The setting might be a first date, a cocktail party, or a small social gathering. People give information about where they live, how many children they have, what trips they have taken, and so on. They behave "correctly," criticize others only cautiously, and generally behave formally. The *exploratory affective-exchange* stage is characterized by greater spontaneity, discussion of more personal relations, and some cautious exchanges of status and love, such as complimenting a hostess on her superb cooking. *Affective exchange* is characterized by considerable exchanges of status and love. Close friendships and courtship relationships are at this stage. The exchange is freewheeling, and people feel quite comfortable teasing each other, touching each other, evaluating each other, and communicating about their fears, loves, and foibles. *Stable exchange* is achieved in only a few relationships, such as a good marriage. People can predict each other's next behavior, trust each other, exchange freely and spontaneously, and use much nonverbal behavior, such as touching, kissing, and gesturing. They allow each other to use their "private" belongings, such as items of clothing, and they don't hold back information about their private thoughts.

The process of interpenetration is characterized by exchanges involving deeper and deeper "layers" of the person. The superficial layer involves clothes and the face that people display to manipulate the impressions that others acquire about them. The deepest layer involves information about our needs, values, feelings, and physiological processes. Love and hate for important others, such as parents and spouses, are found only in "deep" layers.

The Social Component

Cultures differ in their prescriptions of how people should behave along the intimacy/formality dimension. Lewin (1936) analyzed differences between American and German culture. Americans tend to be very easy to meet. They exchange freely and readily in the superficial layers of the person; but exchanges at deeper layers are made only with a few people. For example, meeting at a cocktail party, Americans are quite likely to discuss where they come from and where they're going but unlikely to talk about how much they earn or how much they spent on their shirt. Germans are more difficult to meet. They are less likely to interact with a complete stranger and are more dependent on a formal introduction before they can engage in social interaction. However, after a given period of time, if interpenetration has taken place beyond the public layer of the person, Germans open up and are quite willing to discuss intimate matters that most Americans would not discuss except with very good friends. Thus, the process of interpenetration is different in the two cultures. Americans penetrate the outer layers easily and quickly but stop for a long time before moving to the inner layers. Germans are difficult to penetrate in the first place, but, if pierced to the middle layers, are more open about many matters than are Americans.

These differences in norms can, of course, cause a good deal of misunderstanding. The American's casual approach to the superficial layer is likely to offend the German who is not ready for interaction; if interaction does take place, the German may be willing to open up just at the point when the American is closing down!

Norms about touching, smiling, kissing, and interpersonal distance are also important. As mentioned in Chapter 2, Watson (1970) has summarized the literature and has presented data that show that there are "high contact" and "low contact" cultures. The high-contact cultures, such as the people around the Mediterranean, Arabs, and South Americans, tend to touch a lot, to speak to each other at a close distance, and to permit males to hold hands. Low-contact cultures, such as Northern and Western Europeans and East Asians, do not touch but bow, keep at greater distance from each other, and consider holding hands between males quite inappropriate. Hall (1959, 1966) has presented numerous examples of cultural differences in proxemic behavior. It is clear that people in high-contact cultures are more likely to act intimately, because high-contact behaviors are often intimate.

The norm of reciprocity seems to hold in interpersonal exchanges. When O reveals intimate thoughts to P, P is likely to reveal intimate thoughts to O, if appropriate. Altman and Taylor (1973, pp. 52–56) review several studies that support the reciprocity hypothesis.

Affective Factors

Intimate exchanges with others who are liked are more enjoyable than formal exchanges. Formal exchanges tend to be boring—too structured, too controlled. Intimate exchanges are more interesting, stimulating, and rewarding.

Foa and Foa (1974) suggest that people prefer particularistic to universalistic interactions. Altman and Taylor (1973) have shown that, the greater the rewards and the lower the costs of interpersonal relationships, the greater the interpenetration. As long as a relationship remains viable, it is likely to shift to more and more intimate layers of exchange. Superficial interactions continue at the same level, over time, but intimate interactions increase with the age of the relationship.

Acquiring information about important O's is often particularly useful and enjoyable to P's. The fascination that people have with biographies of famous people must be, in part, the outcome of their trying to understand what makes such people "tick." Perhaps it is also a reflection of the fact that many of the items of information that they are exposed to are quite intimate. Gossip often involves information about the intimate affairs of others. The fact that so much of it goes on in most societies is an indication that it is enjoyable.

The Perceived Consequences of Intimacy

The Altman and Taylor (1973) analysis shows clearly, through a review of several studies, that reward/cost factors—that is, the anticipation of positive and negative consequences—are important in the interpenetration process. The rate of development of a relationship varies over time. Exchanges in the least intimate areas are easy, in the sense that they don't cost much to the individual. In contrast, exchanges in the most intimate areas can be very costly. A person becomes vulnerable when others know his or her innermost thoughts. Thus, at the early stages of development, social penetration is fast; at later stages, it slows down.

When the negative consequences of revealing one's inner thoughts are remote or nonexistent, one is more likely to present intimate thoughts than when the consequences are likely. This fact explains, in part, the phenomenon called "stranger-on-a-train" or "passant." Altman and Taylor (1973) review several studies that show that people are more likely to reveal intimate thoughts to another with whom they do not expect future interaction, such as a fellow passenger on a train or plane, than with another whom they expect to see frequently.

Facilitating Conditions

The absence of anticipated future interaction can also be considered a facilitating condition for intimacy. Another condition is isolation of a pair from their social environment. Altman and Taylor review several of their own studies on the effects of social isolation. In some studies, two men lived and worked in a small room, completely cut off from the outside world for ten days. In such situations, when the subjects were compatible they exchanged intimate information, but when they were incompatible they often were "at each other's throats." In both kinds of dyads, there was a good deal of evidence of territorial behavior, with each man defining some of the furniture as his and objecting to the other's use of it. Dyads who spent much time together in the first day were most likely to complete the experiment, while dyads who did not build their interpersonal relationship in the first days were more likely to abort. High degrees of territorial behavior in the early phases helped the dyads stay together until the end of the experiment. For those who completed the experiment, as intimacy developed, territoriality dropped. Over time, territoriality increased among those who aborted.

Individual Differences

There is considerable evidence of individual differences in willingness to reveal intimate thoughts. Tuckman (1966) found that System III persons in the Harvey, Hunt, and Schroder (1961) classification of personality types were particularly likely to be high revealers. System III persons are the types whose socialization consistently included a good deal of information (explanations) about why they should or should not behave in certain ways. Most of this information which tended to be superficial, concerned the effects of their behavior on interpersonal relations. System IV persons were socialized inconsistently; that is, sometimes they were given information about other people and sometimes they were not. Such socialization tends to make people information seekers. Consistent with this theoretical interpretation was the finding that the System III subjects gained much information from a casual acquaintance (the superficial relationship) but were not high in seeking information from intimate friends, while consistent with their information-seeking tendencies, System IV people were lowest in revealing but highest in probing information from others. Taylor (1968) used an individual-differences measure of tendency to reveal information. He showed that, over a 13-week period, high revealers consistently revealed more and low revealers consistently revealed less to their close friends.

There is some evidence that subjects who do not achieve an identity cannot establish intimate interpersonal relationships (Orlofsky, Marcia, & Lesser, 1973). Those characterized by identity diffusion may become "playboys" or become aimless, aloof, drifting, and empty. Orlofsky and his associates argue that there is a great difference between the intimate and the isolate and that identity diffusion is a partial cause of nonintimacy.

OVERT VERSUS COVERT BEHAVIOR

The fourth dimension of social behavior concerns whether the behavior is overt or covert. There are a number of factors that suppress overt behavior. These include norms about silence, dislike of the behavior, and negatively perceived consequences.

Among the most important covert behaviors are attributions—interpersonal evaluations of decisions and behavioral intentions. In later chapters, we'll examine the determinants of attributions, interpersonal attraction, and behavioral intentions and show that they do have social, affective, and cognitive aspects similar to those suggested by the model presented in Chapter 1.

One interesting phenomenon is the suppression of social behavior. Behavior that is often punished or is associated with tension is often suppressed. If this happens frequently, a habit of continual suppression of this behavior may develop. For example, *to criticize* might often have negative consequences, and our well-considered decision to avoid criticizing might be associated with the reduction of the unpleasantness of social situations. If this happens frequently, we will eventually suppress the behavior without even thinking.

The Social Component

Cultures have norms that make certain behaviors taboo. A person may like the behavior and may perceive many desirable consequences of it but, because of social norms, may not engage in it. One's feelings, however, may be closely in correspondence with the suppressed behavior. For example, in American culture, one normally does not criticize another at the home of a mutual friend. One may feel like criticizing and might perceive some desirable consequences and yet not act. Under some conditions, *not acting* may be associated with positive affective states. For example, a person may feel very good about keeping silent.

Perceived Consequences

One of the most common determinants of inaction is anticipated punishment. A person may feel like doing something, but the probability that the action will lead to punishment may be seen as very high. In that case, the person may have all the feelings consistent with the behavior, and yet no behavior may be seen. For example, a boy may feel like kissing a girl but may perceive the consequences as negative. His feelings would be associative, coordinate, and intimate—but the behavior covert.

Individual Differences

One of the major dimensions of personality is extroversion/introversion. Individual differences on this dimension determine, in part, the probability that social behavior will be expressed rather than covert.

A Note on the Social Psychology of Suppressed Behavior

It is notable that no references are included in the present section to specific studies concerned with suppressed behavior. One reason is, of course, that such behavior is difficult to study. This is a virtually unexplored area of social psychology and should become the focus of future research. The absence of behavior can be just as interesting as the presence of behavior. We need to know why some people don't marry, don't vote, don't invite people to dinner, don't criticize, and so on just as much as we need to know why they do help, do aggress, and do conform.

SUMMARY

In this chapter, we examined behaviors characteristic of the four dimensions of social behavior that form the typology presented in Chapter 1. We examined associative behaviors (helping) and dissociative behaviors (aggression). We examined the superordination/subordination dimension by looking at studies of conformity behavior and looked at the intimacy/formality dimension in terms of the interpenetration process. Finally, some thoughts were presented about the covert/overt dimension. In each case, it was possible to show that habits, social factors such as norms, the affect toward the behavior, the perceived consequences of the behavior, and personality differences are among the important factors that determine whether the behavior will occur.

4

THE OTHER AS A STIMULUS TO THE PERCEIVER

In the previous three chapters, we focused primarily on the kinds of responses that the actor makes in relation to others. We discussed different types of responses—attributive, affective, overt. I presented a model that interrelates the major determinants of these responses and gave examples of how these determinants influence helping behavior, aggression, conformity, and interpenetration.

In these chapters, we discussed the effects of norms on behavior. However, it should be clear that, in order for particular norms to be evoked, the actors must perceive that the situation calls for these norms. The situation usually includes the other, the other's behavior, the assumed characteristics of the other, the setting in which P and O are interacting, the norms of the groups to which P and O belong, and so on. Understanding the person's perception (distal) of the interpersonal situation, then, is crucial in understanding which determinants of behavior (proximal) will be evoked. In short, in the previous chapters we discussed proximal determinants of action. Now we will discuss more distal determinants of interpersonal behavior. We can consider the person's perception of the elements of the interpersonal situation to be more remote (or distal) determinants of interpersonal behavior than the components in Equation 2 are because they affect action through those components.

There are three major foci for discussing the distal determinants. First, the actual characteristics of the other, the other's behavior, and the situation in which the behavior takes place are perceived selectively. The perceiver notices only some aspects of the total situation. What the perceiver does notice depends on many of his or her own characteristics; the second focus concerns how *P*'s characteristics modify what is perceived. Finally, the third focus concerns what *P* does with the several cues that he or she picks up about the interpersonal situation. *P* usually does not respond directly to objective stimuli but *constructs* the situation out of the elements that he or she has perceived.

The way people construct the situation out of elements that they have perceived and remember it later has been a focus of attention among psychologists for a long time. One of the classic studies was published by Sir Frederic Bartlett in 1932, in a book titled *Remembering*. Bartlett used the method of repeated reproduction, in which a story is presented to a person who reads it twice and reproduces it about 15 minutes later. The subject is asked to reproduce the story again and again at later points in time. Bartlett found that, as the story is reproduced, it becomes considerably shortened (mostly by omissions), the wording becomes more consistent with the subject's normal vocabulary, and the story becomes more coherent and organized.

Bartlett also used the method of serial reproduction, in which one person tells the story to another, who tells the story to still another, and so on. In these experiments, again, the tendency toward simplification was clear, but there was also a tendency to construct a new story—a more meaningful one in terms of the culture of the subjects—by changing the unfamiliar to make it familiar. If the original story came from another culture and had many elements that made no sense to the subjects, it was likely to be elaborated and reconstructed so that it made sense to those who told it. There was also a tendency for certain incidents to become dominant, with all others grouped about them.

Bartlett gives many examples of reconstruction, some of which are now classic. He tells the story of the Paramount Chief of the Swazi people of Africa who visited England to settle a long-standing land dispute. When he returned, the local British settlers in Swaziland asked him what he had found most impressive during his visit. The Chief indicated that he was most impressed by the English policemen regulating traffic with uplifted hands. It turns out that Swazis greet their fellows in the same manner. Thus, the policemen seemed to be unusually friendly, and the behavior fitted well in an already established familiar framework, so it was well remembered.

Cognitive construction of a situation often involves *attributions* made by the perceiver concerning the characteristics and the

causes of behavior of the other. Such attributions are very important because they give meaning to what is perceived.

PERCEPTION OF THE CHARACTERISTICS
OF THE OTHER

The other has millions of characteristics, in the sense that he or she
differs from other people in innumerable ways. These differences obviously
include dress, physical characteristics, behavior patterns, voice quality, and
so on. The perceiver notices only some of these characteristics. For example,
most people do not see the size of the ears of others unless the ears are in
some way extremely abnormal.

It is much easier to attend to characteristics of the other for which the
language of your culture has a word than to attend to characteristics for
which there is no culturally defined concept. For example, the Greeks consider the most important characteristic of a person to be whether he or she is
philotimos (Vassiliou & Vassiliou, 1973). The word *philotimos* corresponds to
the idea that the person is highly reliable in behaving in ways specified by his
or her family and close friends. English speakers don't have such a term or its
equivalent, hence will have difficulty perceiving this characteristic. In fact,
English speakers might not even consciously check the extent to which people behave as they are expected to behave by their ingroup, since such
behavior is not always considered desirable or important.

Each culture classifies experience in ways that are functional for life
in its particular environment. Since environments differ, each culture encourages the development of different maps of reality. These maps of reality
guide the perception of interpersonal cues. A cue from another person is
more likely to be perceived if it is (a) consistent with existing habits of en-
coding reality, (b) vivid, (c) associated with pleasant rather than unpleasant
events, and (d) familiar than if it does not have any of these qualities
(Campbell, 1967). In short, expectations, needs, and values guide the selective processing of cues.

A more detailed analysis of perceptual processes (Gibson, 1969)
suggests that perceptual selectivity is a function of both the extent to which
stimuli contain familiar (previously learned) stimulus patterns and the extent
to which they contain distinctive features. The organism is exposed to extremely rich stimulation, which already contains homogeneities and local-
ized heterogeneities; for example, P might see that most O's go to church but
that one O does not. The organism learns to attend to the distinctive features of the stimulus array. As perceptual learning takes place, what was
meaningless becomes differentiated, meaningful, and readily recognizable.

Stimulus generalization—for example, thinking that all Orientals are alike—decreases as stimulus differentiation—for example, noting that the Orientals you know are very different from one another—increases. During perceptual learning, the organism extracts dimensions of difference across stimulus arrays (for example, notices that some people play with their fingers and some don't) and learns to identify the distinctive features that characterize different events. Differentiating a stimulus pattern from other patterns creates a perceptual habit that can be transferred to new situations, with the transfer being best when the new situations allow for maximum contrasts and provide several sharp and distinctive features as well as several clues of similarity with previously learned stimulus patterns. For example, if the *O* who doesn't go to church also has other traits that distinguish him from those who do go, *P* may notice other traits of this *O* that make him different. Thus, the mechanisms of perceptual learning involve extraction of the distinctive features of stimulus arrays and the filtering out of irrelevant variations of stimulus input. Neither reinforcement nor knowledge of results is essential for a person to learn a perceptual habit. What is important, according to Gibson, is the reduction of uncertainty.

In person perception, any interpersonal behavior or attribute that stands out is likely to be selected, particularly if it permits greater predictability of the environment. Thus, if, in a given culture, Blacks behave just like Whites and people never discriminate between a person who is Black and one who is White, there will be no information carried by a person's racial characteristics. In such a society, people would probably not notice a person's race but would instead focus on other characteristics of persons. Klineberg (1954) claims that one of his Brazilian roomates did not notice the race of persons he encountered.

We now turn to a more detailed discussion of cue utilization, including discussion of the stages of perception.

Stages in the Process of Perception

In their discussion of the relationship between perception and personality, Eriksen and Eriksen (1972, p.14) distinguish four stages:

1. the initial response of the receptors,
2. the integration of receptor information,
3. categorization of the integrated percept on the basis of distinctive features (categorization involves treating somewhat different stimuli as though they were identical), and
4. labeling of the percept or some motor response to it or both (labeling involves using a verbal response associated with the category).

It is important to remember that the receptors receive a great deal of information but that only some of it is integrated in the brain to the extent that it can be categorized. The categories may be labeled by the perceiver, who then, upon perceiving certain characteristics of another, says to himself or herself that the other is *intelligent, malicious,* or what have you; or the categories may involve responses such as avoidance.

There is debate concerning whether all four or only some of these stages should be called perception. If perception is defined as "the extraction of information from the stimulus energy impinging on human sensory receptors" (Eriksen & Eriksen, 1972, p.2), then only the first three stages can be called perception, since the last stage concerns the perceiver's response. This distinction is helpful in detailed work on perception, but for our purposes perception includes all four stages.

The Determinants of Cue Perception

The initial response of the receptors is the result of stimulus energy hitting the receptors. The other (O) emits innumerable cues, which may or may not be noted by the perceiver (P). Among the most important of O's cues are his or her color (at least in race-conscious cultures), type of hair, accent, rate of speech, loudness of speech, clothes, and, of course, behavior.

The eye is capable of making about 7,500,000 discriminations among colors alone (Brown & Lenneberg, 1954), and the ear can discriminate millions of sounds. The receptors receive this rich input, but the brain selects only some of this information for further processing. Electrophysiological work with various animals suggests that integration of receptor information occurs soon after the energy activates the receptors. Integration involves sorting the input into distinctive bundles of features (Gibson, 1969). The sorting is done on the basis of similarities in *physical* features of the stimuli. In the final stage, the physical features are "translated" into human categories, which involves attaching verbal labels, such as *intelligent* and *anxious*, to the visual image (Eriksen & Eriksen, 1972, p. 14).

To sum up, the other emits innumerable potentially discriminable stimuli, only a small fraction of which are sorted by the brain into patterns of physical categories. And only some of the categories are labeled. The labeled categories constitute cues concerning the other.

These cues are likely to be perceived in proportion to the extent to which they "stand out." The perceiver holds some point to be the average for any human attribute. For example, you may consider persons of a certain size average, while persons who are very different from this "level of adaptation" (Helson, 1964) you see as very tall or very short. The *level of adaptation* is the geometric mean (a kind of average) of all of your experience with this attribute. This means that people who live in a culture in which most people are very tall (for example, the Watusi of Africa) are likely to have a high level of adaptation, and people who live in a culture in which most people are very short (say, the Pygmies) are likely to have a low level of adaptation. People notice deviations from their level of adaptation for any human attribute, including size, color, loudness of speech, and various behaviors. For example, behaviors that are normal might not even be noticed; a person who says "Hello" might not be characterized as "polite," but one who typically growls when seen in the street and fails to greet others might be considered rude. But even greeting behavior is subject to cultural variations in level of adaptation. In most rural environments, particularly in Europe, people greet each other even if they've never seen each other before, but in urban environments one greets only those with whom one is acquainted. Hence, a greeting from a stranger in an urban environment is likely to be noticed. Inferences may range from "This is an unusually friendly type" to "He/She is probably trying to get something from me," depending on other cues.

As noted above, a person emits too many cues for P to perceive, so that P must select the cues he or she will notice or be overwhelmed with information. What P considers relevant is most likely to be perceived. Relevance is largely a function of whether the cue makes a difference for P's behavior or understanding; a cue is particularly relevant if it reduces P's uncertainty concerning who the other is and how he or she should react to the other (Gibson, 1969).

In addition, the relevance of the cue depends upon whether it has value for the perceiver. If it is known by P to lead to rewards, P is more likely to notice it. For example, a dress designer is likely to note what the other person wears, in part because he or she experiences rewards when O wears one thing and not when O wears another. For a professor, what a student wears may have a zero "cue validity," and hence the professor may literally "not see" what the student wears. Cue validity refers to the extent to which the cue predicts some event that the perceiver considers in some sense important.

A cue is also more likely to be perceived if it is familiar than if it is unfamiliar. For example, if O has a slash on his cheek, it may indicate to those familiar with it the African tribe to which he belongs. But if P knows nothing about such things, he or she will just see a slash and assume that it is due to an accident. In short, if P does not have an appropriate category for thinking about the cue, he or she may not even notice it or may categorize it incorrectly. We can make a more general statement: the greater the availability of a concept in the perceiver's language, the more likely it is that P will perceive cues that are labeled by this concept. Familiarity, then, is likely to aid the perception and correct categorization of a cue.

Postman (1953), in his analysis of motivational factors in perception, summarizes studies that demonstrate the importance of *frequency* (familiarity), *recency,* and *effect* in determining perception. Frequently encountered, recent, or rewarding stimuli are more likely to be perceived than rarely encountered, remote in time, or punishing stimuli. One can analyze some of the phenomena described under the label of "set" (for example, you are told that you are going to see a "fat lady," and, when a woman of ordinary weight appears, you still "see" a "fat lady") in terms of the recency of a cue in the history of the perceiver. Campbell (1967), in his well-known analysis of stereotyping also discusses how perceptual thresholds are affected by the perceiver's drive, the value of the cue, and the familiarity of the cue. Drive and value are, of course, related to the rewarding aspect of the cue.

The impact of a new piece of information is greater when P does not expect it than when P does expect it. For example, Gollob, Rossman, and Abelson (1973) presented adjectives describing a person (kind, cruel, and so on) and also acts (for example, antagonizes, meets, helps) attributed to this person. Subjects were asked to judge the likelihood that the person described with the adjective behaved in the particular way. Information affected the judgments of likelihood more when it was inconsistent with other information.

It is worth noting the paradox that both familiar and unexpected cues tend to be noticed. If a cue is entirely unfamiliar, it may not even be categorized, so it will not be noticed. For example, suppose that a person who belongs to a certain tribe wears an earring that is worn only by members of this tribe. Most observers who do not know about the relationship of the type of earring to the tribe will not notice the *type* of earring and may not even notice the earring at all. An observer who is familiar with the type of earring is more likely to notice that this one is of that type. Now, suppose that there are several cues consistent with tribal membership, but one cue that is not. The inconsistent cue will be unexpected and will stand out. In this case, if the earring is consistent with all sorts of other signs of tribal membership, it may not be seen. Thus, both familiarity and unexpectedness may be important in increasing the probability that a particular cue will be perceived.

In addition, negative information is generally given more weight than positive information. For example, in an interview, negative information is correlated with the decision to hire or not to hire to a greater extent than is positive information (Webster, 1964). This is apparently a rather general phenomenon in human judgment, according to Kanouse and Hanson (1972). They review studies that show that, when objects have both good and bad characteristics, the overall evaluation given them is closer to the bad than to the good characteristic. In addition, negative adjectives (such as *heartless, unscrupulous*) modify nouns much more powerfully than do positive adjectives (such as *holy, sincere*). For example, consider the noun *landlady* and the extent to which *heartless landlady* and *sincere landlady* differ in meaning from *landlady*. It is intuitively true that *heartless landlady* indicates somebody very far removed from the neutral point, in the direction of negative affect, while *sincere landlady* is not very different from *landlady*. The same is true for negatively valued nouns—for example, *heartless thief* versus *sincere thief*. Furthermore, when a description of a pair of immoral deeds is presented to subjects, the subjects' evaluations tend to be appropriate to the worse of the two deeds. A person described with several positive adjectives is liked only a little, while a person described with the same number of negative adjectives is disliked very much. Positive verbs, such as *helps* and *loves*, do not have as much impact as negative verbs, such as *hates* and *avoids*, in producing an impression of another person.

Kanouse and Hanson went on to examine several possible reasons for this so-called "negativity bias." One explanation is that in life most outcomes are good but not very good (for example, we don't win sweepstakes every day), and extremely bad outcomes (for example, the death of a loved one) are more frequent than extremely good outcomes. An examination of probable distributions of outcomes led these authors to suggest that the neutral point for the evaluation of outcomes is somewhere between the mean and the median outcome. This implies that most outcomes will be evaluated as positive. Now, a negative outcome will not change the neutral point much, but a very positive outcome will. When the latter happens, the person becomes "spoiled" and experiences many intermediate outcomes as negative. This reduces P's overall level of happiness. People learn through experience to avoid negative outcomes rather than seek positive outcomes, because they learn that the pursuit of highly positive outcomes is illusory. Happiness depends on a high proportion of nonnegative outcomes rather than on a few highly positive outcomes. "Keeping out of trouble" is more valuable than "trying to make it big." Thus, any sign of "trouble" is very bad news.

Other explanations are also possible. Perhaps negativity is due to the fact that negative attributes interfere with enjoyment of positive attributes, while positive attributes seldom reduce the experience of negative ones. For example, fine spices do little to alter the taste of rancid soup. Kanouse and Hanson also point out that a gambler who goes broke may not be able to have future gains, while great gains do not prevent the gambler from having great losses in the future. Finally, they argue that, if life's outcomes are such that there are more extremely negative than extremely positive outcomes, a negativity bias is adaptive, in the Darwinian sense. The personnel director who pays great attention to negative characteristics may save himself or herself from much criticism, while one who looks mostly at positive characteristics may never receive much positive feedback from colleagues, since most feedback is negative (in the form of complaints).

Responses after the Cue is Perceived

The discussion above examined the effects of certain variables on the probability that a cue will be perceived. Once a cue is perceived, a number of additional processes take place. First, cognitive elements related to the cue may become activated. Second, the cue is likely to be actively related to other cues so that P can draw inferences concerning the characteristics of O. Thus, P might classify O according to race, sex, or social class or might attribute particular motives or personality characteristics to O. Once this happens, P is also likely to compare himself or herself with O on these same attributes and to do a computation of the extent to which P and O are similar or different on attributes that are valuable (relevant). If P judges the other to be very similar, P may feel good about O; we've already noted that perceived similarity is strongly related to interpersonal attraction. Similarity is also related to many other responses, including a predisposition to be friendly and intimate with the other. Elsewhere, I have compiled a detailed discussion of how cues of similarity/difference are used by people in different cultures to react to O's (Triandis, 1967).

Apparently there are individual differences in the number of cues perceived. For example, Bodalyev (1972) found that actors used 2.9 times more different elements concerning another person's appearance than did engineers. The actors inferred 8.5 times more consequences from these elements than did the engineers. An actor, of course, has to observe details of other people's appearance and behavior in order to portray different types in the theater; engineers have a much smaller requirement of interpersonal sensitivity in their work.

The perception of cues will vary with culture, occupation, and personality. For example, in the United States, where race is a very important determinant of interpersonal behavior, it is difficult to conceive of people who do not notice the race of the other. In Brazil, where race is less important, it is more likely that the most perceivable cue will be related to social class, which in turn is the attribute that has most importance in social relationships. My review (Triandis, 1967) shows that race, social class, religion, and nationality may have more or less importance in social perception, depending on P's culture. Both P's occupation and P's personality will have sensitization effects. For example, a person who is highly talkative may look for cues of a good listener.

There is considerable empirical evidence that both culture and personality can affect the relative importance of cues in person perception. For example, in a study by Korten (1974), Ethiopians and Americans were asked to describe several kinds of persons, such as "a university student you know very well" or "a villager you know very little." Content analysis of the descriptions showed that Americans tended to mention the competence or knowledge—generally, the abilities—of the person described; Ethiopians tended to mention mostly the person's opinions, beliefs, values, and interpersonal interactions.

Davis and I (Triandis & Davis, 1965) studied the behavioral intentions of 300 students with respect to persons who were White or Black, male or female, and supportive of the 1964 Civil Rights law. (The study was conducted during a period when the particular law was being debated in Congress.) Similarities in the patterns of answers of these 300 students to the various stimuli were obtained through factor analysis. Students who had similar points of view were identified. One point of view was characterized as "conventionally prejudiced." This view rejected Blacks, regardless of their position on the Civil Rights law. These students considered civil rights an *unimportant* issue and indicated that they would follow leaders who opposed it. They were more authoritarian (as measured by the F scale), less tolerant of minorities, and less critical of established social institutions than were the majority of students. They were also characterized by other opinions and beliefs that were consistent with extreme antiliberalism. Another point of view, obtained in the factor analysis, was characterized as "belief prejudice." Subjects with this point of view responded according to the beliefs of the stimulus person. Blacks who were against the Civil Rights law were liked as much as Whites. These students considered the Civil Rights issue *very important* and many political and civil-rights issues (for example, the John Birch Society and segregated schools) *very important*. Here, then, is a case in which one group of students "zeroes in" on the race of the other, while another group focuses on the opinions and beliefs of the other. These two sets of people are similar in some of their attitudes but attribute vastly different degrees of importance to certain controversial issues. In short, we can expect a good deal of variation in what cues are perceived and how they are processed, depending on cultural, occupational, and personality factors.

THE ACCURACY OF PERCEPTION

Several studies, reviewed by Warr and Knapper (1968, p. 298), show that the level of accuracy attained in interpersonal judgments is relatively low. These studies deal with a range of topics from the perception of emotions to the perception of dispositional characteristics such as *intelligence* and *masculinity*. If there is any trend in such studies, it is that, the greater the amount of information at the disposal of the perceiver and the smaller the extrapolations that the perceiver is asked to make, the more accurate are his or her judgments likely to be.

Certain traits have highly visible aspects. For example, in Moslem cultures, the trait *pious* can be inferred from the number of times a person prays each day. Since praying is done in public and by means of behaviors that are easily identified (turning toward Mecca, and so on) it is relatively easy to be accurate in judging this particular trait (Schuman, 1966). Identifying this trait, then, in this setting, requires little extrapolation on the part of the perceiver. Other traits, however, may require a great deal of extrapolation. In fact, some traits, although frequently referred to in our conversations, may be very difficult to identify. For example, *masculinity* is a trait that is difficult to identify, and psychologists have had only modest success in finding measures of this trait that correlate with each other. There is a strong possibility that the trait is situation-bound, because there are so many cases of masculine-looking male athletes who like to cook and sew and feminine-looking females who fight like men. It is most likely that there is no general trait but that a person may be masculine in certain situations and feminine in other situations.

Perceiving Emotional States

The earliest investigations of the accuracy of person perception concerned the accuracy of the perception of emotional states. As early as 1872, Darwin argued that expressive movements associated with emotions have no functional value per se but only represent what remains of movements that were once functional for a certain species. In short, emotions are correlated with biologically determined movements, and an observer should have no difficulty recognizing such movements, no matter what his or her culture.

This argument makes two assumptions: (1) that each emotion always has certain features associated with it and (2) that humans can correctly identify emotions because they know, without having to learn it, which features go with which emotion.

A typical test of these assumptions involves the presentation of pictures of emotional expressions to judges, who try to identify the expressions. Work done at the turn of the century suggested that judges are rather poor at identifying some emotions, although they do a relatively good job with other emotions. Still later, some psychologists argued that cultural factors determine what people do when they are in particular emotional states. However, by the mid-1950s, it became clear that the difficulties that judges had in correctly identifying emotions were due, in large part, to the difficulty of applying a particular label to a particular photograph; but people could do a very good job of judging where a picture should be placed on a particular *dimension*. While judges may have trouble telling whether a picture represents *surprise* or *fear*, they have little trouble seeing that the first is closer to the *pleasantness* end of the pleasantness/unpleasantness dimension than the second.

Schlosberg (1954) proposed a theory of emotion that had three dimensions: pleasant/unpleasant, attention/rejection, and sleep/tension. Any emotion can be represented by a combination of (technically, a set of coordinates on) these three dimensions. The sleep/tension dimension represents the intensity of the emotion; the other two dimensions are combined, as shown in Figure 4.1, to produce emotions.

Lambert and I (Triandis & Lambert, 1958) explored the applicability of this theory to another culture by using the Schlosberg pictures with samples of Greeks, some of whom lived in an isolated village and had had no exposure to movies, television, or other media that provide opportunities for judging emotions. The Schlosberg theory was found to hold for the Greek data. In short, the villagers were able to correctly place the pictures on the three dimensions, and their placements correlated well with the placements of American college students. Work in Taiwan reported by Lambert and Lambert (1973) suggests that Chinese villagers behave much like Greek villagers on this task. Ekman, Sorenson, and Friesen (1969) have also found much agreement among observers in the identification of emotions. Izard's (1971) and Ekman's (1972) major reviews of these and other studies leave little doubt that the similarities in the perception of emotion across different cultures are much greater than the differences. This finding, of course, supports Darwin's original point.

Other support comes from animal studies showing some similarity in expression across species and greater expressiveness in animals that hunt together than in animals that hunt alone. In addition, studies have shown that all neonates, when placed in certain settings, express themselves similarly, using expressions that can be identified correctly by observers. Finally, studies show that the congenitally blind express emotions in much the same ways as sighted people. These three types of studies are reviewed in Izard (1971).

It should be clear, however, that, while there is a good deal of agreement on dimensional judgments, there is much less agreement in the way

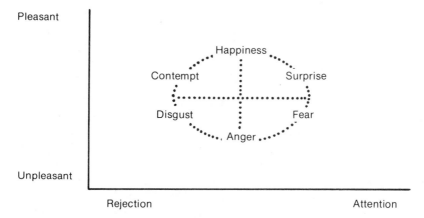

Figure 4.1   The structure of emotional experience, after Schlosberg.

particular labels are applied to particular pictures. Furthermore, an emotional state is often transitory, and judges have difficulty making an accurate evaluation of a transitory condition of the other (Warr & Knapper, 1968).

Our judgments of another's emotions are influenced by our own emotions. In an experiment by Schiffenbauer (1974), subjects were emotionally aroused and then asked to judge a set of facial-expression slides. The judgments of another's emotional state were influenced by the emotions of the subjects. Thus, there is a "projection" of our own emotion onto others.

As we move to evaluating perception of more enduring characteristics of the other, we should find more accuracy. Yet this is not necessarily the case; several other factors complicate the picture. As we shall see below, the amount of information that the perceiver has available to him or her, the extent to which the trait being judged is highly visible or covert, the extent to which the judgment requires extrapolation from the information, the tendencies of the perceiver to use responses that have particular biases or to commit "errors" in judgment, and several other factors can influence the accuracy of perception.

Accuracy of Perception of Other Traits

After World War II, one of the most important topics of investigation in social psychology was the problem of accuracy in the perception of others. This is a problem with important practical consequences. Personnel managers often decide whom to hire solely on the basis of impressions gained in interviews. Supervisors judge workers on how satisfactory and promotable they are, professors interview students, social workers and clinical psychologists interview their clients, juries form impressions of a defendant's innocence or guilt, police officers arrest individuals whom they suspect of having committed a crime, and so on. In all of these examples, a person forms an impression of another and acts according to this impression. If the impression is accurate, all is well; but, if it is inaccurate, behavior that follows from it will be ill-advised.

The popularity of this area of investigation was great not only because of its social significance but also because psychologists discovered an easy method for studying it. They asked a person O to describe himself or herself and a person P to predict what O would say. The experimenters reasoned that, if P were an accurate perceiver, he or she would be able to predict O's ratings. The correlation between O's actual ratings and P's predictions of O's ratings could be considered a measure of accuracy. Armed with this simple procedure, researchers published many papers until, ten years later, devastating critiques by Gage and Cronbach (1955), Cronbach (1955), and others brought this work to a halt. The problem with the methodology was that, if P assumed himself or herself to be similar to O and if P *happened* to be similar to O, P would get a perfect score—not because he or she was an accurate observer, but because of a tendency to consider others to be similar (a tendency called assumed similarity).

Figure 4.2 is taken from Gage and Cronbach's discussion. Consider a self-rating item such as "intelligent/unintelligent." If most people rate themselves as intelligent, and, if P assumes O's similarity, P will predict that O rated himself or herself as intelligent, which will turn out to be true. But this does not mean that P accurately *detected* O's intelligence. If we call P's self-description a, O's self-description b, and P's prediction of O's self description c, we can graph the possible situations as shown in Figure 4.2.

One ideal situation, in terms of accuracy of predictions, occurs when $a = b = c$. This situation is called *warranted assumed similarity*. However, $b - c$ does not give the accuracy of the perception; one must take into account the extent to which $a = b$—that is, one must control for real similarity. Another situation, which is called *warranted assumed dissimilarity*, occurs when $a \neq b = c$. Again the $b - c$ measure is not sufficient in itself; it must be corrected by a control for real dissimilarity. Accuracy of perception is measured by the correlation between warranted assumed similarity (taking into account real similarity) and warranted assumed dissimilarity (taking

	$a \neq b$ Real Dissimilarity (RD)	$a = b$ Real Similarity (RS)
$a = c$ Assumed Similarity	Unwarranted Assumed $a = c \neq b$ Similarity	Warranted Assumed $a = b = c$ Similarity
$a \neq c$ Assumed Dissimilarity	Warranted Assumed $a \neq b = c$ Dissimilarity	Unwarranted Assumed $a = b \neq c$ Dissimilarity

a = P's self-description

b = O's self-description

c = P's prediction of O's judgments

Figure 4.2 Possible combinations of assumed and real similarity of any dichotomous item. From "Conceptual and Methodological Problems in Interpersonal Perception," by N. Gage and L. Cronbach, *Psychological Review*, 1955, *62*, 411–412. Copyright 1955 by the American Psychological Association. Reprinted by permission.

into account real dissimilarity). Gage and Chronbach indicated that, since most previous researchers had not controlled for similarity and dissimilarity, their results were invalid.

Gage and Cronbach also pointed out that there are different kinds of studies of interpersonal perception. One can consider the extent to which P and O are acquainted with each other and the extent to which P must make a judgment that requires little or much extrapolation. For example, when a high school counselor is asked to agree or disagree with the statement "The majority of adolescents say they have conflict with their parents," the counselor makes a small extrapolation about people he or she knows well; but, if you ask a clinical psychologist to predict from a projective test, the scholastic performance of a client he or she has seen for an hour, you ask the psychologist to make a large extrapolation about a little-known person. Gage and Cronbach showed that perceivers bring different abilities to bear in their judgments, depending on the degrees of acquaintance and extrapolation. Specifically, when there is much acquaintance and little extrapolation, the perceiver uses mostly knowledge from past experience; when there is little acquaintance and little extrapolation (for example, when a judge interviews strangers and rates their command of English), the perceiver uses his or her ability to observe. When there is much acquaintance and much extrapolation (for example, husbands predicting the personality-test responses of their wives), the judge uses the ability to infer; when there is much extrapolation and little acquaintance, the judge uses both the ability to observe and the ability to infer. In short, person-perception situations involve differential difficulty for the judge. Furthermore, the other can be "people in general," "people in a particular category" (for example, Blacks), a particular individual, or even a particular individual in a particular situation. Again, the perception process requires different abilities, depending on which of these situations is under investigation.

Other problems with assessments of perceptual accuracy concern the fact that most accuracy scores include several kinds of factors. Bender and Hastorf (1953) identified (a) *projection:* the difference between the judge's own response and his or her prediction (a judge who predicts scores of the other similar to his or her own may be projecting his or her own characteristics onto the other), (b) *similarity:* the difference between P's response and O's response, (c) *raw empathy:* the difference between P's prediction and O's response, and (d) *refined empathy:* a score obtained by subtracting raw empathy from projection. Using the notation of Figure 4.2, we can say that projection is $a - c$, similarity is $a - b$, raw empathy is $c - b$, and refined empathy is $(a - c) - (c - b) = (a - c - c + b) = a + b - 2c$.

Cronbach (1955) identified four components of perceptual accuracy: elevation, differential elevation, stereotype accuracy, and differential accuracy. *Elevation* concerns that part of the accuracy score that is the result of

P and *O* using different parts of rating scales. For example, *P* might tend to use the high end and *O* the middle of the scales. A difference between *P*'s prediction and *O*'s response may reflect simply these "response sets" and have nothing to do with inaccuracy in perception.

Differential elevation concerns *P*'s ability to rank correctly the means of the responses of different *O*'s. For example, O_1 might make average ratings of 3.5 on a seven-point scale, O_2 might average 4.0, and O_3 might average 3.0. A perceiver who correctly guesses how these *O*'s use the rating scales will be more accurate, but it is a special kind of accuracy.

Stereotype accuracy concerns *P*'s ability to correctly identify that certain traits are rated high by particular *O*'s and not by other *O*'s. For example, if *P* can guess that professors will rate themselves as *intelligent* more often than they will rate themselves as *aggressive*, *P*'s perception scores will reflect a particular kind of accuracy.

Differential accuracy is "true" accuracy. It is the accuracy score that remains after the "response bias" components (elevation, differential elevation, and stereotype accuracy) have been removed. It concerns the ability to predict differences among *O*'s for each trait.

Crow and Hammond (1957) showed that the various response sets are more stable over time for different *P*'s than is differential accuracy. This finding suggests that accuracy depends much more on the ability to accurately stereotype others than on the ability to correctly identify how a particular *O* reacts to a particular scale. Other studies also have suggested that sensitivity to the generalized other, which is similar to stereotyped accuracy, is a more important determinant of accurate perceptions than is differential accuracy.

Following the critical evaluations of the earlier work, there was a dramatic shift in the methodology of research on the accuracy of perception. Many sophisticated methodologies were developed. A review of the later work can be found in Cline (1964).

Most of the results of work on perceptual accuracy have been disappointing. Apparently, humans are poor judges of people who are not similar to them. If a person is very similar to us, we can judge that person accurately not so much because we can accurately judge another but because we can accurately judge ourselves.

In judging another—say, for fitness to do a certain job—is it better to examine a great deal of information about the other and make a "clinical judgment" or to use a computer, place all the information about others in regression equations, and place an individual on some dimension on the basis of "statistical judgments"? The evidence favors the statistical judgment, although Cline argues that, when judging persons who have identical actuarial scores, clinicians can improve prediction by bringing into play the additional information at their disposal. That is, after we select a person on purely objective bases (such as test scores or grades), we can look at the additional, fine-grain information (such as letters of recommendation and interview impressions) and improve our prediction.

An optimal way to combine human and computer judgments might involve having several judges make *component* rather than global judgments. For example, in selecting graduate students, professors would not only judge globally (accept, reject) but would also make separate ratings of the students' motivation, stated goals, character references, and so on. These partial judgments would be combined by computer with more objective elements (such as grades and GRE scores). Using a concrete criterion (for example, success in graduate school), one could "validate" the judgments of each judge and find that some do very well in judging motivation while others do well in evaluating other aspects of the applicant. A final selection procedure would use the best judges for each attribute (Einhorn, 1972).

The information can be combined into a final judgment in different ways, using different rules. One way is simply to add the numbers that represent each component. For example, one might have the high school grade-point average, college-aptitude test scores, and ratings of letters of recommendation and determine a student's admission to college from the sum of these three numbers. This is a linear rule. Dawes (1964) has described two other rules: the conjunctive and the disjunctive. The conjunctive rule requires that a person meet minimum standards on each component. For example, the college may set minimum levels for grade-point average and college-aptitude scores and take all students who do better than both these minima. The disjunctive rule requires that a person pass at least one of the cutoff levels on one of the components. Thus, if a person has grades that are above a certain level *or* aptitude scores that are above a certain level, the person is admitted. Dawes points out that there is an infinite variety of such rules, but the three mentioned above are the ones that are most widely used. The strictest (admits the smallest number) rule is likely to be the conjunctive; the easiest is likely to be the disjunctive, with the linear being intermediate in the number of cases that are admitted.

In the case of college admissions, one could defend all three rules. One could argue, for instance, that, if a student has good grades, that is an indication of good potential, and the fact that his or her aptitude test scores are poor may be an indication of the invalidity of the test or the nervousness of the student when taking the test. If the student has good aptitude scores, he or she is bright, and poor grades may indicate a poor teacher. On the other hand, one might argue that any one piece of information is likely to be in error and that only when the information agrees should one admit the student. One could also argue that, if the student does well in one thing and not so well in another, it is likely that the sum of the two will give the best prediction of his or her potential, since the sum allows the student to compensate for a deficiency by doing well in some other area.

The extraordinary difficulty of making accurate interpersonal judgments can be understood when we analyze the process a little more carefully. As mentioned earlier, a person emits thousands of cues, but only some of them have validity for a given trait. For example, a student who wants to go to graduate school may ask a professor to write a letter of recommendation. Of the thousands of cues emitted by the student, only some have relevance to whether or not he or she will make a good graduate student. The set of correlations of the criterion "good graduate student" with each of the cues varies a good deal. Some cues are excellent predictors (for example, grades in senior year of college), while other cues are poor predictors (for example, length of hair). In short, cue validity varies a great deal. We can call the set of correlations between the criterion "good graduate student" (Y_e) and the predictors ($e_1, e_2, \ldots e_n$) the cue validities and symbolize the correlations $r_{e1}, r_{e2}, \ldots r_{en}$.

The next question is whether the cue will be incorporated into the perceiver's judgment. For each cue, the correlation between the presence of the cue and the perceiver's final judgment is quite variable. One professor may base this judgment entirely on grades, another on the rate of speech (using it as an indication of IQ), and another on a combination of half a dozen cues. If we represent these correlations between a cue and the perceiver's judgment as $r_{s1}, \ldots r_{sn}$, we have another set of correlations.

Now we have two sets of correlations. One set of correlations ties the cues to events in the "real" or objective world—for instance, tying undergraduate grades to success in graduate school. The other set ties the cues to events in the subjective world of the professor's head—for instance, tying undergraduate grades to the professor's judgment. The success of the professor's judgment will depend on *both* of these. In fact, there are mathematical ways of predicting the "achievement" of the professor.[1]

---

[1]Tucker (1964) and Hammond and Summers (1972) showed that the correlation between a trait (for example, being a good graduate student) and the accurate perception of that trait (for example, the professor deciding that a student is likely to be a good graduate student) is expressed by the equation

$$r_a = GR_eR_s + C \cdot \sqrt{1 - R_e^2}\, C \cdot \sqrt{1 - R_s^2}$$

where r_a is the correlation of trait and judgment, which they call *achievement*, G is the correlation between the least-squares linear prediction of Y_e and Y_s from the n traits, which they call *knowledge*, R_e is the multiple correlation for predicting Y_e from the n traits, which they call *task uncertainty*, R_s is the multiple correlation for predicting the judgment Y_s from the n traits, which they call *control* or *utilization of knowledge*, and C is the correlation between the variance in the task system and the variance in the judgment system that is unaccounted for by G.

A simplifying assumption is that C is zero—in short, that there is a perfect correlation between the variance in the task system and the variance in the judgment system. Then the achievement of accurate judgment, r_a, is simply equal to GR_eR_s.

This analysis shows clearly that achievement r_a is the product of several correlation coefficients. Even under the most favorable conditions, the correlations would not exceed ordinary reliabilities—say, .8—and hence r_a would be smaller than $.8 \times .8 \times .8 = .51$. This

Achievement will be high if the professor predicts correctly who will be a good graduate student. It can be shown that, even under the most favorable conditions, if the correlations approach the limits of the reliability of the measurement of the variables, the "achievement" will account for less than a quarter of the variance in the useful aspects of the actual cues. But the most favorable conditions seldom prevail. There is a lot of evidence that perceivers do not make the best possible use of available information. Goldberg (1970) did an empirical study in which 29 psychologists rated 861 MMPI profiles. The MMPI is a psychological inventory that requires a subject to answer several hundred questions. It is scored by computer, and several scores are given for each subject. These several scores constitute a profile. The psychologists were required to make judgments, from these profiles, about the psychological characteristics of the 861 subjects. Goldberg had much other information about the subjects, so he could check the "achievement" of the psychologists. The correlation between cues and judgment was only .28; that is, only about 8% ($.28^2 = .08$) of the variance in the cues was utilized in the actual judgments of the psychologists.

What was even more interesting in Goldberg's study was that a computer was able to beat the psychologists in making these complex judgments. The reason for this is that people do not stick to a consistently correct strategy when utilizing information. Sometimes they use the right strategy, but at other times they shift to other approaches. A computer instructed to use the best strategy makes a set of judgments that is more correct than that which most humans can make.

One way to improve human judgments is to instruct judges about true cue validities and about the way they utilize information. One can train people to use the more valid cues and to pay little attention to the less valid cues. One can also make them aware of how they presently use information and how this affects the total "achievement." Unsophisticated judges tend to jump to conclusions on the basis of invalid cues or to use the less valid of several cues in making judgments. For example, people often use stereotypes, their own ideas of how human traits are interrelated, or cues that have nothing to do with what is being predicted and, in addition, give the wrong weights to these cues.

As a result of studying psychology, I have become much more modest about my ability to predict human behavior or traits just from "talking" to

---

means that only about 25% of the variance in the useful part of a cue is likely to be common with the variance in the judgments, even under the most favorable conditions.

Hammond and Summers analyzed performance in cognitive tasks as acquisition of knowledge (R_e) and control over knowledge already acquired (R_s). They reviewed studies of multiple-cue probability learning, clinical judgment, and interpersonal conflict and concluded that incomplete cognitive control is a more important problem than incomplete knowledge. In short, perceivers do not make the best possible use of available information.

people. The interview is one of the least useful sources of information about applicants for employment. If you want to know whether a person will do a good job, give the person a chance to do a sample of that job. That is the most valid cue. Don't look at whether the person is "shifty eyed," well groomed, or wearing polished shoes. The chances are that a person will not come for an interview looking his or her usual self but rather will put on a show. And even if you've used a high-validity cue, you should not expect complete success. Human judgments are simply not good enough.

Other obstacles to accurate perception include various "errors" that judges typically make when judging others. These include the so-called "halo effect" (Thorndike, 1920), which is a tendency to generalize a positive impression about O to all aspects of O's behavior, and the "logical error" (Newcomb, 1931), which is a tendency to make impressionistic judgments about the other that reflect popular stereotypes or popular logic, (for example, if he is athletic, he probably drives a sports car).

The perceiver's conception of what traits are frequently related to other traits is called an implicit personality theory. A person may think that fat people are happy, skinny people are neurotic, tall people are intelligent, intelligent people are honest, and so on. Thus, a whole network of connections among traits may exist. Such a personality theory can distort what is perceived. For example, a skinny person might be seen as neurotic in the absence of any objective evidence.

The Practical Significance of Perceptual Inaccuracy

The inaccuracy in person-perception judgments has important implications. It means that people should discount a lot of the information they receive from interviews and similar informal procedures and base their judgments to a much greater extent on objective evidence. That the interview is subject to undesirable influences has been well documented by Webster (1964). One source of error is the use of an ideal-applicant stereotype as a basis for comparison of each applicant. Those applicants who are hired fit this stereotype. Unfortunately, there is little evidence that such stereotypes have validity. Thus, interviewers may make consistent judgments, but they often end up making wrong judgments.

A study illustrating these problems was published by Hakel, Hollmann and Dunnette (1970). These authors constructed a test that had 21 items that are known to differentiate between Certified Public Accountants and men in general and 36 items that do not so differentiate. Three samples—CPAs, experienced employment interviewers who were not CPAs, and introductory psychology students—were asked to identify interests and activities that differentiate accountants from men in other professions. The maximum possible score was, of course, 21. There were no differences in the number of correct identifications among the three groups: the CPAs averaged 12.2, the employment interviewers 12.3, and the students 11.5 correct items. In short, there was no evidence that the CPAs had a more accurate stereotype than the students. Further analysis showed that the CPAs had a *different* stereotype. This means they would select a different applicant from the type of applicant selected by the students, but neither group would be particularly successful.

In conclusion, the available evidence suggests that person perception is often inaccurate. While certain factors, such as extensive acquaintance with the other, small extrapolation from cues to judgments, and cognitive feedback about the validity of certain cues and the way we use information can improve our interpersonal perception, the accuracy is usually not high, and we should use information derived from our person perceptions with the greatest caution. On the other hand, it must be conceded that we cannot do without interpersonal judgments; they are too much a part of our routine of life. The only reasonable approach is to be very cautious and to give more weight to interpersonal judgments when we have reason to believe that we are similar to the other, when we know the other well, and when we are making a small extrapolation than when these conditions do not prevail.

DEVELOPMENT OF AND INDIVIDUAL DIFFERENCES IN CUE UTILIZATION

The Development of Social Perception

The evidence appears to support the idea that children begin by looking at the world in an undifferentiated fashion. First they learn to differentiate between self and other, then between sexes, and finally between generations (ego's generation or older). This differentiation leads to a particular pattern of cognitions. For example, people of the same sex or same generation are seen to be more similar to one another than people of different sex or different generation (Foa, Triandis, & Katz, 1966).

The environment also contributes to perceptual effects, so that a person perceives another's characteristics differently, depending on the environment in which the other is perceived. For example, an American is not likely to perceive the characteristic "American" in another person he or she meets in the United States but is very likely to perceive that characteristic if he or she meets that same person in France.

At early stages of a child's development, perception is concrete, focusing on superficial characteristics, such as dress and appearance. As children grow older, they pay less and less attention to such superficial characteristics and greater attention to personality dispositions and hypothetical traits of the other person. This emphasis on perceiving internal dispositions appears earlier for upper-class than for lower-class subjects. For example, a study by Levy-Schoen (1964) shows an increase in attention to internal dispositions after age 6 for upper-class and after age 9 for lower-class French children.

Individual Differences in Cue Utilization

Wiggins (1971) has reviewed several studies that show individual differences in human judgment and that are relevant to an analysis of the manner in which individuals react to stimulus persons. There is ample evidence of different strategies in cue utilization. For example, Wiggins, Hoffman, and Taber (1969) studied the cues that people use in making judgments about the intelligence of the other. They found several kinds of people; three of these types were most frequent. Types 1 and 2 were highly intelligent subjects. Type 1 used, almost exclusively, information about the high school standing of the other (which is, of course, a reasonable correlate of intelligence). Type 2 used the high school standing but also the English effectiveness of the other. Type 3 judges were not so intelligent and they tended to be authoritarian. They gave weight to high school standing and English effectiveness but also placed heavy emphasis on "character variables" such as responsibility and study habits—variables that are unrelated to intelligence. All subjects of these three types also gave some weight to the number of credit hours attempted per semester by the stimulus person.

Ehrlich and Lipsey (1969) measured "affective style" by means of a scale defined by statements such as "When I meet people for the first time, I immediately have a strong reaction to them" and "It takes more than one meeting for me to decide whether I like or dislike a person." They found that strong reactors had more stable person perceptions, used less information, showed more vigilance, and accepted a greater number of other persons into intimate relationships.

Kelley and Stahelski (1970) examined the responses of subjects in a Prisoner's Dilemma Game and found differences between "cooperators" and "competitors." Cooperators tended to believe that some people are cooperative and some competitive, whereas competitors tended to believe that others are always competitive. The cooperators tended to be low on the F scale, while the competitors tended to be high. Thus, there is evidence for different views of interpersonal relationships involving different assumptions about the distribution of the characteristic "competitive" in the social world.

Several studies suggest that cognitive complexity influences person perception. Jones (1954) studied differences in perception associated with high F-scale scores and found that the high F-scale subjects were more insensitive than nonauthoritarians to the personality characteristics of others. They were also more likely than nonauthoritarians to differentiate the social environment in terms of power-related concepts. Halverson (1970) showed that people who do not differentiate much see traits as going together if they are desirable and as not going together when they are unequal in desirability. In other words, the evaluative connotations of the traits determine which traits are seen as going together by the low-complexity subjects. High-complexity persons were not so strongly affected by the evaluative connotations.

The above examples indicate that there are numerous differences in cue utilization; most of them relate to some measure of cognitive complexity. In many of these studies, the F scale was used as a measure of individual differences. A high score on this scale reflects, in part, an unsophisticated perceptual style and utilization of the concrete aspects of a stimulus. It seems safe to guess that some aspect of cognitive differentiation is involved, as a major determinant of style, in interpersonal perception.

Cognitive Complexity and Perceptual Style

In terms of the Harvey, Hunt, and Schroder (1961) typology, concrete individuals (that is, those who are cognitively simple) show few differentiations and have an inability to be neutral about issues. They do not introspect. They are egocentric and nonanalytical. They fail to plan, and they show ritualistic and fatalistic response patterns. There is some correlation between high scores on the F scale and these characteristics. Furthermore, Harvey and his associates looked, for an explanation of their types, at the behaviors of the parents of subjects who later were found to perceive at different levels of abstraction. Concrete subjects had parents who punished them consistently without explanations. The argument is that punishing consistently gives the child no information; and, of course, explanation involves giving information. Inconsistent punishment is likely to result in greater information processing simply because children who receive it have to explain to themselves why sometimes they are punished and sometimes they are not punished. The analysis of cognitive development in terms of the amount of information received by the child seems to be quite promising.

Streufert and Streufert (1969) examined the reactions of subjects to success and failure. It was found that subjects take increasing credit for success as success increases but do not take similar credit for increasing failure. This effect is more pronounced for cognitively simple than for cognitively complex persons.

One area of future research that appears particularly promising involves the concept of a *match* between the complexity of the environment and the complexity of the individual. The argument is that, when the environment is very complex, only a complex individual can deal with it, and, when the environment is very simple, a simple individual is likely to be more effective in it. Environmental complexity can be indexed in several ways. One way is following the suggestions of Streufert and Driver (1967) and Schroder,

Driver, and Streufert (1967), who consider, in their measure of environmental complexity, information load (the quantity of information impinging on the organism per unit of time) as well as the success and failure of the organism. The less the frequency of success and the greater the frequency of failure, the more information must be processed by the organism to successfully deal with that environment.

It seems reasonable that children exposed to a complex environment in which success is rare and failure is frequent will become exceptionally vigilant and utilize a complex cognitive structure to process the information they receive from the environment. In contrast, children who grow up in a simple and highly protected (success-guaranteed) environment may develop a simple cognitive structure.

When discussing environmental complexity, one should consider, however, the domains of the stimuli. Some environments are extremely complex in one domain and very simple in another. For example, survival in the financial circles of Wall Street requires a high level of discrimination among different types of stocks, bonds, futures, treasury notes, and so on that is unnecessary in a rural environment, where discrimination among plants and animals is more likely to be useful. Social systems show differentiations at different points. For example, the family may be highly differentiated as in extended-family structures in one setting and very simple (nuclear) in another. Cultures also can vary in differentiation (for example, in number of roles found), as already discussed in other chapters. Determining the optimal match between the cognitive structure of the individual and aspects of his or her environment would require an examination, by domain, of the complexity of the cognitive structures, on the one hand, and the complexity of the significant others, the institutions, and the total environment, on the other hand.

As people become exposed to increasingly complex environments, they can be expected to develop more cognitive dimensions to deal with them. Some evidence that this is the case is presented in a study by Friendly and Glucksberg (1970), who examined the relationship between the amount of experience of Princeton undergraduates with the Princeton culture and the number of dimensions utilized in responding to Princetonians. A two-dimensional solution of a multidimensional scaling task provided a satisfactory fit for the freshman data, while a three-dimensional solution was needed to provide a satisfactory fit for the data obtained from seniors.

The analysis of child rearing in terms of information loads seems promising for the understanding of cognitive development. For example, in a study by Thomas (1972), it was found that highly authoritarian subjects had been exposed to repressive control of sexual and aggressive behaviors during childhood as well as to a great deal of sex-role differentiation. One could argue that repressive parental behaviors involve establishing rules for the child's behavior that may appear entirely arbitrary to the child and that may therefore discourage the child from seeking underlying rules and hence from developing cognitive complexity. Socialization utilizing information, such as telling a child what other people think, expect, or need, is likely to be less repressive. Low levels of sex-role differentiation require a more complex reaction to the social environment, since typically they require the child to learn that some behaviors, some of the time, are appropriate for males and the very *same* behaviors, under other conditions, are appropriate for females. Rigid sex-role differentiation matches the behavior with the role and thus does not require the child to examine the environmental conditions in order to decide on an appropriate behavior. Thomas also argues that societies that are "tight" (Pelto, 1968)—that is, formal, rigorous, orderly, and disciplined—develop these characteristics because of high population density and a requirement that economic activities be highly planned and rigidly organized. Agricultural societies sometimes require large organizations for irrigation or defense; they are likely to develop a tight cultural style. In contrast, in societies where economic activities require individual initiative and flexibility, the style may be loose. Tight societies have an advantage in large-scale operations (for example, in modern warfare), but loose societies have an advantage when the environment is changing quickly. We can assume that in tight societies the child receives less information and therefore develops less cognitive complexity than in loose societies. There will be greater frequencies of highly abstract cognitive structures in the loose societies, brought about by the necessity to cope with an unstructured environment. This higher frequency of complexity will in turn facilitate adjustment to fast-changing environments.

Cognitive complexity is a very popular area of research in psychology. Common to most conceptions is the notion of cognitive differentiation, which was greatly used by Werner (1948). Werner emphasized that acts differ in kind, from reflex, to trial-and-error-based behavior, to assimilation-controlled behavior (behavior that keeps changing as a result of rewards), to practical judgment, to conceptual thought, and finally to logical-mathematical analysis. In terms of the model discussed in Chapter 1, reflex and trial-and-error behaviors are under habit control and logical-mathematical analysis completely under intentional control. Other acts may be controlled by both habits and intentions.

Witkin and his associates (Witkin, Dyk, Fatuson, Goodenough, & Karp, 1962), in a development of Werner's thinking, measured psychological differentiation by determining field dependence and field independence. Field-independent individuals discriminate stimuli to a greater extent than do field-dependent people. Field-dependent people appear to be more concrete and to conform to authority, while field-independent individuals have been trained for independence by parents who rewarded early independence, set clear standards, and used much praise.

Kelly (1955) examined the responses of subjects to a test in which a subject lists traits or attributions of significant others and indicates the extent to which the attributions are appropriate as a description of these others. For example, suppose that a subject is presented with three stimuli: your mother, your father, and a female friend. The subject is asked to pick the one that is different from the other two and give the dimension on which they differ. One subject might say that mother and friend are alike and father is different because of the attribute sex. Another subject might say that father and mother are alike and friend different because of age. Still another might say that father and friend are alike because they are extroverts and mother is different because she is an introvert. Subjects continue making such judgments for several triads of stimuli. After the subjects finish this first phase of the test, the psychologist has a long list of attributes generated by each subject. The next phase of the test requires the subjects to judge the extent to which each attribute applies to each stimulus person used in the first phase. In other words, the subject rates each person on each attribute. If subjects make such ratings so as to suggest high correlations among all the attributes, they have used only one major dimension in thinking about people. For example, if all stimuli are rank-ordered the same way on all attributes, it would indicate that there is only one major factor underlying all judgments. If the correlations among the attributes suggest that there are several factors underlying the judgments, the implication is that the subject has a more differentiated cognitive field when thinking about other people than does the person using only one factor. Thus, the number of dimensions underlying judgments can be used as a measure of differentiation. Crockett (1965) has reviewed many studies that utilize this measure of cognitive differentiation. There is much evidence that, the more information a person has, the greater the differentiation (Miller, 1968).

Even more complex views of differentiation have been proposed. One commonly found in the literature distinguishes three aspects of cognitive complexity: *differentiation* (number of dimensions used), *discrimination* (the fineness of the use of each dimension), and *integration* (the organization of the several dimensions into coherent structures). For example, a person might judge others using one factor (say, goodness), while another might use three uncorrelated factors (say, goodness, strength, and level of activity); the first shows no differentiation, while the second shows some differentiation. Moreover, the number of gradations on any factor may be different: one person may use good and bad, while another may use excellent, very good, good, slightly good, and so on, suggesting more discrimination on that dimension by the second person. Finally, one person may see no relationship among the three factors (low integration), and another may believe that good people are weak and passive, except when they are mad, in which case they are strong and active. The latter person has a cognitive structure that interrelates factors (high integration).

Scott (1969) has also done work on cognitive complexity, using the concepts *dimensionality* (differentiation) and *attribute articulation* (discrimination). Most of Scott's research shows that, the more information a person has about a cognitive domain (say, people, or nations), the greater the dimensionality and attribute articulation of this domain.

There is a good deal of disagreement among theorists about the relationships among the various aspects of cognitive complexity. Schroder, Driver, and Streufert (1967) appear to consider differentiation and integration positively related from low to medium levels of differentiation, while Scott proposes an even more complicated set of relationships.

A review of the literature on cognitive complexity by Streufert (1972) has a major section on the relationship between complexity and impression formation that suggests that there are very few well-established relationships. However, it does appear to be confirmed that complex subjects utilize many traits when describing others and are capable of reconciling inconsistencies among such traits so as to produce a creative integration of the information. Frequent contact between a person (P) and another (O) results in some traces of increased complexity in the cognitions of P about O.

The evidence is contradictory concerning whether others who are liked are perceived in a more complex or a more simple fashion than those who are not liked. The weight of the evidence appears to favor a "vigilance hypothesis," according to which disliked others are perceived in a more complex way. However, there are several studies that are inconsistent with that generalization. Harvey, Reich, and Wyer (1968) found that subjects differentiated best among neutral stimuli. In sum, while it would be interesting to find out whether liked and disliked others are perceived in a more complex manner, the evidence so far is not conclusive, and we must wait until more research has been completed on this topic. This is certainly one area that could benefit from student research.

Implicit Personality Theories

In the sections above, I argued that there are individual differences in cue utilization, that these differences are related to cognitive complexity, and that cultural as well as developmental factors can account for an individual's level of cognitive complexity. Remember the ways in which a person can be cognitively complex. Complexity can involve differences in differentiation, discrimination, and integration. Now, the individual's *implicit personality theory* is the theory about how traits found in other people are organized. Different people's theories show different degrees of differentiation, discrimination, and integration.

One reason why it is important to study implicit personality theories is that they provide data on the way a person transforms stimulus information about other people into conceptions that guide his or her action toward them. In other words, the implicit personality theory provides the basis for interpretation of the actions of the other that a person uses to decide how to react to specific behaviors of the other. In this section, we will see that both culture and personality affect these implicit personality theories. But first we need to consider how we can study such "theories."

An illustration of the methods of study of implicit personality theories is the work of Asch (1946). Asch presented a list of traits, such as *intelligent, skillful, industrious, warm, determined, practical,* and *cautious* twice to subjects, who were then asked to use an 18-item checklist to describe the characteristics of the individual they had just heard depicted by the experimenter. In half the conditions, the word "warm" was changed to the word "cold." The subjects responded very differently to the "warm" and "cold" lists. Specifically, the warm person was seen as higher in *generosity, happiness, humor, sociability,* and *popularity* than the cold person.

Asch argued that the warm/cold dimension is more important than the other traits and used the concept of *cue centrality.* This phenomenon can be seen both in the kinds of items subjects check and in the kinds of sketches of the person that they produce after hearing the descriptions. However, Wishner (1960) argued that the centrality of the trait depends on the nature of the checklist. If the checklist consists of items that correlate with the trait, then the trait will appear to be central. He found that, when a dependent variable is highly correlated with the cold/warm scale, there is a large difference between people's perception of the "warm" person and people's perception of the "cold" person. Such differences were also found by Kelley (1950), who presented a man to a class at MIT and told the students that he (Kelley) was interested in how classes react to instructors. Kelley passed out information about the instructor prior to his lecture. Some students received the information that the instructor was cold; others were told that he was warm. The subjects wrote three descriptions of the instructor after they heard his lecture. The "warm" instructor was seen as more *considerate, informal, sociable, humorous,* and *popular* than the "cold," but there were no differences on *knows his stuff, self-assured, intelligent,* and *important.* Interestingly, there was a behavioral difference: the subjects who received the "warm" preinformation asked the instructor more questions than the subjects who received the "cold."

Schneider (1973) has reviewed numerous approaches to the study of implicit personality theories. One of these was to have the person rate, on many trait-descriptive scales, a large number of people. Factor analysis revealed the dimensions underlying these judgments (that is, what traits went with what other traits). One of the by-products of such a study is the opportunity to assess the complexity of the implicit personality theory.

Norman (1969) showed that peer ratings of a person agree with that person's self-perceptions and suggest the structure of implicit personality theories. Five factors appear to define independent dimensions structuring implicit personality theories: (1) extroversion, (2) agreeableness, (3) conscientiousness, (4) emotional stability, and (5) culture. In other words, people think of others and themselves as occupying some point in a five-dimensional space—a point defined by one's standing with respect to these five characteristics.

Extroversion refers to the tendency to get involved in relations with others—to talk, to try to meet others, to be friendly. The opposite pole is *introversion*; the person avoids others, is shy, likes to be alone.

Agreeableness refers to the tendency of the person to avoid picking a fight, to smile, to support. The opposite pole is characterized by "difficult" people—people who tend to disagree, criticize, and find most of what is around them disgusting and objectionable.

Conscientiousness refers to personal traits associated with getting jobs done well, being on time, working carefully, meeting one's obligations, and producing high-quality work. The opposite pole is characterized by a person who couldn't care less about getting things done well or on time and who is not likely to meet his or her obligations.

Emotional stability refers to the quality of not showing many variations in emotion—in other words, having an even temper. *Instability* implies the kind of manic-depressive episodes that are often associated with certain kinds of mental illness.

Culture refers to the idea of cultivation, good manners, *savoir faire*—knowing what to say to whom, where, and when. The opposite is boorishness, impoliteness.

Comment. Note that the extroversion/introversion dimension has something in common with the initiating-interaction dimension that we found related to superordination/subordination. The agreeableness dimension has something in common with the association dimension we have discussed already, suggesting that implicit personality theories have something in common with the major dimensions of the typology of social behavior that I presented in Chapter 1.

One of the big issues in this area is whether correlations among ratings obtained from subjects are produced by their implicit personality theory or by correlations among the real traits of the stimulus persons. The evidence (for example, Hakel, 1969) suggests that people will produce reliable cognitive structures reflecting implicit personality theories in the complete absence of stimulus persons. Lay and Jackson (1969) argue that there is a clear correspondence between measures of real personality and perceived personality and that, therefore, implicit personality theories validly reflect the state of the world. Norman (1969) discovered that peer ratings, self-ratings, and questionnaire data concerning expected peer perceptions show a great deal of consistency. In several studies conducted by D'Andrade (1970), the matrix of correlations among classes of behaviors rated immediately after social interaction did not correspond with the correlations when the classes of behavior were rated from memory some time later. The "memory matrix" was closely related to the linguistic similarity matrix (that is, the matrix of correlations based on the similarity in the meaning of the traits), while the "immediate-rating matrix" was not. This suggests that ratings made from memory are distorted by conceptions of what goes with what—that is, by implicit personality theories, which strongly reflect linguistic structures.

Individual differences in implicit personality theories have been studied, although there is some dispute about whether they constitute a highly significant phenomenon. One major correlate of such individual differences has again been found to be authoritarianism.

Even though no important personality differences have yet been correlated with implicit personality theories, there is evidence that different cultures have somewhat different implicit personality theories. Compare results obtained by Warr and Haycock (1970) for a British personality differential with those obtained by Tzeng (1973) from a Japanese personality differential. A personality differential asks people to rate person stimuli (for example, "my mother") on trait scales (for example, warm versus cold). The British results suggest the presence of evaluation, potency, and activity dimensions, as do the Japanese. However, additional factors don't seem to show much correspondence, suggesting that the British implicit personality theory is not the same as the Japanese.

Specifically, the British evaluation scale includes the characteristics *polite, kind, honest, cooperative,* and *nice;* the Japanese includes *liked, reputable, honest,* and *good,* showing a good deal of correspondence. The second factor of the British is related to *forceful, large,* and *sturdy,* while the Japanese is related to *strong, energetic,* and *high.* The third factor for the British is related to *agile* and *fast* and for the Japanese *vivid* and *flexible,* suggesting variations of the activity factor. But then the two solutions part company. The fourth, fifth, and sixth British factors emphasize (a) *careful, quiet,* and *rational,* (b) *ambitious, lucky,* and *unusual,* and (c) *religious.* The Japanese emphasize (a) *busy, tense,* (b) *individualistic, unusual,* (c) *tangible, predictable,* (d) *calm, logical,* and *rational,* and (e) *sophisticated, logical,* and *unhappy.* While some traces of similarity appear even in these later factors, it is clear that the implicit personalities theories used in the two cultures are not identical.

INFORMATION PROCESSING

The previous section examined the general problem of what information reaches an individual about the other person. In the present section, we will examine how this information is combined, integrated, and used.

Some Early Work

Some of the earliest work on this subject was inspired by Asch's (1946) study concerning the formation of impressions of personality. As mentioned earlier, students were typically presented a sequence of personality traits, such as *intelligent, industrious, warm,* and so on, and were asked to make judgments about or write descriptions of the person so described. Later work was dominated by attempts to test various cognitive-consistency theories. Some of the ideas behind these theories were mentioned in earlier chapters, but a brief review is in order.

The basic notion is that consistency among cognitive elements is pleasant while inconsistency among elements is unpleasant. When inconsistency is present, there is a tendency for some aspect of the cognitive structure to change in order to reduce the inconsistency. For example, the situation "Jim likes George, George likes John, and Jim dislikes John" is unbalanced. Such unbalanced structures are more difficult to learn, more unpleasant, believed to be less likely, and more apt to change than are balanced structures.

Inconsistencies lead to some sort of cognitive change.[2] Abelson (1959) suggested a number of different ways in which people deal with inconsistency: they might stop thinking, bolster one element, differentiate, or transcend the inconsistency.

---

[2] The interested student should consult other publications for more details. Overall reviews can be found in Insko (1967), Kiesler, Collins, and Miller (1969), and Triandis (1971). More details can be found in monographs and papers discussing cognitive balance (Heider, 1946, 1958; Newcomb, 1953, 1956; McGuire, 1966), affective-cognitive consistency (Abelson & Rosenberg, 1958; Rosenberg, 1960; Fishbein, 1965), congruity (Osgood & Tannenbaum, 1955; Tannenbaum, 1967), and cognitive dissonance (Festinger, 1957; and innumerable others). A major summary volume by Abelson, Aronson, McGuire, Newcomb, Rosenberg, and Tannenbaum (1968) is a sourcebook for information on this topic.

Cognitive elements that are consistent with P's emotional state are less likely to change than elements that are inconsistent with this state. (That is, the individual strives for cognitive-affective consistency.) Cognitive elements are likely to shift to a new balance that is somewhere in between the position of the two inconsistent elements, with the more important element shifting less than the less important element. A behavior that is inconsistent with one's cognitive structure leads to dissonance, which is unpleasant; a person experiencing dissonance is likely to change his or her cognitions and even feelings about the situation. For example, if a woman is induced to make a speech that is inconsistent with her attitudes, she is likely to change these attitudes to bring them into line with her behavior. Dissonance is particularly strong when there is a large discrepancy between the cognitive elements, when the cognitive elements are very important, when the person has acted freely (was not forced by others to act), and when P was committed to the act. When people make a choice between two positive stimuli, they experience dissonance. For example, if a man likes both Ann and Mary, and he chooses to have a date with Ann, the fact that he did not have a date with Mary is inconsistent with the positive features of Mary. He can reduce dissonance by thinking of the good features of Ann and finding some undesirable features in Mary.

Balance is important in our impressions of others. When subjects in Gollob and Fischer's (1973) study were asked to make judgments such as "If Bill likes Pete, how likely is he to humiliate Pete?" their responses indicated that acts that were consistent with the dispositions of the actor were considered more likely. In the early 1960s, there was much discussion about the adequacy of such models in accounting for the phenomena of integration of information into a single impression. Among the issues that aroused considerable debate was the question of whether *averaging* or *summation* models were better.

In averaging models of impression formation, the values of each perceived trait are added and the sum is divided by the number of traits, while, in the summation models, the values are added, and no division by the number of traits is required. In symbols, and for the simplest case, the final judgment (J) is determined from the equation $J = \frac{1}{n}(X_1 + X_2 + \ldots + X_n)$ for averaging and from $J = X_1 + X_2 + \ldots + X_n$ for summation, where the $X_1 \ldots X_n$ symbols stand for the value of each trait. Theorists usually consider the weights attached to each value also, so that the general formula for averaging models is

$$J = \frac{1}{n}\left[\sum_{i=1}^{n} (w_i V_i) \right],$$

and the general form of summation models is

$$J = \sum_{i=1}^{n} (w_i V_i).$$

We can use the symbols *H, M,* and *L* to refer to adjectives describing a person. These symbols stand for high (for example, sincere), medium (for example, inoffensive), and low (for example, cruel) values (here, likeability values). Suppose that several such adjectives are used to describe a person, and we ask subjects to judge the likeability of this person. A crucial test of the validity of averaging and summation models involves comparisons of judgments of likeability for stimuli such as *HH* and *HHMM.* According to averaging models, the *HHMM* person should be less likeable than the *HH* person because the average value of the four traits is smaller than the average value of the two traits. The summation models predict that the *HHMM* person will be more likeable than the *HH* person because the *HHMM* person has all the excellent traits of the *HH* person and a couple more moderately good traits. For example, compare these two stimulus persons:

HHMM: sincere, loyal, bold, suave

HH: sincere, loyal

Whom do you like more? Averaging models would expect you to like the second; summation models would expect you to like the first. In general, more people conform to the predictions of the summation models.

A study I did with Fishbein (Triandis & Fishbein, 1963) compared congruity theory (a special kind of averaging theory) with Fishbein's summation theory. The latter was found to be superior at prediction. Fishbein and Hunter (1964) also examined summation versus averaging, finding support for summation.

Since these early studies, several other models have been proposed. Among the better known is the model of Manis, Gleason, and Dawes (1966), which takes into account the number of traits used and counts traits presented early in a sequence more than traits presented later. Dustin and Baldwin (1966) take into account the redundancy among traits. Rokeach and Rothman (1965) argue that the traits should be weighted by their perceived importance. In sum, a large number of different models have been proposed.

As the available models increased in number, the typical studies tried to compare several models at once (for example, Triandis, 1968). Warr and Smith (1970) compared six models, finding relatively good results for all of them and a slight superiority for one of them. They ended their paper with the suggestion that an averaging model may be the best because it combines simplicity and good results.

The weighted-averaging model has been supported in very extensive work done by Anderson (reviewed 1974). Anderson examined, in meticulous detail, averaging versus summation models and found more support for the averaging models.

Anderson's Integration Theory

The broad components of integration theory are the value of the stimulus (s) and the weight of the stimulus (w), the latter depending on the relevance of the stimulus for the particular situation. *Integration* refers to the processes whereby the stimuli are combined to form an overall response. In some situations, s and w are independent, but in others they are related. For example, in judgments about (diagnoses of) mental illness, an extreme behavior (which has an extreme negative value) will be given more weight in the diagnosis. However, in general, the two elements must be considered separately.

The weighted-averaging model. Two stimuli, with values s_1 and s_2 are presented to a person so that he or she can make a judgment based on them. For example, the subject is told that another person is *wise* and *active* but that he or she must judge this person on *likable*. The response to these two stimuli is given, in Anderson's model by

$$R = \frac{w_1}{w_1 + w_2} S_1 + \frac{w_2}{w_1 + w_2} S_2,$$

where $w_1 + w_2 = 1.00$.

This is a very simple case. The model is actually designed to handle the more general case—when there are N stimuli.[3]

---

[3]In the general case, a set of N stimuli with values s_i and weight w_i are related to a response by

$$R = C + \frac{\sum_{i=0}^{N} w_i s_i}{\sum_{i=0}^{N}} + e,$$

where C is an additive constant and e the error term. Assuming that $\Sigma\, w_i = 1.00$, that the error is negligible, and that the constant is zero, the model simplifies to

$$R = \sum_{i=0}^{N} w_i s_i .$$

When the organism has an initial impression of the stimulus person, this is shown as s_0 and weighted by w_0, and the summation includes w_0s_0.

Empirical support for Anderson's model has been obtained with a wide range of materials and in a wide range of situations and problems. In general, work on models of impression formation has supported averaging rather than adding models, although on certain occasions adding models proved superior.

Anderson has had many critics, perhaps the most damaging being Fishbein and Ajzen (1975). They present several objections to Anderson's conclusions and argue that many of the studies that he claims support his model really do not. The argument does get rather complicated and will not be reviewed here.[4] Some of the objectors to his model argue that the model does not do a good enough job of predicting the way people make judgments and integrate information.

Some objections. One objection to Anderson's model concerns the set-size effect. For example, in one of his experiments, Anderson found that the response to an *HHHH* stimulus was 79.4 and to an *HH* stimulus 72.8. When the stimulus values are about equal, Anderson's model predicts equal responses, regardless of the number of stimuli. There should be *no* difference between the *HHHH* and the *HH* stimuli. He handled this difficulty by introducing an internal-state variable, I_0, with value s_0 and weight w_0. For k adjectives of equal value and equal weight, the response becomes

$$R_k = \frac{w_0s_0 + k\,w_1s_1}{w_0 + k\,w_1}.$$

Anderson has reviewed experiments (Anderson, 1972a, pp. 32ff.) in which this formulation has worked well. Fishbein and Ajzen have criticized him for reformulating his model to fit the data; they argue that *ex post facto* changes can always make a model look good.

Another problem is the effect of context. When a subject judges an *O* who has been described by positive traits and then is asked to evaluate each of the traits individually, the context tends to increase the positivity of such judgments. Anderson presents evidence that this is due to a generalized halo

---

[4]The argument gets complicated because Anderson has a theory of measurement, which he calls *functional measurement* (Anderson, 1970), that he believes is especially well suited for tests of the goodness of fit of models and that he claims has wide applicability to many areas of psychology (Anderson, 1972a, 1974). There is skepticism about his claims and also criticism of the fundamental assumption that different pieces of information about an object are averaged. Wyer (1973) argues that these pieces of information are neither averaged nor summed; rather, the information is used to circumscribe several categories to which the object can belong. The object is then assigned to the most representative of these categories.

effect—good people's good traits are seen as even more good than other people's good traits.

Some of Anderson's critics (for example, Wyer & Watson, 1969) have argued that stimulus elements change their meanings in different contexts. His model assumes that they do not. Anderson has generally been successful in answering these criticisms with empirical demonstrations that what changes are the weights of the elements, not their values.

Still another problem is the tendency for the first piece of information received by *P* to control *P*'s judgments. That is, first impressions are given a larger weight than later impressions. This is called a *primacy*, as opposed to a *recency, effect*. Anderson presents evidence that this is due to a lesser attention to the later-presented traits. But this phenomenon implies unequal weights. Anderson agrees that weights are sometimes unequal, and he even presents some studies that estimate the weights on the basis of the size of the scale values.[5] The critics again counter that this is no longer the development of a general model but "curve fitting"—that is, making the model change to fit the data, rather than designing a model that will *predict* the data.

Weight changes. There is a great deal of evidence that stimuli are given unequal weights. For example, Bugental (1972) presented to subjects positive and negative messages in a positive or negative tone of voice. The tone of voice had more weight than the content of the message. Dutton and Arrowood (1971) studied whether the *content* or the *form* of a speech had greater importance in determining ratings of attraction. When a subject had argued consistently her own position on an issue, her liking for a confederate depended on whether the confederate had agreed with the content of her talk rather than on whether he had liked the way she had argued the case (form); but, when she presented a position that was inconsistent with her attitude, she gave much greater weight, in her liking judgment, to the opinion of the confederate about the form of her argument. In short, the subject's liking for the confederate and the weight given to information about him depended on her goals.

Negative information is generally likely to be given more weight than positive information. Redundancy, as when several pieces of similar information are perceived, reduces the weight of an element of information, but consistency, as when similar information is received from different sources, tends to increase the weight of the elements in determining judgments. Extremely inconsistent information, as when someone says that the President of the U.S. is a communist, may be discounted and given a zero weight.

---

[5] For example, Anderson (1972b) used the equation $W = 1 + as + bs^2$, where a and b are parameters that have to be estimated from the empirical information. In this study of clinical judgments, he shows that the process is "configural" because the weight of each element depends on the weight of the whole set.

Other Models of Information Processing

An important theory of differential weighting was proposed by Chalmers (1969). It is based on five assumptions:

1. An adjective elicits the very same meaning response in an information (task) sequence as it does in isolation.

2. The degree of meaning intensity of the adjective that is attached to the person stimulus depends on the meaning of the stimulus. If the stimulus has accumulated positive affect, a negative adjective will have less impact than if the same negative adjective were used to describe a neutral person, and vice versa.

3. The *solidity* of an impression is a function of the number of traits of like scale value and of the number of unlike traits constituting the sequence. For example, *HHHH* has more solidity than *HHH*, which has more than *HLH*.

4. Facilitation occurs when the new adjective is consistent with the previously accumulated meaning of the person. For example, *industrious* has more weight when presented after *intelligent* than when presented after *dirty*.

5. Interference occurs when the new adjective is inconsistent with the previously accumulated meaning. For example, *industrious* has less weight when it follows *dirty* than when it follows *intelligent*.[6]

A very serious challenger to Anderson's model is Fishbein's expectancy-value model. According to Fishbein, the individual's reaction to an attitude object can be measured by the individual's expectations that the attitude object has certain attributes and his or her evaluation of these attributes. Specifically, each attitude object is associated with a number of beliefs about its attributes, and the cognitive bond between an attitude object and a belief can be represented by B_i. Each belief about an attribute of the attitude object has an evaluative aspect, represented by e_i. The total affect toward the attitude object is then

$$A_o = \sum_{i=1}^{k} B_i e_i,$$

[6]From these assumptions, Chalmers arrives at a formula that predicts the weight of a given element as a function of the number of similar adjectives (n_s) and the number of adjectives of opposite scale value (n_o), such that $W_n = a + b (n_s - n_o)$, where W_n is the weight of the adjective in the nth ordinal position and a and b are constants. For example, reactions to the stimulus *LLHHHL* can be computed on the basis of the weights a, $a + b$, $a - 2b$, $a - b$, a, $a - b$.

The weights also depend on the range of values of the stimuli (Warr, 1974). Warr used the expression $C = (1 - k) L + kS$, where C is the value of the composite, L is the "larger" of the values, S is the "smaller" of the values, and k is the relative importance of S. He shows that k depends on the difference between L and S. The k value is generally larger when $L - S$ is where A_o is the attitude or affect toward object o, B_i is the strength of the belief about the attitude object having an attribute i, e_i is the evaluative aspect of these beliefs, and i takes the value from 1 to k beliefs.

Fishbein and Ajzen (1975) have presented an impressive review of the field of attitude and attitude change in which the above formulation is the central building block. The argument is that attitudes, impressions of others, and behavioral intentions can all be conceptualized in terms of cognitions associated with them. The cognitions are probabilistically related to the attitudes, and each cognition has an evaluative aspect. Fishbein and Ajzen review Anderson's work, challenge it on a number of points, and present evidence that the expectancy-value model makes more accurate predictions of the way people integrate information.

Concluding Comment

Information processing is likely to remain an important research area. I am not in a position to take sides, and you will probably want to read the original sources and decide on your own which model is the most promising. I feel that, at this time, both the Anderson and the Fishbein formulations have strong points, one of which is that, although the models are simple, they can account for a wide range of phenomena.

While the Anderson and Fishbein models are the ones that have received most attention, there are numerous other models in the literature.[7] Among the most interesting are models that take into account the multidimensional nature of evaluation (Einhorn, Komorita, & Rosen, 1972) and can deal with different kinds of inferences, over and above likeability judgments. Such models may finally prove even more powerful than Anderson's. This remains to be seen.

THE RELATION OF PERSON PERCEPTION TO THE MODEL OF INTERPERSONAL BEHAVIOR

This chapter has examined the effects of O as a stimulus to P. We saw that O has a myriad of characteristics, only some of which are selected and

---

large, but it also depends on the evaluative direction of these elements. For some combinations, S can be weighted more heavily than L. Warr argues that Anderson's model applies best where the range of L–S is large, since then the elements are truly different. When $L - S$ approaches zero, there is little integration, since L is essentially another way of saying S.

[7]The number of models in the literature is now substantial. Students interested in further reading might find papers by Himmelfarb (1970), Willis (1971), and Warr (1974) of particular interest. Another topic that a serious student may wish to investigate is the relationship between integration and attribution theories (see Lopes, 1972; Anderson, 1974). I will discuss attribution theory in the next chapter.

used by *P*. Several characteristics of *P*, such as *P*'s culture and personality determine which cues will be selected. The accuracy of person perception is low. However, you will do better if you know much about the other and have to make judgments that require only small extrapolation from the cues.

The impact of the other on the perceiver will activate several of *P*'s behavioral tendencies. In terms of the model of interpersonal behavior, the cues selected by *O* might influence the social, affective, or cognitive components of Equation 2 and hence *P*'s behavioral intentions.

Figure 4.3 summarizes in a single diagram many of the relationships reviewed in Chapter 1 and in this chapter. The right-hand part of the figure depicts behavior and its antecedents—behavioral intentions and habits. Behavioral intentions are determined by the social, affective, and consequences components. Outcome-behavior contingencies, of course, modify the subjective probability that a behavior will have certain consequences. The social component depends on inferences made by *P* concerning (a) characteristics of *O* and (b) characteristics of the social situation. Inferences about *O* are determined by what clues are perceived, how these clues are integrated into an overall impression, and the nature of *P*'s implicit personality theory. Inferences about *O* also have consequences: the attributions that *P* makes about *O*. Many cues are emitted by *O*, but *P*'s expectations, values, and skills in perceiving filter many of these, so that only a few of the cues are perceived. A similar process takes place with the perception of the social situation. Cues received from *O* can activate habits that will have a direct effect on behavior. The past experiences of *P* in the presence of *O* will influence the affective component. This figure shows how the elements of the model present in Chapter 1 are but the final stages of a long process that determines the way *O*'s behavior and other attributes will influence *P*'s behavior.

Further details might be filled in. Specifically, cues about *O*'s membership in particular groups (such as *P*'s ingroup) might activate particular norms of behavior. Cues about *O*'s position in the social groups to which *P* and *O* jointly belong might activate particular roles. *P*'s self-concept might be affected by comparisons with *O*. Cues received from *O* might suggest that the interdependence of *P* and *O* calls for mutual support or for competition. Some cues may lead to interpersonal contracts. The cues will suggest which of *P*'s behaviors might be consistent or inconsistent with the situation. The perceived consequences of certain behaviors might be suggested by the selected cues.

In short, each of the elements of the model has the potential to be affected by cue selection. Thus, an understanding of cue selection and utilization is very important to an understanding of interpersonal processes.

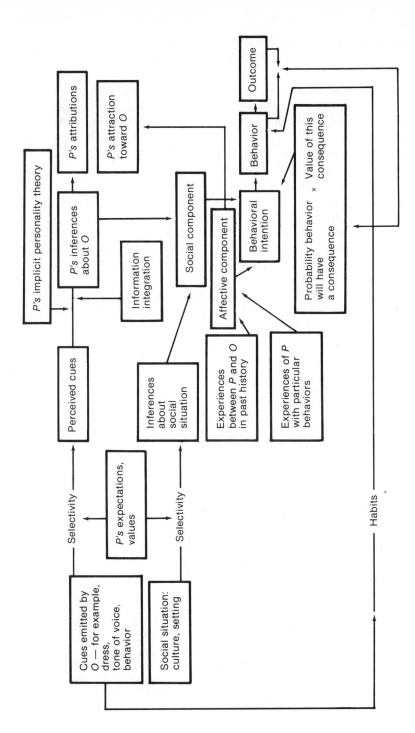

Figure 4.3 The interrelation of social perception and social behavior.

133

SUMMARY

We started this chapter by discussing selectivity in perception. We saw how the perceiver's culture and personality dispositions, his or her values and concerns, contribute to this selectivity. Cues of the other that reduce uncertainty and that are vivid, relevant to *P*, associated with rewards, and familiar have a greater probability of being perceived than do cues without these characteristics. The accuracy of interpersonal perception is low. However, extensive acquaintance with the other, small extrapolation from cues to judgments, and feedback about the validity of cues can improve interpersonal-perception accuracy. Individual differences in the utilization of cues received from the other are numerous. Degree of cognitive complexity—a major way that people differ—has an impact on cue utilization. People differ also in the kinds of implicit personality theories that they use. A review of the work on the manner in which information is processed concluded that Anderson's and Fishbein's models are the most attractive at this point. Finally, I showed that person perception affects the different determinants of interpersonal behavior.

5

THE ANTECEDENTS OF ATTRIBUTION

In the previous chapters, we examined first a model of social behavior, then a number of proximal antecedents of social behavior, such as the social, affective, and perceived-consequence components, and, finally, a number of distal antecedents, such as the cues received from others. The distal antecedents include the characteristics of the other, the way these characteristics are selectively perceived, and the way the information is processed.

In this and the next two chapters, we will go into greater detail; specifically, we will discuss the proximal antecedents of attributions, attraction, and action.

The perceiver makes attributions about the characteristics of the other and about the causes of the other's behavior on the basis of different kinds of information that he or she has about the other. One important class of information is the other's membership in different groups, including O's sex, race, and age groups. There are stereotypes concerning what characteristics go with membership in such groups. So, one of the first topics we will discuss will be stereotyping.

In terms of the elements of Figure 4.3, in this chapter we are in the upper left-hand corner.

STEREOTYPING

Humans frequently assign traits to other groups of humans. A set of characteristics assigned by a group to another group of humans or to themselves is called a stereotype. Stereotyping is a direct consequence of our inability to handle the complexity of information reaching us; we simplify our job by categorizing experience, or stereotyping.

For example, a description of American sex stereotypes can be found in the work of Bem (1974) and in that of Spence, Helmreich, and Stapp (1974). Certain traits, such as *acts as a leader, dominant,* and *self-sufficient,* are considered both likely and desirable in a male by both males and females; other traits, such as *affectionate, cheerful,* and *loyal,* are considered likely and desirable for females. Males are assumed to be more aggressive, independent, and competitive than women, and women are considered more emotional, gentle, and helpful to others than men—again, by both males and females. Numerous traits have been found that fit this pattern of results—that is, that are considered more appropriate, desirable, and likely for one sex than for the other by both males and females.

The study of stereotyping is very popular in social psychology. The voluminous literature has been reviewed by Cauthen, Robinson, and Krauss (1971), Brigham (1971), and myself (Triandis, 1971). Disagreements on the definition of the term do exist. For example, Brigham (1971, p. 31) defines an ethnic stereotype as "a generalization made about an ethnic group, concerning a trait attribution, which is considered to be unjustified by an observer." The problem is to establish whether the observer does consider the attribution unjustified. The broader definition, given in the first paragraph of this section, doesn't require this step. However, it does require that a distinction be made between *sociotypes* and *stereotypes.* As I said in Chapter 1, accurate characterizations (for example, "Northern Blacks are supporters of the Democratic party") are sociotypes; what people *believe* about a group is a stereotype. There may be some overlap between the two; some of the traits included in a stereotype may validly describe the particular social group. Thus, the approach used here permits easier measurement of the stereotype than Brigham's approach but still requires further work: establishing the validity or invalidity of some aspects of the stereotype. The correlation between stereotype and sociotype is often close to zero, and, generally speaking, stereotypes have very little validity, except insofar as they make attributions about traits that are very visible.

Distinctions among Stereotypes

Edwards (1940) distinguished four dimensions of stereotyping: uniformity (clarity, definiteness, agreement among subjects), direction (favorable or unfavorable), intensity (degree of affect), and quality (content). Cauthen and his associates (1971) have reviewed studies that indicate relationships between several pairs of these dimensions.

In general these four dimensions are unrelated to one another. However, there is a tendency for uniformity to be related to intensity and for direction to be related to quality. In other words, when a group agrees about the way they stereotype other groups, they are likely to feel quite strongly about their stereotypes, although they may use both desirable and undesirable traits to stereotype some groups, thus reducing the relationship of uniformity to direction and to quality. Quality and direction are usually related because, when there are predominantly desirable traits in the content of the stereotype, the direction is favorable, and, when there are predominantly undesirable traits in the stereotype, the direction is unfavorable.

Later discussion will indicate that it is important to distinguish autostereotypes (what people think about their own group) from heterostereotypes (what people think of other groups). One can also distinguish between attributions that are considered to be purely one's own (personal attributions) and attributions that are considered to be widely shared by other members of one's group (social attributions). Brigham (1971) has shown that measures of stereotypes differ, depending on whether people are asked to give their own stereotype or to characterize what they believe to be the opinions of others.

It is also important to consider the tendency of people to use their implicit personality theory (see Chapter 4) when making judgments that amount to stereotypes. For example, Triandis and Triandis (1960) have pointed out that, when Whites respond to the word *Negro,* they often think of a lower-class person; hence, there is a need to find out whether the subjects respond to the race, to the social class, or to the nationality of a stimulus person. Feldman (1972) showed that American students have similar stereotypes for Black and for working-class persons. It is important to measure these stereotypes separately by considering the reactions of the subjects to Black professionals, White working-class people, Black working-class people, and White professionals. Feldman showed that the Black stereotype is, in reality, a lower-class Black stereotype and that, when contradictory information is presented (for example, that the stimulus is a Black professional), it takes precedence. For example, Black professionals are seen as even more "professional" than White professionals. Professionals were stereotyped as more *persistent, foresighted, well-dressed, resourceful, striving, independent, complex, creative, intelligent,* and *leaders* than working-class persons. Working-class persons were stereotyped as more *coarse* than professionals. By determining the number of traits associated with the subjects' professional stereotype, Feldman was able to examine the degree to which a stimulus is seen as a professional. He presented many stimuli to his subjects, some characterized as "a White professional" and others as "a Negro professional." He found that the Black professional was seen as having more of the previously determined professional-stereotype traits than the White professional.

Several different procedures are available for the measurement of stereotypes. The most widely used is that introduced by Katz and Braly (1933), which requires subjects to select from a list of traits those they believe describe a target group. Zavalloni (1973) asked French subjects to supply traits in response to sentences such as "They (the French) are . . ." and "We (the French) are . . ." These responses were content analyzed. Zavalloni showed that these two forms elicit rather different stereotypes. The semantic differential (Osgood, Suci, & Tannenbaum, 1957) has been widely used to study stereotypes. For example, Vassiliou and I (Triandis & Vassiliou, 1967) used stimuli such as "Americans tend to be" and scales such as intelligent/unintelligent to obtain ratings of these stimuli. Gardner, Wonnacott, and Taylor (1968) developed a special set of semantic-differential scales suitable for tapping the stereotypes of Canadians concerning their various ethnic groups.

Some Factors Determining Stereotypes

Stereotypes are determined by a number of factors. First, familiarity with another group is related to stereotyping. For example, Berry (1970) studied the relationship between familiarity and uniformity. He measured familiarity of Australian students with the six Australian states by considering the area of the state, the population of the state, and the distance of the state from the subject's state. The assumption underlying this index was that the larger, more populous, and nearer states would be the more familiar. He measured uniformity by considering the number of traits that were ascribed to a particular state by 40% or more of his respondents. He found a statistically significant rank-order correlation of .54, indicating that familiarity and uniformity were positively related. He also measured the differentiation of the stereotype by considering the number of words used, the number of different words used, and the number of words used only one or two times by subjects when writing down adjectives to characterize each state. He found that familiarity was also related to differentiation.

Second, stereotyping depends on the amount and quality of contact.

Contact and stereotyping. A major concern in social psychology has been the reduction of prejudice. One hope has been that this could be accomplished by making sure that people come in contact with one another, the argument being that people will thus discover the human qualities of others and develop more positive stereotypes, affect, and behavioral intentions toward them. Amir (1969) reviewed the evidence in favor of this hypothesis, but his review of the literature indicates that *only under certain conditions* does contact reduce prejudice. Contact with persons from another group whose status is equal to or higher than *P*'s may reduce *P*'s prejudice. Still other favorable circumstances may be: if authorities favor the contact, if the contact is intimate rather than casual, if the contact is rewarding, and if the contact involves superordinate goals that are more important than the individual goals of each of the groups.

In the modern world, there are many contacts between groups that have a high standard of living and groups that have not yet achieved a high standard. The perceived discrepancy between living standards can cause problems.

Vassiliou and I (Triandis & Vassiliou, 1967) and Vassiliou, Triandis, Vassiliou, & McGuire (1972) showed that, when unequal achievement is apparent in intergroup contact, the group that has successfully achieved will "explain" its own success by giving itself more favorable attributions (developing a more favorable autostereotype) than it gives the other group. The low-achievement group will show a favorable heterostereotype, suggesting admiration for the high-achievement group.

Contact may increase the uniformity of the stereotype. This prediction was supported for Americans living in Greece but not for Greeks living in the United States. Vassiliou and I assumed that this difference was due to the nature of the stereotypes of these groups before the contact. We argued that Greeks had a clear stereotype of Americans before contact because the U.S. is an important country and Americans are featured in the Greek press and in films shown in Greece, while Americans had a less clear stereotype of Greeks. Accordingly, contact increased the clarity of the American heterostereotype (since there was room for change). Gardner, Taylor, and Santos (1969) interpreted our results differently. They argued that Americans live in narrowly defined neighborhoods in Greece, hence have relatively similar experiences with Greeks, from which they develop more uniformity (clarity), while Greeks in the U.S. (in this case, college students) have different and more diffuse experiences and hence have less opportunity to show a clear change in stereotyping. In support of this argument, they presented data collected in the Phillipines, which suggest that, when a group has diverse experiences, there is no increase in the clarity of their stereotype with contact, but, when a group has focused experiences, there is a change. Of course, the two interpretations are not incompatible. Further research is needed involving measures of the stereotype before and after the contact.

Vassiliou and her associates (1972) and I (Triandis, 1971) also presented the argument that contact makes the stereotypes converge on the sociotypes. Such a view suggests that, when the sociotypes are very different on specific attributes (for example, one group in fact is very pious, and the other in fact is not), the qualities reflecting these attributes (here, piousness) are particularly likely to appear in the stereotype. I reviewed evidence that supports a "kernel of truth" interpretation of stereotypes. The shifts in stereotypes that occur with political events suggest that people use stereotypes as explanations of what goes on in their environment. People also use them as justifications for particular kinds of action. For example, the Japanese in 1941 were seen by Americans as aggressive, which justified fighting them; the Japanese in 1975 are seen as friendly, which justifies current policies. In fact, the traits *aggressive* and *friendly* do not apply to the Japanese in a reliable way; some Japanese are aggressive and most are friendly. But in certain situations the friendly become aggressive, and in other situations the aggressive become friendly. Nevertheless, there may be a "kernel of truth" in the characterizations for these particular periods, in terms of international relations.

A couple of other phenomena suggest the presence of a kernel of truth: a group's autostereotypes often agree with the heterostereotypes assigned to it by others, and attempts at validation of stereotypes have sometimes shown certain aspects of stereotypes to be valid.

There is much evidence (see Triandis, 1971, pp. 107–108, for a review) that autostereotypes are often similar to heterostereotypes of the same group held by other groups. For example, a detailed study of the stereotypes of the Swiss (Fischer & Trier, 1962) showed large convergences among the French-Swiss stereotype of themselves and the German-Swiss stereotype of the French-Swiss. Vassiliou and I (Triandis & Vassiliou, 1967) found much similarity in the auto- and heterostereotypes of both Americans and Greeks. Similarities can be due to a kernel of truth in the stereotype or to similar correlations of objective traits, such as wealth, with other traits, such as efficiency. For example, if both groups use the same correlation among traits, then, starting from the observation of an objective trait (poor) they might agree on another one (inefficient).

Although there is evidence of a kernel of truth in some stereotypes, it should be stressed that this can happen only for those traits that are public. For example, reckless driving by the members of a group will convey the accurate impression that the group is reckless. Other traits are much less public, and stereotyped attributions about them are likely to be inaccurate.

In any case, stereotypes are poor ways to judge groups of people, for several reasons, which have been brilliantly analyzed by Campbell (1967). First, stereotypes imply that all of the members of the group have a particular characteristic. This is obviously nonsense. Not *all* Japanese are friendly. In fact, it is not possible to find a label that applies to all members of any nationality. Furthermore, perceivers are typically not aware of the selective distortion of their perception of another group nor of the extent to which their own needs and desires determine their stereotypes. We see our stereotypes as "the truth." Second, people see great similarity among members within their ingroups and within their outgroups and great dissimilarity between their ingroups and outgroups. In fact, on most traits, there is a large overlap. Third, there is a confusion of causes. If two groups are shown to be different on a trait, we assume that the characteristic that we see as distinguishing the two groups is the cause of the observed difference in the trait. An example can be found in the current controversy about racial differences in intelligence. Blacks generally score about one standard deviation lower on intelligence tests than do Whites. Some people infer from this that race is the critical factor responsible for this difference. In fact, Blacks and Whites differ in a myriad of characteristics, race being only one. One cannot infer anything about causality without random assignment of people to two groups (which is impossible in this case) or control of the myriad of relevant characteristics (which is completely impractical). In spite of this obvious methodological difficulty, certain social scientists, such as Jensen (1972, 1973), have acquired notoriety by making statements to the effect that race *is* the relevant variable—that it explains the observed difference.

Groups that are in conflict with each other often develop stereotypes that justify the conflict. Thus, a stereotype is often an explanation of the hostility generated by conflict and must be viewed as a correlate of a bad relationship. Furthermore, when a group exploits another for economic gain, it develops stereotypes that justify its exploitation. If members of the other group are lazy and irresponsible, they need to be bossed around; exploitation is often rationalized by the exploiter as "providing leadership." The relationship between hostility and stereotyping is well documented by Campbell and LeVine (1968) and LeVine and Campbell (1972).

The latter offer the hypothesis that "the more ethnocentric the ingroup, the more it should perceive outgroups as strong, aggressive and effective rather than despising them as weak, cowardly, stupid and lazy" (p. 40). Other variables, however, may also influence such attributions. LeVine, for instance, posits a relationship between the nature of the social organization of a society and the way the society stereotypes outgroups. He contrasts "socially divisive" with "socially integrated" societies. The former have structural features such as patrilocality (when young people get married they live in the area in which the father of the groom lives) and local-group endogamy (choice of a spouse is limited to the local group), which encourage a parochial loyalty structure. Socially integrated societies, on the other hand, disperse males to wider areas and hence develop loyalties to wider groupings. In the socially divisive societies, there is suspicion, malicious gossip, and witchcraft, but outgroups are *not* seen as inferior and immoral, while, in the more socially integrated societies, such stereotypes of outgroups are more frequent (LeVine & Campbell, 1972, p. 54).

In their book, *Ethnocentrism*, LeVine and Campbell offer a large range of hypotheses about ethnocentrism in general and about the content of stereotyping in particular, derived from a wide range of theoretical traditions. Some of these propositions are contradictory, so that empirical tests can pit one theoretical view against another. A sample of these propositions is presented below to give the reader some appreciation of the range of predictions. Any serious student of ethnocentrism must consult the original publication.

From frustration-aggression and displacement theories, the authors derive the notion that frustrations of the ingroup are displaced onto the outgroup. Hence, the outgroup is perceived as frustrating, inhibiting, and depriving (p. 133) and will be stereotyped as order demanding, law enforcing, and work demanding (p. 133). The outgroup is perceived as doing the things the ingroup members feel guilty about having done or having wished to do (p.134). From psychoanalytic theory, the authors derive the hypothesis "Stereotypes of outgroups will correspond to motives that are being inhibited at the ingroup level" (p. 146). Hence, "the more a group inhibits sexuality the more it will perceive outgroups as sexually immoral." Chapter 10 of their book is devoted to hypotheses that are derived from perceptual theory. For example: "When socioeconomic differentiation is concomitant with ethnic differentiation, ethnic images emerge that reflect the social and economic roles." Or, more specifically: "Rural groups are seen by urban groups as unsophisticated, guileless, gullible and ignorant" while "urban groups are seen by rural groups as sophisticated, urbane, avaricious, dishonest and immoral" (p. 159). Much of the discussion is summarized by the hypothesis "The greater the real differences between groups on any particular custom, appearance, item of material culture, the more likely that cultural trait is to appear in the stereotyped imagery each group has of the other" (p. 167). This position is parallel to the arguments of Vassiliou and me (Triandis & Vassiliou, 1967) and Vassiliou and her associates (1972) that contact makes the real differences more visible, and hence the stereotypes begin to converge with the sociotypes. The data we presented support Campbell's arguments.

Part Summary

Stereotyping is one of the major factors in person perception that is supplied by the perceiver. The perceiver *constructs* his or her image of the other out of some real and some imagined traits. The real characteristics of O are selectively perceived and processed by the perceiver. The perceiver constructs the stimulus by using an implicit personality theory and by stereotyping. Finally, P looks at O's behavior. However, it is not the behavior itself but the meaning that P gives to the behavior that determines how P will react to O. In the next section, we will examine how P makes attributions about the causes of O's behavior.

ATTRIBUTION THEORY

Attribution theory is concerned with the attributions that people make about their own motives and the motives of others on the basis of behavior. More specifically, it is concerned with factors that increase or decrease the probability that a particular factor will be seen as the determinant of behavior.

To get a complete picture of this situation, we need to consider not only the behavior but also its actual consequences. Suppose that *O* does something that *P* perceives; *P* may also perceive the consequences of *O*'s behavior. *P* then uses these perceptions to infer the causes of *O*'s behavior.

The model of social behavior that was presented in Chapter 1 can be used to classify the attributions that people make. Specifically, *P* might attribute *O*'s behavior to the *social* component, including norms, roles, *O*'s self-concept, and *O*'s moral obligation to behave in a certain way, to the *affective* component, such as *O*'s liking for the behavior, or to the *value-of-the-consequences* component, such as *O*'s perception that valuable consequences will result from the behavior. Furthermore, *P* might believe that *O*'s behavior is habitual (automatic) and not intentional or that it was due to unusually high facilitating conditions, such as high levels of ability (rich people are able to contribute money to charity more easily than poor people), arousal (he bought too many cookies because he was very hungry), or knowledge (she saw the important official because she knew someone who could introduce her).

The attributions that a person makes affect how the other's behavior is perceived. For instance, if *P* believes that *O* gave him money because *O* is very rich, he will appreciate *O*'s gesture less than if he did not have such a belief. If *P* thinks that *O* enjoys giving money, that will also reduce the appreciation. If *P* is seen as giving money because of his role or because of perceived consequences, that too will reduce the appreciation. On the other hand, if *P* sees that *O* gives him money to prove that she is a good friend of his, *P*'s appreciation will increase. In short, attributions influence very much the perception of the meaning of social behavior.

The Major Theoretical Statements

Some of the most influential work on the question of attribution was initiated by Heider (1958). Later development on this work by Jones and Davis (1965) and Kelley (1972a) stimulated a great deal of research on this topic. In this section, we will examine the main trends.

Jones and Davis (1965) examined the action of *O* and its effects, from which *P* can infer something about *O*'s intention and disposition. Such inferences are dependent on *P*'s perception of the extent to which *O* had (1) the *knowledge* necessary to foresee the effects of his actions and (2) the *capacity* to bring about the effects. Jones and Davis present a theory of *correspondent inferences*; the theory is concerned with the extent to which a behavior is seen as reflecting underlying intentions and dispositions. In the terms of my model, the greater the perceived correlation between behavior and intention, the higher the degree of correspondent inference, or correspondence.

When the act is predictable from the social component (norms, roles, interpersonal contracts), it gives us little information about the unique characteristics of the individual. For example, when a wife kisses her husband, we cannot be sure that it really tells us something about the way she feels. Similarly, if the situation (facilitating conditions, in my formulation) makes the act very probable, we cannot infer very much from it. For example, the fact that someone invites you to a large party does not necessarily mean that the person likes you. Inviting one more person to a big party is easy. Maximum inference is possible when the individual does something unique and unusual and when the effects have low social desirability. In other words, when *O* does something unusual that has undesirable consequences for him or her, we can infer more from that situation than when *O* does something usual or something that leads to desirable outcomes. For instance, if *P* invites *O* to an expensive restaurant, *O* could be justified in assuming that *P* likes him or her a great deal.

If *O*'s actions have an effect on *P*, *P* is likely to be greatly influenced by whether or not these effects are beneficial or harmful. The more beneficial *or* harmful the effects, the greater the *hedonic relevance* of *O*'s behavior for *P*. The more hedonically relevant the behavior, the greater the perceived correspondence between the act and the intention or disposition (Jones & Davis, 1965, p. 239). The greater the positive hedonic relevance and perceived correspondence, the more *P* will like *O*. However, these effects can be moderated by *personalism*—the extent to which *P* believes that *O*'s actions were uniquely intended for *P*. The greater the personalism, the greater the perceived correspondence between act and intention. Jones and Davis review empirical evidence suggesting that personalism is more important for the interpersonal relationship when *O*'s behavior has negative effects for *P* than when it has positive effects.

Many of the studies done to test attribution theory have used the simple distinction of *internal* versus *external* determinants of the action. Internal determinants are characteristics of the person, such as the actor's habits or intentions, while external determinants are characteristics of the social situation, such as pressure from others, or facilitating conditions. The main equations of the model presented in Chapter 1 have both of these determinants; the first equation considers habit and behavioral intentions (internal) and facilitating conditions (external), and the second equation considers social pressures (external) and affect toward and perceived consequences of the behavior (internal). Of course, the perceived consequences also depend on external factors, since perceptions generally correspond to reality. Most of the attribution-theory research hasn't made such fine distinctions but has considered simply internal versus external factors. When external factors are very strong, *P* infers very little about internal factors; when external factors are very weak, *P* infers more about internal factors. For example, if *O* is forced to sing a song at a school assembly, *P* is not justified in assuming that *O* is in a good mood, but, if *O* sings while entering a classroom, *P* might have reason to make that inference.

Kelley (1972a) has argued that internal factors can be inferred from consistencies in behavior. Specifically, if *P* sees *O* acting in a certain way in the presence of some stimulus but not in the absence of this stimulus, particularly if *O* acts consistently over time and in different situations, *P* will infer that the stimulus causes *O*'s behavior. Furthermore, if there are several *O*'s who behave the same way in the presence of the stimulus, this will also cause *P* to attribute the behavior to the stimulus. On the other hand, when there is little consistency of action toward a particular stimulus, *P* will not think that *O* acted under the influence of the stimulus and will attribute *O*'s actions to events within *O*.

Kelley has analyzed both social perception and self-perception in terms of attribution theory. Of particular interest is his discussion of biases, errors, and illusions in attribution. Such biases seem to be of several kinds. Among the most important is the tendency that people have, when they make attributions concerning the behavior of another, to ignore the relevant situation. The implication is that they tend to give internal causes more weight than external or situational causes in making their attributions. This bias corresponds to Heider's observation that "the person tends to attribute his own reactions to the object world, and those of another, when they differ from his own, to personal characteristics in [the other]" (Heider, 1958, p. 157). We shall return to this point below. Another bias involves egocentric assumptions—*P*'s assumption that the way he or she evaluates the world is and always has been shared by others. For example, an antifeminist may see most men, in all historic periods, as agreeing with his views about women.

Another bias concerns the affective consequences of an act. The larger the magnitude of these consequences, the greater is the effect of this act on the attributions. Finally, in impression-formation, negative information is given more weight than positive information. For example, negative traits are often given greater weight than positive traits. As you saw earlier (Chapter 4), Kanouse and Hanson (1972) consider this a relatively widespread bias, having implications not only for impression formation but also for the attribution of evaluations to others and for other phenomena. Webster (1964) obtained a similar result in studies of the interviewing process. Negative information, particularly if it is received early in the interview, is likely to lead to a "no hire" decision, even when it is embedded in highly positive information so that the total amount of information received is overwhelmingly positive. An explanation of this phenomenon is that personnel managers receive criticism for poor choices but do not receive criticism for failing to hire good people. A similar phenomenon may operate in other situations. A girl who rejects boys who have a single undesirable trait may never know what she missed, but accepting a boy with such a trait may lead to serious regrets.

To understand this phenomenon better, look at Figure 5.1, which shows a hypothetical case in which the judgments of an interviewer have been found to correlate with the final judgment of effectiveness of employees hired by this interviewer. Each point on this figure represents an employee. The total pattern of points shows a correlation between interviewer judgments and outcome. However, there are four sets of people, designated with the letters *A, B, C,* and *D*. The *A* people are those who were accepted and turned out well, the *C* people are those who were rejected and would have turned out badly, the *B* people were rejected but would have turned out well, and the *D* people were accepted and turned out badly. The interviewer is likely to receive criticism for selecting the *D* people but not for failing to select the *B* people. Nor does the interviewer generally receive much praise for successes (the *A* + *C* group). In short, the only feedback the interviewer receives concerns the *D* people, so it is not surprising that he or she is exceptionally sensitive to any cues that may suggest that an applicant should be rejected.

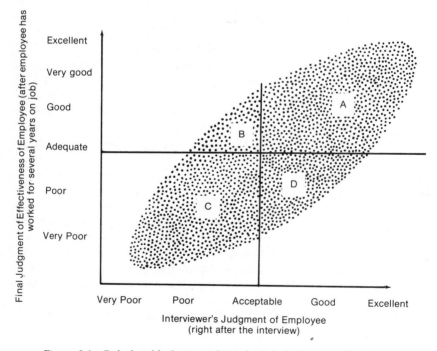

Figure 5.1 Relationship between interviewer's judgment of employee and final judgment after employee has worked on the job for several years (hypothetical case).

In two additional papers, Kelley (1972a,b) examines several other influences on the attribution process and, in particular, the way causal schemata are used in making attributions. A major point in both the Jones and Davis and the Kelley analyses is that, when P does something in relation to O, P is directing his or her behavior primarily at changing O's intentions rather than at changing O's specific behavior. Thus, our reaction to another person depends much more on our inferences concerning the person's intentions than on the behavior per se. For example, an American host family was offended when the foreign student they invited to their home gave a loud belch after finishing dinner. Now, in some parts of the Middle East, belching at the end of the meal is considered a compliment to the host. Obviously, if the host family had had this information in hand, they would have been able to attribute the behavior to the intention to compliment the host rather than to rudeness.

My analysis of interpersonal behavior across cultures (Triandis, 1975a) makes this very point: much intercultural interpersonal behavior leads to serious interpersonal difficulties because the perceiver makes the wrong attributions. I said that, when P makes attributions about O's behaviors that are similar to the attributions that O makes about his or her own behavior, the attributions are isomorphic. I suggested methods, which we will review in Chapter 8, for training people to make isomorphic attributions.

The Jones and Davis formulation has some implications that may not be obvious. Some of these will be mentioned here. One implication is Kelley's (1972a) discounting principle: the role of a given cause in producing a given effect is discounted if other plausible causes are also present. In other words, if P can attribute O's behavior to O's habits, P may not attribute it to O's intentions; or, if P attributes O's behavior to social pressure, he or she may not feel that the action was prompted by O's attitudes.

Empirical Evidence

Numerous studies have obtained results that are generally consistent with the theoretical formulations of Jones and Davis and of Kelley. I'll review two studies to give you the flavor of the findings.

A recent study by Chaikin and Cooper (1973) checked on the implications of the Jones and Davis (1965) analysis by having P's read anecdotes about O's behavior, which was either in role (low correspondence) or out of role (high correspondence). The behavior was positive, negative, or neutral for the P's; thus, it differed in hedonic relevance. The subjects were students. They were given booklets containing stories and were asked to read each story and rate the main character, using the information in the story and whatever they could infer from this information. Here are some examples. An in-role, positive story was: "Dan Z. is the son of a Boston physician. He was raised in a fashionable suburb of Boston. In two years, Dan will get his medical degree from Columbia Medical School." An out-of-role, positive story was: "Juan S. is Puerto Rican. His father is a custodian, and his family lives in the part of New York City called Spanish Harlem. In two years, Juan will get his medical degree from Columbia Medical School." An in-role, negative story was: "Joel T. is the son of an Alabama mill worker. His father is an officer in the local Ku Klux Klan chapter, and his uncles are all members. Upon reaching the required age of 18, Joel joined the Klan."

After reading the stories, the subjects were required to indicate the degree to which they agreed with statements such as "I admire [the target] very much," "I respect . . . ," "I like . . . ," "I would definitely enjoy having . . . as a friend."

The first finding that we need to consider is that the P's differed in the responses they gave to scales measuring respect and scales measuring liking or friendship. In other words, respect and friendship were found to have different determinants. The second finding was supportive of the Jones and Davis analysis. Specifically, respect was found to be influenced by both hedonic relevance and correspondence, while liking and friendship were influenced only by hedonic relevance. More specifically, the role manipulation influenced the ratings that P's gave concerning O's sincerity—out-of-role behavior led to the attribution of greater sincerity than in-role behavior. Positive hedonic relevance resulted in judgments both of high liking and of high friendship, while negative hedonic relevance resulted in low ratings of friendship. For the respect ratings only, there was a significant interaction between role and hedonic relevance, with the out-of-role O's rated more extremely than the in-role O's.

The second empirical study that we'll examine is that of Ajzen (1971), who presented O's, faced with a choice among alternative behaviors, to several P's. Each situation varied in two ways: in the O's apparent decision freedom (high versus low) and in the utilities of the behavioral alternatives (high versus low). P's judged the probabilities that the O's would act in particular ways. Then the P's were told which alternative had been chosen by the O and were asked to attribute attitudes or personality traits to the O on the basis of O's choice. Both the O's freedom and the utilities of the behaviors were found to have significant effects on the probabilities assigned to O's behaviors. The strength of the after-the-fact attributions was negatively correlated with the predicted behavior probabilities.

An important point that is demonstrated by Ajzen's data is that attribution of a disposition to an actor depends on the observer's knowledge of what people do in similar situations and what the consequences of the behavior are. Also, the observer infers that the actor has traits that are similar to the traits that the observer knows people like the actor usually have. The observer takes all this information into account in making judgments about the reasons for the actor's behavior. So when P is told that O acted in a certain way, P will attribute certain traits to O. In Ajzen's study, the greater the utility of O's chosen behavior, the less P inferred from it. However, P inferred a great deal when O did not choose behaviors that would have benefited O; in fact, the greater the benefit, the stronger was P's inference. This effect of behavioral utility was greater when there was little freedom than when there was a lot of freedom.

Thus, doing something that benefits you, particularly when you have little choice in the matter, does not give much information to P. This is consistent with the theoretical analyses presented earlier.

Attributions of the Actor and the Observer

An interesting phenomenon, discussed first by Heider (1958, p. 158) and later much more extensively by Jones and Nisbett (1972), is the difference between what actors and observers feel are the causes of behavior. Briefly, there is a differential bias in such perceptions: the actor (O) sees his or her behavior as largely under the influence of external causes, while the observer (P) sees O's behavior as largely under the influence of causes internal to O. Kelley puts it slightly differently, arguing that the bias is for the observer to put too little weight on external causes.

The theoretical explanation is straightforward: O has a great deal of information about his or her own behaviors, including the fact that he or she has not behaved in the particular way under other circumstances, at other times, or in other places. The observer sees the behavior and has little else to guide his or her inferences. So, P assumes that the behavior is "typical of" O, while O knows better and focuses on the situational factors that produced that behavior in that particular case.

Jones and Nisbett (1972) and Nisbett, Caputo, Legant, and Marecek (1973) reviewed several studies, which I'll mention only briefly. One such study is the now classic one by Jones, Rock, Shaver, Goethals, and Ward (1968), which examined the attributions of ability made when P's observe an O whose performance is correct, in a problem-solving task, 15 out of 30 times. In one experimental condition, the correct trials were spaced randomly, while in two others they were in ascending or descending patterns. The researchers found a strong primacy effect; that is, an O who performed well in the early trials and later performed poorly was considered much more intelligent than an O who performed poorly at first and later performed well, or an O whose pattern of successes was random. Apparently, when P observes a successful O, he or she forms a favorable impression that persists when O is much less successful, and, when P observes an unsuccessful O, he or she sticks to uncomplimentary attributions regardless of the later success of the *O*. The implication is that making a good impression in the beginning is vital in creating the impression of high intellectual ability.

The remarkable finding was that the pattern of attributions was reversed when *P* was placed in the experimental situation and asked to make attributions concerning his or her *own* ability. Here, an ascending pattern of successes led *P* to think that the problems were getting easier and that he or she was very good at solving them, while a descending pattern demoralized *P*. Note that, when *P* judges that the problems are getting easier, he or she is attributing success to an external cause.

In another actor/observer situation, an experimenter apparently forces someone (an accomplice *O*) to perform counterattitudinal acts, such as giving a speech that is inconsistent with his or her attitudes. The observer (*P*) is asked to estimate the relative importance of personality and situational influences on this behavior. In such experiments (for example, Jones & Harris, 1967), *P* sees a stronger influence of the personality factor—*in spite of* the fact that he or she is aware that *O* was forced to perform the act. We might extrapolate that an audience that sees an American POW making a pro-Communist statement will consider him pro-Communist, in spite of the presence of his captors.

An interesting study by McArthur (1970) points to the same bias. McArthur asked *P*'s to judge sentences describing *O*'s performance of a particular act and to attribute the act to conditions in *O* or outside of *O*. For example, the act described in the sentence "George translated the sentence incorrectly" can be construed as due to the difficulty of the sentence or as due to George's inability or stupidity. In this study, 44% of the attributions were person related. In addition, McArthur induced some *O*'s to perform an act and then asked the *P*'s to judge the reasons and the *O*'s to give theirs. A content analysis of these reasons showed that *O*'s gave external influences and *P*'s gave internal predispositions as the causes of the observed behavior. In one study, when *O* participated in a survey, he or she was likely to say that the survey was important, while observers were likely to say that *O* is the sort of person who enjoys taking part in surveys.

Nisbett and Caputo (1971) asked male college students to write brief essays stating why they had chosen their major field of concentration and why they liked the girl they dated most frequently. In addition, the students were asked to do the same for their best friends. For both topics, when discussing the choices of their best friends, the subjects used three times as many person-related as stimulus-related causes; when answering about themselves, they used an equal number of these two types of causes.

The theoretical explanation for these kinds of findings focuses on the different types of information available to the actor and the observer and on the different consistencies of the information. Kelley's analysis, which we discussed earlier, predicts such differences. The observer lacks both the distinctiveness and consistency information that is available to the actor about his or her own history. Furthermore, the actor sees his or her environment, while, for the observer, the actor's behavior is the central element of the perceptual field.

These observations are of profound importance for psychology because they challenge the emphasis given the trait concept by certain psychologists. It is interesting that actors seem to behave like Skinnerians, while observers seem to have studied mostly Allport. Perhaps observers posit traits as determinants because this gives them the feeling that other people's behavior is predictable, while actors see their behavior as highly contingent on a large number of situational determinants in order to avoid the blame for any undesirable consequences of their behavior.

Mischel (1968) has argued that a few human traits, such as intelligence, are transsituational; however, most traits do not predict behavior in different situations. Rodin (1972) showed that descriptions using traits are not particularly informative. In a communication task requiring subjects to identify well-known persons from trait information, the performance of the subjects was shown to be poor. Thus, given that descriptions using traits are of dubious reliability and result in poor communication, why do humans use them? Several answers are plausible. First, the definitions of most traits are so vague that, even when the traits are used to characterize the wrong targets, the perceiver may have the impression that the traits communicate information. For example, in experiments in which a psychologist prepared a standard "personality description" (with mostly complimentary traits) and asked people to indicate their satisfaction with this description of them, most subjects indicated that they were "very satisfied." Second, traits constitute an easy way to characterize a complex stimulus. A lazy P would rather use traits than try to summarize detailed and confusing information about O. Third, traits allow P's to let their needs shape their perceptions of O. In short, no matter how poor they may be for communication, or how invalid, traits will continue to be used because they satisfy real needs that people have in interpersonal situations.

Mischel (1968) has advocated a deemphasis of the trait concept in psychology and has provided a balanced discussion of the dependability of traits (Mischel, 1973). He points out that intellectual traits such as IQ, cognitive complexity, cognitive style (Witkin, 1965), and self-ratings of personality are highly reliable. It is appropriate to make inferences from intellectual traits to behavior in a variety of different situations. However, other kinds of traits, particularly those measured by indirect procedures such as projective tests, do not appear to have predictive utility. Indirectly measured predispositions don't predict behavior better than the person's own direct self-report, simple indexes of directly relevant past behavior, or demographic variables. Mischel argues that estimates of mean past behavior (what I call habit) are the best predictors of future behavior in similar situations, especially when there are no other bases for prediction. However, in new situations, the predictive limitations of past behavior become evident. The traditional viewpoint is that traits are internal factors that "cause" behavior. Mischel's position, however, is that they are summary terms (labels, codes, organizing constructs) applied to observed behavior (1973, p. 264). In short, traits are stable behavior patterns inferred from past behavior. Mischel provides a model of behavior that has much in common with the model I presented in the first chapter.

Attribution theory, as well as helping us understand interpersonal perception, can help us understand some of the phenomena of intergroup relations. For example, Aboud and Taylor (1971) found that people use role determinants (external cause) to explain the behavior of a member of their own ingroup, while they use ethnic personality traits (internal cause) to explain the behavior of a member of their outgroup. In intergroup perception, then, the self-perception of the ingroup is similar to the actor's perception of his or her own behavior, while the ingroup's perception of the outgroup is similar to the observer's perception of the actor.

Taylor and Jaggi (1974) studied the attributions that Hindus make about the causes of the behavior of ingroup (Hindu) and outgroup (Muslim) members performing desirable and undesirable acts. There was a strong tendency for these subjects to make internal attributions when they explained the behavior of ingroup members who were doing something desirable and to make external attributions when they perceived ingroup members doing something undesirable. Conversely, when Hindus saw the behavior of Muslims, they attributed desirable acts to external determinants and undesirable acts to internal determinants.

The study was done in southern India. The subjects were presented with one-paragraph descriptions of an actor behaving in a social context. The subjects were asked to imagine themselves in a particular situation and to imagine that the actor was directing the behavior at them. The situations involved a shopkeeper who either was generous or cheated the subject, a teacher who praised or scolded the subject, a householder who sheltered or ignored the subject when the subject was caught in the rain, and so on. The actor was described as a Hindu or a Muslim. The responses made by the subjects were internal (for example, the shopkeeper is generous) or external (for example, the shopkeeper was required to do this by others; or, there was a misunderstanding between the shopkeeper and the subject) attributions.

On the average, the subjects attributed the desirable behavior of Hindus to internal causes about half the time; they attributed the undesirable behavior of Hindus to internal causes
only about three percent of the time. Conversely, they attributed
desirable behavior of Muslims to internal causes about ten percent of the time and undesirable behavior of Muslims to internal
causes about a third of the time.

Self-Attributions as Determined by Own Behavior

There is a good deal of evidence suggesting that people attribute to
themselves attitudes that are consistent with their behavior. This argument
has been made most forcefully by Bem (1965, 1967). He has argued that people look at their own behavior toward some attitude object and infer their attitude toward the object. Nisbett and Valins (1972) review several lines of
research that can be summarized in the following principle: "A belief inference may result from the observation of one's behavior if the behavior is
perceived to have been elicited by one's intrinsic reaction to the stimulus
toward which the behavior was directed, but a belief inference will not result
if the behavior is perceived to have been elicited by some aspect of the circumstances extrinsic to the stimulus" (p. 70). The principle applies not only
when we look at our own behavior but also when we note our emotional
reactions to a situation (autonomic behavior).

Purely cognitive information about the behavior, supplied by an experimenter, is sometimes sufficient to produce a change in attitude. For example, Valins (1966) showed slides of nude females to male college students.
Dummy electrodes, which allegedly measured heart rate, were placed on the
subjects, who were allowed to "overhear" their heart rates while they looked
at the nudes. The heartbeats that the subjects heard were arranged so that
subjects thought that their hearts beat harder than normal in the case of
some of the nudes. For some nudes, the heart rate was experimentally made
to decrease and for others to increase. The experimenter randomly paired
certain nudes with "changes" in heart rate. Subjects rated the attractiveness
of the nudes much higher when there was a *change* in heartbeat from whatever the subjects thought was normal than when there was no such change.
The subjects were also told that they could take some of the slides home. The
slides they chose to take home were those associated with changes in
heartbeat.

Inferences resulting from observation of behavior may take the form of
a hypothesis (for example, I acted that way; it must mean I like to act that
way), which the individual may confirm (I acted that way again). Then the

individual may establish his or her attitude (I do like to act that way). But the crucial point is that the attributions that the individual makes about the *causes* of his or her own behavior determine whether or not the behavior will lead to attitude change. When people see their behavior as arising from within them, they may infer an attitude, but, when people see their behavior as determined by the situation, they will not make such an inference. Since, as you saw in the previous section, people see their behavior as determined by the situation as often as or more often than they see it as determined by their attitude, we must conclude that Bem's argument is true only some of the time.

Two illustrations of the processes described above will be offered. Ross, Insko, and Ross (1971) investigated the effects of previous behavior on subsequent reports of attitude. Subjects were asked to respond to a 76-item questionnaire, which they marked with an identifying mark. This mark enabled them to retrieve the questionnaire one week later. During the week, the experimenters changed one of the pages of the questionnaire by randomly marking response scales for a particular attitude "agree" or "disagree." During the second session, the subjects were asked to read carefully two parts of their previous questionnaire, including the one that was altered, and to respond on a different attitude scale. The new attitudes measured at that time were consistent with the phony attitudes that the subjects had just read and believed to be their own. Of course, this experiment has some problems. It may be that this effect can be obtained for non-ego-involving attitudes, but it is questionable that it would be obtained for attitudes that are ego-involving. Furthermore, in our culture, there is a norm that people should behave consistently. Breaking this norm may be more painful to the subjects than showing a change of attitude for the benefit of the experimenter.

A more convincing demonstration of the effect was published by Schopler and Compere (1971). In the Schopler and Compere experiment, subjects were asked to serve as experimenters in a learning task. Each subject was instructed to be kind to one accomplice and harsh to the other accomplice of the experimenter. The subjects then rated their attraction toward the accomplices. It was shown that being kind to someone, in comparison with being harsh, leads to the self-perception of greater liking for the target of the behavior.

In terms of the model, when subjects see their behavior, they sometimes form hypotheses regarding the factors that determined it. They may ask themselves "Did I do it out of habit, because it was easy to do, because of social pressures, because I'm the type to do it, because it gives me a big kick, or because I thought it would get me something?" If an explanation is not to be found in our habits (I always do that), social pressure (other people think I should do it), self-image (I am the sort of person who does that) or expected outcomes (this will lead to an advantage), we are likely to infer that it gives us pleasure (a big kick). In the Schopler and Compere experiment, it appears that the subjects did not attribute their behavior completely to following the instructions of the experimenter (which was the true cause of their behavior) but thought of themselves as sufficiently "free" to behave in ways that they determined. This required another explanation for their behavior. Clearly, there is nothing in their past history (habits) consistent with giving only kind or harsh treatment to the other. In fact, they probably never functioned as experimenters in psychological experiments and hence had no established habits. The perceived consequences would be seen as about the same for the harsh and the kind treatments: the experimenter will simply thank them for following instructions. So, the only explanation of their own behavior that they could entertain was that they liked (or believed in) doing what they did.

Perceived Freedom

Note that, in the previous analysis, I argued that the subjects perceived themselves as free to act as they liked. This is an important variable in the attribution process. If we do not perceive ourselves as free to act, then the act will have no influence on the self-perceptions of our attitudes. Perceived freedom is also important when P looks at O's behavior. When P can give a complete account of the causes of O's behavior, then P does not see O as free; but, if P does not understand O's behavior, P sees O as free. For example, if P decides that O's behavior is due to the social pressures received by O, then P is likely to see O as not free.

A series of studies by Steiner (Steiner, 1970, 1973; Davidson & Steiner, 1971) explored the attribution of freedom to the other. For example, when the other sometimes rewards us, but we do not understand why, we are likely to attempt to win his or her approval; if the other punishes us in an unpredictable manner, we are likely to fear and avoid him or her. If the rewards and punishments are completely predictable, then we do not see the other as free to act, and we feel less positive or negative toward him or her.

Steiner argues that people make distorted attributions of freedom to others. For example, poor people imagine that rich people are infinitely free, when in fact rich people may behave compulsively under social pressures that are even greater than those brought to bear on the poor. Blacks may see Whites as free, and Whites may see Blacks as free, on the basis of different behaviors.

Steiner believes that people are free only when they make decisions among behaviors that are equally attractive. In terms of my model, when the social pressures, affect toward the behavior, and perceived consequences add up to a level of behavioral intention for one behavior that is about the same as for another, then people perceive that they are free. If the behavioral intention for one behavior is much higher than that for an alternative behavior, the person does not feel free. The person feels that he or she must do that which has the higher behavioral intention—and usually does do it.

Evidence consistent with this argument was found in some of Steiner's experiments. In an experiment by Davidson and Steiner (1971), an accomplice administered rewards and punishments in a predictable or unpredictable manner. When the subjects who received these rewards or punishments later judged the freedom of the accomplice, the predictable accomplice was judged to be less free than the unpredictable. Furthermore, the students tried to ingratiate themselves with the unpredictable accomplice. A replication of this experiment, using a videotaped session with a predictable or unpredictable actor, resembling the experimental situation just described obtained essentially the same results. In still other experiments, it was shown that accomplices who reward 75 or 25 percent of the time are seen as about equally predictable and considerably more predictable than accomplices who reward about half the time. The more predictable are seen to be less free than the less predictable accomplices.

In short, we attribute freedom to a person whose behavior we either do not understand or cannot predict.

Ingratiation

Ingratiation can be analyzed in attributional terms. Here O tries to get P to attribute good causes to O's behavior. This was done in a fascinating way by Jones and Wortman (1973). They say that there are four basic ways in which O can ingratiate himself or herself with P. O can compliment P, conform to P, render favors to P, and present positive information about himself or herself to P.

Each of these acts is likely to be analyzed by P: "Why did O act that way?" There are many explanations that P may use to account for O's behavior. For example, suppose O, a man, complimented P, a woman. P can say: "He's a nice guy" or "He was forced to do it" or "He's trying to manipulate me" or "It was appropriate for him to say that in that situation" or "He really means it!" Knowing which of these attributions P makes is crucial to understanding how P will react to O's compliment.

Jones and Wortman suggest that the most effective O's flatter P's behind their backs. You can imagine how effective that can be. Suppose that you overhear a conversation between two of your friends in which one of them says something complimentary about you. It is difficult to attribute the compliment to attempts at manipulating you, and it is not obvious that the person was forced to make the compliment or that the situation called for such action. Hence, it is likely that you will think that the person really means what he or she said. Another powerful tactic is to mention an attribute that the other would like and hopes to have but is not sure that he or she does. For example, complimenting a hostess who would like to be thought of as a good cook but who is unsure of herself will make a great hit.

Praise, however, can also have negative outcomes. It can, for instance, make a person feel awkward. This might happen if the hostess is bashful and does not want her cooking to become a subject of extensive conversation. Or it might suggest that one who praised expected low performance and was pleasantly surprised. Or it might create apprehension about being able to continue to be a good cook in the future.

Conformity to another is another technique of ingratiation. Here the effective approach is to disagree with someone about several trivial topics and to agree on those topics that really matter. Conforming on a rare belief is particularly valuable. For example, if P believes that "the world will end next Monday," and O approaches and says "You know, I am convinced that the world will end next Monday," this is likely to be particularly welcome to P. A famous study by Festinger, Riecken, and Schachter (1956) dealt with just such cases of groups holding unusual beliefs.

Rendering a favor will have desired effects if the donor is seen as intending to give it. The effectiveness of the act in ingratiating the giver is greatly reduced if other attributions are made by the receiver, such as unwillingness to give it, being forced to do so by others, or deriving great pleasure from it.

How should O present information about himself or herself? Obvious boasting is counterproductive. Indirect ways of communicating are more effective. The best strategy is to present the self as P would like O to be. It is best for O not to emphasize his or her weaknesses unless it is *obvious* that he or she is being unnecessarily modest. For example, if, after O wins the Nobel Prize, he or she were to say "You know, I was very *stupid*. I could have done that experiment differently," that would be a perfect self-presentation!

These valuable suggestions from Jones and Wortman are tempered by considerations about the relative status of P and O. The greater the difference in the status of P and O, the more indirect should O be in presenting positive information about himself or herself, in complimenting, in conforming, or in rendering a favor to P. Low-status O's should use conformity; high-status O's should use favors or compliments. High-status O's must commit slight errors to increase their attractiveness when they say good things about themselves.

Attribution of Responsibility

Suppose that P sees O drive down the street and hit another car. Will P consider O responsible for the accident? The answer to this question is that it depends on both the context of the accident and the kind of person that P is.

Heider (1958) proposed five levels of responsibility: (1) *association*: the actor is held responsible for all effects that are in any way associated with him or her, (2) *commission*: the actor is responsible if he or she was instrumental in producing the observed effects (even if they could not have been foreseen), (3) *foreseeability*: the actor is responsible only if he or she could have foreseen the effects, even if there was no intention to produce them, (4) *intentionality*: the actor is responsible only for those acts he or she intended to commit, and (5) *justification*: the actor is held responsible only to the extent that the intended behavior was not caused by factors beyond his or her control.

Fishbein and Ajzen (1973) have shown that these levels should be applied to *both* the context of an event and the perceiver of the event. Children and unsophisticated perceivers tend to make attributions of responsibility at the associative or commission level, while more sophisticated judges employ "higher" levels. For example, suppose that, during a robbery, the victim accidentally shoots and kills a neighbor who has come to help. At the associative and commission levels, the victim is guilty; he did the shooting. At the foreseeability and intention levels, he is not guilty, since he did not intend to kill his neighbor. But let us imagine another situation, in which he did intend to kill his neighbor, who was being used as a hostage by terrorists holding many hostages. The killing of the neighbor resulted in the killing of all terrorists and the freeing of the other hostages. A judge who operates at the highest level of moral development might conceivably find him not guilty, since he did what he did intentionally but for a higher purpose and under the influence of factors beyond his control.

A similar analysis of levels can be done using the context of the act. In the U.S. judicial system, guilt is determined by such contextual factors. The law in most states treats intentional killing (murder), unintentional killing (manslaughter), and justified killing differently from one another.

The point made by Fishbein and Ajzen, in analyzing several studies of attribution of responsibility, is that both the level of development of the perceiver and the level of the context must be considered in order to make sense out of the results. When one considers both of these factors, the data do suggest a very clear pattern of attributions. Simple people are likely to attribute responsibility at a lower level than sophisticated people; the context can vary in the extent to which intentionality or justification are important elements. Furthermore, as predicted from attribution theories, the desirability of an outcome influences the strength of the attribution when the action was intended to a much greater extent than when its results were foreseeable but it was not intended.

Walster (1966) found that, the more serious the outcomes of a person's acts, the more an observer holds the person responsible for the outcome. Lerner (1965) proposed that people must believe there is an appropriate fit between what they do and what happens to them (their outcomes). Lerner argues that, for the sake of their sanity, people cannot afford to think otherwise. To believe that the world is governed by a schedule of random reinforcements is likely to lead to great anxiety. People need to believe in a *just world*. Given this general belief tendency, if *O* is suffering, *P* is likely to think that *O* did something that makes him or her deserve to suffer.

Lerner and Simmons (1966) tested the just-world hypothesis by arranging for female students to observe a peer (victim) participating in a paired-associate learning task. The victim, as a result of making the usual errors, appeared to receive severe and painful electric shocks. In describing the suffering victim, subjects rejected and devalued her when they believed they would see her continue suffering and when they thought they were powerless to alter her fate. In short, the subjects explained the suffering by derogating the victim. This is a general tendency. Many analysts of the condition of the ghetto, for instance, blame the ghetto residents rather than the exploitative conditions that result in the particular characteristics of the ghetto residents. There appears to be a cognitive bias to derogate the victims.

The rejection of the victim is particularly extreme when the victim is a martyr. This hypothesis was tested by Lerner and Simmons by having the "innocent victim" (actually a confederate of the experimenters) reluctantly agree to be given severe electric shocks so that the subjects could observe her and thus satisfy a course requirement to participate in an experiment. The martyr in this case agreed to suffer for the benefit of the subjects. A staged sequence was used in which the experimenter pointed out that the victim's refusal to participate in the shock condition of the experiment would create great inconvenience and trouble for the subjects but that of course the decision to participate was up to her. After a few minutes of hesitation, the victim agreed to take part so that the students could get course credit. Ratings of the attractiveness of the victim on 15 scales such as likable/unlikable and mature/immature were combined to get an index of attractiveness. The martyr was seen as less attractive than victims, in a control condition, who had not agreed to receive shocks.

In short, the just-world hypothesis does a reasonably good job of predicting the attractiveness of victims.

Attributions of Intelligence

The attributions that people make about the intelligence of others depend in part on whether others can be easily persuaded. Cialdini, Braver, and Lewis (1974) tested the hypothesis that a person will consider those whom he or she is able to persuade easily more intelligent than those who are hard to persuade. They found that, relative to observers, persuaders attribute more intelligence to yielders and less to nonyielders.

Attributions of Causes of Success and Failure

Weiner and Kukla (1970) provided an attributional analysis of achievement motivation and Weiner and his associates (1972) an analysis of the causal attributions associated with success and failure. They consider four causes of the outcome of an achievement-related event: ability, task difficulty, effort, and luck. Two of these causes are internal (ability and effort), and two are external (task difficulty and luck); two are stable (ability and task difficulty), and two are unstable (effort and luck). Weiner and his associates showed that people tend to evaluate an achievement-oriented outcome more positively the greater the effort expended by O and the lower O's ability. In other words, when a person of modest ability accomplishes something extraordinary, his or her behavior will be evaluated positively, since it will be seen as due to "superhuman" effort. (Incidentally, there were differences between the social classes in the way that they evaluate such events. For example, a sample of upper-class college students saw a student O who was failing to do well in school as deserving more punishment than did a sample of lower-class high school students.) A student who gets excellent grades will feel the most pride, according to student teachers, if he or she has high motivation, regardless of ability. One who fails will feel the most shame if he or she has the ability but does not have the motivation; having no ability, an individual will feel less shame for failure. In short, rewards and punishments are seen to be connected with effort more than with ability. Effort is, of course, under the actor's control.

Other studies by Weiner show that attributions of luck and effort (unstable causes) increase with increasing discrepancy between an outcome and the prior performance of an individual. In contrast, attributions to the task and to ability (the stable characteristics) increase with increasing consistency between the outcome and previous performance. Stability in performance is thus seen as due to the stable determinants of the outcome; instability is seen as due to the unstable determinants of the outcome. Success is seen as associated with effort and ability (internal), while failure is seen as associated with task difficulty (external).

An analysis of achievement motivation led Weiner and his associates (1972) to the following conclusions. Individuals high in achievement motivation (a) approach achievement-related activities, (b) persist in the face of failure, (c) select tasks of intermediate difficulty, and (d) perform with great vigor. Individuals low in this trait (a) do not approach achievement-related activities, (b) quit in the face of failure, (c) select easy or difficult tasks, and (d) perform with relatively little vigor. These results follow from their theory of achievement motivation, which posits differences in the way information is processed by these two types of people.

Specifically, the high-achievement people attribute success to high ability and effort and attribute failure to lack of effort. They welcome self-evaluative feedback, which is available only after undertaking tasks of intermediate difficulty, and they work hard because performance at tasks of intermediate difficulty is indeed greatly influenced by effort. Those low in achievement motivation attribute success to external causes and failure to lack of ability; they avoid self-evaluative feedback, and, because they believe that outcomes are comparatively independent of effort, they exert little.

Cultural Determinants of Attributions

The discussion in the previous section suggests that different kinds of people make different attributions about the causes of similar behavior. This phenomenon can be approached in a number of ways. Both personality and cultural factors can influence the choice of attributions. Among the cultural factors are the relative weights that cultures place on various components of the model.

Some cultures use social attributions more than attributions to other components of the model. Consider, for example, relatively stable agricultural cultures, such as the Temne. Much of their life is a repetition of well-learned behavioral patterns. Obedience to the chief, doing what is prescribed by tribal norms, and not doing what is proscribed are highly valued. Under these conditions, we will observe few interpersonal behaviors that are novel. Hence, according to the model, behavioral intentions will have a small importance as determinants of behavior. People habitually do what is correct according to the customs of the society. Behavior is predictable from norms, and people do not feel free to do much that is not prescribed. Norms are converted to stable habits that control behavior.

Consider, in contrast, modern industrial societies. Norms no longer have consistent influence on behavior. Rather, the perceived consequences may determine rational behaviors, while, on occasion, people do what gives them great satisfaction, regardless of consequences. In such a setting, habits will carry less weight in attributions of causes of behavior than the affect associated with the behavior and the perceived consequences.

Variations in attributions can also be introduced by subcultural norm differences concerning what is proper behavior, by differential emphases of the various components of the model, by the perception of different degrees of affect associated with particular behaviors, by the perception, both realistic and illusory, of different outcomes as following from behaviors, and by differential evaluations of these outcomes. Thus, in a complex industrial culture such as the United States, there might be literally thousands of subcultural groups utilizing different combinations of these parameters as determinants of their social behavior. While these statements concern the "objective" relationships between determinants and behavior in different cultures, attributions too will depend on cultural myths and ideologies. For example, people who believe that "all men are created equal" may distort their attributions in a direction consistent with this assumption and may see more equality than there really is. As a result, they may assume that differences in outcome are related to differences in effort and hence consider the poor to be lazy and "good for nothing." Thus, Americans are *more* likely than members of less egalitarian societies to look down on the poor among them.

One of the major ways in which cultures differ is in their complexity (Lomax & Berkowitz, 1972). In very simple cultures, most interpersonal behaviors are determined by very few factors; in very complex cultures, several more factors may determine behavior. There is some correspondence between this argument and the argument we have just presented concerning cultural differences in the determinants of behavior. If habits are the only determinants of the behavior, attribution is much simpler than if the other factors of the model, with different weights according to the social situation and the type of behavior, combine in different patterns to determine interpersonal behavior. These arguments are also parallel to the concept of tight versus loose cultures (Pelto, 1968). In tight cultures, such as theocracies, people tend to do what they believe to be consistent with the will of some high authority. Good outcomes are seen to come from gods, saints, or good spirits, while unfavorable outcomes come from devils or evil spirits. With such a cosmology, the individual is likely to associate rewards and punishments with theological events, and hence his or her behavior will be determined by what is prescribed (customs, habits). The other components of the model, then, will be relatively weak or have zero weights.

In many simple cultures, tasks are very easy, and people believe that events are determined by external factors. In such a case, the most important determinant of events will be seen as luck (which is external and unstable). This belief leads to *kismet* among Moslems or, more generally, to fatalism—the doctrine that all things happen according to a prearranged pattern. Fatalism assigns no place, in the determination of outcomes, to the initiatives of the individual or to rational processes. It can be found in the history of human thought from Homer to the present day.

When gods or spirits are assumed to determine a person's success, the person feels less responsible for failure. In contrast, in a society that expects people to be successful and attributes success mostly to a person's efforts, failure is very difficult to live with. In studies I did on the self-concept of Blacks and Whites of different social classes and different ages, I found that some subgroups in American society consider themselves *unimportant* to a much greater extent than is normal in America (Triandis, 1976). These subgroups were unemployed Blacks and the old (age 35 to 50) working class, both Black and White. The unemployed feel rejected by society; members of the old working class know they are no longer likely to "make it." People in other societies with similar job status probably do not feel as negative about themselves because, attributing their status to the will of the gods, they don't have to blame themselves.

SUMMARY

The perceiver attributes characteristics to the other on the basis of *O*'s membership in different groups and on the basis of *O*'s behavior. Attributions made entirely on the basis of group membership are called stereotypes. *P*'s perceptions of the causes of the other's behavior gives meaning to this behavior. *P* may attribute *O*'s behavior to any of several causes. The kinds of causes are internal—habits, behavioral intentions, ability—or external —luck, task difficulty, and the situation. The actor and the perceiver emphasize such causes differently; the actor emphasizes the situational elements, while the perceiver emphasizes internal dispositions of the actor. When *P* can give a complete account of the causes of *O*'s behavior, then *P* tends to see *O* as not free; when *P* cannot fully understand what causes *O*'s behavior, *P* tends to see *O* as free. The perceiver will attribute responsibility to *O* for his or her actions differently, depending on *P*'s level of development and the context of the interaction. Cultural factors determine, in part, what particular causes are likely to be perceived as important determinants of *O*'s behavior.

6

INTERPERSONAL
ATTRACTION

In the previous chapter, we examined some of the determinants of attributions. In this chapter, we will examine the determinants of interpersonal attraction. The student who wishes to conceptualize where interpersonal attraction fits in the broad scheme of things should remember that we are here concerned with the upper right-hand corner of Figure 4.3.

Attraction is a very popular topic in social psychology. One of the reasons is that most of the research in social psychology is done in the U.S., and attraction is an exceptionally important aspect of the way American society functions. This is not true of all societies. In African societies, for instance, tribal membership is a more significant basis of interpersonal relationships than is attraction. But there is no doubt that, in the U.S., attraction is a key variable. Political candidates want to be liked; school teachers want to be liked. Even police officers want to be liked. You name the group and think about it, and the chances are that most of its members want to be liked. There are a few exceptions, such as those who prefer to be respected or feared rather than liked, but these can be found mostly in prisons and other unusual social settings.

Interest in interpersonal attraction has increased so rapidly in the last few years that there is now a voluminous literature dealing with this topic. A good review can be found in Huston (1974). A recent review by Byrne and Griffitt (1973) covered only a small part of this literature but used four major headings that will also be used, among others, in the present chapter: (1) types of measure, (2) antecedents of attraction, (3) consequences of attraction, and (4) theories of attraction.

Going back to the model presented in Chapter 1, we see that attraction is related to the affective component. In my discussion of this component, I argued that its weight is determined by the extent to which a behavior is associated with pleasant or unpleasant events. In the case of interpersonal attraction, it is the other person (O) that is associated with the pleasant or unpleasant events. We can make the general statement that, the more rewarding O is to P, the more P will be attracted to O. As you go through this chapter, you will see which factors make O rewarding to P and hence contribute to P's attraction to O.

One of the reasons the literature on attraction is so large is that attraction is used as an overall label to describe many phenomena that are qualitatively different from just *liking*. Studies that really belong under other labels are often described as studies of attraction. Specifically, studies of stereotyping, of attribution, and of social distance should not be considered studies of attraction. There is empirical evidence that liking is unrelated to many dimensions of attribution and to many dimensions of behavioral intention (see Triandis, 1967, for a review).

Two studies of the relationship between affect and behavioral intentions were presented by my associates and me (Triandis, Fishbein, Hall, Shanmugam, & Tanaka, 1968). In the first study, the subjects were American and Indian students. They rated stimulus persons both on scales measuring affect (healthy, good, beneficial, clean, wise) and on scales measuring behavioral intention (would invite to my club, admire the character of, date, treat as equal, teach, and so on). Factor analyses were done, and three factors of behavioral intentions (respect, friendship, and marital acceptance) were obtained from each sample of subjects. The second study, with American, Indian, and Japanese students, also obtained these three factors. Correlations between affect and behavioral intentions, for the respect factor, ranged (depending on the sample of subjects) from .08 to .48; between affect and the other two behavioral-intention factors they ranged from .09 to .39. The data for American females resulted in the highest correlations; data for the Indians and the Japanese showed the lowest correlations. It is clear that these correlations preclude the assumption that attraction is a unitary concept that can be measured just as well with one as with another instrument. It does make a difference whether we are interested in voting behavior, friendship, sexual attraction, or deep love.

Before I review the literature on attraction, I'll describe how researchers measure this concept. Then you'll be able to visualize some of the operations that take place in the experiments we discuss.

TYPES OF MEASURES

Verbal Measures

The most widely used procedure for measuring the attractiveness of O is the Interpersonal Judgment Scale (Byrne, 1971). This is a six-item Likert-type (strongly agree to strongly disagree) rating scale on which subjects evaluate target persons on seven-point scales of intelligence, knowledge of current events, morality, adjustment, likeability, and desirability as a work partner. Scores on the last two items are summed to yield an index of attraction that has a split-half reliability of .85.

Other procedures include adjective checklists, in which a subject is asked to indicate which traits apply to another person, semantic differentials (Osgood, Suci, & Tannenbaum, 1957), in which the target person is rated on a series of bipolar scales, behavioral differentials (Triandis, 1964), in which the subject is asked to indicate his or her behavioral intentions toward a target, and sociometric tests. In sociometric tests, the subject is asked to name a specified number of people from a particular group whom the subject would like as friends, as travel companions, as co-workers, or in some other social relationship. People who are chosen very frequently (by many subjects) are considered more attractive than people who are not chosen. There are many variations of the approach (for details, see Lindzey & Byrne, 1968, pp. 454–460).

Most researchers writing about attraction assume a high correlation among these different measures, because they expect results from one to be consistent with results from another method. However, making this assumption is a mistake; in many cases, the correlations are low. Careful work has shown that several independent dimensions underlie these types of judgments. For example, work with the semantic differential has typically found the three dimensions of *evaluation* (good, clean), *potency* (strong, heavy), and *activity* (active, alive). However, when only person stimuli are used, additional dimensions often emerge; for example, "personality differentials" have discovered dimensions such as *morality* and *aesthetic satisfaction* (with the target person). Komorita and Bass (1967) found three factors: *functional evaluation* (wise, valuable, beneficial), *pure affect* (pleasant, attractive), and *moral evaluation* (clean, honest, trustworthy, sincere). Bryson (1974) found two factors, reflecting *social* (friendly, outgoing, and warm versus unfriendly, introverted, and cold) and *responsibility* (responsible, reliable, and conscientious versus irresponsible, unreliable, and undependable) dimensions of social evaluation. Work with the behavioral differential has similarly led to several dimensions, such as *respect* (admire the ideas, admire the character, ask for the opinions), *marital acceptance* (marry, fall in love, go on a date with), *friendship* (eat with, gossip with, accept as intimate friend), *social distance* (exclude from the neighborhood, prohibit from voting, not invite to my club), and *superordination* (treat as a subordinate, command, criticize). Kiesler and Goldberg (1968) replicated the distinction between *respect* and *friendship*. In short, there is much evidence that we should not consider attraction a single dimension; it involves at least two independent dimensions.

Bogus Pipeline

Many investigators have questioned the use of verbal measures of attraction (for example, Jones & Sigall, 1971) because of the supposed tendency of the subjects to hide their "true" feelings. Assuming that "true" feelings exist, that subjects are aware of them, and that subjects would rather reveal their feelings than have them revealed by a machine, Jones and Sigall proposed the use of the "bogus pipeline" technique as a sensitive index of attraction. This technique involves convincing subjects that physiological measures obtained by the experimenter provide an accurate measure of their true feelings. The subjects are then asked to estimate what the machine is showing to the experimenter. Preliminary findings suggest that attraction measured in this fashion differs from verbal measures of attraction and shows great sensitivity to experimental manipulations (Sigall & Page, 1971).

On the other hand, Cherry, Byrne, and Mitchell (1975) report that the bogus pipeline is more rather than less susceptible to bias from experimenter demands. When demand characteristics were made salient by the introduction of experimental hypotheses, subjects high in social desirability (the personality trait of trying especially hard to please others) used these cues when responding to the bogus pipeline but not when responding to simple rating scales.

Nonverbal Measures

A number of nonverbal measures of interpersonal attraction have been used by researchers, including visual contact (Goldberg, Kiesler, & Collins, 1969), physical proximity (Byrne, Ervin, & Lamberth, 1970), body posture and arm positions (Mehrabian, 1968), placement of felt figures in hypothetical social situations (Little, 1965), and physiological responses (Gormly, 1971). There are a very few studies relating the verbal and nonverbal measures to each other, and the general finding has been that the relationships are complex. A great deal needs to be done, in terms of additional research, in order to discover the systematic determinants of these relationships.

ANTECEDENTS OF ATTRACTION

Similarity of P and O

A major research tradition has developed that examines the similarity between characteristics of P and O as a determinant of attraction. One of the most widely used procedures for manipulating similarity in attitudes is the "phantom other" procedure developed by Byrne. Subjects are asked to give their opinions, on a questionnaire, during one experimental session. They return to a second session, where they are presented with the answers of "another person" to a questionnaire like the one the subject answered at the previous session. During this second session, the subject is asked to study the answers of the "other" carefully and then to respond on the Interpersonal Judgment Scale, which I described earlier. Between the first and second testing session, the responses of the "other" are made by the experimenter, who arranges them so that they overlap with the subjects' own answers to the same questionnaire by, say, 0, 20, 40, 60, 80, or 100%, thus providing a stimulus of maximum dissimilarity, intermediate similarity, or maximum similarity.

Similarity has been found to exert a major influence on attraction. The best-researched relationship is the one between the *proportion* of similar attitudes held by P and O and the attraction of one for the other. Byrne and Griffitt (1973) refer to numerous studies that show that this relationship is a linear one. Other kinds of similarities that have sometimes been shown to result in attraction are similarities in economic status, similarities in task performance, similarities in emotional states, and similarities in certain kinds of personality characteristics.

Similarity, as I will show later in more detail, is rewarding. The greater the similarity between P and O, the more likely it is that O will do what is rewarding for P. It would seem intuitively obvious that, the more important the attitude on which two people agree or disagree, the greater the effect of the agreement or disagreement on their attraction for each other. However, this has not been found in most studies that have tested this hypothesis.

The importance of similarity in interpersonal relationships is well documented by anthropologist Russell Bernard, who studied interpersonal behavior on an oceanographic-research ship. Bernard (personal communication) noted that the scientists on the ship used one area of the ship for relaxation, while the crew used another. The sailors commented contemptuously, about the scientists, "These characters come out here to get the wrinkles out of their bellies. But they don't know the first thing about the sea. . . . They don't even know how to put on a life jacket. They ought to make every one of these doctors take a course in horse sense so they don't kill themselves."

Several cases of sabotage of the work of scientists were reported to the anthropologist. For example, one scientist locked prawn specimens in a freezer that the crew used to cool their beer.

During the night, the freezer was broken into, and $50,000 worth of specimens, representing the young man's doctoral dissertation, went overboard.

The anthropologist commented: "There is a gulf of values that seems almost unbridgeable between those two groups. I don't mean that one group is more intelligent than the other—just that they view things differently. For instance, scientists, as a rule, avoid prostitutes, and crewmen seek them . . . and they talk about different things."

The importance of the attitude has generally not been found to be a very important determinant of attraction; that is, agreement on an important issue does not seem to improve attraction much more than agreement on a relatively unimportant issue. Only certain kinds of experimental designs have yielded effects on attraction that can be traced to the importance of the issue. Specifically, when (1) the proportion of agreement between P and O is intermediate between 0% and 100%, (2) the attitudinal items are heterogeneous in their importance, and (3) the items of different importance are systematically associated with the similarity/dissimilarity manipulation, the importance of the issue *does* become a significant effect, and important issues exert three times as much weight as others (Byrne, London, & Griffitt, 1968).

Disagreement leads to physiological arousal (Gormly, 1974) and to negative responses on scales measuring attraction. The level of abstraction of the issue on which there is disagreement is relevant. When P and O disagree on values, which are at a high level of abstraction, the disagreement has a major impact on their interpersonal attraction. In contrast, when they disagree on less abstract matters, such as norms, roles, or how to get things done, the impact of these disagreements is less severe. For example, a disagreement between husband and wife about *how* to wash the dishes will produce minimum trouble for their relationship. However, if they disagree on *who* should wash the dishes, they have a more acute problem. Furthermore, if they disagree on *whether* the dishes should be washed at all, the results can be very serious. Finally, suppose they cannot agree on whether *cleanliness* is important. This last phase of the argument is the most abstract and will lead to maximum interpersonal conflict. My associates and I (Triandis, Weldon, & Feldman, 1974) have found that, for White subjects, abstract disagreements decrease attraction more than disagreements at concrete levels. However, Blacks were most upset by the more concrete disagreements on roles. This may reflect the historical significance of role disagreements in White/Black relations, such as various restrictions imposed by Jim Crow laws.

Complex relationships emerge when different kinds of similarities are considered. One very important variable is whether or not *P* and *O* have common goals; if so, *P* is likely to expect *O* to facilitate him or her in reaching his or her goals.

A study by Johnson and Johnson (1972) manipulated attitude similarity and goal facilitation in such a way as to be sure that these two variables were independent. In addition, they manipulated actual goal facilitation. In other words, in some conditions, persons who expected to be helped were not helped, and in other conditions they were helped. Attitude similarity was related to attraction *only* when a person did not expect goal facilitation. When a person expects another to help, and the other in fact frustrates this person, attraction decreases very little; but, when a person expects the other to frustrate goal accomplishment, and the other in fact helps, there is an increase in attraction. In short, similarity leads to attraction only under some conditions, and goal facilitation leads to attraction mostly when the person did not expect the help.

This experiment shows that, if *O* rewards *P*, *P* will like *O*. The reward does not have to be attitudinal similarity; it can be goal facilitation. Later in this chapter, we will examine several theories that may explain why attitudinal similarity is rewarding. At this point, it is sufficient to remember that similarity is not always strongly related to attraction. There are factors that decrease the relationship—for example, when the agreeing other is described as emotionally maladjusted (Novak & Lerner, 1968) or when a disagreeing other is an effective co-worker.

A further complication concerns whether the agreement is on beliefs or on values. There is some evidence that, if *O* is *dis*similar, people are more rewarded if *O* agrees with them on a belief than if *O* agrees with them on a value. If *O* is similar, people are more rewarded by *O*'s agreement on a value. This difference may be due to the redundancy of the information that a similar other has similar ideas. When it comes to values, on the other hand, we like to know that others feel the way we do. Goethals and Nelson (1973) showed the importance of distinguishing between similarity in beliefs and similarity in values. When a belief is at issue, agreement from a *dissimilar* other increases *P*'s confidence in his or her own judgments; however, when a value is at issue, agreement from a *similar* other is most likely to increase *P*'s confidence. Subjects judged the relative academic success of two students (belief) or indicated which of the two they liked more (value). In addition, they were given the opinions of another student whom they assumed was similar or dissimilar to themselves. When a belief was involved, this other student's opinions had more influence when the other was dissimilar. When a value was involved, the opinions had more influence when the other was similar. Agreement from dissimilar others increases our confidence in some cases because we sense that dissimilarity eliminates biases that might reduce the accuracy of our judgments.

People who think about their environment in similar ways tend to be attracted to each other. I studied the cognitive similarity of supervisors and workers in industry by examining the similarity in the ways they categorized stimuli (persons and jobs found in their environment) and in the ways they rated stimuli on the semantic differential (Triandis, 1959). I also measured perceived interpersonal-communication effectiveness and attraction between worker and supervisor, using specially constructed scales. I found that both the perceived communication effectiveness (my boss understands me) and the attractiveness of the supervisor were correlated with similarities in the cognitive structures of the supervisors and the workers.

More recent work has confirmed that having different cognitive structures produces barriers to interpersonal communication. People who have different definitions of key terms used in a discussion stop participating in the discussion (Back, Bunker, & Dunnagan, 1972). A match between individuals can be obtained by selecting people who answer personality scales similarly. Slack and Cook (1973) studied pairs of subjects who had similar or different F-scale scores. The subjects played a game that has many similarities to real-world conflict. With this game, it is possible to obtain measures of performance (outcomes), such as points earned by each player, and measures of conflict, such as the number of moves that hurt the other player but did not help the actor. In general, the best performance and least conflict was observed when both subjects were low on the F scale. Those pairs who were both high on the F scale were intermediate in performance; those pairs who had mixed F-scale scores (one high and the other low) performed most poorly. This finding suggests that matching for ideology improved the performance of the pair.

The racial membership of P and O can also influence attraction. In general, there is greater attraction between people of the same race than between people of different races—at least in the U.S. However, again, many complexities can be found. One complexity is that this general rule is not equally true for men and women. White females and Black males react to Blacks and to Whites about equally favorably; White males, on the other hand, very clearly prefer Whites over Blacks, and Black females very clearly prefer Blacks over Whites (Triandis, 1976). The number of White female/Black male dates one observes on liberal campuses in the North, relative to the number of Black female/White male dates, seems to correspond to these observations, although there are as yet too few such pairs to allow us to be sure that it is a stable trend.

Another complication concerns the relative importance of attitudinal similarity and race. For intimate behaviors, such as dating, similarity of race is a more powerful determining variable than belief similarity; for superficial behaviors, such as those that maintain an acquaintanceship between two people (greeting, joking, smiling), race has very little importance, while attitudinal similarity is a crucial variable. Even for ordinary friendship (which tends to be superficial), race is less important than belief similarity. The relative importance of race and belief as determinants of attraction depends on (a) the extent of the differences in beliefs, (b) the type of behavior, and (c) the type of person (Triandis & Davis, 1965; Goldstein & Davis, 1972). In short, racial membership is related to attraction in a complex way.

There are obviously many kinds of similarity; the effects of each kind on attraction may depend on characteristics of the perceiver. An interesting illustration of this point is the experiment reported by Touhey (1972), who obtained the religious values and sexual attitudes of 100 male and 150 female undergraduates from a questionnaire. He then arranged 300 matches of males and females, making four combinations: similar in religious values, similar in sexual attitudes (both persons permissive or both conservative), dissimilar in religious values, and dissimilar in sexual attitudes. Names and phone numbers of the matches were mailed to the students. When a couple reported a date, they were tested with a modified version of Byrne's Interpersonal Judgment Scale. Males were more attracted to females with similar sexual attitudes than with similar religious values, but females were attracted to males of similar religious values. Furthermore, females were most attracted to males who had sexually dissimilar attitudes and had similar religious values, while males were most attracted to females who had dissimilar religious values and had similar sexual attitudes. In other words, similarity is not always a source of attraction. In some cases, discrepancy leads to more attraction. A similar conclusion can be derived from the study of Aboud and Taylor (1972), which suggests that people *like* those who are ethnically similar to them but are *interested in* those who are ethnically dissimilar to them.

Finally, Wright and Crawford (1971) reported six studies that generally suggest that males are most attracted to people who agree with them on specific day-to-day activities, while females are most attracted to people who agree with them on abstract values and generalized areas of interest. These findings are consistent with the data reported by Touhey. There are apparently sex-related differences in the kinds of similarities that lead to attraction.

While similarity seems to be a highly desirable trait in another, whether it is in the area of attitudes or of status, it is not always a desirable trait when it concerns personality. For example, a person who likes to talk a lot is not necessarily attracted to other people who like to talk a lot, particularly if these other people take over and don't let him or her talk! For certain kinds of personality traits, such as dominance, complementarity rather than similarity seems to lead to attraction. For example, a dominant person is most often attracted to others who are submissive. Some evidence favoring the need-complementarity hypothesis, first formulated by Winch, Ktsanes, and Ktsanes, (1955), has been reported by Kerckhoff and Davis (1962). The research focused on college couples as their relationship progressed toward marriage. The dependent variable was the progress made by the couple towards a permanent union. It was found that, in the early stages of the relationship, social-status variables, such as similarity in religion and socio-economic status, were most predictive of whether or not the relationship would continue. After the first few weeks of the relationship, consensus on attitudes and values became most critical. Only very late in the relationship did need complementarity become the most important determinant. This study suggests, then, that both similarity and complementarity are important—but at different stages.

Related to similarity is the concept of compatibility. Schutz (1958) hypothesized three major interpersonal needs, which can be observed in either a passive or an active mode. In the passive mode, they are inclusion (a person wants to be included in the group), affection (a person wants to receive affection), and control (a person wants to be controlled, dominated). In the active mode, the person wants to include others, to give affection, and to control others. Compatibility exists when the person who is high on the active mode of a given need interacts with a person who is high on the passive mode of the same need.

Haythorn (1968) reviewed several studies of group composition and attraction and concluded that three independent principles may be assumed to operate simultaneously: congruity, complementarity, and compatibility of needs, attitudes, and values. He suggested that all three may influence attraction. The effect of the likeability of the other's personality, for example when the other is said to be sincere, nice, and agreeable can be separated from the effect of similarity on attraction (McLaughlin, 1971). A person who is both likeable and similar is more attractive than one who is only similar; but a person who is dislikeable and similar is more unattractive than one who is dislikeable and dissimilar. Taylor and Mettee (1971) had females interact with a female confederate who was represented as either similar or dissimilar to them and who behaved in either a pleasant or an obnoxious manner. They found that the obnoxious-similar was disliked more than the obnoxious-dissimilar other.

Similarity in certain kinds of attitudes leads to much more attraction than similarity in other kinds of attitudes (Batchelor & Tesser, 1971). People hold attitudes for different reasons. First, some attitudes have a knowledge function; that is, they help us understand the world around us. Second, they may have an ego-defensive function, helping us to protect our self-esteem by making it possible for us to avoid unpleasant truths about ourselves. Third, attitudes may have an adjustive-utilitarian function, helping us to adjust to our world by making it more likely that we will get rewarded by others in our environment. Finally, some attitudes have a value-expressive function; that is, they allow us to express our fundamental values. I'll give an example of an attitude serving each type of function: I might favor a particular political official because the things I have read about his behavior all hang together in a neat package and make sense. I might dislike skating because I do not want to make a fool of myself. I might favor a particular person as the new head of my department because many of my friends favor the same person. And, finally, I might favor construction of a new concert hall because I like music. Batchelor and Tesser found that similarity on value-expressive attitudes leads to more attraction than similarity on ego-defensive attitudes.

It should be obvious from the above that similarity is a very important determinant of attraction. The exact mechanism that underlies the relationship, however, is not completely understood. Several theoretical positions can be found in the literature; some emphasize cognitive consistency (for example, Newcomb, 1971), and others emphasize the frequency of rewards, the ratio of rewards to costs or to inputs, and distinctions among types of rewards.

Cognitive Similarity and Attraction

By *cognitive similarity,* I mean similarity (a) in the categorization of events occurring in the environment, (b) in the perceived relationships among categories of events, (c) in the perceived antecedents and consequences of environmental events, and (d) in attributions about interpersonal behavior.

Categorization means treating stimuli that are different as though they were alike. There are literally billions of discriminable stimuli. We deal with our complex environment by simplifying it, which involves ignoring most of the differences among the stimuli. If two people differ on one or more of the four aspects of cognitive similarity, disagreements will arise, and the potential for a rewarding relationship will be reduced.

The following examples will serve as illustrations. A husband and wife will have difficulties if one categorizes a quiet evening at home with a book as fun while the other considers going to a loud party fun, or if one regards reading a book as acquiring wisdom and the other sees it as a waste of time. If they perceive different consequences of going to a party—one thinks of meeting interesting people and the other thinks of committing some terrible faux pas—again we can anticipate troubles. Finally, consider what would happen if the attributions about the causes of behavior were different. Say, the husband is late from work, and he attributes this to the work load, while the wife acuses him of lack of interest in her. Again, we can expect an interpersonal problem.

Detailed studies of how people analyze their social environment (Triandis, Vassiliou, Vassiliou, Tanaka, & Shanmugam, 1972) have suggested that each of these differences can produce interpersonal problems. Both theoretical (Rommetveit, 1974) and empirical work (Runkel, 1956; Triandis, 1959; Tesser, 1972; Back, Bunker, & Dunnagan, 1972; Duck & Spencer, 1972) suggest that this analysis is correct.

Rommetveit (1974) points out that, when we hear a sentence, we take a point of view that corresponds to the other's subjective world. Thus, when a person says "I too was invited; I went to the ball . . ." we expect to hear what happened at the ball. However, a schizophrenic sometimes has a different subjective world from the one we expect. The schizophrenic may continue the sentence with ". . . and it rolled and rolled away." This is a jarring stimulus; we didn't expect to hear that. Rommetveit talks about the "architecture of intersubjectivity"—the area of agreement between two speakers. He stresses the need to establish common interpretations and shared strategies of attribution in order to have good communication.

Duck and Spencer (1972) found that frequently interacting female subjects had similar "personal constructs" (that is, used similar attributes to categorize others). Friendship formation was determined by similarity in such constructs.

In analyzing the similarity in the attributions that people make concerning another's behavior, it is useful to use the model I presented earlier. The model would predict that, if P and O have similar habits or behavioral intentions, they will make similar attributions. That is, if similarity exists in the weights given the various elements of the model, the two people will analyze social situations in similar terms. As I mentioned in Chapter 5, if P makes attributions about O's behavior that are similar to the attributions that O makes about his or her own behavior, the attributions are *isomorphic* (Triandis, 1975a). Isomorphic attributions are likely to lead to attraction because O will appear predictable and P and O will both be in good positions to reinforce each other.

Consider a simple example: a police officer stops a citizen for speeding. While the officer is approaching the citizen, the latter moves his hand under the seat to reach for a pack of cigarettes. The behavior is moving the hand to a position under the seat. Two possible attributions are "he is getting cigarettes" and "he is getting a gun." Imagine the consequences if the officer makes the second attribution. The citizen who knows that a police officer might make the attribution "He is getting a gun" will keep his hands showing. Miscommunication is less likely to happen under these conditions. In short, making an isomorphic attribution would save the citizen from much trouble. This simple example can be extended in many ways and reveals an important principle of interpersonal relations.

Isomorphic attributions are desirable in order to have good interpersonal relationships. However, they are unlikely, for several reasons. For one thing we learn to look at the world in particular ways, as a result of the kinds of experiences that we have in our environments. There are large variations in norms, roles, values, and so on in different social environments (Triandis,

Vassiliou, Vassiliou, Tanaka, & Shanmugam, 1972). Furthermore, we don't always communicate. For example, we generally avoid giving bad news to others, and, when we make evaluations of others, we often avoid communicating them. Blumberg (1972) asked subjects whether they would communicate evaluations of others under various hypothetical circumstances. He found that evaluations are communicated freely among most friends, but both positive and negative information tends to be withheld from the person being evaluated. Positive evaluations circulate more freely than negative, and more is communicated to close friends than to acquaintances. Apparently, there is a social norm devised to keep people from learning too much about what others think of them.

Another factor that makes communication difficult is that different groups have different styles of communication. The work of Heider (1971) will serve as an illustration. She used abstract figures and faces as stimuli and asked middle-class and lower-class Black and White children to describe a stimulus so that another child could pick it out from a set of similar stimuli. She found substantial differences between the middle and lower-class children but no differences between races or sexes. Specifically, the middle-class children used many more words in describing the stimuli, used substantially fewer whole-inferential judgments (that is, judgments that referred to the whole drawing and made an inference, such as "the face is intelligent"), made many more part-descriptive statements (such as "the top part has a line sticking out at a slant"), and made many more part-inferential statements. The largest difference was that the lower-class children used mostly whole-inferential and the middle-class children used mostly part-descriptive statements. Heider also studied the accuracy of identification of the correct stimulus. The middle-class children were correct 58% of the time in identifying abstract figures, while the lower-class children averaged only 45%. In the case of the identification of faces, the middle-class subjects were correct 53% of the time and the lower-class only 43% of the time. The middle-class descriptions were generally better understood than the lower-class descriptions because the middle-class children gave not only more information but also more *relevant* information. These results imply greater difficulties in communication and poorer interpersonal relations among the lower classes. This poorer communication may contribute to the higher divorce rate of this group (Bumpass & Sweet, 1972).

Heider's results support some of the arguments presented by Bernstein (1971) about particularistic versus universalistic communication in the lower and middle classes. Bernstein believes that some communications are heavily dependent on the context in which they occur, while other communications are more or less independent of context. Particularistic communications are those whose meaning is closely tied to the context, while universalistic communications do not require the context to be understood. Working-class mothers train their children by rewarding or punishing them in particular contexts and do not infer general principles of morality in the course of engaging in socialization practices. Middle-class mothers, on the other hand, spend much time talking about general rules of human behavior and about morality. Working-class children, then, learn to rely on context. In fact, much of what they learn takes the form of a demonstration: "This is the way you do this." In contrast, middle-class children learn much from books if the context (such as the chair they're sitting in) is constant.

Particularistic communication can be very efficient, but it requires that two people attend to the same context. A dog that barks in front of a door communicates very effectively that it wants to go out; the same sound in the context of a food bowl would indicate that the animal is hungry. Here we have an extreme example of how context can communicate. Furthermore, if the context is clear, communication is very efficient, since a single bark can stand for a long message equivalent to: "Please open the door for me; I want to go outside." When two people have identical contexts, their communication will be very effective and they may well be attracted to each other. However, a person who learns to depend on context will communicate in a way that many members of society may find deficient. The communication will be elliptic (partial) and will utilize a "restricted code" as opposed to an "elaborated code." Written communication is usually elaborated, and middle-class speech is often similar to written communication, while lower-class speech is often "missing" parts of sentences. The point is that, in certain cultures, people do not *have* to learn to communicate universalistically, since all the people they communicate with are very similar to them and make the same assumptions (use the same context). However, middle-class culture requires people to operate differently in order to be effective. Thus, a middle-class man might "define his terms" before explaining a problem, which is something that is quite unnecessary when the context is strong.

Dependence on context can make a child appear "verbally deprived," and communication between a middle-class teacher and a working-class pupil may be ineffective if the teacher does not understand the elliptic talk. The attraction of the teacher to the student will suffer. Likewise, a working-class student may not be attracted to a teacher who spends much time defining terms; the student may find such activity pedantic and boring.

In experiments such as Heider's (1971) on communication, it becomes evident that middle-class communicators take into account what the other person knows or does not know; working-class communicators are more likely to *assume* that the other has the same context and, hence, fail to communicate. In different cultures, also, emphases on context may differ. For example, in cultures where most communication is about concrete events, there is much dependence on context. A good example can be found in studies described by Cole and Scribner (1974). In a communication experiment, two people are seated at a table on which there are ten pairs of sticks, and each communicator has one member of the identical pair. A barrier prevents each from seeing the other's sticks. The task is to describe a stick so that the other person can pick its mate out of his or her pile of ten sticks. Kpelle farmers (from Africa) do very poorly on this task. They use communications such as "one of the sticks," "not a large one," and "a piece of bamboo." In contrast, middle-class subjects use more effective messages, such as "the thickest, straight wood with one thorn." In short, the middle class takes into account the information needed by the other side.

We can generalize, then, as follows: People are attracted to those with whom they can communicate effectively. If the communication can be heavily dependent on context, then particularistic communication by both communicators can be satisfying. However, if the communication cannot depend on similar contexts, universalistic communication is needed for success in the communication task. In general, when one person uses particularistic and the other universalistic communication, there will be communication difficulties, and interpersonal attraction will suffer.

Characteristics of O

O's behavior is often an important determinant of P's attraction toward O. Generally speaking, behaviors that are rewarding to P increase P's attraction to O. Such behaviors may include the giving of love, status, information, money, goods, or services to P. In Chapter 5, I focused on how O gets P to attribute good causes to O's behavior (ingratiation). Here, my main focus is on whether O will do what P will find rewarding. The two analyses are, of course, related. We noted earlier that O can compliment P, conform to P, render a favor, or present good information about himself or herself as means of ingratiation. Here, I point to these processes using the theoretical terms of Chapter 2. To give a compliment or to conform is to give status; to render a favor is to give a service. The general point is that the giving of needed resources to P by O will increase O's attractiveness.

One could find many examples, but only two will be mentioned here. Lombardo, Weiss, and Buchanan (1972) showed that yielding (agreement preceded by a disagreement) leads to greater attraction than simple agreement. Presumably, yielding gives more status to P than does mere agreement. In another test of attraction-provoking behavior, Rosenfeld (1966) asked female undergraduates to win approval or to avoid approval. In the approval condition, subjects smiled and used gestures much more frequently than in the avoid-approval condition. Note here the *costs* (efforts) of these subjects expended in order to please (reward) the other. Again, when O does something that rewards P (for example, smiles), O's attractiveness increases.

Negative behaviors, such as withdrawing rewards or providing punishment, typically tend to decrease attraction; however, there are many complexities. One such complexity has to do with the expectations that people have concerning how much they should be rewarded. Other complexities concern how equitable it is seen as being to receive rewards.

Negative behaviors can sometimes be very subtle. For example, simply staring can be annoying. As mentioned in Chapter 2, in a series of field studies, an experimenter stared at people stopped at a traffic light and measured their speed across the intersection when the light changed. Presence versus absence of staring, sex of experimenter, and sex of subject were systematically varied. In all experiments, crossing time was significantly shorter in the stare condition (Ellsworth, Carlsmith, & Henson, 1972). Another subtle effect concerns the timing of the disclosure of one's own good fortune. When a person reveals, very early in a relationship, that something nice has happened to him or her, *P* is likely to find him or her less attractive than if he or she discloses it later (Jones & Gordon, 1972). The same information that, when presented early, may appear as boasting, when presented later may seem to be a modest afterthought.

More obvious relationships between behaviors and attraction are also found in the literature, such as the findings that the aggressiveness of *O* tends to depress *P*'s attraction to *O* (Hendrick & Taylor, 1971).

Physical attractiveness is an obvious and important determinant of *P*'s attraction to *O*. Walster, Aronson, Abrahams, and Rottman (1966) found that the most important determinant of liking for a date was the date's physical attractiveness. In other experiments, it was found that people have different ideas about who is attractive; the correlations among ratings of attractiveness obtained from four raters were relatively low, running between .49 and .58. In spite of this low reliability in the measurement of physical attractiveness, however, the average physical-attractiveness ratings given a person did correlate with the extent to which students liked that person as a date. Also, the individual's ratings of attractiveness of and liking for his or her date correlated about .7 (Berscheid & Walster, 1969).

Wiggins, Wiggins, and Conger (1968) discovered different points of view concerning physical attractiveness. They presented female silhouettes to male undergraduates and asked them to make preference ratings. They found four distinct points of view, such as preferences for large breasts, for large buttocks, for small legs, and for large legs. They also found some personality correlates of such preferences; for example, males who like large breasts are higher in need for achievement than males who prefer small breasts.

A variety of other characteristics and behaviors of *O* have been found to influence *O*'s attractiveness to *P*. One phenomenon that has recently been studied (Walster, Walster, Piliavin, & Schmidt, 1973) is the playing-hard-to-get pattern of behavior. It was found that a woman's desirability to a man is a function of (1) how hard she is for the subject to get and (2) how hard she is for other men to get. The most preferred woman is the one who is easy for the subject to get but hard for all other men to get. One can see how this pattern would be the most rewarding. By being easy to get, the woman reduces the *costs* to the man; by being hard for all other men to get, she increases her value.

Characteristics of the Environment

The environment in which *P* and *O* meet has been found to have some influence on interpersonal attraction. Crowding, high humidity, and high temperature can depress interpersonal attraction. For example, Griffitt and Veitch (1971) put college students in rooms that were either at 90 degrees Fahrenheit or at 73 degrees Fahrenheit, and they placed either a few (3 to 5) or many (12 to 16) students in such seven-by-nine-foot rooms. The subjects were required to make judgments of interpersonal attraction utilizing the Interpersonal Judgment Scale. The results show more attraction in the normal-temperature than in the hot rooms and more attraction in the low- than in the high-density conditions.

When people live and work next to each other (propinquity), this similarity between them becomes a particularly important variable. If they happen to be similar in the first place, they are likely to experience greater rewards from interacting with each other than if they are dissimilar. If they are not similar, they will attempt to exchange views in an effort to increase similarity. If they are able to increase their similarity, their attraction to each other will increase. So, the relationship among similarity, propinquity (opportunities for interaction), and attraction is that similarities and propinquity increase attraction, and attraction leads to more exchanges of views, which leads to more similarity. Many field studies, done in neighborhoods (for example, Whyte, 1956), dormitories, factories (Festinger, Schachter, & Back, 1950), and hospitals, show that interpersonal-attraction patterns are highly correlated with propinquity; that is, one is attracted to people who live or work close to one.

Zajonc (1968) presented evidence that mere exposure to a stimulus can increase the attractiveness of this stimulus, provided the exposure is experienced frequently. For example, a figure the subjects have not seen before, such as a Chinese ideograph, elicits neutral responses, but, after repeated presentations, it can elicit positive responses. The effect of mere exposure appears to be independent of the context in which the stimulus is presented. Saegert, Swap, and Zajonc (1973) presented subjects with other people in either pleasant or unpleasant contexts (circumstances). The number of encounters varied from one to ten. There was a trend for the number of encounters to be positively related to attraction, although there were no effects due to context. This suggests that, when O is presented to P numerous times, P acquires a positive response to O that is independent of the context.

Saegert, Swap, and Zajonc (1973) varied the number of times people met others under pleasant and unpleasant circumstances. In one study, female undergraduates were required to rate the taste of solutions contained in beakers. The solutions had a pleasant taste, such as Kool Aid, or an unpleasant taste, such as vinegar, quinine, or citric acid. The subjects were scheduled in groups of six. The purpose of the experiment was explained to the subjects as the study of the perception of tastes "which differ from each other in specific ways and which you will taste in different orders." It was explained that, since the bottles could not be moved, the subjects had to be moved to the bottles. This allowed the experimenters to manipulate the encounter of two students, who worked during a given trial in the same cubicle. A general-information questionnaire was used to assess the subject's attitudes toward the experiment, the cubicle, and the other subjects.

The results showed that there were minor differences between the pleasant- and unpleasant-substances treatments. The major factor determining the ratings of the attractiveness of the other subjects was the frequency (0, 1, 2, 5, 10 times) of encounter with the other subject. Similar results were obtained in a second experiment using a somewhat different procedure.

Comment. Note that here the pleasantness/unpleasantness concerns the task in which the person is involved and not the actions of the other. One would have expected very different results if the other had been responsible for the pleasantness/unpleasantness.

Characteristics of the Perceiver

The kind of person that P is can affect his or her relationship with O—in particular, his or her attraction toward O. Insecure people tend to be attracted to those having similar interests to a greater extent than secure people are (Goldstein, 1969). When P is afraid, he or she may find others more attractive than when he or she is unafraid; however, this is not always the case (Schachter, 1959). A series of experiments was conducted in which a subject entered the laboratory and was surrounded by electrical equipment. The subject was greeted by the experimenter, who posed as a member of a university department of neurology and explained that the experiment was to study the effects of electric shock. In one condition, in order to induce a high level of fear, the experimenter described the shock as terribly painful and at the limits of human endurance, although not causing permanent damage. In another condition, the shock was described as a mild tickle or a tingle. The experimenter then asked the subjects to wait for ten minutes while he prepared the equipment. The subjects were told that they could wait in very comfortable rooms alone or with others in a classroom. The subject's preference for the "alone" or "together" waiting condition was a measure of his or her *affiliation*. The results show that, under conditions of high fear, the subjects preferred to be together, while, under low fear, this tendency was not present. This suggests that the attraction of the generalized other is higher when a person is fearful than when he or she is not.

Schachter also discovered an important relationship between birth order and the strength of the need to affiliate with others. Firstborn and only children, when afraid, have an even greater tendency to affiliate than later-born children. This suggests the existence of a personality variable that predisposes certain persons to be attracted to others. One possible explanation for the greater affiliation of the firstborn and only child is that their parents spend more time with them than they would if there were more children. Spending time means, in many cases, greater frequency of rewarding, loving, and comforting behaviors. This means that firstborn and only children get more rewards from their parents and thus learn to depend on other people for reward and support. In short, they experience relationships with their parents that lead to greater affiliation than usual toward the parents, and they generalize this feeling to others.

Some environments require the subject to do things that are extremely difficult for him or her and thus cause the person to lose some self-esteem because of failure to perform adequately. When this happens, the person shows different patterns of attraction than under normal conditions. Subjects whose self-esteem was lowered by fake personality-test feedback responded more positively to an accepting target than did subjects whose self-esteem was raised (Jacobs, Berscheid, & Walster, 1971).

CONSEQUENCES OF ATTRACTION

One of the obvious consequences of attraction is the increased tendency to approach another. This can be manifested in more looking, closer sitting, and greater amounts of touching behavior. Liked persons are generally evaluated more positively than disliked persons. A person is more likely to conform to the behavior of, or agree with, or use as a model another who is attractive to him or her. Experimenters who are liked have more effect in producing high rates of task performance and persistence than do disliked experimenters. Several studies that support these points are summarized by Byrne and Griffitt (1973).

THEORIES OF ATTRACTION

Why does similarity lead to attraction? Three models that account for the relationship between similarity and liking were considered by Insko and his associates (1973). Model 1 suggests that similarity has both an impact on liking and an impact on implied evaluation (the assumption that people whom we like will like us). Model 2 suggests that similarity leads to liking, which leads to implied evaluation, which then increases liking. The third model says that similarity and implied evaluation, as independent variables, lead to "positive information," which leads to liking. The data of this paper suggest that Model 2 is most likely to be the correct one. In other words, people experience a direct link between similarity and liking; liking another implies that the other person will like you also, and that increases the liking you feel for the other person.

Exactly why similarity should be connected with liking has been the subject of considerable debate. One viewpoint, generally supported by Byrne and his associates, is that similarity is a form of reinforcement.

Byrne and Clore (1967) assumed that the relationship between similarity and attraction would be stronger when the subject was highly aroused, as in an unpredictable social situation. However, this hypothesis was not supported; instead, the highly aroused subjects showed less of a relationship between similarity and attraction than the moderately aroused. One possible explanation for this result is that the highly aroused subjects experienced cognitive restriction, so that they did not take strong positions on any issue. Byrne and Clore argued that disagreement elicits negative affect because it threatens a person's sense of competence. Deductions from this theory were tested by Johnson, Gormly, and Gormly (1973), who worked with variations in the level of disagreement and in the level of self-esteem and found support for this position.

Exchange Theory

The general viewpoint that reinforcement is an important determinant of attraction is found in the so-called exchange theories (Thibaut & Kelley, 1959; Homans, 1961). The idea is that a person who receives more rewards than costs from a given relationship will find the relationship more agreeable than otherwise and thus will experience more attraction toward the other.

One theoretical perspective is that interpersonal attraction is a learned response and follows the well-known laws of learning. For example, it is well known that a person learns a response more readily and emits the learned response more intensely if the rewards received in the course of learning are delivered immediately. Delays in reward weaken learning. Lott, Aponte, Lott, and McGinley (1969) demonstrated that there was more liking toward a stimulus person consistently associated with immediate reward than toward one consistently associated with delayed reward. Lombardo, Weiss, and Buchanan (1972) showed that subjects learned a response when they were reinforced by agreement or yielding (agreement preceded by disagreement) of another person. In other words, agreement or yielding has the same effect on humans that food has on rats in the learning laboratory.

However, what is conceived of as *reinforcement* can be conceived of equally well as *information*. Kaplan and Anderson (1973) present a number of arguments in support of the view that the information conceptualization is more useful. For example, they point out that the most elementary fact of learning is the growth curve in mean habit strength. The idea is that, the more reinforcements received by an organism, the greater is the habit associated with an act that was followed by these reinforcements. This "habit strength" increases the chances that the act will occur in the future, increases the size of the response (the organism acts more strongly), decreases the latency of the response (the organism acts more quickly), and so on. Yet, when the same trait is repeated many times, there is no evidence that attraction increases. For instance, if a subject is told that O is good-natured, he or she tends to like O, but if the subject is told many times that O is good-natured, this does not increase his or her liking for O. On the other hand, if O is described as good-natured and pleasant by two different acquaintances, O's attractiveness does increase. In information terms, the fact that two different persons make a similar judgment increases its reliability. Another aspect of the Kaplan and Anderson argument concerns the set-size effect, which I reviewed in Chapter 4 and which refers to the fact that a stimulus person who is described by many equally desirable traits is seen as more desirable than a stimulus person who is described by just a few, equally desirable, traits. Kaplan and Anderson argue that this effect can be handled by information-integration theory but not by reinforcement theory.

The reinforcement theorists, on the other hand, are not convinced by such arguments. Clore and Byrne (in press) review much evidence in support of their position. Lombardo, Weiss, and Stich (1973) and Lombardo, Tator, and Weiss (1972) presented additional support for the reinforcement theory of attraction. For example, they showed that reinforcement through agreement on high-interest items leads to faster responding by subjects than does reinforcement through agreement on low-interest items. Thus, the theoretical arguments are likely to continue for some time to come.

Thibaut and Kelley (1959) used the so-called comparison level —CL—as a standard of what the person expects to receive in a relationship and reviewed several studies in which different CL's were expected to exist. They showed that, when the person receives more than he or she expects, he or she is more satisfied with that relationship.

The CL corresponds to what we called, in Chapter 2, P's expectation of the behavior of O. Thibaut and Kelley conceive of CL as an average value of all the outcomes of the given social situation known to P by virtue of personal or vicarious experience. Each outcome is weighted by its salience—in other words, by the degree to which it is instigated at the moment. With this concept, the authors are trying to define a neutral point on a scale of satisfaction. If the other gives more than the CL, P will be satisfied; if O gives less than the CL, P will be dissatisfied. For example, a worker who works for a very demanding supervisor would expect to receive criticism frequently and praise rarely. If a new supervisor came in and provided a little more praise, the worker would be extremely satisfied with the relationship. In contrast, another worker, who had been employed by someone who was very lavish with praise, would be extremely dissatisfied with the new foreman. The *identical* amount of praise would lead to satisfaction for the first worker and dissatisfaction for the second worker. In short, it is not so much what O does, but how much P expects of O that determines P's satisfaction with O's behavior.

Bridgeman (1972) examined the hypothesis that both reinforcement and expectancy are important determinants of attraction. Maximum attraction, according to this analysis, will occur when a person receives somewhat more reinforcement than he or she expected. In Figure 6.1, we see Bridgeman's theoretical analysis, which shows attraction as a function of reinforcement (a linear function) and as a function of expectancy (an inverted U function, with the maximum attraction at the point of expected reinforcement). The figure also shows the combined function, which is a compromise between the two functions and which reaches a maximum at a point at which a person receives somewhat more reinforcement than he or she expects. Figure 6.2 shows some of Bridgeman's empirical results from two groups that expected 25% and 50% reinforcement. The data suggest that expectations do play a substantial role in attraction.

Specifically, Bridgeman worked with male sophomores in a game situation depicted as a test of a student teacher's (actually a confederate of the experimenter's) skills. The students received four levels of reinforcement (0%, 25%, 50%, and 100%) from the teacher and were led to expect to win either 25% or 50% of the game trials. After the game trials, the subjects evaluated the "teacher." The students thought that the game was designed to assess the

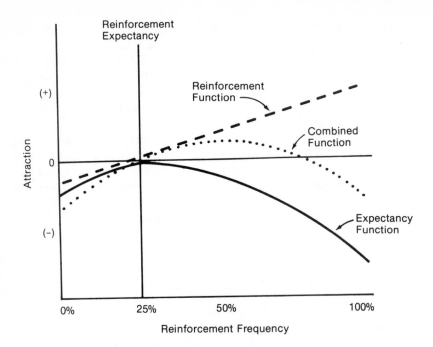

Figure 6.1 Schematic illustration of the hypothetical relationship of attraction, reinforcement frequency, and expectation of reinforcement frequency. From "Student Attraction and Productivity as a Composite Function of Reinforcement and Expectancy Conditions," by W. Bridgeman, *Journal of Personality and Social Psychology*, 1972, *23*, 249–258. Copyright 1972 by the American Psychological Association. Reprinted by permission.

teaching competence of student teachers. Figure 6.2 shows that those who expected 25% reinforcement found the teacher most attractive when they received 25% reinforcement and somewhat less attractive when they received 50% or 100% reinforcement; similarly, those who expected 50% found the teacher less attractive when they received 100% than when they received 50% reinforcement. Thus, there was a strong effect of expectation on the perceived attractiveness of the teacher.

One problem with this study, as pointed out by its author, is that the major deviation from the simple reinforcement hypothesis (the more *O* reinforces *P*, the more *P* likes *O*) is due to the 100%-reinforcement group. It is possible that these subjects found the situation in which they always won difficult to believe and found the teacher less attractive as a result. On the other hand, the students in the 0% group are equally likely to find the situation unbelievable (why did they fail to win on *all* trials?) and might be expected to show *very* negative attraction scores, which did not

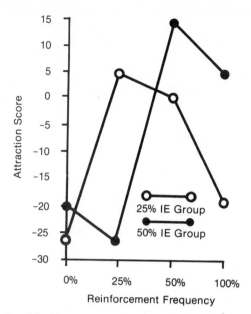

Figure 6.2 Empirical interrelationship of reinforcement expectation, reinforcement frequency, and attraction. From "Student Attraction and Productivity as a Composite Function of Reinforcement and Expectancy Conditions," by W. Bridgeman, *Journal of Personality and Social Psychology,* 1972, *23,* 249–258. Copyright 1972 by the American Psychological Association. Reprinted by permission.

happen. In general, the data supported the importance of expectations, but the study needs to be replicated, with other aspects of the situation varying, to be sure that this is a dependable effect.

Baron (1966) has presented a theory of social reinforcement that considers the impact of the individual's history of social reinforcement on his or her receptivity. He suggests that the person's history produces an internal norm or frame of reference, which he calls the Social Reinforcement Standard (SRS). This can be considered the person's social reinforcement thermostat, and it functions as a determinant of the way the person will react to social reinforcements. Disparities from SRS produce a negative affective arousal. Large disparities, regardless of their direction, produce negative affect. For example, if a man is not used to receiving compliments, and he receives many, he will feel highly embarrassed. Furthermore, receiving greater rewards than expected may produce guilt feelings. Similarly people with low self-esteem are often less able than persons with high self-esteem to accept favorable evaluations from others. This difference suggests the existence of individual differences in acceptability of reward that may be traceable to the history of interpersonal rewards of the individual.

Weiss (1966) has shown individual differences in reinforcement tendencies. Firstborn and only children do more reinforcing in interpersonal relationships than later-born children do. This finding is consistent with the Baron analysis, since, as we discussed earlier when reviewing Schachter's work, firstborn and only children are likely to have received more reinforcements from their parents, which means that they have developed greater expectations for the reception of reinforcement (higher SRS). Since people believe that reciprocity in interpersonal relations is a dependable principle, they may try to increase their received reinforcements by providing more reinforcement to others. Following this logic, we can conclude that firstborn and only children provide more reinforcement to others in order to instigate greater rates of reinforcement by others to them and thus maintain their high level of reinforcement.

Several conditions of the child-rearing environment may be responsible for differences in the experienced reinforcement. In addition to the number of children present in an environment, which affects the number of reinforcements that any one child is likely to receive, the parents' total stock of resources (available reinforcements) and the presence of an extended family (grandmothers, aunts, and others) will affect the frequency of reinforcements received and thus will affect the SRS of the children. Cross-cultural work (for example, Ziller, Long, Ramana, & Reddy, 1968) has shown that children from extended families have higher SRS levels than children from nuclear families, other things being equal.

Social-Comparison Theory

Another theoretical orientation has emphasized the importance of social comparisons for self-evaluation and for the evaluation of issues. Festinger (1954) has argued that, on many issues, people cannot find objective standards that will help them evaluate the issue. Since objective standards are not available, people choose others as the sources of their standards. If a lot of people think the same way, you may think, I must be right. When a person compares himself or herself to others who are thought to be similar, he or she is likely to receive an evaluation of the issues that agrees with his or her viewpoint. This theoretical perspective can be tied with ideas of reinforcement by considering that, the greater the similarity of P and O, the more likely it is that P will be rewarded by discovering that O has the same views on issues that P happens to hold. This discovery will lead to a self-evaluation that will be complimentary for P and therefore rewarding. This analysis suggests that people seek others who are similar so that they can make social comparisons that are more complimentary to themselves. When a person discovers that another is not similar, he or she is likely to communicate with the other in order to make the other similar. In other words, attraction is, in part, determined by the other's ability to act as a standard of comparison.

The other also acts as a standard of comparison when P judges the equity of social-exchange situations. Wicker and Bushweiler (1970) found that equity theory does very well in predicting the perceived pleasantness and fairness of a social situation. Equitable social situations ($I_o/O_o = I_p/O_p$) are seen as both more fair and more pleasant than situations that are not equitable.

Social-comparison theory (Festinger, 1954) has been under careful scrutiny by social psychologists (Latané, 1966), and the making of social comparisons has been found to be complex. Wheeler (1974) presents a summary and review of the literature on social comparison. He states that the evidence suggests that P's who are uncertain about their opinions are likely to seek O's with whom they can compare opinions; generally, P's will choose O's with whom they expect to agree and O's who are likely to be correct. If there have been disagreements between P and O, when O agrees with P, P feels more attracted toward O than if the history of disagreements did not exist, particularly if the issues are nonverifiable and nonobjective. If O is seen as dissimilar by P, and O agrees with P on a belief, this agreement is given more weight than if O were seen as similar. On the other hand, when the issue involves an agreement on values, a similar O is more believable. In general, emotional arousal (such as fear) leads P to seek the company of O's who are responding with similar emotional intensity. Uncertainty about one's ability often leads one to seek comparison with others of relatively low ability. As we have seen, there is some evidence that firstborns have stronger affiliative needs when they are emotionally aroused than do later borns. Extroverts have been found to affiliate under stress more than introverts. Such findings suggest that there are strong tendencies toward comparison with others and this is one of the bases of affiliation. People get together to find out who they are.

Self-Esteem Theory

There is also evidence that people select their comparison others so as to maximize their self-esteem. There is a good deal of information available concerning the way individuals maintain a high self-esteem (Rosenberg, 1967). Rosenberg found that people who, by objective standards, had accomplished very little did have, nevertheless, extremely good opinions of themselves. They accomplished this by cleverly selecting the dimensions on which they judged people (for example, if they were good students, they considered good grades important; if they were good athletes, they considered athletics the most important dimension), by selectively interpreting their own behavior (for example, I did this, therefore I am good), by selecting the standards to apply to their behavior (for example, one should not be too good or too bad on this skill; my level is best), and, finally, by selecting their friends. They were found to select friends who use similar dimensions and standards to judge people. Using all of these strategies does maximize one's self-esteem.

O's Predictability

The predictability of the other can be a source of attraction. When O is predictable, he or she is more rewarding than when unpredictable. When the behavior of the other is highly predictable, P feels that he or she can control O and thus feels more attracted to him or her than when O's behavior is inexplicable. A related phenomenon is whether P knows how to behave appropriately in relation to O. If P does not know how to behave, he or she can become quite anxious. This is the reason that *status incongruity* can cause lack of attraction. Status incongruity can take place in two different ways.

First, at the *individual* level, a person might be incongruent if his or her statuses are highly inconsistent. For example, if your instructor in college math happens to be a 17-year-old Ph.D., you may not know whether to relate to him as an instructor or as a 17-year-old. Status is ranked on many dimensions in most societies, including wealth, education, age, sex, race, religion, family background, amount of foreign travel, type of housing, type of car, and so on. A person is *status congruent* if he or she is consistently high or consistently low on all of these statuses and incongruent if he or she is both high and low across such statuses. When a person is status incongruent, the other person does not know how to relate to him or her and therefore often feels less attracted to him or her than to status-congruent people.

The second form of incongruence, which has been called status disequilibrium, occurs when the status of *two* individuals is not consistent, as for example, when one person is rich and the other is poor. Societies develop norms about appropriate behavior that are tied to status; when this kind of status incongruence occurs, it is unclear which norm should operate. Therefore, the social encounter becomes less comfortable, and people in such situations perceive each other as less attractive. This type of incongruence is theoretically indistinguishable from interpersonal dissimilarity.

DEEPER RELATIONSHIPS

Most of the discussion presented so far in this chapter is relevant to the early phases of interpersonal relationships. Levinger and Snoek (1972) have distinguished three levels of relationship: awareness, surface contact, and mutuality. At the first level, a person notices the other. Surface contact refers to the stage at which people are in interaction and are experiencing the fruits of this interaction. With mutuality, a relationship has achieved unique interpersonal qualities. Levinger and Snoek make the case that most of the results of interpersonal-attraction research are applicable to the first two stages but not to mutuality. This is because, for reasons of convenience, laboratory studies have focused on the relationships between strangers—and, in some cases, only on the relationships between bogus strangers.

During the awareness stage, superficial traits and characteristics, such as physical attractiveness, competence, warmth, and interest in similar activities, lead to attraction. During the surface-contact phase, such characteristics may be less important; the kinds, frequency, and intensity of rewards and costs received from the other determine attraction. At this phase, similarity in attitudes, as well as role behavior determined by social categories, are the more important determinants of attraction. During the mutuality phase, there is much self-disclosure concerning personal feelings. Information is shared, concern for the other's well-being is expressed, and unique pair norms are constructed. Responsibility for protecting and enhancing the relationship is assumed, and there is much emotional investment. Pairs moving toward greater intimacy tend to do so by increasing reciprocal self-disclosure (Taylor, 1968). This is a level of relationship at which mutually understood contracts are the most important determinants of behavior.

In the terms of my model, the early phases of the relationship involve behaviors that are determined by the other's potential for reinforcement; hence, the A and C components control behaviors. In the middle phase, there is more stereotypic and norm- and role-controlled behavior. In the later phase, there is a shift to unique interpersonal contracts as major determinants of social behavior. In the early phase, P looks for cues that O will be able to reward him or her. In the middle phase, P evaluates O's behavior on whether it is rewarding or costly to P. In the last phase, a joint construction of a unique relationship is accomplished that sometimes results in a feeling of deep satisfaction. During the later phases, attitude, value, and need compatibility are crucial.

Walster's (1971) analysis of passionate love emphasizes the physiological-arousal factor as well as P's use of a label to explain his or her arousal. She argues that passionate love can result from gratitude, anxiety, guilt, loneliness, hatred, jealousy, or confusion. As long as these states intensify emotional experience and this experience is labeled by the individual as "love," the subject does experience "passionate love."

Murstein (1971) provides a theory of marital choice. He suggests that couples seriously considering marriage show greater than chance similarity in physical attractiveness and in their hierarchy of values concerning marriage. He assumes that the chosen partner will be close to the ideal self; hence, low self-acceptance subjects will see less similarity between themselves and their partners, while high self-acceptance people will see more similarity between themselves and their partners. He proposes that members of couples who are likely to make good "courtship progress" (*CP*) are more accurate in their predictions of the partner's self and ideal self at the beginning of the study of the pair than poor *CP* couples are. Individuals tend to choose partners whose level of self-acceptance and/or neuroticism is similar to their own. Murstein has some data that suggest that couples in which the sex drive of the male is high show less compatibility than couples in which the sex drive of the male is low. When the male sex drive is below the median, it approximates the female view of an ideal partner. Males high in sex drive are less accurate in estimating how their partners perceive them and how their partners perceive themselves than are low-sex-drive men.

As mentioned in Chapter 3, the rate of interpenetration—that is, the rate at which two people become intimate—depends on the rewards and costs of their exchanges. Altman and Taylor (1973) reviewed several studies that show that "people become more or less open to others in terms of level of intimacy of exchange, number of things told about themselves and length of time they talk, as a function of satisfactions and dissatisfactions experienced in interpersonal exchange" (p. 102). Openness to others is especially affected by rewards. When males were placed in isolation, under conditions that are often found in scientific expeditions in the antarctic or in remote naval installations, they tended to use territoriality responses, such as "This is *my* chair," which apparently helped in the development of intimate interpersonal relationships. In fact, those dyads that did not use territoriality responses in the early phases of the study aborted the study, while those who did use such responses in the early phases completed the eight-day study and used fewer territoriality responses in the later phase of the study. The growth of a relationship requires the development of "contracts" that will eliminate some of the costs but eventually involves the gradual elimination of physical interpersonal boundaries as the parties literally come to use one another's "places" and "things" (Altman & Taylor, 1973, p. 115).

SUMMARY

Broadly speaking, interpersonal attraction is dependent on the rewards that one person gives to the other. Rewards are of many kinds. Physical attractiveness can provide aesthetic rewards. Similarity between *P* and *O* is often rewarding. Similarity in goals is particularly rewarding, since what the other does helps the perceiver. If *O*'s behavior is predictable, *P* is likely to be attracted to *O* to a greater extent than if *O*'s behavior were unpredictable. Status congruence implies predictability and is therefore related to attraction. Complementarity in certain behavior patterns, such as when *P* is talkative and *O* is a good listener, also leads to attraction. Value and need complementarity are crucial to deep and long-lasting relationships. When relationships grow, *P* and *O* develop "contracts" that eliminate some of the costs of the relationship. Costs include all elements that annoy, embarrass, create anxiety, or arouse guilt. These include antagonistic, competitive, superordinate, and coldly formal behaviors, unpredictability, and incompatibility of needs. Rewards and costs make an impact on the perceiver that is moderated by his or her expectations of what rewards and costs are likely to occur in a social relationship.

7

THE ANTECEDENTS OF ACTION

The previous two chapters examined attributions and affective responses; in this chapter, we turn from sentiments to action and examine the determinants of action. The model presented in Chapter 1 is designed to account for overt behaviors and, therefore, for the substance of the present chapter.

In Chapter 1, I presented the model. In Chapter 2, I showed how to use the model to deal with interaction. Chapter 3 attempted a synthesis of much of the literature on social behavior on the basis of the elements of the model. Since the model appears to be useful, this chapter will discuss it in greater detail, answer some of the frequently asked questions about it, and provide a review of literature that supports it.

REVIEW OF THE MODEL

It will be recalled that the model consists of two basic equations:

$$P_a = (w_H H + w_I I)F \qquad \text{(Equation 1)}$$

and $\quad I = w_S S + w_A A + w_C C. \qquad \text{(Equation 2)}$

The probability of an act is a function of the number of times the response has occurred in the history of the organism (H, or habit) and the intention to behave in that way (I), both multiplied by facilitating conditions (F). The intention is a function of social (S), affective (A), and cognitive (C) factors. The social factors include norms, roles, the self-concept, and interpersonal contracts. The affective factors include the emotions elicited by the thought of the behavior. The cognitive factors are the subjective probabilities of perceived possible consequences of the behavior multiplied by the value of these consequences.

The facilitating conditions include the organism's *ability* to perform the act, the organism's level of *arousal* in regard to the act, the *difficulty* of the act, the organism's possession of the *knowledge* required to perform the act, and environmental factors that increase the probability of the act.

One characteristic of the model should be made clear at this point. While the model is a reasonable and convenient way of summarizing a lot of information, precisely how the elements of the model should be assembled to provide the best prediction and understanding of behavior remains to be worked out. There is very much we do not know yet—for example, the best way to combine the information that is included in the facilitating-conditions component (F) or in the social component (S). Should we think of the organism's ability, arousal, and knowledge as additive or as multiplicative terms? At this time, I believe that each of these terms has a value of from 0 to 1. If the organism has zero ability, arousal, or knowledge, the probability of the behavior is zero. So the multiplicative conception is probably correct. Similarly, if environmental factors make the behavior impossible, then $P_a = O$. While this is current thinking, it does not prevent future research from suggesting other ways of conceiving of the problem.

All of the elements of Equation 1 are in 0 to 1.0 scale units, which means that the P_a term is a probability. Even though the measures may originally be in some other units, they can be converted into 0–1.0 through the use of simple nomographs, as illustrated in Figure 7.1. Looking at the figure, assume that the difficulty of the task is measured on a nine-point scale. Maybe several people rated the difficulty of the task on that scale; the mean value of these judgments is entered in the X axis. Figure 7.1 shows how any numbers on the X axis can be converted to numbers ranging from zero to one on the Y axis. If all other aspects of the F component were constant, whatever is measured on the Y axis would be entered in Equation 1 as the F value.

According to the discussion above, F is zero under the following circumstances: (a) when the organism has inadequate ability, (b) when the organism is asleep, (c) when the task is impossibly difficult, (d) when the organism has no information about how to perform the behavior, or (e) when the environment precludes the act.

When we determine the probability that a particular act will be performed, we should also consider the probability of each alternative to it. The prediction is that the act that has the largest P_a value is the one that will occur. Of course, when we *measure* the components and predict P_a, the value of P_a includes measurement error. Thus, we have $P_a \pm$ error. If the error associated with P_a's for two acts is large, we may not be able to call these

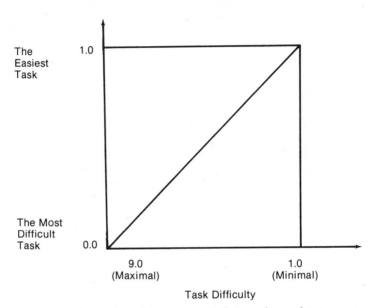

Figure 7.1 Illustration of a nomograph that can be used to convert a
1–9 scale into a 0–1 scale.

probabilities significantly different. The final outcome of the model is still a
probability statement, such as "Given the information we have in hand,
there is a probability of .8 that act *A* rather than act *B* or *C* will be observed."
If too much error is involved in the measurement, we may not be able to
make a useful statement, since a statement such as "There is a probability of
.5 that act *A* rather than act *B* will be observed" communicates exactly zero
information!

One other point is important. For best prediction, it may be necessary
to consider not only how Equations 1 and 2 deal with a particular act but
how they deal with nonaction. To do nothing is sometimes a behavior. For
example, to decide *not* to take a particular vacation is just as much a decision
as to decide to take the vacation. Dulany (1974) has argued that it is important to consider both the act and the absence of the act in computing the
equations and in making predictions. Whether doubling the data gathering is
justified by increased predictability is a matter that needs to be subjected to
empirical tests.

One could make the model more dynamic by considering changes in
the weights over time. Future developments should permit us to write equations that will relate the weights to other variables. At this time, the presentation of such developments would be speculative.

The weights of the social, affective, and cognitive components are subject to three sources of variance: the person, the behavior, and the situation.

The social component's *strength* (the value of S in Equation 2) reflects the clarity of the norms, roles, self-concept, and interpersonal contracts. The *weight* of the S component partially reflects the extent to which the person believes that he or she will be discovered if he or she deviates from the norm, and it reflects the strength of the person's moral development. Thus, under conditions of surveillance, the social component has a large weight. When the behavior is overt, it has larger social weights than when it is covert. In societies in which a particular behavior is functional, there are institutional arrangements that maximize the weight of the S component and thereby maximize conformity. Furthermore, a highly socialized person would use larger weights for the S component than a less socialized person.

The affective component's *strength* depends on the intensity, frequency, and recency of associations of the behavior with positive or negative events. (A classical conditioning of the behavior to positive or negative feelings is assumed.) The longer the behavior goes on, however, the more fatigued and satiated is the organism, and hence there can be a reduction in the size of the A. The *weight* of this component is higher when (a) the individual is "impulsive," (b) the weights of the social and cognitive components are low, and (c) the culture has developed weak S-component elements for the particular behavior.

The cognitive component's *strength* is high when the behavior is frequently and consistently connected with consequences and when these consequences have high value (positive or negative). The *weight* of the C component reflects (a) the extent to which the person exhibits a personality variable related to internal control (Rotter, 1966), (b) the extent to which the culture provides frequent, clear connections between a particular behavior and consequences, and (c) the extent to which the social situation contains weak cues for activation of the social or affective components. Note that I assume that $w_S + w_A + w_C = 1.00$. Future research may show that this assumption is incorrect.

An important area of research related to the C component is the problem of willingness to delay gratification (see Mischel, 1974, for a review); this is studied by asking children whether they prefer a small reward immediately or a large reward later. There are both individual and cultural differences associated with this phenomenon. Theoretically, immediate gratification implies an emphasis on the affective component, while delay means an emphasis on the cognitive component, which does have a time dimension. The finding that there is less willingness to delay in families in which the father is absent (Mischel, 1974) fits with this analysis. When the father is present, events in the family are more predictable, since some rules need to be developed to take into account when the father will be coming back from work, who is going to do which household chores, and so on. Theoretically, predictability implies greater emphasis on the C component. However, complications arise from the fact that one of the best ways to make a child delay gratification is to distract the child (Mischel, 1974). This means that one may best delay a child's gratification by making some other attractive act salient. Thus, in such a case, it is not the relative weights within Equation 2 for the same act but the relative weights across acts that predict the child's actions.

This analysis suggests that there are two ways to delay gratification. This theoretical distinction may justify some empirical tests.

Cultural differences in tolerance of delay of gratification have been observed. For example, unemployed Blacks living in a Black ghetto have often been found to be less willing than other Blacks to delay. Research by me (Triandis, 1976) has shown that this sample experiences "ecosystem distrust": they do not trust people or the predictability of events in their environment. That outlook is consistent with a small weight on the C component. Cultural influences on the weights may be observed when it is especially functional for the particular culture to have clear norms and when this is possible because the population is relatively homogeneous. For example, when the population density is very high, it is especially important to regulate human behavior with strong norms; when the population is homogeneous, it is possible to have a single set of norms. Thus, in high population density, homogeneous societies (say, Japan) the weight of the S component should be higher than in other societies. In societies that are stable, the connection between behavior and consequences will be clearer than in societies that are constantly changing (for example, societies that are frequently involved in wars). When neither the S nor the C component is important, the A component will probably be high, reflecting the immediate, hedonistic side of human nature.

Some of the assumptions underlying these statements are parallel to the well-known arguments advanced by Freud. Psychoanalytic theory considers the *id* a set of drives and emotions controlled by attempts to maximize pleasure. The *ego* consists of psychic structures in contact with reality that attempt to harmonize pressures from the id and the requirements of reality. The *superego* is supposed to evaluate the impulses that come from the id and the activities of the ego in terms of standards and values acquired as a result of the individual's experience in social groups, particularly the family. These Freudian concepts are infinitely richer and more complex that the corresponding affective, cognitive, and social components of the present model. However, since there is a definite correspondence, and, since Freud was a very shrewd analyst, it is likely that some of the arguments that he presented will work with the present, much less complicated attempt to account for social behavior. The general point I've made is that, when the social and cognitive components are not particularly important determinants of social behavior, the affective is likely to take over. This argument is parallel to Freud's argument that an underdeveloped superego and a weak ego are likely to let the id control behavior. The difference is that I have ways of measuring my posited components and thus subjecting these speculations to empirical tests.

Anomic conditions prevail in societies in which the strength of the S, A, and C elements of Equation 2 is small or the elements are inconsistent. Seeman's (1959) classic analysis of alienation postulated five dimensions of alienation. (Note how they correspond to the model.) The first dimension is *powerlessness,* a condition in which individuals see little connection between what they do and what happens to them. This condition can also be described by saying that the P_c term of $C = \Sigma\, P_c V_c$ is close to zero or that the C component has a zero weight. The second dimension is *meaninglessness,* a condition in which the person is unclear concerning what he or she ought to believe. One could say that, in this condition, there are several P_c's of equal strength, and the person is not clear how his or her behavior might be connected with the various consequences, if at all. *Normlessness* is a condition in which the S component is close to zero, or one in which there is inconsistency between the S and C component, so that socially disapproved behaviors are needed to reach valuable goals. *Isolation* is a condition in which the individual has few V_c's that correspond to the values of his or her society. *Self-estrangement,* the fifth dimension of alienation, is the inability of the individual to find activities that are enjoyable and is a condition in which the A component is close to zero for many behaviors. In other words, we have one or another of the dimensions of anomie when the S, A, and C components are close to zero or when there is inconsistency among these components.

Ehrlich (1969) has made the case that, when there is great inconsistency between the behavioral intentions and the norms, the individual may not act. One can assume that other kinds of inconsistency may also lead to nonaction, as well as to anomic behavior. I have argued that, when there is inconsistency among the components of Equations 1 and 2, it is difficult to predict the behavior (Triandis, 1971). Norman (1975) reported empirical support for this argument.

The Concept of Attitude

One of the problems with the literature on the relationship between attitudes and behavior is that different researchers have used different measures of attitude. The best measure for behavior prediction is behavioral intention. However, since behavioral intentions are related to affect (see Equation 2), we can also consider studies in which the affect toward the behavior was measured suitable for the illustration of the relationship of attitudes to behavior.

In the standard social-psychological literature, the distinction among different aspects of the attitude concept is not always made. I argued, in an earlier publication, that *attitude* is a nonexpert's concept and should be used by social scientists in a loose way, as nonexperts use it (Triandis, 1971). For precise discussions, scientists should use three terms: behavioral intention, affect, and beliefs about the attitude object. I thus defined an attitude as "an idea charged with affect, predisposing action." This definition includes the (a) belief, (b) affect, and (c) behavioral intentions toward the attitude object.

Fishbein has used the concept *attitude* to denote only affect. This is a "scientific" use of the concept, as opposed to an everyday use. There are some advantages in using lay terms when communicating with nonexperts, but there are also advantages in using precisely defined terms when communicating with scientists. In any case, Fishbein has provided a very clear analysis of behavioral intentions, attitudes, and beliefs (see Fishbein & Ajzen, 1975). According to him, behavioral intention depends on the attitude toward the act; attitude toward the act depends on beliefs about the act and on the evaluative aspect of each of these beliefs. For example, all the beliefs that a person has about an act and the affect attached to each belief together determine the attitude toward the act; attitude is

$$\sum_{i=1}^{n} B_i a_i,$$

where B_i refers to the strengths of the beliefs and a_i to the affective aspect of each belief. There are n beliefs. For example, a person might believe that hitting another is enjoyable, and the affect attached to the idea "being enjoyable" is multiplied by the strength of the belief. Other beliefs and their affective aspects may also be salient. The corresponding B and a elements are multiplied, and the products are added. The Fishbein formulation subsumes the affective and cognitive components of my model under one concept: the attitude toward the act.

We turn now to evidence that supports my model. In this review, I will use the concept *attitude* loosely because most researchers do not distinguish affect from behavioral intention and often include elements of both in their index of attitude. When I can be more precise, I will be. First I will mention broad support for the model, and then I'll discuss more detailed studies, including some that specifically tested the model.

GENERAL EVIDENCE SUPPORTIVE OF THE MODEL

There is an extensive body of literature that is concerned with the prediction of behavior from attitudes. Much of this literature has already been reviewed by Ajzen and Fishbein (1969, 1970, 1973); they reviewed the relationship between behavior and behavioral intentions, on the one hand, and the relationship between behavioral intentions and normative beliefs and attitudes toward the act, on the other hand.

The major points of these papers are that (a) specific behaviors are predictable from behavioral intentions and (b) behavioral intentions are predictable from the attitude toward the act (that is, from the affective and the cognitive components) and from the perceived normative expectations of the subject's reference groups multiplied by the person's motivation to comply with these expectations. Ajzen and Fishbein further maintain that certain variables influence the attitude toward the act or the normative component (expectations of reference groups multiplied by motivation to comply with these expectations). Traditional measures of attitudes are variables external to the Fishbein theory, and the relationship of these measures to behavior is mediated by the attitude toward the act and by the normative component. In short, Fishbein does not necessarily expect such measures to predict behavior.

Ajzen and Fishbein (1973, p. 45) presented a table that summarizes ten studies that observed 21 samples of subjects using the Fishbein model. The multiple correlations between behavioral intention and the two elements of the Fishbein model range from .38 to .92, with a median value of .80, and the correlations between behavioral intentions and behavior range from .21 to .97, with a median value of .68.

There is considerable literature suggesting that attitudes are not related to behavior. Most of the studies showing no relationship, however, upon careful examination, prove to be methodologically unsound. For example, the classic LaPiere (1934) study would be rejected by any reputable journal today because of its poor methodology (see Triandis, 1971, pp.14–15 for a critique).

In any case, the model of Chapter 1 does predict that, when habits have all the weight, or facilitating conditions make the behavior impossible, attitudes will be unrelated to behavior. Thus, only under some conditions, specified by the model, are attitudes related to behavior. A number of other papers are also relevant; for example, Ajzen (1971) has shown that different kinds of communications can have an impact on the normative and the attitudinal components and thus differentially affect behavior. Howard and Sheth (1969) applied a similar theoretical analysis to buying behavior, and my associates and I (Triandis, Vassiliou, Vassiliou, Tanaka, & Shanmugam, 1972) have attempted to summarize much of the cross-cultural evidence concerning subjective influence on behavior utilizing a variation of this model.

Evidence in Support of the First Equation

Behavioral Intentions. There is much evidence, in addition to the studies of Fishbein and his associates, suggesting that behavioral intentions are good predictors of overt action. For example, intent to buy is an excellent predictor of purchasing (Gormley, 1974). Wicker (1969) indicates that, in one of his studies, students' participation as subjects in a psychology experiment was predicted from attitudes toward participating in such experiments. Goldstein, Gleason, and Korn (1975) found behavioral intentions to be good predictors of drug use eight months later. Frideres, Warner, and Albrecht (1971) found a strong relationship between attitudes toward marijuana (the measure of which included several items tapping behavioral intentions) and the use of marijuana. It was further shown that the congruence between overt behavior and attitudes was greater for those individuals whose immediate group had attitudes similar to their own. Kothandapani (1971) found a closer relationship between behavioral intentions and behavior than between other components of attitude and behavior. In a study of who volunteers for companionship with mental patients, Fischer (1971) obtained a strong relationship between behavioral intentions and behavior.

Habits. That past behavior predicts future behavior is widely believed, and hence the importance of habit is widely acknowledged. A simple observation of the behavior of individuals who are professionally concerned with the prediction of the behavior of other people suggests that they rely almost entirely on the concept of habit. For example, law-enforcement officers find that the more reliable clues in the detection of a criminal are idiosyncratic patterns of behavior that are known to be associated with a particular criminal and that occur as habitual patterns of behavior in almost every one of that person's crimes. Such almost ritualistic behavior, if it is sufficiently idiosyncratic, can provide excellent clues concerning the identity of a particular criminal, at least in those social settings in which the police are very familiar with individual criminals. While law-enforcement officers, the courts, educators, and business leaders tend to discriminate very little among their "clients," when they do discriminate, they are particularly likely to use previous behavior as a predictor of future behavior. What we know from learning theory and from the massive literature on behavior modification is also consistent with the concept that habit is a major determinant of behavior.

Most nonverbal behaviors, such as the choice of the distance one sits from a moderator in a discussion session (Hendrick, Giesen, and Coy, 1974), are probably under the control of habits. In other words, as far as nonverbal behaviors are concerned, we act without thinking about how to act.

In a study by Landis, Triandis, and Adamopoulos (1975), teachers were observed in classrooms during three different periods of time. Teacher behavior toward Black and White, male and female students was classified into a system of categories. The frequency of the behavior at time 1 was correlated with the frequency of the behavior at times 2 and 3. These correlations provided an estimate of the importance of the habit component. Correlations of the order of .42 were obtained when predicting behavior from habits. Habits had consistently the most important weight, while behavioral intentions, in this case, were unimportant.

Habits and Intentions. Pomazal (1974) predicted whether or not students would give blood at a blood clinic from the students' behavioral intentions and habits (the number of times they had given blood in the past). In this case, the behavioral-intentions component had the larger weight. Pomazal's findings and those of Landis, Triandis, and Adamopoulos are consistent with this analysis: teachers behave in classrooms according to well-established habits, while students at a blood clinic do not.

In still another study of volunteering behavior, Adamopoulos and Brinberg (1975) tested the model by means of a questionnaire that assessed the views of psychology students regarding participation in psychological experiments. The purpose was to see whether the subjects actually participated in an experiment that took place several days after the assessment of the intentions. The time and place of the possible participation was experimentally manipulated, to obtain some variation on the facilitating-conditions (F) component. Four levels of F were used. The most easy was for the students to be interviewed in their homes on any day of their choosing during a given week. The most difficult was for the students to come to the Psychology Building on a specified day and hour during that same week. The habit component was assessed by asking the subjects how many times they had participated in psychological experiments as volunteer subjects.

The social determinants were obtained by asking the subjects to rate statements measuring norms—"Most of my classmates feel that participating in psychological experiments is important"—and statements measuring roles—"As a student, I have to do certain things. Participating in experiments is one of them." The affect was obtained by asking the subject to respond to several semantic-differential scales, in connection with the statement "I find participating in psychological experiments. . . ." The subjects marked *pleasant, interesting, valuable,* and so on. The probability of the consequences was assessed by means of statements such as "If I participate in a psychological experiment, I will be harmed or hurt" rated on seven-point scales of choices from "very likely" to "not likely." The value of the consequences was assessed by questions such as "How important do you think is the chance that you might be hurt in a psychological experiment in determining whether you will participate in the experiment?" Subjects answered on a "very important" to "not important at all" scale. The behavioral intention was obtained after the subject was told about the second study and the conditions of participation in that study. The subject was then asked to respond to an "I am absolutely certain that I will participate" to "I am absolutely certain that I will not participate" scale.

The results show that the affective component was given the largest weight in determining the behavioral intentions of the subjects. The regression weight was .30 (significant at the $p < .01$ level), while the regression weights of the S and C components were only .12 and .13 (and reached significance at the .05 level only with a one-tailed test). The multiple correlation was .43. In short, subjects indicated willingness to participate in experiments when they anticipated that participation would be enjoyable, and they refused to participate when they expected the experiment to be unpleasant or boring.

In another analysis, subjects were separated into two groups, according to whether they actually participated in the second study (that is, fulfilled the criterion of behavior). An interesting finding emerged: those who participated in the second study weighted the C component most heavily, while those who did not participate weighted the A component most heavily. Since the majority of the subjects did not participate, the greater importance of the A component in the overall results is understandable. It turns out, then, that students who do *not* participate are those who think of experiments as boring and unpleasant; those who *do* participate are those who see desirable consequences, such as helping science, learning something useful, getting a better grade in a psychology course, and so on.

The S, C, and A components were also used to predict behavior directly. The correlation was only .27, which suggests that these components predict behavioral intentions better (.43) than they predict behavior, as would be expected from the model.

The next question is how well did behavioral intentions and habits predict behavior? In this case, the behavioral intentions predicted very well, with a correlation of .59. Habit made no contribution. The model further predicts that, for the highly facilitating conditions (the possibility of being interviewed at home any day), the prediction should be best and for the least facilitating condition (having to come to the Psychology Building on a specific day) the prediction should be worst. This is in fact what happened. The multiple correlations were .81, .67, and .18 for the three levels of facilitating conditions for which there were enough subjects to do separate analyses.

A major question now is why, in some studies, habit is the only important predictor of behavior (for example, for the behavior of teachers) and, in other studies, intention is the only important predictor (for example, volunteering for a psychological experiment) and, in still other studies, both are important. First, it should be remembered that, theoretically, intention and habit are related. If intentions are relatively constant over time, they will cause the same behavior over and over. Habit reflects the frequency of this behavior. As behavior repeatedly takes place, habit increases and becomes a better predictor of behavior than behavioral intentions. When two predictors are highly correlated, the one that is highly correlated with the criterion (in this case, the behavior) will take all of the weight, and the other will have a zero weight. This follows from the mathematical relations that determine regression weights. In other words, when habit and intention are highly correlated, the one that is more highly correlated with behavior will take all the weight, and the other variable will contribute nothing to the prediction. The studies reviewed above, then, simply tell us that teacher behavior is rather stable and that learning about teacher intentions does not increase the accuracy of our prediction of behavior; in contrast, the behavior of students volunteering for psychological experiments is mostly under intentional control, since in this case habits have not yet been formed. For volunteering to give blood at a blood clinic, the situation is intermediate; at least for the sample tested by Pomazal, the habit component was beginning to be operating, but the intention component was still the stronger of the two.

To summarize, two major components determine behavior: habit and behavioral intentions. The question is when does one or the other have the greater weight? Our analysis suggests that, when a behavior is new, untried, and unlearned, the behavioral-intention component will be solely responsible for the behavior, while, when the behavior is old, well-learned, or overlearned and has occurred many times before in the organism's life span, it is very likely to be under the control of the habit component. In addition, when the person is highly emotionally aroused, habit rather than intention controls behavior.

Zajonc (1965) utilized the distinction between learning (the acquisition of new responses) and performance (the emission of previously learned responses) to explain the conditions under which social facilitation or impairment of performance can be observed when a person acts in the presence of an audience. The argument is that an audience increases the *level of arousal* of an individual performing. When the task is easy or the behavior has been overlearned, arousal has the effect of making the emission of dominant responses (those for which $w_H > w_I$) more probable, which means that responses that are habitual are more likely to occur, causing social facilitation. When the task is new and difficult, the arousal inhibits performance, since the dominant responses interfere with the responses that must be emitted for successful completion of the task and which are under behavioral intentional control. Consistent with these points, when the person is aroused, performance is sharper, more intense, and quicker. The activation of behavioral intentions presumably requires cognitive processing of information, which takes more time than the activation of habits.

A potential explanation of the audience effect is that the subject anticipates that he or she will be evaluated by other people, and this anticipated evaluation leads to higher arousal and the emission of dominant responses. A study by Paulus and Murdoch (1971) manipulated audience presence and anticipated evaluation in a 2×2 factorial design and found greater emission of dominant responses when the subject anticipated evaluation. The presence or absence of an audience alone did not significantly affect the dominant responses.

We now turn to studies in which measurement of the habit component was found to improve prediction. Crespi (1971) analyzed the success of preelection surveys in the prediction of election outcomes. He presents a summary that suggests a highly successful overall prediction of behavior. Furthermore, in a study of movie attendance, a multiple r squared of .85 was obtained from four attitudinal variables. In most market surveys, about one-half the variance of buying behavior is predictable from attitudinal variables. This contrasts sharply with the difficulties in relating attitudes and behavior reported by Wicker (1969) and others. Crespi argues that the discrepancy between the two sets of results can be accounted for by, first, the specificity of the corresponding behavior. That is, the "successful" attitudinal questions often involve a behavioral intention that is very similar to the behavior, such as "If tomorrow you had to vote in an election in which X and Y are running, which one would you choose?" Second, the closeness of the time of measurement of the attitude to the behavior affects the results. Third, the consistency between habits and attitudes is important. For example, in the analysis of voting, accuracy of predicting increased dramatically when the sample was dichotomized into those voters who had voted in the past in similar elections and those who had not voted. In the case of movie attendance, general information about the frequency of movie attendance (habits) can be combined with specific attitudes toward specific movies to produce an excellent prediction of behavior. In the buying-behavior study, success required that the analysis be restricted to those persons who qualified as "likely users" on the basis of their reported actual use of the product in the last four weeks.

Improved prediction can also occur when we add to information about attitudes the person's prediction of his or her own future behavior, in which case past behavior is probably an important source of information for the subject. A study by Juster (1966) showed that this is true for buying behavior, and a study by Holman (1956) showed it to be the case for attendance at football games.

The conclusion, then, is that, when the behavior is institutionalized or routinized—that is, when it has a significant habit component—adding this information to the information about behavioral intentions greatly increases the predictability of the behavior.

Facilitating Conditions. At any level of habit or behavioral intention, the absence or presence of facilitating conditions will affect the likelihood of a behavior. In an extreme case, the person's habits and behavioral intentions have no relevance if the situation does not permit him or her to behave. A trivial example is a prisoner, whose hands are tied, wanting to punch somebody in the nose. Explicit recognition of the importance of such facilitating conditions in the design of research on the attitude/behavior relationship is highly desirable. Consider the relative success of predictions made on the basis of indexes, of facilitating conditions obtained directly from the subject, as in the previously mentioned study by Holman (1956). Here, the subjects were asked their attitudes toward attendance at football games and were asked to make a specific prediction concerning which games they would attend. Such specific predictions presumably took into account information that had nothing to do with attitudes or habits, such as that the date of a game coincided with the subject's mother's birthday. The result was that the subject's prediction and the actual attendance correlated .8, while the attitude towards football games and attendance correlated .41, and a multiple correlation reached .96.

The person's ability to carry through the behaviors that he or she has the intention to perform must be considered as part of facilitating conditions. For certain kinds of behaviors, a good deal of skill is needed. In addition, the expectation that the behavior will be effective may be an important aspect of the C component. Rosen and Komorita (1971) obtained a measure of effectiveness by asking subjects to rate how effective each of several acts would be in bringing about changes consistent with their position on a given issue. When this index was multiplied with their intentions, it resulted in what the authors called an Action Potential Index. In my terms, their probability formula is $P_a = I P_c V_c$, which is different from my own. This index predicted behavior much better than did conventional attitude scales. Furthermore, the index appears to be relatively consistent across behaviors, thus providing a measure of "activism"—a personality variable. There are, as yet, no empirical tests comparing the Rosen and Komorita with other models.

The importance of general arousal can be seen in studies in which the person's arousal is not directly related to the behavior. For example, Jaffe, Malamuth, Feingold, and Feshbach (1974) arranged for subjects to read erotic passages and to have the opportunity to deliver shocks to an experimental confederate as punishment for incorrect responses in a bogus extrasensory-perception task. Those who were sexually aroused (both males and females) delivered more intense shocks than nonaroused subjects.

Wicker (1971) analyzed the influence of other variables on attitude/behavior inconsistency. His conclusion strongly supports the notion that facilitating conditions must be assessed in order to predict behavior, and he suggests a number of approaches that may lead to effective assessment of facilitating conditions.

Facilitating conditions may include the total situation in which a subject (P) and another (O) find themselves. For example, in the Altman and Haythorn (1965) study, members of dyads placed in isolation revealed more intimate topics to the other than did controls, although they revealed less in this situation than they would to a best friend. It appears, then, that the environment in which two people find themselves increases the probability of certain kinds of behaviors and decreases the probability of others. In terms of the model, this effect can sometimes best be considered under facilitating conditions, but it may also appear as an aspect of the S component of Equation 2, as, for example, when there is a norm developed among people in isolated conditions that it is "right" to talk about intimate topics.

Evidence in Support of Equation 2

There are several studies that support the model's second equation. The best review is provided by Davidson, Jaccard, Triandis, Morales, and Diaz-Guerrero (1976). The data come from Illinois and Mexico City women and concern fertility-relevant behaviors. Samples of women from both upper-middle-class and lower-class backgrounds in both locations supported the model, with multiple correlations, corrected for shrinkage, exceeding .6 and sometimes reaching the upper .80s, depending on the reliability of the data from a particular sample. The cognitive component was most important with the upper-middle-class samples, while the social component, particularly personal beliefs about the appropriateness of the behavior, was most important for the lower-class Mexican sample.

Jaccard and Davidson (1972) obtained a multiple correlation of .83 for predicting behavioral intentions from the social and cognitive components alone. Thus, there is strong evidence that the second equation of the model is useful, and the importance of each of its elements is supported by studies not specifically related to the model.

The S Component. The environment in which P and O find themselves is an important determinant of behavior. The influence of the environment is best analyzed in terms of the concept of the behavioral setting (Barker, 1968). Some behaviors are "pulled" by the environment (for example, praying in church). Much of the work of Wicker (for example, Wicker, 1972) examines the relationship between behavioral setting and behavior. A review of the work on human environments can be found in Moos (1973).

The importance of norms as determinants of behavior is too well supported in the literature to require much review. Numerous norms have been explored in detail, such as the norm of reciprocity (Gouldner, 1960; Pruitt, 1968). Heise (1973) presents a systems approach to the analysis of the relationship of attitude and behavior in which norms are a critical element.

Norms, such as retributive justice and self-defense, have been used in an analysis of violence by Blumenthal (1972). The work of Linn (1964/1965), particularly his analysis of the reasons people give for behavior that is inconsistent with their attitudes, clearly shows that norms control behavior. Finally, DeFriese and Ford (1969) studied racial attitudes related to the willingness of White individuals to accept Blacks as neighbors. The prediction of overt responses was better when both attitudinal position and norms were employed than when one or the other alone was used for the prediction. An analysis of the characteristics of the social environment by Jessor and Jessor (1973) and their review of their findings on reported marijuana use by seventh- to ninth-grade students show the S component to account for more than 50% of the variance of this behavior.

There are several experiments in which a confederate of the experimenter did a favor for a naïve subject and then asked the subject to cooperate with him or her in a project. Compliance was higher in such a condition than in control conditions. However, the attraction of the subject to the confederate was unrelated to compliance (Nemeth, 1970; Reagan, 1971). In other words, the experimental manipulations changed the norms but not the affect toward the confederate. Changing the norm, through bringing to bear the reciprocity norm, was sufficient to get the change in the behavior; changes in attraction did not have to take place in order to arouse the change in behavior. In short, the S component affected the behavior independently of the A component.

In an analysis of role perceptions among Americans, Greeks, Indians, Peruvians, and Chinese, Triandis, McGuire, Saral, Yang, Loh, and Vassiliou (1972) found three dimensions necessary and sufficient for the descriptions of role perceptions. The dimensions were named *solidarity* (love, cooperation, nurturance, no hostility, and formal acceptance), *giving versus denying status* (control, envy, and superordination), and *intimacy*. These three dimensions seem to provide the contrasts needed to characterize the major differences in role perceptions. One can argue that, when the role between P and O is salient—as, for example, when a father talks to his son with the awareness that he is acting as a father in relation to his son—the role can control most of the variance in interpersonal behavior. Since both roles and behaviors can be located, conceptually, in the same three-dimensional space defined by the dimensions of solidarity, status, and intimacy, it is possible to say that any role occupies a particular point in that three-dimensional space and that any behavior also occupies a point in the same space. The probability of a behavior occurring is inversely proportional to the distance between these two points (Oncken, 1968).

The demographic characteristics of P and O also can have a significant influence on the probability that certain behaviors will occur in the particular interpersonal relationship. An analysis of responses of samples around the world to a variety of hypothetical social situations (Triandis, 1967) suggests that American subjects pay much attention to race similarity when considering *respectful* behaviors such as "admiring the ideas of the other," or "admiring the character of the other." High occupational level of the other is also a factor leading to these behaviors, as is similarity in religion. High occupational level is also important in most other samples of nationalities studied. Similarity in religion, however, is not always important. Similarity in sex is not important in American samples, but it is important for Japanese males.

Associative intimate behaviors, such as kissing on a date, are highly dependent on similarity of race, age, and, to some extent, religion for American samples, while a high occupational level is important for Japanese and Indian samples. *Associative coordinate* behaviors, such as eating or gossiping with another require similarity of sex, age, and race, and/or similarity of belief systems among American subjects. Again, a high-status occupation is conducive to such responses among Japanese males and females, as well as among Indians. *Dissociative* responses occur when the other is different in race, religion, or beliefs or holds a low-level occupation, for American samples. A low-level occupation is a primary factor leading to dissociative behavior for German and Japanese males. Race is much more important as a factor among Americans than among other samples around the world. Among American samples, *superordinate* behaviors are particularly likely when O is of a low occupational status, of a different race, or holds different beliefs.

What are the bases for the formation of groups whose norms are likely to affect the individual? In traditional societies, three bases are apparent (Bruner, 1972): descent (belonging to the same clan; having common ancestors), territory (coming from the same part of the country), and alliance (being related by marriage). In highly industrialized societies, these bases of group formation are sometimes less potent, and similarities in professional affiliation or in political or religious orientation are more potent. In general, similarity in beliefs results in interpersonal attraction and group formation in industrialized settings.

Whether a person will comply with the norms of his or her group depends on the relationship between the reference group and the individual. When the relationship involves common goals (promotive interdependence), people tend to do what is specified by the norms; when the relationship involves different goals (contrient interdependence), people tend to find ways to deviate from the norms. Thibaut, Friedland, and Walker (1974) subjected these ideas to empirical test and found support. Individuals were found to observe rules more closely in promotive than in contrient interdependence situations. When an individual participates in the making of rules and the situation is promotive, he or she is particularly likely to follow the norms;

when the rules are general rather than specific and the situation is promotive, the individual is again more likely to follow the rules. The reverse pattern was obtained by Thibaut and his associates when the situation was contrient. In that case, people followed the rules only when they were under surveillance, while, in the case of promotive interdependence, surveillance had no effects. In other words, people followed the rule without being checked by others.

The self-concept is another part of the S component. The self is the individual as known to the individual (Murphy, 1947). It is a complex pattern of thoughts and feelings and behavioral dispositions of which the individual is aware and which are summed up by "I am the kind of person who does that." Such cognitions are among the determinants of behavioral intentions found in the S component.

Ziller (1973) has presented a scholarly review of the literature that deals with the self. His analysis suggests that people with high self-esteem will behave more according to their self-concept and less according to norms, while those low in self-esteem will conform to external norms. Those high in social interest (feeling of being included in a group) will follow the norms of the particular group more rigidly than those low in social interest. Both self-esteem and social interest apparently increase with age, up to age 40 (Ziller, 1973, p. 100). This suggests a greater weight of the S component for older than for younger persons.

Empirical evidence suggests that the self-image can be related to significant aspects of a person's behavior. Epstein (1973) summarizes much of this evidence. He conceptualizes the self-concept as a theory that the individual has constructed about himself or herself (self-theory). It includes major postulates on the nature of the world, the nature of self, and their interactions. The purpose of the theory is to optimize the pleasure/pain balance of the individual over the course of a lifetime. By maintaining the individual's self-esteem and by organizing the data of experience in a manner that can be coped with effectively, the theory permits the individual to maximize his or her rewards. Self-theories can be narrow or extensive, parsimonious or multifaceted, empirically valid or invalid, internally consistent or inconsistent, testable or not testable, and useful or not useful. Individuals characterized as mentally disturbed often have narrow, multifaceted, invalid, inconsistent, not testable, and not useful self-theories.

McArthur, Kiesler, and Cook (1969) obtained further evidence in support of Freedman and Fraser's (1966) suggestion that the self percept may affect the likelihood that individuals will act on a given attitude. Freedman and Fraser had discussed the idea "I am the kind of person who does this sort of thing" as a determinant of behavior. Schwartz and Tessler (1972) demonstrated that the person's self-image predicted whether a person would volunteer to become a bone marrow donor. They showed that a person's beliefs about the correctness of behavior can be powerful predictors of behavior.

Apparently, even small changes in self-concept can alter behavior. For example, Kraut (1973) found that subjects who were arbitrarily labeled charitable by an experimenter gave more to charity and subjects labeled uncharitable gave less than corresponding control groups who were not labeled. One can imagine how powerful labeling can be when a person is labeled "guilty" (criminal) by a court or "mentally deficient" by a school psychologist.

Changing the self-concept will change the attributions that a person makes about his or her own behavior, and as you will see in the next chapter, this is one way to change behavior.

There is a good deal of evidence that people act in ways that are consistent with their self-concept. Eisen (1972) discovered that persons high in self-esteem behave more honestly than people low in self-esteem, while Shotland and Berger (1970) found that people who considered themselves honest were more likely to return a pencil that they had borrowed than people who did not stress honesty as part of their self-concept. Aronson and Mettee (1968) suggest that people whose self-esteem was made low through an experimental manipulation cheated more than people with high self-esteem. Snyder and Cunningham (1975) approached subjects with a small request (virtually sure to lead to compliance) or a very large request (virtually sure to lead to noncompliance). Later, when the same subjects were approached with a request of intermediate magnitude, those who had complied were more likely to comply (52%) than those who had not complied (22%) and more likely than controls who had not had the experience of complying or not complying (33%). In other words, people developed the self-concept "I am the type of person who complies" or "I am the type of person who does not comply," and later behavior was consistent with this self-percept.

Self-regulatory systems and plans of action are also important in determining behavior. The individual regulates his or her own behavior by self-imposed goals (standards) and self-produced rewards and punishments (Mischel, 1973, p. 273). The concept of a self-imposed achievement standard can be found in Rotter's (1954) "minimum goal" construct and in formulations of self-reinforcing functions (Kanfer, 1971; Kanfer & Marston, 1963), all of which refer to people rewarding themselves. The central characteristic of these systems is the subject's adoption of contingency rules that guide his or her behavior in the absence of external situational pressures. Such rules specify the behavior that is appropriate, the goals that must be achieved, and the consequences of achieving or not achieving those goals.

This theoretical analysis is consistent with Snyder's (1974) research on *self-monitoring*. According to Snyder, people differ in the extent to which they engage in self-observation and self-control or are guided by situational cues of social appropriateness. He has developed a self-report instrument of self-monitoring. Theater actors scored high on this scale. Those high in self-monitoring, when compared with those low in this attribute, were better able to communicate an arbitrarily chosen emotion to naïve judges, were more sensitive to the expression and self-presentation of others, and used more cues to monitor their own expressions.

So-called "moral character" (Hogan, 1973) is sometimes an important determinant of behavior. Hogan's analysis suggests a sequence of moral development in which moral knowledge (knowing the rule but not accepting it), socialization (acceptance of the rule), capacity to take the point of view of others, the development of a conception of what are useful rules of behavior, and the ability to function independently of these rules are characteristics of different stages of moral development. In his review, he stresses parental behaviors as antecedents of the development of moral conduct. In terms of the model, his review suggests that, at early stages of development, the child stresses the S component of Equation 2, while, at higher levels of development, the child emphasizes the C component, particularly concerning the effects of his or her behavior on the welfare of others; at the highest level of development, the A component of Equation 2 becomes integrated with the S and C components, and the three become consistent.

Kohlberg's (1963) well-known developmental sequence emphasizes the perspectives of individuals, who are seen as focusing on themselves, their role, their ingroup, their community, and the world at different stages of development. At the lowest stage, the emphasis on immediate gratification is egocentric; at the highest stage, the emphasis on consequences of one's action for people in general (the world) reveals the broadest perspective. His Stage 6 involves abstract concepts that are applicable to everyone, such as equity, universality, and justice and represents the point of view with the broadest historical and geographical perspective.

Recent evidence linking moral reasoning and participation in protest demonstrations such as sit-ins (Fishkin, Kenniston, & MacKinnon, 1973) suggests important linkages between the self-image and behavior. Jones (1973) showed the power of self-esteem theory in the prediction of interpersonal evaluations. He found that, the higher an individual's evaluation of himself or herself, the less his or her tendency to evaluate others as they are perceived to evaluate him or her.

Two other influences of the S component can be mentioned: interpersonal agreements and general intentions. Interpersonal agreements are, of course, quite specific to a particular P and O and therefore not particularly predictable. However, general theories of interpersonal behavior must have a place for them, since a good deal of social behavior is under the control of such agreements. The instructions that an experimenter gives to a subject, for instance, must be conceptualized as an aspect of the S component, and a good deal of the social psychology of the experiment operates through this component.

An illustration of how interpersonal agreements influence social behavior can be found in a study reported by Moriarty (1975). This researcher examined the probability that bystanders would intervene to stop a theft if they had committed themselves in advance to the victim. During the summer of 1972, thefts were staged (a portable radio taken from an unattended beach blanket) at Jones Beach, New York. Subjects who had agreed to watch the victim's belongings (an interpersonal agreement) were more likely to notice the theft, and, compared with other subjects who noticed, "agreement" subjects were more likely to stop the theft. Similarly, thefts were staged at automat cafeterias in New York City (a suitcase was taken while the owner was absent). Again, those who had made an interpersonal agreement with the victim were more likely to stop the theft.

In the interpersonal-agreement condition at the beach, the request of a confederate, who left a radio tuned to a rock station on a blanket located about five feet from the subject, consisted of the following: "Excuse me, I'm going up to the boardwalk for a few minutes. Would you watch my things?" The subject answered "Yes." In the no-agreement condition, the request was: "Excuse me, I'm here alone and have no matches. Do you have a light?" Thus, in both cases, some interaction took place between the confederate and the subject. When there had been an interpersonal agreement 95% of the subjects intervened if they noticed the theft; when there had been no interpersonal agreement, only 20% intervened.

Comment. The theoretical perspective of the researcher who did this study was that the commitment of the subject to watch the object of the theft was the critical variable. Commitment constituted a decision to intervene, and, when an emergency occurred, a prior decision to intervene reduced the subject's indecision and conflict concerning whether to respond. In my theoretical perspective, interpersonal agreement changes the behavioral intention, which changes the probability of action. The predictions from the two theoretical perspectives are the same, and therefore we cannot distinguish one from the other.

Finally, broad general intentions are determined by the social situation, which provides a framework for the interpersonal relationship. That is, whether the behavior is associative or dissociative, superordinate or subordinate, intimate or informal is determined by the social situation. I pointed out earlier that associative/dissociative behaviors are determined by the goal interdependence of one individual P and another O. When goals are promotive—that is, when the reaching of the goal by one person means that the other person also reaches his or her goal—cooperation is high and associative behaviors are much more probable than when there is contrient interdependence—that is, when the reaching of one person's goal precludes the reaching of the other's. In addition to the quality of interdependence, several other factors may determine whether behaviors will be associative or dissociative. For example, similarity and interpersonal attraction are likely to increase the frequency of associative rather than of dissociative behaviors. The membership of P and O in particular groups may lead to associative or dissociative behaviors; for example, when both are members of the same family, norms of cooperation are likely to prevail. Within the ingroup, behavior is much more likely to be associative than to be dissociative, although dissociative behaviors are by no means rare. In some cultures, the ingroup consists of the extended family and persons with whom an individual has developed promotive interdependence. In other cultures, it is much broader, consisting of people with similar interests, professional commitments, or ideals. Typically, in traditional cultures the ingroup is narrower than in modern industrialized cultures, stopping at the level of the family or the tribe.

The superordination dimension reflects differences in the relative power of P and O. Again, demographic characteristics can have an influence on the likelihood that behaviors will be superordinate or subordinate, since, in many societies, sex, age, family background, and other such variables are associated with superordinate or subordinate behavior.

The intimacy/formality dimension reflects, in part, the age of the relationship. Intimate behaviors, such as revealing intimate thoughts, discussing one's sex life, or discussing the members of one's family, are more likely when the P-and-O dyad has existed for a long time or when P and O suddenly find themselves isolated from the environment and with a lot of time on their hands (Altman & Taylor, 1973). In addition, people who are complete strangers and meet under circumstances that suggest that they are not likely to meet again, such as at a railway station or airport, may exchange behaviors at a level of intimacy that is higher than that between people who know that their behavior may come back to haunt them in the future. This phenomenon can be analyzed in terms of the second equation of the model. A person may be preoccupied with a personal problem but feel unable to speak about it to people he or she knows well, since this might lead to embarrassment or to other undesirable consequences. When such a person meets a stranger whom he or she will not meet again, the relationship occurs in zero time perspective, and, therefore, the cognitive component of Equation 2 drops out, since it requires a time dimension. At the same time, there are often no norms about what is an appropriate topic of conversation between strangers; at any rate, there are no groups to monitor the conversation and provide sanctions against deviance from norms. Under such conditions, the person's self-image is the only powerful aspect of the S component, while the pleasure of discussing the suppressed topic may strongly influence the affective component and determine the behavior. Thus, inhibitions about expressing oneself are dropped, in this particular situation, and a highly intimate exchange may take place.

The A Component. The A component refers to the extent to which a behavior is seen by the subject as exciting, entertaining, enjoyable, interesting, disgusting, nauseating, or depressing. Such adjectives can describe a subject's feelings relatively well. (Byrne, Fisher, Lamberth, and Mitchell, 1972, reported a study that used these adjectives to measure affect.) Topics that elicit emotional responses may also elicit a variety of behaviors consistent with such responses. For example, in extensive work on the potability of water, Dillehay, Bruvold, and Siegel (1967) reliably measured potability on a purely affective scale ranging from "horrible" and "sickening" to "delightful" and "delicious."

Fishbein (1967b) was the first to stress the significance of the affect toward the behavior as a predictor of behavior. More recent work has supported this view. For example, Weinstein (1972) shows that, while most attitude researchers use attitude toward the object rather than attitude toward the behavior as the predictor of behavior, both of these attitudes are needed for good prediction, and, in fact, attitude toward the behavior is more important.

The C Component. The C component is widely used by decision theorists and by industrial psychologists interested in the prediction of employee performance (for example, Vroom, 1964; Porter & Lawler, 1968). In most studies, subjects are asked to indicate the consequences of particular behaviors. Later, these subjects are presented with an opportunity to judge the truth of statements of the form "If I do X, Y will happen." Following this, subjects are asked to rate Y on evaluative scales such as good/bad and valuable/harmful. The probability and evaluation ratings for each Y are multiplied, and the products for the several Y's are summed. Thus, C is an index that reflects both the perceived probability that certain consequences will follow a behavior and the value of these consequences.

Heneman and Schwab (1972) and Mitchell and Biglan (1971) have provided extensive reviews of the literature that show that, under a large number of conditions, for different populations, the C component (the sum of the products of probability of a consequence times the value of the consequence) predicts behavior. For example, Jorgenson, Dunnette, and Pritchard (1973) manipulated the performance/reward contingency for a sample of male college students, with the expected effect on performance and on the perceived probability that effort is connected with pay. On the other hand, there are many conditions under which C does not predict behavior, such as when the S or the A component is more powerful.

Locke's critique of current studies clearly shows that the C component, *by itself,* is not always a sufficient predictor of behavior. Locke (1975) indicates that the C component is a version of hedonism, in which human action is seen as an attempt to maximize pleasure and minimize pain. The individual uses the course of action that he or she believes will maximize pleasure. Locke argues that this is not the only factor that determines behavior. There are circumstances in which people will do what will lead to pain, in order to do their duty, as they see it. The existence of individuals, such as St. Francis of Assisi, who deliberately renounce pleasure obviously points to the inadequacy of a theory that uses only the C component.

These kinds of arguments suggest that theories that use only the C component are inadequate. On the other hand, the extensive success of such theories in predicting some of the variance of behavior suggests that the C component is likely to be important in any adequate theory of behavior.

An illustration of the way the C component predicts actual behavior can be found in the work of three Japanese researchers (Matsui, Osawa, & Terai, 1975). They were interested in two aspects of a supervisor's behavior: *consideration* and *initiating structure* (Fleishman, Harris, & Burtt, 1955). *Consideration* involves behaviors that pay attention to the feelings of one's subordinates. *Initiating structure* concerns behaviors designed to get the work done. For example, a supervisor who sets definite goals and deadlines and checks the quality of the work is high on this behavior pattern. Both self-ratings of 150 first-line supervisors and the ratings of their subordinates were obtained. There were from 50 to 20 subordinates per supervisor.

For each of 46 items, the supervisors had to indicate, on a five-point scale, how often (from *very seldom* to *always*) they showed that behavior. Subordinates rated the frequency of their supervisor's behavior on the same 46 items. The correlations of self and subordinate descriptions of supervisor behavior were .54 for consideration and .67 for initiating structure.

The supervisors were also asked to indicate whether particular behaviors would lead to particular consequences. They were asked, for example, "Does helping subordinates with their personal problems lead to spoiling of subordinates?" Ratings were obtained on a + 4 (highly possible) to 0 (impossible) scale. These are, of course, the P_c measures. In addition, the supervisors rated the desirability of outcomes (V_c measures). They were asked, for example, whether spoiling of subordinates is extremely good (+ 4), indifferent (0), or extremely bad (− 4). By multiplying the P_c and V_c measures for each outcome and summing the products, the researchers obtained $\Sigma P_c V_c$ measures for each behavior. Since there were several behaviors representing consideration and several representing initiating action, these $\Sigma P_c V_c$ indices were further summed across behaviors—$\Sigma(\Sigma \ P_c V_c)$—to obtain a total index for the consideration and for the initiating-action behavior patterns.

The correlations between the estimates of the C component and self-ratings of behavior were .26 for the consideration and .32 for the initiating-structure behavior patterns. The correlations between the C component obtained from the supervisor and the ratings of the supervisor's behavior obtained from the subordinates were .20 for consideration and .36 for initiating structure. An interesting aspect of the data was that, at high levels of the C component for consideration, there were almost no changes in subordinate ratings of supervisors' behavior, suggesting that subordinates are only sensitive to differences in behavior when the supervisor is inconsiderate. Once a supervisor reaches a certain level of consideration, the subordinates see no more differences in the amount of consideration. The opposite effect was obtained with initiating structure. Here, at low levels of structure (C component), the subordinates gave similar ratings to the supervisors, but, at high levels of structure on the C component, the higher the level of the C component, the higher the rating on structure, and the relationship was very sharp (steep). To put it differently, an eager-beaver supervisor was rated high in initiating structure; a *somewhat* more eager supervisor was rated *extremely* high in initiating structure.

Comment. This study is interesting for several reasons. First, it is nice to have a behavior pattern rated from two points of view—the viewpoint of the supervisor and of his or her subordinates. Granted, the overlap between supervisor and subordinate ratings of supervisor behavior is not very high (there is only about 30% common variance); it is good enough to suggest to us that something real is being measured. Second, the correlations of the C component and the behavior rating are significant. Again, the relationships are not too strong, but remember that in this case there is no measure of the S or the A component. It is reasonable to assume that, had the Japanese researchers used these other components of the model and also some measures of habit and facilitating conditions, they would have predicted the behaviors much better. Third, the relatively low correlations between C measures and P_a ratings in this study are in part due to the curvilinear relationship between C and P_a. This kind of curvilinearity makes sense. One can see that, once a supervisor is considerate, increases in consideration will make little difference to the subordinates; similarly, at very low levels of initiating structure, a relaxed supervisor is seen as low on structure, and it makes little difference *how* relaxed he or she is. One can guess that the subordinate ratings reflect subordinate needs. A subordinate does not need to worry about his or her supervisor being too relaxed or too considerate. Supervisory behavior really makes a difference to the subordinate if the supervisor is not considerate enough or is too much of an eager beaver. In other words, the ratings obtained from the subordinates are not necessarily the best measures of supervisory behavior. Of course, self-ratings have problems too, since people tend to misperceive the frequency of their own behavior and to give ratings that are socially desirable. Ideally, the researchers would have used direct observations of the behavior of the supervisor. However, to get much stability, such observations would have to take place over a long period of time. To get that many observations from 150 people would have been enormously expensive. So, I can sympathize with my Japanese colleagues for not observing directly. Furthermore, even direct observations might be biased, since, when people know they are being observed, they have a tendency to behave in more socially desirable ways. To get good data, the observer has to become part of the woodwork, and that takes a lot of time and money.

Parameters Determining Differential Weighting of the Components of the Model

There are probably three sorts of parameters that can modify the weights of these components: (1) the type of behavior, (2) the type of person, and (3) the type of social setting, including the culture.

Type of behavior. The review, presented earlier, of my typology of social behavior suggests that the weights may be quite different for associative, superordinate, and intimate behaviors. Empirical demonstrations of the differential weights can be shown in the literature dealing with the question of whether race, as such, or belief dissimilarity, as such, is the basic determinant of prejudice and discrimination (see Triandis & Davis, 1965, and Triandis, 1967, for details). Rokeach, Smith, and Evans (1960) argued that belief dissimilarity is the most important determinant of prejudice. To test this idea, they asked subjects to rate stimulus persons differing from themselves in race, religion, and beliefs on scales defined by the statements "I can't see myself being friends with such a person" versus "I can very easily see myself being friends with such a person." Friendship preferences were found to be determined primarily by congruence in beliefs rather than by similarity in race or religion. I accepted these findings on the friendship variable but argued that prejudice involves more than nonacceptance as a friend (Triandis, 1961). It involves negative behaviors, such as excluding someone from one's neighborhood. In an empirical study, I showed that race rather than belief dissimilarity determines the rejection of hypothetical stimulus persons from intimate social situations.

Stein, Hardyck, and Smith (1965) presented a study designed to reconcile these differences. On some scales, they obtained a strong belief effect and on others a race effect. They concluded that both race and belief are important determinants of prejudice. Such inconsistencies (some findings stressing race and others differences in beliefs) are easily accounted for by the fact that the items used in these studies are not unidimensional. Factor-analytic studies have shown that the friendship component or factor is only one of the several dimensions of behavioral intention (Triandis, 1964).

Davis and I showed that people give different weights to belief dissimilarity and race dissimilarity, depending on the kind of behavioral intentions under investigation (Triandis & Davis, 1965). Specifically, on social behaviors that are quite intimate, all subjects rejected others on the basis of race and not on the basis of belief dissimilarity. For behaviors intermediate in intimacy, both race and belief were important. For behaviors that are formal, belief dissimilarity was the only important determinant of rejection.

Other differences in the weights, depending on the type of behavior, are suggested by experiments in which the relationship among verbal attitudes, voice tone, and behavior toward Blacks was investigated (for example, Weitz, 1972). The data show a general pattern of overt friendliness and covert rejection. The friendliness of attitude expressed on paper was negatively related to the friendliness of voice tone and to behavior directed toward Blacks, while voice tone was positively related to behavior. This suggests that the overt cues are under S control in the environment of a "liberal" White college in the North but that the covert cues are under H control. The behaviors used in this experiment were (1) the selection of a task requiring different levels of close interaction with another person, (2) the subject's choice when asked whether he or she wished to wait with or apart from the others, (3) the subject's willingness to return for future interaction, and (4) the placement of chairs. Thus, in this experiment, we have evidence of differences among specific behaviors in terms of determination by the S or H component.

Type of Person. Much evidence of individual differences in the weights of the normative and affective components has been provided by Fishbein and Ajzen (1975). They review a number of studies that show sharp differences. For example, in one study, students were asked about their intention to engage in premarital sexual intercourse. These intentions were predicted from the affective component (regression weight of .76) better than from the normative component (weight of .23), in the case of females, and better by the normative component (.95) than by the affective (regression weight of zero), in the case of males.

Davis and I found that the relationship between social stimulus and behavior depends on the kind of person behaving (Triandis & Davis, 1965). Some people were particularly sensitive to the race differences and were called "conventionally prejudiced" in our study, while others were particularly sensitive to belief dissimilarity and were called "belief prejudiced." The conventionally prejudiced showed greater rejection of Blacks in situations of intermediate intimacy than did other subjects and gave some importance to race in formal situations. The belief prejudiced did not show this pattern. In short, knowing both the type of response that the subject is asked to make and the type of person making the response is essential in order to understand the relative weights that are given to race and belief. Replications of the essential aspects of this study by Insko and Robinson (1967) and Goldstein and Davis (1972) suggest that this conclusion is quite firm. However, the matter is further complicated by the fact that it is likely that racial prejudice leads to anticipated belief differences and anticipated belief differences lead to racial prejudice (Dienstbier, 1972).

Highly authoritarian subjects are likely to use higher weights than less authoritarian subjects for the S component (Kirscht & Dillehay, 1967). They tend to behave in ways that they perceive to be consistent with the norms of their ingroup to a greater extent than subjects low in authoritarianism.

As discussed earlier in this chapter, there are also individual differences in willingness to delay gratification (Mischel, 1974). Persons who are unwilling to delay gratification may emphasize the A component more than the other components.

Finally, there are individual differences in the extent to which people are internally controlled (Rotter, 1966). Those who are internally controlled tend to persuade, while those externally controlled tend to use power (force) when faced with the problem of how to influence another (Goodstadt & Hjelle, 1973). Presumably, this reflects different expections about being successful when using persuasion. Those who are internally controlled see a strong connection between what they do and its consequences; that is, they emphasize the C component (Broedling, 1975). External control apparently is a complex variable that has four separate dimensions: belief in a difficult world, belief in an unjust world, belief in a world that is governed by luck, and belief in a world that is politically unresponsive (Collins, 1974). The first dimension is measured by items such as "Sometimes I feel that I don't have enough control over the direction my life is taking" and "Most people don't realize the extent to which their lives are controlled by accidental happenings" and reflects the belief that there is little connection between what one does and what happens to one. This is related to a small emphasis on the C component. The next two dimensions (belief in an unjust world and in luck) have little to do with the strength of the C component because they do not concern connections between behavior and outcomes. However, the last dimension, political responsiveness, does concern this component but is limited to behaviors that have political significance.

Among the hard-core unemployed Blacks in the U.S., there is an orientation that has been called ecosystem distrust (Triandis, 1976). It involves distrust of people, things, and institutions in one's environment. The orientation includes moderate to small connections between behavior and consequences, which suggests that these people are not sure that behavior has clear consequences. I argue that the orientation develops when parents promise a toy or special event and find themselves unable to deliver it because of a lack of resources, when rewards are decided by social agencies or governments in apparently mysterious ways, and when most outcomes are negative because of discrimination. It is reasonable for ecosystem distrust to arise from these experiences. For this group, much behavior *is* disconnected from consequences. The reality in which they live calls for distrust of others and for distrust of institutions. It is reasonable for these people to reject authority figures and to feel powerless. The person with ecosystem distrust will deemphasize the C component and, in all probability, will emphasize the A component.

One of the broad personality syndromes isolated in recent years is called *modernity* (Inkeles & Smith, 1974). Modern people have a particular pattern of attitudes and values. Modernity, as defined by Inkeles and Smith, includes (a) openness to new experience, (b) readiness for change, (c) a predisposition to form and hold many opinions on many topics, (d) interest in the world, (e) concern with the here and now and the future rather than with the past, (f) a belief in the ability of human beings to control nature, (g) emphasis on long-range planning, (h) willingness to trust others, (j) positive evaluation of technical skills, (k) an emphasis on education and skills, (l) an emphasis on the rights of weaker people, and (m) an analytic perspective. This syndrome should correlate with emphasis on the C component, since many of its elements (particularly e, f, g, h, and m) reflect aspects of this component.

Type of Situation. Situational factors may increase the weight of the S component. For example, if the individual is under threat or if the connection between a norm and a behavior is clearly visible, the weight of the S component will be great.

Threat presumably increases the tendency of the individual to do what authority figures dictate. Fromm's suggestion that the rise of Nazism was an attempt to "escape from freedom" under the extreme stress brought about by adverse economic and political conditions in the Weimar republic, or the finding that, when economic conditions are adverse, people tend to join authoritarian churches (Sales, 1972) may be interpreted in this manner.

When the connection between a norm and a behavior is clear, the person cannot ignore the norm. If the behavior is covert or the connection unclear, the person can ignore the norm. Hence, the weight of the S component is greater when there is an obvious relationship between the norm and the behavior.

The weight is higher in situations in which the visibility of the behavior can make deviation from the norm easily identifiable. In such situations, the group can easily impose sanctions, and, therefore, the S component is likely to be given much weight. In a recent study by Boyanowsky and Allen (1973), an investigation of the contributions of race and belief factors in social interaction showed that prejudiced White subjects discriminated against Blacks on all tasks calling for self-description, and the effect was magnified under conditions of ingroup surveillance (by other Whites) with threat of censure. In short, the possibility of ingroup retaliation made itself felt on those behaviors on which surveillance was possible; on those on which there was no surveillance, this influence was not observed. A similar study by Warner and DeFleur (1969) took explicit note of the extent to which a behavior is likely to be known to other people and showed larger weights of the S component in situations in which the behavior was known. These writers used the concept of social constraint, which is similar to the idea of visibility of norm-governed behavior. The attitude under study was prejudice toward Blacks. The overt behavior under observation was a response to a letter that was received by several hundred subjects. This letter came in several versions, all requesting the recipient to sign a pledge and mail this pledge back to the sender. The pledges committed the subjects to engage in one of several varieties of behavior involving Blacks. These behaviors ranged from dating a Black to making an anonymous contribution to a Black charity. Obviously, the visibility of the dating behavior is very high; doing something anonymously is least visible. For each condition of the experiment, the researchers subtracted the percent of the subjects refusing to comply with the request from the percent complying with the request. For the least-prejudiced subjects and the low-visibility condition, this index was 21%. For the most prejudiced in the low-visibility condition, it was 4%. For the most prejudiced in the high-visibility condition, it was −69%. The difference between the +4 and the −69 is obviously dramatic. It shows clearly that the visibility of behavior does influence compliance rates.

Part Summary

The findings of the Triandis and Davis (1965) study can be described in terms of the model. For intimate behavior between members of different races, the S component is strong; the norms about it are definite and are likely to be very powerful in determining behavioral intentions and behavior. For other kinds of behavior, such as association, the norms are not strong; the anticipated rewards and costs from the interaction with a member of another race, rather than the norms, will now be the important determinants of behavior. In other words, the affective and the cognitive components will be stronger than the social. If a person anticipates that the other will be dissimilar in beliefs, the C component will make dissociative behaviors more probable. If the person experiences a negative emotion at the thought of a member of another race, this will activate the A component and lead to avoidance.

If a White man and a Black woman decide to marry, the chances are, given the American norms, that the two families will object. If the families have enough influence to prevent the marriage, the social component will have dominated the behavior. However, if the positive emotions of the pair are very strong, the affective component may overwhelm the social. The perceived consequences of getting married may include anticipations of future social difficulties, as well as visions of a long and happy life together. The relative strengths of these and other anticipations will finally determine the strength of the C component. The three components together will determine the behavioral intention.

The importance of the weights of the three components is determined by personality variables. Some people (such as those high on the F scale) give much weight to the social component, others give weight to the affective component, and still others weight the cognitive component. Belief-prejudiced people are those who anticipate very negative experiences from interaction with persons who have dissimilar beliefs. When the dissimilar-belief cue (for example, a member of another race) is present, the belief-prejudiced person may have a negative C component for many possible behaviors.

CULTURE AND BEHAVIOR

A major taxonomy of culture by Lomax and Berkowitz (1972) was based on the Human Relations Area Files and on recordings of songs and dances from a wide range of cultures. Specifically, a thousand cultures were examined, and 4000 recorded song performances from 400 cultures were analyzed. Both sets of data suggested that the major dimension in the taxonomy be *differentiation*. At the lowest level of differentiation are African gatherers and at the highest level are modern European and the older, higher cultures (for example, India). At the intermediate levels of differentiation are the Australian gatherers, Siberian cultures, and American Indian cultures and a little higher are the Polynesian, Melanesian, and Black African cultures.

In the cultures low in differentiation, food is obtained mostly by gathering or fishing, settlements are small, social stratification is nonexistent or low, and there is an absence of high gods. In high cultures, agriculture and cattle milking are the chief sources of food, settlements are large, stratification is complex, and high gods are important.

There are two variables that may change the strength of the social component, as a society is characterized by higher and higher levels of complexity. First is the need for some groups to impose their views on other groups. When a society is simple and homogeneous there is no such need. As a society gets to be more complex, groups pressure each other more. In a society such as the U.S., pressures exist between many groups—between consumer and producer, farmer and worker, politician and citizen, labor and management, teacher and student, and so on. In short, this cross-pressures variable is linearly related to complexity and causes the strength of the S component to increase with complexity. The second variable is the size of groups. In simple societies, groups tend to be small and can impose their norms with little social pressure. In more complex societies, groups tend to be larger, but in very complex societies groups are again smaller. For example, extended families are found in societies that are relatively high in complexity, but in extremely complex societies the nuclear family is again the norm. Thus, the second variable has an inverted U relationship to complexity. Small groups do not have to impose norms as much as large groups because they can allow their members much individual freedom without this leading to disruption of the group. Thus, at low levels of complexity and at very high levels of complexity, we expect smaller strengths of the social component. We therefore speculate that the relationship is as shown in Figure 7.2. In other words, the S component will increase with cultural complexity, so that African gatherers will have a weak S component and Australian gatherers will have a somewhat stronger one. Black African cultures will have a strong S component

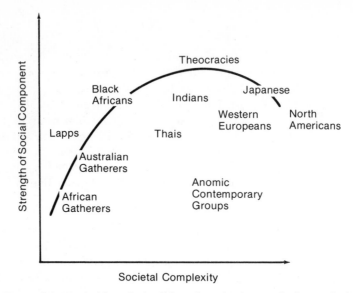

Figure 7.2 Probable relationship of societal complexity and the strength of the social component.

and India a very strong one; in Western Europe and North America, it will be strong, with certain samples that show anomie having a weak component.

The highest levels of the S component occur in theocratic cultures, which Pelto (1968) has characterized as "tight." As mentioned in Chapter 1, in tight cultures, interpersonal behavior is often formal, orderly, unemotional, and cooperative. People are docile and conforming. The Hutterites and the Japanese have relatively tight societies, in Pelto's classification. Loose societies are characterized by individualistic, expressive behaviors with little regimentation; norms have wide ranges of alternatives, departure from norms is tolerated, and there is little development of organization and solidarity. Typical cultures include those of the Lapps and the Thais. The tightest cultures are theocracies, which show corporate control of property, corporate ownership of stored food and of production power, religious leaders, hereditary recruitment into priesthood, high levels of taxation, and so on. The loose societies do not meet most of these criteria.

Determinants of tightness, according to Pelto, include unilateral kinship (only the father or the mother determines a person's identity), dependence on food crops (versus hunting or herding), and high population density. One can argue that, when there is unilateral kinship, norms can be sharper, while, in bilateral kinship situations, norms can conflict; thus, the S component is stronger in unilateral situations. Dependence on food crops means that the group must cooperate in such tasks as developing an irrigation system and, therefore, is more likely to have a complex social organization in which norms are clearly stated and strongly imposed. In a hunting and herding society, such norms are not quite as important for the survival of the group, so that lower strengths in the *S* component can be tolerated.

Finally, high population density means that people are likely to run into each other and produce difficulties for other people unless their behavior is strictly governed by norms. In short, the taxonomy proposed by Pelto suggests that the tight cultures are high on the *S* component while the loose cultures are not. The relationship between tightness and differentiation is positive; however, it is suspected that, at very high levels of differentiation, tightness breaks down. Thus, modern industrial societies are not as tight as theocracies and do not impose norms as clearly as do the tightest of societies on record.

Blumberg and Winch (1972) found that familial complexity was minimal when the society was either very low or very high in complexity. That means that hunting and gathering societies and urban industrial societies have similar levels of familial complexity, generally adopting the nuclear family and giving the individual a good deal of freedom for his or her behavior. In short, hunting, gathering, and urban industrial societies appear to utilize the *S* component less strongly than traditional agricultural societies. Maximum familial complexity was found in societies with agriculture that used irrigation and had a system of hereditary aristocracy and one or two levels of political hierarchy beyond the local community. One can visualize such societies as sufficiently integrated to impose the norms developed by the hereditary aristocracy, while not so complex as to lose the possibility of imposing sanctions on those who deviate from those norms.

Variations in Value Orientations

Many social scientists believe that variations in value orientation are the most important type of cultural variations and therefore the central feature of the structure of culture (for example, Kluckhohn & Strodtbeck, 1961, p. 28). Among the major variations in such orientations are the five discussed by Kluckhohn and Strodtbeck. (1) Is innate human nature basically evil, good and evil, or good? Is innate human nature mutable or immutable? (2) Is the relation of people to nature one of subjugation, harmony, or mastery? (3) What is the temporal focus? Is human nature oriented toward the past, the present, or the future? (4) What is the action orientation of people? Is it toward intensive appreciation of experience (being), toward total development of the person (being-in-becoming) or toward accomplishment (action)? (5) What is the human orientation toward other humans? Are people to do what seems right to them (individualism), what is mandated by their social group (collaterality), or what is correct from the point of view of the elites of their social group (lineality)?

In different cultures, one finds different profiles of these value orientations. For example, Americans place the greatest emphasis on individualism, then on collaterality, and then on lineality. The future is emphasized more than the present and the present more than the past. Mastery over nature is valued more than subjugation to or harmony with nature. The stress is on doing rather than being. Human nature is evil but mutable. This last orientation tends to lead to particular emphases, such as the great reliance on legislation to change people from evil to good and on education to change the ignorant into well-informed citizens. The American use of legislation and education as a panacea for social problems appears ridiculous to people from some other countries. The emphasis on individualism results in the glorification of private enterprise and in suspicion of schemes that depend on group action. The emphasis on the future and the deemphasis of the past result in the continuous rebuilding of cities, the construction of relatively impermanent houses, the continuous cycle of changing car models, and appliances with built-in obsolescence. The mastery-over-nature orientation results in broad modifications of the face of the landscape, as exemplified so well by the U.S. Corps of Engineers and their penchant for building dams redirecting the flow of rivers, creating artificial lakes, and so on. In other cultures, people feel perfectly happy to adjust to the natural contours of their environment. A brochure describing a newly constructed bridge in the Austrian Alps boasted that it had been built in harmony with nature. Doing rather than being or being-in-becoming results in emphasis on accomplishment rather than on aesthetic experience. Thus, people who change the immediate material world, such as business leaders and industrialists in the U.S., are often honored much more than those who have made great cultural or intellectual contributions, such as musicians or painters. For most Americans, Henry Ford has made a greater contribution than George Gershwin.

Variations in values are of course reflected primarily in the V_c element of the C component. Behaviors that lead to legislation or education, for instance, will be valued because of their connections with these outcomes. The emphasis on the future makes the C component, which has a temporal dimension in it, important. Emphasis on individualism makes the self-concept more important than roles or norms as a determinant of behavioral intentions.

In short, while the major implication of different value orientations concerns the kinds of values that will be important as consequences of action (V_c), an additional factor is the variation in the weights of the S, A, and C components. The values emphasized by different societies determine, in part, the weights of the S, A, and C components. For example, a society that emphasizes the being orientation is likely to have many people who give a large weight to the A component.

Interactions of Culture, Person, and Behavior

The weights of the model are not only determined by culture, personality, and the type of behavior, but also by the interactions of these three. A good illustration comes from the work of the Whitings. Whiting and Whiting (1975) studied social behaviors in children by means of five-minute observations, made over a period of several months, in six cultures. One variable of interest was the child's culture. Two aspects of the culture were important: whether the culture was complex or simple and whether the family was nuclear or nonnuclear.

Complexity of culture was indexed in this study by the number of different occupations, differentiation in settlement patterns, political centralization, degree of social stratification, and degree of religious specialization. Children in simple cultures had mothers who were much busier than mothers in complex cultures. When the mothers are busy, they assign more chores to the children, including taking care of the younger children. Thus, in simple cultures, children do much more child rearing than in complex ones. Children who have child-rearing responsibilities learn to give particularistic resources (love, status, and so on) much more than children who do not have such responsibilities. The result is that, in complex societies, the observations of interaction showed children who were much more likely to take than to give resources, while, in simple cultures, children were much more likely to give than to take resources.

In nuclear families, interaction tends to be more intimate than in nonnuclear families. Thus, children raised in cultures with nuclear families were observed to engage in more intimate interactions than children raised in other kinds of families. The U.S. was characterized by complexity and the nuclear family, so children were likely to take intimate resources (that is, act sociably, seek dominance, seek help). The children from northern India and Okinawa were likely to take nonintimate resources (seek attention, reprimand). Amerindians from Mexico and a sample from the Philippines were likely to give intimate resources (horseplay, touch). Children from an East African sample were likely to give nonintimate resources (suggest responsibility, assault).

The sex and age (3 to 6 versus 7 to 11) of the actor were relevant for certain kinds of behaviors. Finally, the status of the target of social action was also important. Targets were classified as infants, peers, parents, and older adults. A regression analysis suggests that the culture, the characteristics of the actor, the characteristics of the target, and their *interactions* with the type of behavior determine the frequency of behavior. For example, for intimate dependent behaviors, such as seeking help and touching, both culture (complex more than simple) and the target (parents more than others) determined the frequency. In the case of dominance and dependence (seeks dominance, seeks attention), only culture (complex more than simple) was relevant. In the case of nurturance (offers help, offers support), culture, the actor, and the target were important. Simple cultures showed this behavior more than complex cultures, girls showed it more than boys, and when the target was an infant there was more of this behavior than when the target was a peer or an adult. In the case of aggressive behaviors (assaults, insults), culture had some relevance (there was more in nonnuclear), status had relevance (more for young boys), and the target was important (more toward peers). In the case of prosocial behavior (suggests responsibility), both culture (more for non-nuclear) and the actor's age (more for older) were important. In the case of sociability, both culture and the target were important; there was more sociability in cultures with nuclear than with nonnuclear families and less when the target was an infant or a peer than when the target was an adult.

In short, this study shows a highly complex pattern of findings, in which culture, the characteristics of the actor, and the characteristics of the target of action interacted with the type of behavior. This complexity is exactly what the model was designed to handle. Data collected to test the model can be analyzed separately by actor, target, and behavior; we expect the weights of the components of the model to differ across such analyses.

An Experimental Suppression of Components

In an intriguing experiment by Gergen, Gergen, and Barton (1973), several students were put in a room in which there was absolutely no light. They were given no instructions on what to do, and they were observed and photographed with infrared cameras. Their behavior was compared with that of similar groups that operated in a lighted room. Furthermore, some of the groups were explicitly assured that no one in the dark room would meet again at any time in the future. This constitutes an experimental suppression of the S and the C components, since the students had no norms about how they should behave or any expectations for the consequences of their behavior; thus, the behavior would be controlled only by the A component. It was found that 90% of the students purposely touched others, 50% hugged another, and 80% became sexually aroused. It is not difficult to see that these behaviors would have positive affective correlates and therefore be under the control of the A component. When the lights were put on, the frequency of these behaviors dropped dramatically, to 0% on touching and hugging and 30% on sexual arousal.

OTHER MODELS

There are many theoretical models that have features that are similar to those of the model presented in Chapter 1. For example, as mentioned earlier in this chapter, the well-known Freudian analysis of the personality as consisting of id, ego, and superego elements has some similarity to the argument that the *A, C,* and *S* components, respectively, determine behavioral intentions. However, Freud was interested in unconscious behavior even more than in conscious behavior. I consider behavior that is under habit control to be unconscious (unintentional), and, although there is a superficial resemblance between the model and Freud's conceptions, the differences are much greater than the similarities.

The one model that is very similar to mine is Fishbein's, which is not surprising, since it was developed at the University of Illinois in response to work done by Dulany (1962) and by me (Triandis, 1964). My model incorporates many of the innovations proposed by Fishbein, such as an emphasis on affect toward the behavior rather than on the object of the behavior.

The Fishbein Model

Earlier in the chapter, I summarized the main conclusions of the Ajzen and Fishbein (1973) paper. I also mentioned the general form of their model, which states that behavior is predicted from behavioral intentions. Behavioral intentions are a consequence of (a) the attitude toward the act (*Aact*) and (b) normative beliefs (*NB*) about the likelihood that members of the actor's reference group expect the actor to perform the behavior in question, multiplied by the individual's motivation to comply (*Mc*) with each of *i* different expectations. In symbols:

$$\text{Intention} = w_0\,(Aact) + w_1\,[\ \sum_{i=1}^{n} NB_i(Mc_i)],$$

where $Aact = \sum\limits_{i=1}^{n} B_i a_i$, B_i is the strength of beliefs associated with various outcomes of the behavior, a_i is the evaluation of these outcomes, n is the number of beliefs, *NB* is the normative beliefs about the expectations of the reference groups, *Mc* is the motivation to comply with each of these expectations, *i* is an index that goes from 1 to *n* beliefs, and w_0 and w_1 are weights determined from a multiple regression analysis. The studies reviewed by Ajzen and Fishbein indicate that, under highly controlled laboratory conditions, a large portion of the variance of behavior is controlled by the *Aact* and normative components.

Fishbein's model differs from mine in certain respects. First, the two models have somewhat different purposes. Fishbein is interested in account-

ing for the most variance with the fewest variables. I'm just interested in accounting for the most variance. The orientations are in part a matter of
perspective. I believe that accounting for all variance is important because
even a small amount of variance may be socially important, if the phenomenon is a critical one. Second, there are three specific differences between the
models:

1. Equation 1 of my model explicitly takes into account habits and facilitating conditions, while Fishbein simply writes that behavior is approximately a function of behavioral intentions.

2. My model considers roles, the self-image, and interpersonal agreements, none of which is considered in the Fishbein model. Fishbein assumes
that the influence of such variables will be felt through the attitude toward
the act and the normative component.

3. My model uses the *affect* toward the behavior as a separate element.
Fishbein argues that the affect toward the behavior is usually the same as the
sum of the perceived consequences times the value of the consequences.

While Fishbein's position on this third difference may be true in cases
in which behavior is completely rational, it is probably not so under conditions of irrational behavior, phobias, disliked behaviors, or conflicting
goals. For example, if a mother believes that her child will improve his behavior if she spanks him, she may experience the behavior of spanking as extremely unpleasant, while at the same time perceiving the consequences
of the behavior in a very positive light. When the subject thinks about the
behavior, the affective component A taps the emotional response. That
response is not necessarily under rational control (that is, controlled by
considerations of consequences), except in laboratory situations in which the
behaviors are "thought through" and are associated with very little conflict.

For a different example, consider most phobias. The subject is responding to an object with an affective response that the subject himself or
herself can identify as irrational. Typically, the individual says "I know this
is stupid, but I can't do that" or "I know this is stupid, but I am afraid of
that." When the person admits that it is "stupid," he or she is really saying
that there is no rational basis for the action; but, nevertheless, the response is
highly emotional.

To consider each of the differences between the models, then, let's first
consider Equation 1. It seems desirable to be more specific than Fishbein is
about how behavioral intentions relate to behavior. Obviously, there is much
we do not yet know, particularly about the best way to combine information about facilitating conditions, but research is more likely to take place
if a clear statement of what is expected is presented. Furthermore, there is
enough empirical support for the idea that habits or intentions may be the
only determinants of behavior that it is essential to bring this fact into the
open. Finally, it is clear that, in some cases, both habits and intentions are

important, and my analysis has indicated why the relative weights of habits and intentions change, over time, for a behavior.

Second, the normative component of Fishbein's model does, generally, very well in predicting behavioral intentions. However, there are some samples, such as lower-class Mexican women, whose personal moral beliefs are more important than societal norms in determining behavioral intentions. Furthermore, our understanding of the social component is as yet very poor. It would be premature to freeze on a particular form of it and collect data relevant only to that form. Fishbein has done a great service in providing a normative component that does well in predicting intentions, but further work is needed to see how it can be improved. Clearly, this is possible, at least for certain behaviors and certain samples. My formulation is intentionally vague, to encourage further research and avoid premature freezing on a particular form.

Third, the distinction between the affect and cognitive components seems justified by the study of Adamopoulos and Brinberg, which we reviewed earlier. Recall that those who participated in a psychological experiment gave a strong weight only to the cognitive component; those who did not participate gave a strong weight only to the affective component. This would not have been discovered if these components had not been kept separate.

In summary, while the Fishbein model provides an excellent benchmark for further research, my model improves on it in at least three respects, and additional research should lead to even more improvements.

Competitive Tests of the Various Models

An extensive program of research testing the Fishbein model has been summarized by Ajzen and Fishbein (1973). Comparisons of the Fishbein model with my model were made by Davidson (1973). Jaccard and Davidson (in press) present a comparative analysis of the two models, using U.S. data. Jaccard, Davidson, Triandis, Morales, and Diaz-Guerrero (1975) presented a similar analysis with Mexican data. The general results indicate that both models do well in predicting behavioral intentions, although, with lower-socioeconomic-class samples, my model tends to account for more of the variance, while with upper-socioeconomic-class samples, the Fishbein model is to be preferred. The same investigators are currently checking the utility of the models in predicting actual behavior.

Comparisons of the Fishbein model with a model suggested by Wicker (1969) were presented by Brislin and Omstead (1973). The study obtained somewhat more support for the Wicker model; however, Fishbein (1973) has objected to the measurement of some of the variables of his model. Brislin and Omstead concluded that several additional variables must be taken into account, and they explicitly list habits, facilitating conditions, perceived control over the environment, knowledge, and involvement.

There is currently an active effort to test various aspects of these models in different parts of the world. When these tests have been completed, important changes can be expected in the present model that will sharpen its utility.

SUMMARY

This chapter began with a detailed discussion of Equations 1 and 2 of the model. Then evidence supporting the two equations was reviewed. In regard to the first equation, it was shown that behavioral intentions are the most important predictors for new, untried, and unlearned behaviors; habits predict behaviors that have been overlearned or that are carried out by emotionally aroused subjects. In addition, I showed that such facilitating conditions as ability and arousal can affect the likelihood that a behavior will occur. In regard to the second equation, empirical evidence was given for the effect of each component on behavioral intentions. The social component is most important when the behavior is visible and when a person is highly socialized and has developed strong moral views. In societies that are high in complexity, the social component is strong, while, in societies in which there is much anomie, it is weak. The importance of the cognitive component is great when the connection between behavior and its consequences is reliable, consistent, and frequent in a particular environment. When the social or cognitive elements are not important, the affective component becomes particularly strong.

It was shown that the weights of the components of the equations depend on the type of behavior, person, and social setting. More specifically, the effect of culture on behavior was examined, and it was found that the culture, the actor, and the target of the behavior interact with the type of behavior to determine the frequency of the behavior.

Finally, some other models were discussed and some competitive tests described.

8

CHANGING
THE INTERPERSONAL
RELATIONSHIP

So far, we have analyzed the characteristics of the stimulus person (O) and the way these are perceived, categorized, and reacted to by the perceiver (P). We have discussed P's responses in terms of attributions, affect, and overt acts and have seen that implicit personality theories held by P have an effect on the way stimuli are processed.

Now we can turn to the ways in which the relationship between P and O can be modified. For example, if P and O are married to each other and feel that they have a bad marriage, what can they do to change that situation? We'll begin by discussing how change is viewed from the theoretical vantage point provided by my model.

General Considerations Concerning Changes in Interpersonal Relationships

There are three kinds of training that we may expose people to in order to change them. *Attribution training* occurs when we change the typical attributions that a person makes about the causes of his or her own behavior or of the behavior of others. *Affective training* occurs when we change the way a person feels about himself or herself, about other people, or about behaviors. *Behavior modification* occurs when we change either the consequences a person expects from his or her behavior or the value of these consequences. Behavior modification also works through changing habits by associating rewards or punishments with a behavior.

One's cognitions about interpersonal behavior in general and one's cognitions about one's actual behavior constitute a system of cognitions that tends toward balance. People prefer consistency (Abelson et al., 1968); inconsistent cognitive structures tend to be unstable. When people are aware that their actions have been inconsistent with their cognitions about interpersonal behavior, they are likely to change their cognitions. This is particularly true if they are aware that their actions were intentional, that they did not feel forced to act, and that they were committed to their actions (ego-involved). For example, if a person is induced to behave in a manner inconsistent with his or her attitudes, the inconsistency between behavior and attitudes will lead to changes in attitudes. The psychological domains in which the specific changes may occur are suggested by the second equation: $I = w_S S + w_A A + w_C C$. Actors can convince themselves that others approve of their actions, that the actions are particularly appropriate for them, that the actions are enjoyable, or that the actions have positive consequences.

We can easily conceive of several additional kinds of change. First, consider what happens when the S component changes, which can happen when (a) a person changes membership groups, which often implies a change in norms, (b) when a person is promoted or married or becomes a parent (role changes), and (c) when the self-concept changes. Self-concepts are very difficult to change, but certain types of therapists concentrate much of their work on attempts to change them. Second, consider changes in the A component, due to the associations of a behavior with positive and negative events. This association can "condition" the behavior to be affectively positive or negative. Third, consider changes in the C component, due to various events that follow the particular behavior at different times. These consequences may be dependable and clear (high P_c) or undependable and unclear (low P_c) and desirable ($+ V_c$) or undesirable ($- V_c$).

Behavior modification is an approach that is now widely used to achieve change. Typically, the therapist puts the patient in a situation in which the patient receives rewards after certain kinds of behaviors and not after others. Certain behaviors, then, become closely connected with rewards (high P_c), and others lose their connections with rewards (become extinguished). Frequent and prolonged association of the behavior with rewards increases the probability that the behavior will occur. Temporal factors are very important here. In the case of the conditioning of affect, a pleasant event may occur either before or after the behavior but must be in *close* temporal contiguity. In order for the C component to change, the reward must be seen by the person as a consequence of the behavior. However, the time lapse may be long, such as, for example, the nine months connecting sexual intercourse with the expected arrival of a child.

Many events that change an interpersonal relationship can be conceived of as rewards. In an earlier discussion, I pointed out that giving a resource such as love, status, or information is rewarding. Acting toward the other in a manner that is slightly more rewarding than the other expects is maximally rewarding. Agreeing, approving, supporting, or smiling are among the behaviors that a therapist often will use to achieve personal change.

Changes in the components of the model can occur because of the direct experiences that a person has (which modify the A and C components), because of messages received from others (which modify the S and C components), or because of observations of what happens to others (which also may modify the S and C components). The next section is concerned with the way messages are likely to influence the person.

The Impact of Messages

Traditional analyses of the attitude-change process (summarized in Triandis, 1971, Chapters 7 and 8) deal with five stages: (1) *attention,* which concerns whether P becomes aware of changes in his or her environment involving some source of attitude change and/or some message, (2) *comprehension,* which deals with P's understanding of the message, (3) *yielding,* which concerns whether P agrees with the message, (4) *retention,* which involves whether P remembers, at a point in time that is particularly propitious for action, that he or she has agreed with the message, and (5) *action*, which deals with the behavioral manifestations of the attitude change. (See McGuire, 1969, for details.)

For each stage of the attitude-change process, we must consider four elements in order to determine whether a change will occur at that particular stage. The four elements are the source, the medium, the message, and the audience. Sources may be particular individuals. The medium may be a person, a printed page, radio, or television. Messages can vary in style, structure, and content (Triandis, 1971, pp. 182ff.). Audiences can vary on many dimensions, the most relevant of which are their attitudes, the functional bases for holding these attitudes (why they hold them), and their intelligence and interpersonal adjustment. Katz (1960) has described four bases for holding attitudes. The *instrumental, adjustive-utilitarian* basis is the person's tendency to maximize rewards. For example, a worker may hold particular attitudes about unions because unions maximize her income. The *ego-defensive* basis is people's tendency to protect themselves from acknowledging uncomplimentary truths about themselves. For example, a person may have negative attitudes toward athletes to protect himself from the truth that he is crippled. The *value-expressive* basis for attitudes is associated with the idea that an attitude reveals a basic value. For example, a person who has the value orientation that human nature is basically evil may have positive attitudes toward imprisonment. The *knowledge-function* basis is the person's need to understand the universe and to predict events. For example, a person may have a positive attitude toward the U.S. Government Printing Office because, in the past, she obtained from that office much inexpensive literature that helped her understand how the government works.

Different approaches to attitude change are appropriate, depending on which function is the basis for the attitude that is to be changed. For example, information approaches are most effective when a knowledge function is underlying the attitude. Changing the individual's reference and membership group may be most effective when a utilitarian function is served. Self-insight, which can sometimes occur as a result of psychotherapy, is appropriate when an ego-defensive or value-expressive function underlies the attitude. In short, information is not always effective in changing attitudes, because only when the basis of the attitude is a need for knowledge is such an approach likely to work.

Maximum attention is likely to be observed when a competent or expert source sends a message loaded with information that meets the needs of an audience holding an attitude based on knowledge function. For example, if an audience of U.S. citizens needs to understand how an aspect of their federal government works, and an expert on the subject gives a message that contains this information, it is quite likely that the audience will attend to the message.

Other combinations of source characteristics and audience characteristics have powerful effects on the outcome of the attention stage of attitude change. Specifically, the likelihood of attention is high when a powerful source, who is able to give rewards to the audience, presents a message explaining how the audience may obtain such rewards. Such an approach to attitude change will work best when the basis for the attitude is instrumental-adjustive. A familiar source, one that presents the case in a confident and dynamic manner, a source that is physically attractive, or one that has been associated with previous rewards also can create attention. An attractive source giving a message that is consistent with the ego-defensive aspects of an attitude to a highly ego-defensive audience is also likely to be attended. A message that begins with a pleasant communication may lead to great attention, while one that has an unpleasant or strongly anxiety-producing component may lead to inattention. An intelligent audience is more likely to attend than an unintelligent audience, and a neurotic audience is less likely to attend than one that is not neurotic. Finally, a face-to-face relationship between source and audience is more likely to encourage attention than one involving a written message or a televised communication.

Comprehension is maximized when the source presents a clear, well-organized message that fits the categories and ways of thinking of the audience. A message that draws conclusions is more likely to be comprehended than one that requires the audience to draw the conclusions. A face-to-face medium is good for comprehension because it allows the audience to ask questions for clarification. Finally, an intelligent audience is more likely to comprehend than an unintelligent audience. Some early work by me (Triandis, 1959, 1960) showed that, the greater the similarity in the dimensions used by a source and an audience in analyzing their experiences in a particular domain of meaning, the clearer the communication for the particular audience. More recent work by Back, Bunker, and Dunnagan (1972) has further substantiated this point by showing that people who have communication difficulties react to key terms differently. For example, a group of scientists and theologians discussing social issues and having different meanings for the words *model, knowledge,* and *manipulate* found it extremely difficult to have a productive discussion.

Yielding becomes likely when the source is attractive, associated with previous rewards, and/or objective. There also tends to be yielding when the focus of the message is clear and the message advocates a good deal of change or when the message arouses fear. A face-to-face medium is more likely than a less personal medium to lead to yielding, and an insecure audience, of less than average intelligence, is more likely than a secure, intelligent audience to yield.

Retention requires repetition. This can more easily be done on television than in a face-to-face relationship and for a simple message than for a complex one. An audience that is intelligent (its members having good memories) is more likely—and quicker—to retain the message than an unintelligent audience.

Action is most probable when the other components of the model are consistent with the attitude change. Specifically, when norms, roles, self-image, and interpersonal contracts (in other words, the elements of the S component) are consistent with the new attitude, behavior may reflect the attitude. It is obvious that, when inconsistencies exist, the behavior may or may not take place, depending on the weight of the S component in relation to the weights of the A and C components or the weight of the habit component in relation to the behavioral-intentions component. Messages that include details on how to act and urge action in specific terms are more likely to lead to action than more vague messages. A powerful source who will reward future compliance, particularly if it belongs to an ingroup that emits norms consistent with the action is likely to be complied with. Action is most likely when a powerful source is involved or in face-to-face relations in which rewards for conformity to the source are salient.

A summary of the attitude-change factors we've been discussing is provided in Table 8.1. The table shows the source, medium, message, and audience characteristics that facilitate attitude change at each of the five stages. As can be seen from this table, several of the factors that have a positive effect on attitude change at one stage do not have a positive

Table 8.1   Elements of Attitude-Change Processes

	Attention	Comprehension	Yielding	Retention	Action
Source	Expert (competent) Powerful (confident) Familiar Attractive	Clear	Attractive Associated with rewards Objective	Repetitious	Powerful Is member of audience's ingroup and norms of ingroup are consistent with the action Looks over audience's shoulder
Medium	Face-to-face	Face-to-face	Face-to-face	Television	Face-to-face
Message	Draws conclusions Begins with pleasant communication	Fits audience categories Draws conclusions	When issue clear, advocates much change Arouses fear	Simple and repetitious	Urges specific action Gives details of how to act
Audience	Needs are met High IQ	High IQ	Low IQ	High IQ (good memory)	Norms, roles, self-image consistent with behavior that has been yielded to Behavior arouses positive affect Behavior is connected with positive consequences

effect—and may have a negative one—at another stage. For example, an intelligent audience is more likely to attend and less likely to yield than an unintelligent audience. Such factors indicate a good deal of complexity in attitude changes.

A MORE DETAILED CONSIDERATION OF CHANGE

We turn now to an examination of changes in each of the components of Equation 2. It should be understood, of course, that changes in behavioral intentions cause changes in behavior and thus, eventually, changes in the habit component. Thus, it is probable that, after several repetitions, the behavior will become under habit control (become unconscious). If a person sees that a certain behavior can prevent an extremely unpleasant experience, he/she may act that way many times, without ever finding out whether *not* doing the behavior really causes or allows the unpleasant event. For example, a person who has been humiliated in a particular social group may avoid all members of that group, and such avoidance may come under habit control. This person may never find out that the group includes many pleasant people with whom he could form very satisfying friendships. In the case of some forms of abnormal behavior, the symptoms can be explained in that way. That is, the abnormal behavior occurs frequently and is under habit control because, at an earlier point in time, it was a means of avoiding an unpleasant event, and there have been no further chances to find out whether the act still prevents the unpleasant event. A similar process can take place in the case of extreme abnormal behaviors. For example, a woman who fears that she could be induced to have intercourse with almost any male who asks her may develop a breathing disorder that forces her to attend to her breathing, thus reducing the anxiety that she might give in to casual male acquaintances. Since she always has a problem breathing in the presence of males, she does not have a chance to find out that she is able to control her erotic tendencies.

Modifications of the Social Component

The messages that P receives from O often involve requests that P behave in certain ways. When O can clearly make the case that such requests are legitimate because of O's power, expertise, competence, or role in an accepted social structure or because O is representative of either a membership group to which P belongs or a reference group to which P would like to belong, conformity to such requests may be seriously considered by P. The strength of the normative component in Equation 2 of the model reflects, in part, the kinds of membership or reference groups to which P and O belong, the attractiveness of these groups, the clarity of the norms emitted by the groups, and the extent to which the norms can be enforced through sanctions when there is deviation from them.

What has just been said about norms also applies to roles. When *P* and *O* have particular positions in a social structure, certain behaviors become appropriate for their relationship. The clearer the role relationship and the more serious the sanctions that can be applied for deviation from proper behavior, the more likely it is that *P* and *O* will behave as required by their role.

Norms and roles, and hence the *S* component, can change when a person changes membership or reference groups or when he or she changes to a new position within a social structure. The *S* component can also be changed by new information, concerning the appropriateness of behavior, obtained through the mass media. For example, when a law changes, the appropriateness of certain behaviors may change. The self-image of *P* can also change as he or she moves through the development stages of morality, discussed in Chapter 5.

Modifications of the Affective Component

Enjoyment of a behavior is, in part, dependent on physiological processes. For example, eating or sexual intercourse are strongly conditioned by physiological factors. Nevertheless, social inputs are also significant. Some foods may be more attractive than others because of the information we have concerning their nutritive value or because we are more familiar with them. Our familiarity, in turn, reflects culturally determined eating customs.

The affective responses that occur when a particular behavior takes place become strongly associated with this behavior. I assume that a classical-conditioning mechanism operates in many cases. As the person has more and more experiences with a particular behavior that is associated with positive emotional states, the very thought of the behavior produces a positive emotional response.

Behavior in interpersonal relations is usually specific to the particular relationship. Thus, for instance, complimenting a person (*O*) may be generally agreeable, but complimenting a disliked *O* may be affectively negative. To simplify, let's assume that the social, affective, and cognitive components are consistent. In general, *P*'s affect toward the act will determine *P*'s behavior. However, *P*'s affect toward *O* will modify the probability of the act. For positive behaviors, such as giving a resource, *P* is more likely to act if he or she likes *O*; for negative behaviors, such as taking away a resource or hurting *O*, *P* is more likely to act if he or she dislikes *O*. For example, if *P* dislikes hitting others, it is very likely that *P* will not hit anybody, whether he or she likes them or not. If *P* likes hitting others, he or she is more likely to hit disliked than liked others. If *P* dislikes making compliments, *P* is not likely to compliment anybody, whether they are liked or not. If *P* likes to make compliments, he or she is more likely to compliment liked than disliked others. In short, when *P* dislikes the act, the affect toward the other is irrelevant; when *P* likes the act, the affect toward the other is quite relevant, and, when there is consistency between the behavior and the affect toward the other, there is a high probability of the behavior.

The affect toward the other (*O*) depends on many factors, as described in the chapter on interpersonal attraction. Positive changes in this component can occur when *O* is frequently associated with pleasant situations, when *O* is seen as rewarding (for example, *O* helps *P* reach goals), when there is status congruence and equity in the relationship, and when *O* is perceived by *P* as belonging to the same social unit as *P* (family, tribe, or whatever). The extent to which *P* and *O* employ similar cognitive structures in analyzing their social environment, belong to similar demographic categories, have similar status, and have complementary needs also bears on the affect between *P* and *O*.

Modifications of the Cognitive Component

New information about the relationship between a particular behavior and its consequences can modify the cognitive component. Such information has the effect of changing the perceived probability that a behavior has particular outcomes. Changes in the values of the outcomes are also possible, although, in general, values are more stable and reflect relatively enduring personality characteristics of the perceiver.

Some Empirical Support

The classic study by Lewin (1947), which showed that homemakers changed their behavior with respect to serving kidneys when they realized that group norms had changed, illustrates the effects of changes in the *S* component. Until these subjects joined Lewin's groups, they had assumed that norms were unfavorable to serving kidneys. During group discussions, however, they heard about the advantages (nutrition, helping the war effort) of serving kidneys, and they observed a change of norms, with many of the other group members stating that serving kidneys was a good idea and that they planned to do so. Approximately a third of these homemakers did serve kidneys, as determined several weeks after the discussions.

Several of the studies reviewed in Chapters 6 and 7 suggest that interpersonal attraction is a function of rewards received in the presence of the other. In one study (Lott, Aponte, Lott, & McGinley, 1969), individuals liked a stimulus person who was consistently associated with immediate reward considerably more than they liked a stimulus person who was consistently associated with delayed reward—a result consistent with a classical-conditioning analysis of the change in the affective component.

Mikula and Egger (1974) showed that P's evaluated O's who had been silently present in an experiment more favorably if the experiment provided the P's opportunities for successful problem solving than if the experiment provided experiences of failure. When the experimenter was clearly the cause of P's failure, the O was disliked more than in a neutral condition, suggesting a displacement of negative affect to the O. In this experiment, O had not done anything, so that attraction to this person cannot be traced to his or her actions.

Giving information about the consequences of behavior is widely used to change behavior. For example, parents often tell their children that particular behaviors will offend neighbors or other members of the family. The connections between behavior and consequences are often discussed by teachers (for example, if you apply to many colleges, you are likely to get into one). Most advertising campaigns provide connections between behaviors and consequences (for example, if you use toothpaste X, your sweetheart will like you more). The wide use of such approaches, particularly the expenditure of large sums of money, by hardheaded business executives, on advertising, suggests that such strategies are believed to modify behavior at least some of the time.

CHANGING FACE-TO-FACE INTERPERSONAL RELATIONS

We turn now to P and O interacting. Recall the discussion of Chapter 2. Whether interpersonal behavior is rewarding depends on (a) the type of behavior, (b) the perceived causes of the behavior, (c) the needs of the perceiver, and (d) the perceiver's expectations.

It should be stressed again that it is not so much the behavior itself that determines a person's reactions to another but the *meaning* of this behavior to the perceiver. For example, if a professor is asked by a student for an extension of the time to complete an assignment, and the professor believes the student has not finished the job because of laziness, the professor is not likely to agree to the extension. However, if the professor believes that the student was sick, the extension will be granted. The identical behavior is interpreted very differently, depending on the attributions made. In short, it is the meaning of the behavior that determines interpersonal behavior.

The meaning of behavior is highly dependent on the attributions that a person makes about its causes. For example, suppose O compliments P.

How is *P* going to react to *O*? It depends on what *P* perceives to be the cause of *O*'s behavior. He might believe that *O* acted accidentally—she really intended to compliment somebody else. He might assume that conditions facilitated the compliment—that is, everybody was complimenting *P*, so it was awkward not to do the same. He might assume that the compliment was part of *O*'s role—guests often compliment hosts. He might assume that *O* enjoys the behavior itself—she compliments at the drop of a hat because she really enjoys doing it. He might perceive that *O* is trying to manipulate him. Obviously, any of the above attributions will reduce the positive impact that the behavior might have had.

P's expectations about *O*'s behavior also help to determine whether the behavior is rewarding. If the behavior is unexpected, it may be very costly to *P*. Expected behavior that is slightly negative may be more rewarding than completely unexpected behavior that is positive. For example, if a person expects to be severely criticized, a mild criticism will be rewarding, while a compliment may lead to embarrassment.

It follows, from this analysis of rewards and costs, that the relationship between *P* and *O* can be improved, if it is bad, by means of a number of strategies. *O* may be taught to emit more behaviors that *P* finds rewarding. For example, in a marital setting, *P* may be doing something that annoys *O* and *O* something that annoys *P*. A marriage counselor can find ways to develop a "contract" between *P* and *O* to the effect that each will try to reduce the frequency of behaviors that annoy the other. For example, a husband likes to demonstrate his affection for his wife in public, but his wife finds this behavior embarrassing. Once the husband is convinced that his behavior is annoying, and particularly if he is trained to emit other kinds of behaviors that his wife finds acceptable in such situations, he should be able to avoid the annoying behavior.

The development of such contracts requires careful analysis of what is bothering whom. This is not so simple as it sounds, because it requires definitions of terms, discussion of exactly what is categorized as annoying, and understanding of what behaviors are more desirable, and so on. At any rate, this is an example of how a *behavior-modification* program may be used to improve interpersonal relations.

Another way to improve relations is to create pleasant conditions for social interaction. A party, summer camp, or workshop can be used as a basis for *affective training*. All that is needed here are positive experiences in the presence of the other person.

Still another method of producing change is *attribution training*, which can accomplish two goals. It can make the expectations of one person concerning the probable behavior of the other more accurate, and it can make the attributions of *P* concerning *O*'s behavior similar to the attributions of *O* concerning his or her own behavior.

Two studies illustrate the effectiveness of attribution training. Dweck (1975) worked with 12 children with extreme reactions to failure. She provided intensive training over a long period
of time, with one of two training procedures. One procedure
taught the child to take responsibility for failure and to attribute
it to lack of effort. The other procedure provided success experiences only. After the training, the children were tested in
situations involving failure. Those who had received attribution
training (had been taught to attribute failure to lack of effort)
maintained or improved their performance. Those who had experienced continuous success showed severe deterioration of their
performance following failure. Those who had received the attribution training thought, at the end of training, that failure was
due to insufficient effort and not to lack of ability.

Comment. This study is interesting because it shows that the
recommendations of some of the behavior modifiers may be
wrong. Specifically, those who may be wrong are the psychologists who have argued that giving consistent experiences of success to children who show extreme reactions to failure will correct
the problem. Apparently, in this case, attribution training works
better than behavior modification. Note also that it is not the
schedule of rewards but the child's interpretation of the reasons
for success or failure that determines how the child will react after
a failure.

The second study, by Miller, Brickman, and Bolen (1975),
compared attribution training with persuasion. The study consisted of two parts. In the first part, an attempt was made to teach
fifth graders not to litter and to clean up after others. An attribution group was repeatedly told that they *were* neat and tidy people, while a persuasion group was repeatedly told that they *should
be* neat and tidy; a control group was told nothing. Attribution
training proved much more effective in modifying behavior than
the persuasion approach.

In the second part, second graders were repeatedly told that
they *were* very good at or very interested in math, as opposed to
another group that was told that they *should be* good at or interested in math and a control group that was told nothing.
Again, attribution training was more effective than persuasion. A
group that was rewarded for doing well in math also learned to
do well. The researchers in this study make the valuable point
that persuasion involves a negative attribution, because it suggests to people that they should be what they are not. Attribution
training does not have this problem.

The effects of the training persisted for at least two weeks. In the littering experiment, for instance, the experimenter arranged for toy puzzles to be presented to the children as Christmas presents from the Parent Teachers Association. The puzzles were wrapped in a color-coded container, so that classes that were in different experimental treatments could be identified. The experimenter counted the number of wrappers in the wastebaskets, floor, desks, seats, and elsewhere. The attribution-training group discarded about 90% of their litter in the wastebaskets; the persuasion and control groups discarded only about 30% of their litter in the wastebaskets.

Attribution Training

If it is true that the two equations of the model account for interpersonal behavior, it is not too farfetched to assume that people intuitively use some aspect of this model to account for the behavior of others. Accounting for the behavior of another is one of the central processes in any interpersonal relationship. This is so because we respond to the actions of another much more in terms of the perceived causes of these actions than in terms of the actions themselves (Lowe & Goldstein, 1970). For example, when we see a mother spanking her child, our response depends on whether we assume she's doing it because she's vicious or assume she thinks it will improve the child's behavior.

There is a strong tendency for people to attribute the behavior of others to internal personality dispositions. These dispositions, in terms of the elements of our model, can be conceived of either as habits or as relatively enduring patterns of affect or cognition. In short, they represent the H, A, and C components of the model. In contrast, individuals attribute their own behavior mostly to external factors, represented by the F component of the model. The S component is somewhat ambiguous, since it includes both external causes, such as normative pressures, and internal causes, such as a person's self-image. Research on attribution theory, which we reviewed earlier, does not make such fine discriminations and appears to consider only internal versus external determinants of behavior. However, when a person is asked why another behaves the way he does, the person may use explanations such as "That is the kind of person he is" (habit), "Doing this gives him a big kick" (affect), "It makes him feel good about himself" (self-image), and "He thinks he is going to get something out of it" (C component). Similarly, when a person describes his or her own behavior, statements such as "She pushed me to do it" (S component), and "It was an easy thing to do" (F component) are used.

When people come from very different social backgrounds, the attributions they make about the cause of a particular behavior are quite different. An example from the files of Greek psychiatrist George Vassiliou will illustrate the role of attributions in intercultural behavior. It is well known that Greeks perceive supervisory roles as rightfully bossy, while Americans tend to favor participatory procedures (Triandis & Vassiliou, 1972a). When an American supervisor who favors employee participation interacts with a Greek subordinate who expects and wants a bossy boss, the following sequence of behavior, described by Vassiliou, can result:

Behavior	Attribution
American: "How long will it take you to finish this report?"	*American:* I asked him to participate.
	Greek: His behavior makes no sense. He is the boss. Why doesn't he tell me?
Greek: "I don't know. How long should it take?"	*American:* He refuses to take responsibility.
	Greek: I asked him for an order.
American: "You are in the best position to analyze time requirements."	*American:* I press him to take responsibility for his own actions.
	Greek: What nonsense! I'd better give him an answer.
Greek: "10 days."	*American:* He lacks the ability to estimate time; this time estimate is totally inadequate.
American: "Take 15. Is it agreed? You will do it in 15 days?"	*American:* I offer a contract.
	Greek: These are my orders: 15 days.

In fact, the report needed 30 days of regular work. So the Greek worked day and night, but, at the end of the 15th day, he still needed to do one more day's work.

Behavior	Attribution
American: "Where is the report?"	*American:* I am making sure he fulfills his contract.
	Greek: He is asking for the report. Both attribute that it is not ready.
Greek: It will be ready tomorrow."	
American: "But we had agreed it would be ready today."	*American:* I must teach him to fulfill a contract.
	Greek: The stupid, incompetent boss! Not only did he give me the *wrong orders,* but he doesn't even appreciate that I did a 30-day job in 16 days.
The Greek hands in his resignation.	The American is surprised.
	Greek: I can't work for such a man.

What we see here is that each person makes attributions that are quite different from the attributions made by the other. It follows that, if we could train individuals to make isomorphic attributions, we might improve their interpersonal relations. Isomorphic attributions, you'll remember, occur when one person gives the same weight to each of the components of the model as the other person does—or when the weights are at least highly correlated. This condition can occur only when each person makes the same assumptions about the causes of behavior that are made by the other person.

Consider a situation in which members of one group have a very strong norm concerning a behavior, while members of another group do not even know of the existence of this norm. In this case, complete failure in the interpersonal relationship is likely to occur. For example, in a recent attempt by some American employers of Arab oil workers to improve the living conditions of their workers, they produced 300 prefabricated housing units, under the supervision of American architects. The Arabs inspected the houses and refused to use them. Upon further questioning, it was discovered that the toilets had been installed in such a position that people would be disrespectfully turned toward Mecca while using them. The toilets had to be removed and changed in position before the houses could be used. We have here an example of a strong normative determination of a behavior that the architects did not take into account, simply out of ignorance. In a case of isomorphic attributions, the architects would have considered the behavior within the house in the same terms as the Arabs did.

One way to improve the extent to which attributions are isomorphic is to train each individual to make attributions similar to those made by members of another culture. This can be accomplished through a procedure called the *culture assimilator*. This form of training was suggested by Stolurow and Osgood and developed by Fiedler and Triandis, in the course of a research project in which we four psychologists collaborated. An account of the first validation studies involving this approach is presented by Fiedler, Mitchell, and Triandis (1971) and by Mitchell, Dossett, Fiedler, and Triandis (1972).

Briefly, the student of intercultural events is presented with one or two hundred "items" that give information about the other culture. Each item consists of six sheets of paper. On page 1 there is a journalistic description of an intercultural episode in which *P*, a member of culture A, interacted with *O*, a member of culture B, and there was some sort of interpersonal difficulty or misunderstanding. Page 2 presents four interpretations of what went wrong. These interpretations can be considered attributions of the observed behavior. Only one of these attributions is correct, from the perspective of culture B. Thus, a member of culture A has to find the one correct attribution; the other three are plausible and usually consistent with the attributions made by naïve members of culture A, but they are unacceptable and inaccurate from the point of view of the other culture. The trainee selects the alternative that he or she considers correct and is then instructed to turn to the corresponding one of the remaining four pages. If the correct answer was selected, the appropriate page will praise the trainee and tell why the answer was correct. If the wrong answer was selected, the trainee finds on the appropriate page a mild criticism, such as "You did not read the episode sufficiently carefully," and he or she is instructed to read it again and select another answer.

This procedure clearly increases the extent to which a member of culture A makes attributions that are isomorphic with the attributions made by members of culture B. Furthermore, as the trainee learns to make "correct" attributions, it is probable that he or she becomes more and more able to predict the behavior of members of culture B.

As an illustration of the culture assimilator, here is one item from an assimilator prepared by Slobodin, and his associates (1972) to train White supervisors of Black hard-core unemployed male workers.

On page 205–1, we find the following:

> Several hard-core unemployed Blacks had been hired by Jones Tool and Die Company. Mac Grove was one of the supervisors who was supposed to train the Blacks in the procedures of their new jobs. After he had explained the use of one machine, he asked:
> "Are there any questions?"
> One of the Black workers replied: "Yes, Mr. Grove. . ." At which time Mac interrupted, saying: "Oh, call me Mac. Everybody does."
> The group moved on to another machine and Mac explained its function. He was surprised when one of the other Black workers again addressed him as Mr. Grove.

On page 205–2, we find the following:

Why did the Black workers call him Mr. Grove?
1. They thought Whites in positions of authority expect to be called Mr. by Blacks.

Please go to page 205–3.
2. They felt that Mr. was more appropriate under the circumstances.

Please go to page 205–4.
3. They didn't feel comfortable about calling a White by his first name.

Please go to page 205–5.
4. They didn't believe that Mac really wanted to be called Mac. They thought he was just saying the expected thing.

Please go to page 205–6.

Persons studying the assimilator would turn to the page indicated after their selected answer and would find the following feedback:

On page 205–3:

You selected 1: They thought Whites in positions of authority expect to be called Mr. by Blacks.

While this might be true, it doesn't explain why they continued to call him Mr. after he told them to call him Mac.

Please go back to page 205–1.

On page 205–4:

You selected 2: They felt that Mr. was more appropriate under the circumstances.

Yes.

Our data indicate that hard-core unemployed Blacks feel that formal speech indicates mutual respect and provides status. They also feel that establishing this mutual respect indicates friendship and trust. It is a good thing to keep in mind that hard-core Blacks may prefer the more formal use of Mr. until they have established a good relationship with another person. They may prefer to be called Mr. themselves, at first, if the situation is at all formal. Take your cues from the Black workers and maintain formality until it seems appropriate to do otherwise.

Please go to page 206.

On page 205–5:

You selected 3: They didn't feel comfortable about calling a White by his first name.

This is not necessarily true. Hard-core Blacks call friends, White or Black, by their first names. However, they may have felt uncomfortable about calling the foreman Mac until they got to know him better.

Please go back to page 205–1.

On page 205–6:

You selected 4: They didn't believe that Mac really wanted to be called Mac. They thought he was just saying the expected thing.

This is not the best answer. There is no evidence given in the incident to assume this.

Please go back to page 205–1.

On page 206:

SUMMARY

In this section, we saw that some Black workers believe . . . formality is a desirable way to achieve mutual respect between [themselves] and the foreman.

Summary statements, such as the one on page 206, usually include several related points and follow the presentation of half a dozen or so assimilator items.

Foa and Foa (1974) point out that there are two major kinds of communication failure.

1. *Mismapping.* The rule for mapping a message in physical reality may be different for the sender and the receiver. For example, an American might intend to "give love" and might choose a pat on the back as the means. A Thai is likely to read this behavior as "taking away status." Thus, the way the behavior connects with the message is very different in the two cultures, and the difference results in misunderstandings.

2. *Mismatching.* When the degree of differentiation among classes of behavior differs from person to person, miscommunication is likely. For example, if P makes a sharp differentiation between giving love and giving status, while O does not differentiate very well, P might send a message concerning status that is interpreted as a message concerning love. Foa and Foa give the example of the American criticizing an Arab's work. Americans have learned that criticism of another's work (taking away status) is not necessarily related to taking away love. Arabs are not likely to make this distinction and hence are likely to interpret criticism as rejection.

Taking Foa's analysis seriously, I've suggested that too much or too little differentiation can mismatch two persons in a number of ways (Triandis, 1975a). Two people may (a) differentiate unequally within a mode of exchange (for example, within love exchanges, as when a person who is very complex in dealing with love matters interacts with another who is very simple), (b) differentiate unequally across modes of exchange (for example, one person sees a close connection between exchanges of money and of goods and another sees little connection), (c) differentiate unequally among types of people (for example, one person sees many kinds of people and another makes only a one-dimensional differentiation, as in the case of a fanatic who only sees people who agree or disagree with him), (d) differentiate unequally across time (as when one makes fine discriminations such as 10 minutes ago versus 15 minutes ago, while the other makes coarse discriminations such as yesterday and today), and (e) differentiate unequally across space (as in the case of one person seeing South America as a mosaic of cultures while another sees it as a one big, homogeneous hunk of foreigners).

It is obvious from the above that each of these kinds of differentiation situations can cause a communication failure due to a mismatch. In fact, I hypothesize that humans have a limited capacity for differentiation, so that, when they are very good differentiators in one domain, they necessarily are poor differentiators in other domains. If this proves to be a correct hunch, it will be worthwhile to map the differentiations associated with different cultures systematically, in order to predict where communication failures are most likely to occur.

The culture assimilator can provide differentiation training by rewarding judgments that reflect the correct (appropriate for the culture of the target group) amount of differentiation in different domains. Specifically, the culture assimilator provides the following information about the other culture:

1. norms for different kinds of situations,

2. role structures and, in particular, the way role perceptions differ from role perceptions in the learner's culture,

3. the way behaviors express general intentions,

4. the kinds of self-concepts that are frequently found,

5. the kinds of behaviors that are valued and disvalued,

6. the kinds of antecedents and consequents that are frequently associated with valued and disvalued behaviors,

7. the kinds of differentiations that are common among types of people, within modes of exchange, and between modes of exchange, as well as across time and place,

8. the strengths of the norms, roles, self-concept, general intentions, affect toward the behavior, and utility (instrumentality) of the behavior—that is, the weights of the model,

9. the amplitude of the responses that people generally make in various social situations, and

10. the kinds of reinforcements that people expect in different situations and the appropriateness of the exchange of particular reinforcements—for example, that you can exchange love for status but not money for love.

A more detailed discussion of the theoretical basis for a culture assimilator can be found elsewhere (Triandis, 1976).

The effects of the culture assimilator were studied by Weldon, Carlston, Rissman, Slobodin, and Triandis (1975). Culture-assimilator training did increase the extent to which trained persons made attributions isomorphic to those made by members of other cultures. This training increased the range of causes that they used in thinking about interpersonal behavior. Such broadening of perspective also had the effect of decreasing ethnocentric attributions, of forcing the perceiver to search cognitively through a wider range of attributions, and of making the expectations of the perceiver concerning the other's behavior more accurate. In addition, Weldon and his associates showed that culture-assimilator training made the behavior of members of other cultural groups appear more intentional (rational) and less impulsive; trained subjects see less intercultural conflict than untrained subjects in scenes portraying such conflict.

The major benefit of culture-assimilator training is that it increases the extent to which *P* perceives *O*'s behavior in the same way that *O* perceives his or her own behavior. Also, *P* learns to expect *O*'s behavior. Thus, *P* is less surprised by behaviors of *O*'s of the other culture. These changes improve interpersonal relationships.

A more general way to approach the effects of assimilator training is to consider that assimilator training increases cognitive complexity. Complexity can be indexed by the number of dimensions used by a person to think of the stimuli in a specific domain of meaning, the number of discriminations that the person makes along any dimension, and the extent to which the dimensions are integrated into hierarchical systems with different levels of abstraction. There is evidence that people who know more about a particular group of people use more dimensions in thinking about this group.

One can find the number of dimensions used by people by using a procedure called multidimensional scaling. In this procedure, people are asked to make judgments of similarity. For example, suppose we were studying the ways people think about nations. We might ask people "Which country is most different from the other two countries?" and present Brazil, Spain, and Portugal. One person might say that Brazil is different because it is a South American country and the other two are European or because it is larger than the other two. Another person might say that Spain is different because people there speak Spanish, while in the other two countries they speak Portuguese. Still another might say that Portugal is different because it is a very small country, and so on. In other words, different people use different bases for seeing a difference among the stimuli. A person who uses *many* different bases for making such judgments is cognitively more complex than persons who use *few* bases for making such judgments. The statistical procedure is difficult to explain, but you can get an intuitive idea of how it is done if you consider that, when a stimulus is picked as being different, it means that a person places this stimulus further away from the other two stimuli than the other two stimuli are placed from each other. If one presents many stimuli, one gets many judgments placing one stimulus away from two others. When this judgment is made consistently across different sets of three stimuli, this indicates that a particular dimension is being used that causes the contrast between one stimulus and two others. A statistical procedure allows us to find several such dimensions, which may be orthogonal (at right angles) to each other. So if we find that one person uses, say, five such dimensions, while another person uses three, we can state that the first person is more complex than the second.

One can use this procedure to study how a certain group of people, such as Blacks, think about a set of stimuli. For example, Davidson (1975) reports a multidimensional-scaling study involving attributes that are commonly used by Blacks to describe Blacks. Black and White subjects made multidimensional scaling judgments, which established the number of dimensions used by these subjects in thinking about Blacks. It was found that Blacks used more dimensions than Whites. While, for example, both used dimensions such as *militant,* the Blacks used the additional dimensions *slick dude-jive, out of it,* and *self-oriented/black-movement oriented.*

Gardiner (1972) hypothesized that it is possible to train people to increase their conceptual complexity and that that will reduce their prejudice. He presented tape recordings of Black and White applicants for the post of ombudsman in a school government being interviewed and answering a set of questions. The trainees were required to make judgments about the suitability of the stimulus person in the role of advocate (one-concept training) or to first judge the person in the role of advocate and then judge the person in the role of conciliator (two-concept training). Subjects were pretested and posttested with several instruments, including a social-distance scale developed by me (Triandis, 1961) and a Race Relations Paragraph Completion Test measuring conceptual complexity in the area of interracial interpersonal affairs. The results show a slight reduction in social distance (significant only in the one-concept-training condition but in the same direction in the two-concept-training condition) and also a reduction of prejudice, as measured by a projective test. However, the study was equivocal concerning whether the two-concept training was superior to the one-concept training, as had been predicted.

Sensitivity Training

A major method of achieving the goals of affective training is through some form of sensitivity training. This is a widely used procedure and has become a social movement in the United States and in parts of Europe (Back, 1973). There are many kinds of sensitivity training. Back provides a classification including mystic experiences, training associated with pleasant situations (for example, in a summer camp), psychotherapy, education, encounters, recreation, indoctrination, and organizational development.

Sensitivity groups are used for many purposes, one of the most worthy being the reduction of international conflict (Doob, 1970, 1975). Doob has used this kind of training to reduce conflict on Cyprus, in Africa in the conflict between Somalia and Ethiopia, in the conflict between Catholics and Protestants in Northern Ireland, and in other places. He has organized workshops in which representatives from the two sides of a conflict heard lectures, participated in games, and had interviews with members of the opposing group. There is some evidence that people learned the point of view of the other group, learned how to function in groups consisting of members of their own group and of the opposing group, and at times experienced other kinds of change.

A crucial ingredient in such workshops is the intervener, who must be patient, have the ability to withstand frustrations, and have a willingness to become the target of displaced hostilities. Doob (1975) mentions that five assumptions are made by the intervener: (1) that the participants can evolve their own proposals for courses of action, (2) that only certain conflicts, at certain times and certain places, are likely to allow successful intervention, (3) that, within a short period of time, some participants can learn constructive behavior that resolves conflict in relation to people with whom they could not work before the workshop, (4) that the intervener is in a position to arrange optimal conditions for such learning, and (5) that the new learning can and will be utilized under real-life conditions, in ways that constructively affect the conflict.

These workshops are usually arranged at a site that is removed from the conflict—preferably in a neutral country. The participants should be comfortable, well fed, relaxed, rested. A fairly luxurious hotel can be a good site. Learning results from (a) lectures, often given by the intervener, who is an authority on conflict resolution, (b) meetings, centered on specific topics and using parliamentary procedures, (c) games, such as playing the role of members of the other group, (d) observations, in which one group observes the behavior of the other, (e) meetings, in arbitrary groups, designed to train people to interact with those of the opposing group, and (f) interviews, in which participants express their views about the conflict. While the hard evidence about the consequences of such workshops is very difficult to obtain, the importance of conflict reduction in such situations is so great that even small effects might be highly desirable socially.

Turning to more standard sensitivity groups, we note that many different approaches are used. One kind of training involves a weekend session, often starting on Friday evening and lasting until Sunday afternoon. Meetings are usually held in an attractive resort area. After dinner on Friday, people gather in rooms that have been assigned to them and meet people they have never met before, for what they expect will be a unique and intense experience. Each group consists of a dozen or so people—approximately half men and half women. The trainer starts the meeting by giving a vague explanation of what is to take place. Sometimes a game or two is played to warm things up. The trainer encourages people to participate, set limits, and suggests opportunities for activities. More games follow, designed to encourage people to talk about themselves. Particular pairs or triads of people are encouraged to interact—to touch, kiss, talk. Then the group may focus on an individual or a couple. In a group of a dozen or more, it is probable that somebody will talk about one of his or her problems. The personal difficulty that is presented by this person can then be discussed at length, acted out, and interpreted; role playing may be used to explore different facets of it.

The trainer makes sure that the individual with the problem does not take all of the group's time. He or she directs activities so that the focus shifts from member to member. More exercises may be introduced. Some of these are described by Schutz (1968) and involve the acting out of a feeling or need. For example, a person who feels the need for nurturance may be lifted up by the rest of the group and stroked and in this way may feel trust in others and "group support," as well as the experience of being liked. Other exercises may be negative, such as everybody saying something bad about everybody else. This sort of thing goes on until well past midnight.

Saturday is the big day. All that happened the previous night is likely to happen again—but more intensively. People by now know what to expect from others. Exercises may evoke sudden outbursts of emotion, as when a member of the group suddenly expresses his loneliness and his difficult relationship with his wife. Other people may be reluctant to put in such a performance, but the rule of the encounter movement is that everybody must show something of himself or herself during the session. A person does not get accepted by the group unless some intimate side of himself or herself is presented. Crying is a ticket to acceptance.

The marathon session lasts well into the night. People get exhausted. The experience often becomes very intense, with emotional outbursts and behaviors that are normally nonexistent in a person's repertoire becoming evident. At the end, the feeling is that something important has happened during the weekend.

People derive satisfactions from these encounters for many reasons. First, they discover that they are not alone with their personal problems. Everybody has problems, and many have similar problems. Second, they feel accepted by others. In a society in which loneliness is frequent and the opportunity for a deep emotional bond and intimate behaviors is rare, the sensitivity group provides important rewards. Third, a person is given a chance to behave in ways that are often forbidden and to receive rewards for such behavior from the group. For example, a person who is unable to tell people off may be encouraged to do so and then rewarded for it.

Back's (1973) book is important because it shows why the sensitivity-training approach has become a social movement. Modern technological society has certain characteristics that predispose the success of the movement. First, there is a shift away from behaviors that are under *S* control to behaviors that are mostly under the control of the *C* component. Rationality means doing what pays. As cultures change, norms become less clear; punishments are no longer given for breaking the norms. Thus, the individual is freer to do what seems best to him or her, but this also means that there is a reduction in interdependence. A reduction in interdependence is associated with interpersonal behaviors that are more formal and less satisfying. Foa has pointed out that exchanges of love and status are time-consuming. Exchanges of money and information are not. A radio announcer can inform millions in a few minutes; but no one can make love to millions. Thus, modern society, with its emphasis on time saving, favors those interpersonal behaviors that are more universalistic and makes particularistic behaviors less probable. The result is that people in modern societies are starved for love and status. On the other hand, people in less developed countries have the time for love and status; their problem is the need for more money and goods. In short, the sensitivity movement is a useful response to the dilemma of industrialized humanity.

The importance of loneliness in industrial societies can be illustrated with a study on the perceived relationship between loneliness and fear in samples of American, Greek, Indian, and Japanese male students (Triandis, Vassiliou, Vassiliou, Tanaka, & Shanmugam, 1972, p. 205). The Americans and the Japanese (members of industrialized countries) saw a strong connection between loneliness and fear, while the Greeks and the Indians did not. In contrast, the latter saw a strong connection between fantasy and demons and fear, which the former did not see. In short, the meaning of fear is somewhat different in these two types of societies, and loneliness is a factor in the two industrialized countries, while other factors are important in the less industrialized countries.

Back points out that a number of factors contribute to loneliness and lack of intimate relationships in modern societies. First, there is more mobility than in traditional societies. When people move to new regions, they have to make new friends. It takes time to form deep friendships, and some people move so frequently that they never make them. Second, industrial societies are more affluent than nonindustrial societies, and the middle and upper classes are particularly likely to spend money to relieve their loneliness. Participation in the sensitivity movement requires time and money. Third, there is increased secularization. In the past, the church had an enormous influence on people's lives. It provided important social functions and, through devices such as the confessional, made it possible for people to relate intimately to others. As secularism increased, people lost such opportunities for social relationships; the sensitivity movement became a new way to meet human needs.

In short, as societies change and control of social behavior through the S component is reduced, a person is encouraged to control his or her behavior through the C component. But some of the consequences of behavior are remote in time. The sensitivity movement deals with the here and now. It allows a shift from symbols to concrete expression, from intellect to emotions, and from mind to body. The accent is on "gut learning." Some people have talked about the movement providing an "education for ecstasy." The major outcome is a good feeling.

While the importance of changes in the A component must be kept in mind, remember that sensitivity training also changes the other components. T-groups have their own norms, and soon behavior in the group responds to these norms. It is like joining a new culture. The group leader provides some guidance, but, at least in theory, the leader is supposed to make himself or herself unnecessary. Then the "law of the situation" is supposed to guide behavior. That is, behavior will have immediate consequences, and it is these consequences that are to guide it.

Dunnette (1970) believes that sensitivity training can be analyzed into six stages. Most people who join such groups manage to (1) escape from loneliness, (2) receive warmth and support, (3) learn sensory and emotional sensitivity, and (4) learn to tolerate anxiety. Very few find that such groups help them (5) understand themselves and others and (6) learn to change interpersonal behavior and resolve conflicts. Dunnette believes that the first three stages are the recreational phase of sensitivity training. The fourth stage involves learning but is rarely achieved. Many groups never get to stage 4 because they do not spend enough time in stages 1 to 3, which are necessary in order to achieve stage 4. Other groups get to stage 4 but get stuck there.

Attempts at evaluating the effectiveness of sensitivity training have been weak and inconclusive. Few studies are methodologically sound. The study that is probably the best (Lieberman, Yalom, & Miles, 1973) suggests that there is little evidence of behavior change. There is evidence that some people break down and actually develop greater psychological problems as a result of these experiences. The fact that there are such casualties should be of serious concern to the organizers of this training. The study found a 9% casualty rate, partially related to the effectiveness of the leader. Unfortunately, leaders for sensitivity training do not have to be certified, and their competence varies enormously. An incompetent leader can cause much damage because many people who come to participate in sensitivity training are too sick for it and should not be there at all. The leader may not realize this, however, or may not know what to do with a person having a breakdown. Examining the activities of successful leaders, Lieberman and his associates suggest that such leaders engage in sharpening the attributions that people make about the causes of interpersonal behavior. When this happens, sensitivity training is no longer a form of affective training but a form of attribution training.

It should be clear that any kind of training is a mixture of attribution training, affective training, and behavior modification. If a person learns to make accurate attributions about the causes of the behavior of others, learns to feel good about performing some new behaviors, or learns that some behavior will immediately lead to rewards, all three kinds of training were present. While "pure" culture-assimilator training may be attribution training and "pure" sensitivity training may be affective training and "pure" behavior modification may change the *C* component and provide new habits, the fact remains that such pure types of training do not exist in reality. Any training is a mixture of the three ideal types.

Behavior Modification

There are a number of behavior-modification techniques. Among the more important are systematic desensitization (Wolpe, 1958, 1969), implosion therapy (Sherman, 1973), operant therapy (based on Skinner's approach to learning), and aversion therapy. In systematic desensitization, situations that are likely to elicit anxiety are rank-ordered, and the patient is helped to experience increasingly anxiety-producing situations, while at the same time response incompatible with anxiety, such as relaxation, is elicited from the patient. In implosion therapy, the patient is asked to imagine himself or herself in the most anxiety-producing situation, and no relaxation is introduced. The therapist keeps the patient at a high level of anxiety until the patient experiences a spontaneous reduction in anxiety. The principle behind this therapy is that stimuli lose their power to frighten if anxiety is maintained at a high level over a period of time. In operant therapy, a person is rewarded for behaviors that are desirable from the point of view of the therapist (and presumably the patient). In aversion therapy, the patient is punished for behaviors that are undesirable from the point of view of the therapist (and presumably the patient).

Foa and Foa (1974) point out that their circle of six interpersonal exchanges provides ready-made procedures for determining the hierarchy of anxiety-producing exchanges and the course of therapy. For example, if a person is particularly anxious when exchanging love, therapy might start with exchanges of money, later move to exchanges of status, and, still later, deal with the exchange of love. Shaping behavior following Skinnerian principles can also follow the Foa circle. The therapist first determines what exchanges cause most inhibition, for instance, and starts by reinforcing behaviors that are not strongly inhibited; later, the therapist shifts to increasingly inhibited behaviors around the circle, until he or she can provide reinforcement for the behaviors that create the "real" problem. For example, a man might be very inhibited in expressing negative feelings. Assertion training involves teaching him to speak up. It will be difficult to shape this behavior if the behavior does not occur spontaneously in the first place, since shaping requires that the behavior take place so that it can be reinforced. However, it may be easy first to teach him to assert himself in the area of exchanges of goods (say, presents). Once he has learned to assert himself in that area, he might be able to express himself in the exchange of services and, finally, in the expression of a personal resentment. Assertion training also involves learning to reward others. A parent who does not give love to his or her child may first be trained to give information, later to give status (praise), and, finally, to give love.

Most forms of behavior modification involve changes in the A or the C component, which are later manifested in changes in the H component. As implied by the conclusion of the previous section, training does not involve changes in only one component but rather produces differences in emphasis on one or another of the components.

Combining the Methods

In the previous sections, we discussed attribution training, sensitivity training, and behavior modification as though they were competing forms of training. In fact, one can use a combination of them. Attribution training is something one can do on one's own and is essentially similar to reading a book. Sensitivity training requires the presence of a group. Behavior modification usually requires the presence of a skillful therapist.

The motivation of the learner is crucial in determining whether training will be successful. An excellent assimilator might be totally ineffective if the learner is uninterested in reading it. Once the person has learned a new response, it is important that the conditions be right to maintain it. For example, it does not help to have behavior change in one setting if the learner returns to an environment in which the new behaviors are not rewarded (or, even worse, are punished). Thus, changes of the whole milieu are sometimes more important than the training itself.

The various training approaches we've discussed above should be seen as complementary ways of reaching particular goals. One can change the person or the person's environment. One can change the person's cognitions, habits, or way of experiencing others. Each of these changes is accomplished most effectively with a particular technique. For example, one might start with a session of sensitivity training, to create the awareness of a lack of knowledge about the point of view of some class of others. This could be followed by use of the culture assimilator, to inform the learner about the others' point of view, and finally, the environment could be changed so that new behaviors, compatible with the information that has been acquired, will consistently be reinforced. In the final analysis, training people to relate to one another in new ways is an art. What can be done from a scientific point of view is to analyze its elements and determine what antecedents and consequences are most likely for each element. The trainer must decide how to combine the elements to reach the goals of training.

SUMMARY

Interpersonal relationships can change in many ways. A person may behave in ways inconsistent with his or her cognitions about interpersonal behavior. Such inconsistencies often result in an unstable cognitive structure and in cognitive change. A person may be placed in a different group and thus experience different norms or roles. A person may experience pleasant (or unpleasant) associations with a behavior or see different long-range consequences from those seen before. Messages received from others can change a person's perspective. The conditions that maximize acceptance of such messages were reviewed. We considered how modifications in the social, affective, and consequences determinants of behavioral intentions can change behavior. Three kinds of training (attribution, affective, and behavior modification) were considered. Brief descriptions of each kind of training were provided. There is no reason to think that these kinds of training are competing among themselves, but rather it is appropriate to think of them as complementary. Whether to change the person or the person's environment is still another choice of the trainer. Thus, in the final analysis, interpersonal change involves the judicious combination of different elements of training to achieve desirable goals.

9

SOME PRACTICAL IMPLICATIONS

This book has examined social behavior in terms of its major anteced-ents and consequences and has shown how patterns of social behavior can be changed. What are the practical implications of all this?

This chapter will focus on social relationships that vary along the for-mality/intimacy dimension. Formal relationships have little amplitude. That is, they are seldom extreme and don't include behaviors such as screaming or jumping. They are mostly determined by conventions and norms. Intimate relations, in contrast, permit freedom and are complex. My strategy will be to touch rather lightly on formal relationships and to spend much more time on the intimate.

Two examples of formal relationships will be mentioned: interaction across cultures and interaction during the employment interview. Two ex-amples of relationships intermediate in intimacy will also be presented: su-pervisor-subordinate relations and teacher-student relations. However, the major focus of the chapter will be on intimate relations, and for this illustra-tion I've chosen marital relations. This chapter will discuss factors that can lead to "successful" relations in each of these areas. In each case, I'll mention factors characteristic of people involved in a particular relationship and then will touch on how training can help the relationship.

INTERACTIONS ACROSS CULTURES

Most interactions across cultures are highly formal. Diplomats have developed a "third culture," with highly structured rules, norms, and roles —protocol. Behavior is largely under the influence of the S component, which is under the influence of rules or instructions from the diplomat's government. When S control is not possible, because there are no known rules, intercultural behavior is usually under C control. However, as is inevitable, people bring to interactions well-established habits developed in their own culture. When these habits result in behaviors that are unexpected or behaviors that may be interpreted as hostile, much intercultural conflict is generated.

The way perceptions of the other culture can distort our judgment is illustrated by a story told by social psychologist Urie Bronfenbrenner. When he showed slides of Russia to primary-school children in Ithaca, New York, he was asked by the children why the Russians use so many trees along their highways. He turned the question around and asked the children for an explanation. One of the dominant explanations was that the Russians did not want travelers to see what was behind trees; in other words, they planted trees to hide military installations or other objects of importance. Then Bronfenbrenner asked why Americans plant trees along their highways. The children answered that it is for shade. In other words, the same stimulus— trees along the highway—was interpreted very differently, as a result of different conceptions of what people do in the two cultures.

When P and O belong to different cultures, the more dissimilar they think they are, the more likely it is that they will distort the meaning of each other's behavior. Another factor affecting intercultural relationships is how the behavior patterns learned in one culture are transferred to another. We know from studies of transfer of training that, when people learn to make a particular response to a particular stimulus, they can very easily transfer this skilled response to another, similar stimulus. For example, a person who learns to drive a Ford will be able to drive a Chevrolet easily. When a completely different stimulus is present, requiring a completely different response—such as having to say *Yasu* as a friendly greeting instead of *Hi* —there is neither positive nor negative transfer. There is no advantage, but also no interference, from the previous habit. The trouble comes when the same stimulus requires a very different response. Imagine what would happen if you had to drive a car that required you to accelerate and brake by lifting instead of depressing the pedals. This type of problem does arise sometimes in intercultural situations. For example, you may have learned to touch others in your culture, and may find yourself in a situation in which touching is taboo; or, similarly, you may have learned not to touch and find yourself in a situation in which touching is required. Under these circumstances, previously learned habits will make unintentional behaviors wrong.

To take an example, in many cultures people do not say "Thank you." When a person from one of these cultures visits the U.S.—where we often say "Thank you" without even thinking—the visitor appears rude. When we Americans visit these other cultures, we appear excessively polite.

To learn a new correct behavior for every situation is a major undertaking. In that case, the culture assimilator, described in Chapter 8, can be very helpful. In addition, it is helpful to have a good understanding of the way one's own culture functions—its values, biases, and predispositions.

While the culture assimilator can be useful in preparing a person to interact effectively in another culture (Fiedler, Mitchell, & Triandis, 1971), sensitivity training and behavior modification are also good under some circumstances. For example, the Peace Corps and other organizations that function internationally have found some forms of sensitivity training quite useful (Wight, 1969). David (1972) has analyzed the need to condition the traveler to acquire response patterns that will lead to a minimum of disorientation in a new environment.

THE EMPLOYMENT INTERVIEW

The social situation of the employment interview involves contrient interdependence; P wants to find out both the good and the bad behavior patterns of O, and O wants to present only the good ones. P's implicit personality theories determine much of the information that P collects. The accuracy of this information, as we saw in our discussion of the accuracy of interpersonal perception, is rather poor. In fact, there is evidence that the first few minutes of the interview determine the outcome, which suggests that very little information is actually transmitted and processed (Webster, 1964).

Negative information is given much more weight than positive information in determining the outcome of the interview. Major biases can be found in selection decisions. For example, Triandis (1963) found that a woman had to be much more competent than a man in order to receive the same acceptability rating as a man, a Black had to be much more competent than a White, and an old person had to be much more competent than a young person. Of course, this was found before the court decisions were handed down prohibiting discrimination. However, it appears that these cognitive habits persist (Rosen & Jerdee, 1974).

When selection by interviews alone, by objective evidence alone, and by a combination of the two are compared, the results suggest that selection on purely objective criteria is about as good as either of the other methods. However, if the interviewer has much objective information available and considers additional information derived from the interview, he or she can sometimes surpass the purely objective method. For a review of the literature on this point, see Chapter 4.

Training interviewers requires increasing the validity of their judgments by teaching them to use those cues that do have validity and ignore those that are invalid. In principle, it should be easy to train people to pay attention to some cues and to ignore others by using some sort of programmed learning materials, similar in form to the culture assimilators.

SUPERVISOR-SUBORDINATE RELATIONS

Since the literature on leadership is very large, I've selected only one theoretical framework for discussion in this chapter. Fiedler (1967) has presented a theory about the relationship between leader characteristics and the effectiveness of the group led by this leader. He argues that the effectiveness of a leader is contingent on the situation in which the leader finds himself or herself. Hence, it is called the contingency model of leadership.

Fiedler's theory involves correlating a characteristic of the leader with the group's effectiveness. The characteristic used by Fiedler is the leader's attitude toward his or her least-preferred co-worker. This so-called LPC score is obtained by asking the leader to think of all the people he or she has ever worked with and to focus on the least-liked one. Then the leader is supposed to rate this particular co-worker on evaluative scales for such traits as intelligence, warmth, and activity. The leader's LPC score is the sum of the evaluative ratings of the least-preferred co-worker. Some leaders have a low LPC score, which means that they consistently rate their least-preferred co-worker negatively; others have a high score, which means that they see their least-preferred co-worker as having both positive and negative traits.

The second component of Fiedler's theory, group effectiveness, can be indexed by measures of group productivity, creativity, goal attainment, or what not, depending on the purpose of the group. Even if the group's job is rather vague, such as writing a "good" letter to convince people to buy a product, it is possible to get a reliable index of effectiveness. In this example, one can have all the letters produced by several groups rated by a panel of 20 people, and the average rating can be used as an index of effectiveness.

Fiedler's theory concerns the correlation between LPC and the measure of effectiveness. Under some conditions, this correlation is said to be positive, and, under other conditions, it is said to be negative. In other words, under some conditions the high-LPC leader is effective, and under other conditions the low-LPC leader is effective. Fiedler's model spells out these conditions in terms of three parameters: leader-member relations, task structure, and leader power. The first parameter indexes the extent to which the leader feels accepted and respected by the group members. The second concerns the extent to which the leader is able to tell the group members exactly what to do. Some group tasks, such as being creative, are low in task structure; other tasks, such as assembling a machine, are high in task structure. Task structure should not be confused with task difficulty, since one can have a difficult task that is very structured (for example, launching a rocket to the moon). The third parameter reflects the extent to which the leader is able to make all the important decisions concerning the group. For example, leaders who are able to hire and fire without consulting others have more power than those who cannot.

Fiedler argues that, when the leader-member relations are good, task structure is high, and the leader has much power, the situation is very favorable for the leader. He or she is accepted, can tell people what to do, and makes decisions that really count. When the leader has poor relations, task structure is low, and leader power is low, the situation is very unfavorable. For example, the well-liked commander of a military unit that is to dig a trench is in a favorable situation; the hated leader of a voluntary association without goals is in a very bad situation.

When the leader's situation is very favorable *or* very unfavorable, according to Fiedler, a low-LPC leader is most effective; when the situation is intermediate in favorableness, a high-LPC leader is best. This contention is backed by a good deal of evidence (Fiedler & Chemers, 1974b; Chemers & Skrzypek, 1972; Sashkin, 1972; Chemers, Rice, Sundstrom, & Butler, 1975). The difficulty is that we don't know for sure what the LPC score really measures. One view, which seems to be consistent with the literature, is that the LPC score is a measure of cognitive complexity. Remember that low LPC means that the leader rates his or her co-workers consistently negatively. High LPC means that the leader sees both good and bad traits in his least-preferred co-worker, showing that he or she is more complex in thinking about co-workers. Now, consider the most- and the least-favorable situations. Leaders in the most favorable are accepted in every way; they are liked, they can tell people what to do, what they say is accepted, and they can make their commands stick because they have the power. Leaders in the least-favorable situation are rejected in every way; they are hated, their commands probably make no sense, and they have no power to make commands stick. In short, the most- and the least-favorable situations are relatively *simple*. A cognitively simple leader can deal with those simple situations best; there is a *match* (or fit) between situation and leader. Now consider the situation that is intermediate in favorability. Here the leader's situation is mixed; for example, he or she is liked but does not know how to direct the group, or is hated but does know how to direct the group. The situation is more complex. Here, a complex leader (high LPC) will lead best. This analysis, proposed by Foa, Mitchell, and Fiedler (1971), fits relatively well with several known facts, although there are some failures to replicate Mitchell's (1970) finding that high-LPC leaders are high on several other measures of cognitive complexity (Larson & Rowland, 1974). On the other hand, there is much evidence that cognitive complexity is a multidimensional phenomenon (Vannoy, 1965), and it is conceivable that a leader be complex when thinking of co-workers and not complex in any other way. This analysis also fits well with Foa's argument about matching and mismatching, which I presented in Chapter 8.

Research on leadership is at once very promising and very confusing. Sashkin, Taylor, and Tripathi (1974) have presented evidence that LPC is not a stable score but shifts with the situation. They found that the correlations of LPC with other psychological measures may be quite different, depending on whether the leader is in a good or a bad leadership situation. While they replicated Mitchell's finding of a correlation between LPC and cognitive complexity, they note that this correlation is exceptionally high and significant *only* when the leadership situation is good. In unfavorable leadership situations, the correlation is not significant and tends to be negative. In addition, measures of openness to information, on which complex people usually score high, show a strong reversal; they show negative correlations with LPC in favorable and positive correlations with LPC in unfavorable leadership situations. Exactly how to interpret these findings is subject to controversy. One possible interpretation, consistent with my earlier argument, is that, *in general,* LPC reflects complexity. However, in good social situations, when the leader is relaxed, the correlation is particularly strong; in unfavorable situations, when the leader feels anxious, there is cognitive constriction, and the correlation drops to zero. Openness to information is generally desirable. In good situations, the low-LPC leaders are cognitively simple and also open; in unfavorable situations, the high-LPC leaders are open. Openness, as well as the match of leader and situation, relates to effective performance.

One interesting prediction from the contingency model is that, under some conditions, leadership training will hurt the leader. The argument goes as follows. In most favorable leadership situations, low-LPC leaders perform well; in most unfavorable leadership situations, high-LPC leaders perform well. Leadership training improves the favorableness of the situation for the leader. So, to train a high-LPC leader means to take him or her from a relatively unfavorable situation to a favorable situation. However, in a favorable situation, the high-LPC leader performs poorly. Hence, it is undesirable to train high-LPC leaders who are in moderately unfavorable situations. Low-LPC leaders, if they are in a favorable situation, will not be helped by training, since they are already performing well. Only if they are in a moderately unfavorable situation will low-LPC leaders benefit from the training. In short, if one trains leaders without taking into account the favorability of their situation or their LPC score, one can easily make mistakes and hurt some of the leaders. Some of the predictions derived from this reasoning are supported by a study by Chemers and his associates (1975).

Fiedler and Chemers (1974a) have developed a culture assimilator for leaders, to improve their leadership behavior. The approach is as follows. First, the leader is asked to self-administer the LPC measurement. Second, the leader is asked to judge his or her situation in terms of the three parameters of Fiedler's model. Third, the contingency model of leadership is presented, and the leader learns how the constructs of the model are interrelated. Finally, from the leader's diagnosis of the kind of person he or she is and the kind of situation he or she is in, and from an understanding of the model, the leader is supposed to arrive at a conclusion concerning changes to make in order to become as effective as possible.

TEACHER-PUPIL RELATIONS

Much of what we know about supervisor-subordinate relations may apply, with modifications, to teacher-pupil relations.

The literature on teacher-student relations is vast. Here I can only touch on a few points to illustrate the relevance of some of the principles I've developed in earlier chapters.

Teacher behaviors can, of course, differ on all dimensions of social behavior: they can be very associative (help) or dissociative (avoid), superordinate (criticize) or subordinate (ask for opinion), intimate (kiss) or formal (take case to the principal). What behavior will take place depends on several factors, including whether the teacher and the pupils have similar goals (for the pupil to learn), the relative distribution of resources (information), and the age of the relationship (new teacher versus familiar teacher).

Much of teacher behavior is under habit control (Landis, Triandis, & Adamopoulos, 1975). While the behavior is being learned, the training received in college, the views of the principal, and the expectation that certain behaviors will lead to certain goals undoubtedly influence the behavior of teachers; but, once the behavior is well established, knowing the teacher's intentions will not help you predict the teacher's behavior.

Interaction between teacher and pupils can be rewarding or costly. But, as explained in earlier chapters, rewards and costs depend on expectations and attributions. The teacher's expectations about student behavior are important in determining the attributions that the teacher will make. The behavior of pupils will be interpreted by the teacher on the basis of these attributions. For example, it makes a considerable difference whether the teacher attributes relatively poor pupil performance to low ability or to lack of effort. Generally, when poor performance is attributed to lack of effort, the teacher is likely to give a very poor grade, but, when it is attributed to lack of ability, the rating of the pupil is less severe.

The similarity between teacher and pupil can be important in determining how much the pupil learns and how the teacher reacts to the pupil. Runkel (1956) measured an aspect of the cognitive structures of teachers and pupils and demonstrated that similarity of teacher and pupil in such structures is associated with good performance in the classroom.

Teacher training takes the form of teaching how to make accurate attributions of pupil behavior, how to emit more behaviors that are rewarding to pupils, and how to structure behavior so as to reach specific goals. Many of the methods of training we discussed in the previous chapter are relevant to teacher training.

MARITAL RELATIONS

Marriage is a human institution that shows many variations across time and place. While the monogamous ideal is more or less the guide in many parts of the world, there are significant areas of the world in which other forms of marriage prevail. Both polygyny (more than one wife) and polyandry (more than one husband) can be found. In most traditional societies, marriage involves an alliance between two groups—extended families, tribes, or even nations. Under such forms of marriage, much marital behavior is prescribed by the two groups and hence is under the influence of the social component. Of course, it soon comes under the influence of habits.

Ecological factors may determine how the family is organized and also how the parents interact with each other and with their children. For instance, Whiting (1964) has argued that, in tropical environments, where raising cattle is almost impossible because of tsetse flies and other unfavorable conditions, it is functional for mothers to breast-feed their children until they are about 3 years old. Otherwise, malnutrition would be the rule. In such environments, it is necessary to have a long postpartum sex taboo, since this guarantees that the mother will not become pregnant again and lose her milk. Thus, an important aspect of marital relations is controlled by norms that developed in response to the environment. If the society has adopted a long postpartum sex taboo, some form of polygyny may be permitted so that the husband will be able to satisfy his sex drive. Polygyny has implications for the relationship of mother and son, which becomes closer than the relationship between wife and husband. Sons tend to identify with their mothers because of the close relationship. Thus, if the son is to function as an adult, a severe initiation ceremony is required to mark his shift to an adult role. Here we see how ecological factors create a number of conditions that impose particular kinds of interpersonal relationships.

In other kinds of traditional societies, one can also find closer relationships between children and parents than between husbands and wives. For example, in an analysis of role perception in Greece and the U.S., Triandis, Vassiliou, and Nassiakou (1968) found that, on the intimacy/formality dimension, the American husband-wife roles involved more intimacy than the Greek husband-wife roles, but the American parent-child roles involved less intimacy than the Greek parent-child roles.

In societies in which marriages are arranged, parents do a good deal of the work required to locate appropriate spouses for their children. They negotiate about dowries or bride prices. They discuss with the parents of the spouse the development of several kinds of interpersonal agreements specifying how the children are to behave after they marry (for example, that the bride may spend two months a year with her parents). Norms often specify where the young couple is to reside, with whom they are to interact, and so on. For example, in northern India, traditional villagers arrange for a marriage while a boy and girl are still children; a ceremony takes place, and the girl comes to live in the household of her in-laws. The household is an extended family, with women living in a courtyard and the men living in a sheltered section on the perimeter of the house. Inside the courtyard, the oldest woman is in charge. So the child bride comes to live in the yard and work under the direction of this woman. She is allowed to return to her father's home two or three times a year and to stay with her mother for extended periods of time. After the children have reached the age of procreation, there is another marriage ceremony. Now the boy is allowed to come into the women's courtyard at night and have intercourse with his wife. Interaction between husbands and wives is severely limited. A woman is not even supposed to interact exclusively with her own children but rather is supposed to interact with all the children in the courtyard—that is, with the cousins of her own children. In this marital arrangement, husband-wife interaction is rare and limited to specific behaviors permitted by the norms of the culture. We can easily see the predominance of the S component in this kind of family. We can also see that, in such a family, behavior is more formal and less intimate than in the nuclear family (Whiting & Whiting, 1975).

Perhaps the polar opposite of this arrangement is the companionate marriage found on many college campuses today. Much of this marital behavior is explicitly inconsistent with the norms of the culture and is done in secret—without the knowledge of the parents of the young couple. Thus, A and C control of the behavior is likely. Since many of the behaviors do not have a long-range consequence but rather depend on gratifications of the immediate moment, it is safe to guess that many of these behaviors are under the control of the A component. The relationship remains viable if the rewards exceed the costs. Reciprocity, equity, and equality norms derived from the larger culture may have an influence, however, in determining specific behaviors. For example, in deciding who is going to do the cleaning of the apartment, there may be role differentiation (you wash the dishes and I'll vacuum), alternation (you do it Mondays, Wednesdays, and Fridays and I'll do it Tuesdays, Thursdays, and Saturdays), or equity (since I pay more of the expenses, I should clean the floor less often). Thus, while the S component may not be an important determinant of behavior in all situations, it does influence some behaviors.

In any marriage, the expectations that each spouse has about the actions of the other determine in large measure the satisfactions that will be derived from the relationship. One of the reasons the American marital relationship is so unstable—in California, almost one marriage out of every two ends in divorce—is that (a) there are few social ties connected with the relationship (of the type noted in the Indian example above) and (b) the expectations of the partners are often unrealistically high. Unrealistic expectations may be the result of the way the mass media have dealt with marriage. They either focus on extreme problems or present an unrealistically idyllic marriage. In the mass entertainment media, romance and passionate love are important themes. While these are important elements in the modern pattern of *arriving* at marriage, they are not the central ingredients for a good and stable marriage over a fifty-year span of time. Rather, the development of interdependence through appreciation, common interests, complementary needs, and socioemotional compatibility are much more important to long-range success.

In the chapter on interpersonal perception, we noted the importance of physical attraction as a determinant of dating and further progress toward marriage. This is, of course, a factor that is relevant for, at most, 20 years and is obviously not a sufficient basis for a long-term relationship. The importance of compatibility can be seen in a study by Centers (1971) in which 60 engaged couples were given a personality inventory that measures motivational patterns. Centers found that acceptance of the partner was higher when a person was high on affiliation (need for others), nurturance (need to take care of others), deference (need to submit), dominance (need to control), succorance (need to help others), and abasement (need to lower one's position with respect to another) than when the subject was average or low on these motives. Furthermore, people who are high in autonomy (need to be independent) or in aggression (need to hurt others) find their partners less satisfactory than people who are average or low on these motive patterns find theirs. In short, those who need people and have motives involving relating to people rate their partners high; those who tend to go away from others or against others tend to rate their partners low. Such motive patterns develop relatively early in life and probably are more important for long-range relationships than for romantic love.

Speaking of romantic love—what is it?

Berscheid and Walster (1974) present a two-factor theory of the determinants of passionate love. They use Schachter's (1964) theory, which argues that a person feels an emotion if (a) he or she is aroused physiologically and (b) it is appropriate to interpret this stirred-up state in emotional terms. Berscheid and Walster review evidence consistent with the hypothesis that this two-step process is involved in romantic or passionate love. Specifically, they review studies that show that fear, anger, embarrassment, or guilt can increase *P*'s attraction toward an opposite-sex *O*. A girl who is generally hard to get but easy to get for *P* is likely to be more attractive to *P* than a girl who is either hard or easy for anyone to get. Parental interference in a love relationship intensifies the feelings of romantic love between *P* and *O*. Loneliness, deprivation, frustration, hatred, and insecurity are capable, under some conditions, of increasing romantic feelings. Passion demands physiological arousal, and unpleasant experiences are often arousing. Positive emotional arousal associated with sex, need satisfaction, or excitement can also be arousing. Once *P* is aroused, *P* must label the arousal *love*. Cultural norms specify whom it is reasonable to love. Physical attractiveness is a cue that can be used to label the arousal. Such factors help *P*'s label their emotion and lead them to experience passionate love.

From this analysis, it would seem that passionate love is not as desirable a basis for long-term commitments as the mass media and popular literature have often suggested. If the experience of love can arise from an accident such as some frustration, then romantic love is hardly a good basis for the development of long-term commitments. The combination of arousal due to a frustration and labeling of *love* due to physical attraction is truly an insecure basis for a marriage, for, when the frustration is no longer present, or the physical attributes no longer so obvious, the very bases for the marriage will be gone.

Marital adjustment has been found to be related to the way spouses think of themselves and their partners. There is evidence in the literature that, if a husband and wife assign traits to self, ideal self, spouse, and ideal spouse and predict what traits the spouse will assign to these concepts, some of the results are related to marital adjustment. Specifically, the greater the perceived similarity between partners, the greater the marital adjustment. The greater the self-acceptance, the greater the adjustment. The greater the perceived role compatibility, the greater the actual role compatibility. The greater the actual similarity, the greater the accuracy in predicting the spouse responses and the greater the marital adjustment. (See Murstein, 1971, for a review of many relevant studies.) Murstein shows that, for each partner, the more similar the spouse is seen as being to the ideal spouse, the greater is the marital adjustment.

Other work on need complementarity and compatibility was reviewed in Chapter 6. The literature on the subject is vast, and there are even special journals, such as the *Journal of Marriage and the Family*, that focus on this research area. In this journal, one finds many studies concerning the complementarity need theory of mate selection. In one such study (Karp, Jackson, & Lester, 1970), it was found that people select those who are perceived as similar to them on many traits; but, when the mate who is selected is not similar, then the mate turns out to be similar to the rater's ideal self. In short, similarity is found in either the ideal self or the actual self. In another study (Crouse, Karlins, & Schroder, 1968), it was found that couples high on a certain aspect of cognitive complexity (called integrative complexity) reported greater marital happiness than couples low on it.

These kinds of studies bring us close to being able to do a better job of predicting the outcome and stability of a marriage, using information about the characteristics of the two mates, than the two people are likely to be able to do on their own. In the next 50 years, this kind of research may provide reliable information that people can use when they make their decisions to marry or not to marry particular individuals.

There is much statistical evidence (which varies by region and by age of the spouses) that the majority of marriages are considered unsuccessful by those engaged in them. In some states, such as California, almost half the marriages end in divorce (Schoen, 1975). The probability of a divorce is much higher when the mates are very young (say, 16–24 years old) than when they are older (say, 25–35). Divorce is a very difficult experience for most people. Before deciding on this step, and particularly if there are children, people try to improve their marriage with some sort of family counseling.

The three major types of procedure to change interpersonal relations, which we discussed in Chapter 8, provide elements of intervention for the family counselor. Attribution training requires the counselor to teach each spouse to analyze interpersonal relationships not only according to his/her own theory of interpersonal behavior but also according to the partner's theory. The therapist might develop a series of 100 episodes involving family interaction and ask each partner to analyze the causes of the particular activity in the episodes. Discrepancies in such analyses can become the bases for discussion. As the partners realize that there are other ways of looking at these episodes, the range of attributions that they make to such episodes should become larger. Enlarging the range of attributions should increase cognitive complexity, which has been found to be related to marital happiness (Crouse, Karlins, & Schroder, 1968). The extent to which one partner makes a constructive response to actions of the other is related to marital satisfaction (Horowitz, 1970). Sensitivity training can also have some positive effects. Pilder (1972) found that such training improved both interpersonal perceptions and interpersonal skills (behavior). Finally, behavior modification can sometimes be used with success. For example, Azrin, Naster, and Jones (1973) used reinforcement theory to establish reciprocity in reinforcement (if you do X, I will do Y) by teaching reciprocity in several specific areas that were causes of marital unhappiness. The procedure was conducted over 4 weeks, with 12 couples. It was compared with a control procedure, which used catharsis counseling. A comparison of questionnaire responses before and after the treatment showed that the behavior-modification procedure shifted the responses in the positive direction for 96% of the sample.

SUMMARY

The theoretical ideas I presented in Chapters 1 through 7, about the determinants of interpersonal behavior, and the ideas in Chapter 8 about the changes in such behavior, have implications for practical activities designed to improve interpersonal relations. In this chapter, I suggested how some of these ideas can help us improve relations across cultures, in the employment interview, in supervisor-subordinate relations, in teacher-pupil relations, and in marital relations.

10

SUMMARY AND CONCLUSIONS

Social behaviors differ along four dimensions: associative versus dissociative, superordinate versus subordinate, intimate versus formal, and overt versus covert. The kind of interdependence between P and O determines the probability that associative social behaviors will take place between P and O. The more P's resources exceed O's, the more superordinate is P's behavior. The greater the age of the relationship, the more intimate the interpersonal behavior.

Behavior is a function of behavioral intentions and habits. Habits are a function of the frequency, intensity, and immediacy of reinforcements that follow particular acts. Intentions are a function of social, affective, and cognitive influences. Social influences are a function of norms, roles, social contracts, and the person's self-concept. Norms and roles reflect social situations, such as the kind of interdependence, the resource allocation, and the age of the relationship.

Interaction between P and O can be rewarding or punishing. Norms govern the response P will make to O. Reciprocity, equity, and equality are such norms. The expectations that each actor has about the behavior of the other have a strong influence on interaction. The more O behaves as expected by P, the more rewarding is O's action. The more O behaves so as to give resources to P, the more rewarding the action. P reacts to O's behavior according to the meaning that this behavior has for him or her. Propinquity is related to interpersonal attitudes such that, when P and O are similar and interact frequently, they like each other more than when P and O are dissimilar and/or do not interact frequently. When there is inequity in the relationship between *P* and *O*, attempts at compensation or justification for the inequity are likely to take place.

In analyzing social behavior, we must consider characteristics of *O*, characteristics of *P*, and the responses that *P* makes to *O*. Among the characteristics of *O* that are important are *O*'s age, sex, nationality, dress, and behavior.

P constructs an impression of *O* from cues derived from such characteristics, but perception is highly selective and inaccurate and strongly influenced by values and by *P*'s implicit personality theories. The way *P* processes information about *O* can be studied in terms of a number of theoretical models. One promising one is a weighted-average model proposed by Anderson. Another promising outlook comes from Fishbein and Ajzen (1975).

P makes three classes of responses: attributive, affective, and overt. Attribution theory helps us understand the first type of response. Characteristics of *P, O,* and the environment, as well as the similarity of *P* and *O*, account for affective responses. When *P* receives more rewards than costs from interaction with *O*, attraction between *P* and *O* is higher and the relationship is more likely to be long lasting. In addition to similarity, social comparisons (such as those discussed when we reviewed equity theory), status congruence, compatibility, and complementarity are relevant as determinants of attraction and of the quality of interpersonal relationships.

The antecedents of action proposed by the model appear well supported by empirical data. However, the weight of a given element of the model depends on the type of behavior, the type of person, and the social setting (including the culture) within which the interaction is taking place. Empirical demonstrations of these points were presented in Chapter 7.

Changes in the interpersonal relationship can be achieved through attribution training, sensitivity training, or behavior modification. These kinds of training are not incompatible; rather, they are complementary, each achieving a different goal.

Again and again, throughout this book, I've stressed the highly interactive nature of the laws of interpersonal behavior. In the past, many psychological theorists have attempted to develop laws that transcend particular behaviors, situations, or persons. The model of social behavior I've presented is an attempt to take these complexities into account. To do this, I posit shifts in the weights of the components of the model that depend on the type of behavior, situation, and person. The model is different from the typical trait approach (for example, Allport, 1966) and the typical Skinnerian position (1971). The former assumes that there are traits that determine behavior across situations, the latter that situations (described as "contingencies of reinforcement") determine behavior. While Skinner uses residues of learning derived from experience in a particular culture or situation among his determinants of behavior, there is no explication of the interaction of these residues with other inputs. Furthermore, personality is undoubtedly a function of both biological and environmental factors, and a model such as Skinner's which does not allow for personality to be a determinant of behavior, is bound to be oversimple.

Bowers (1973) and Cronbach (1975) have shown the value of an interactionist approach. Bowers, for example, summarized published studies in which the same person was studied in different situations and concluded that approximately 13% of the variance is accounted for by person factors, 11% by differences in situations, and 21% by interactions of persons and situations. However, the sample of studies he used is rather atypical, since most of these studies were done in mental hospitals. We need to do much more research on normal social behaviors in different cultures. Whiting and Whiting (1975) is a good example of the kind of studies that we need (see Chapter 7 for a description).

A more detailed reexamination of a study we discussed in Chapter 7 will serve as a review of the argument that complex interactions must be studied. An empirical demonstration of the interactions among the stimulus, person, and response modes was provided in a paper by Davis and me (Triandis & Davis, 1965). The stimulus mode in that study was manipulated by presenting hypothetical stimulus persons who differed in color (Black or White), belief (in favor of strong civil rights legislation or against it), and sex. The behavior mode was manipulated by asking the subjects to respond to several scales taken from the Semantic Differential (Osgood, Suci, & Tannenbaum, 1957) and the Behavioral Differential (Triandis, 1964). The scales were selected to represent the classic *evaluation, potency,* and *activity* factors of the Semantic Differential and the *respect, marital acceptance, friendship acceptance, social distance,* and *subordination* factors of the Behavioral Differential.

The responses of 300 subjects to these stimulus persons were subjected to a Tucker-Messick (1963) factor analysis, which gives both person factors and stimulus-response factors. Two types of subjects were discovered. One was labeled *conventionally prejudiced* and was characterized by rejection of Black stimulus persons regardless of their beliefs. These individuals were significantly higher on the F scale, less tolerant of minorities, and less critical of established social institutions than were those low on this factor. In addition, they disapproved of a federal law against housing discrimination, the establishment of biracial committees, and the Supreme Court decision on school desegregation. They also responded negatively to the idea of a Negro President and to sit-ins, freedom marches, and interracial marriages. They believed that integrated housing leads to a decline in property values and to slums, that interracial marriages lead to lower morals and a bad society, and that a Negro President would lead to a depression and to injustices to

Whites. In short, several other kinds of measures were consistently associated with this factor, suggesting a very broad cluster of attitudes consistent with race prejudice.

Those low on this same factor tended to be more tolerant of interracial marriages, low on the F scale, tolerant of minorities, and critical of social institutions. They opposed segregation and were only slightly negative with respect to a Negro President, freedom rides, freedom marches, sit-ins, and interracial marriages.

Another type of subject was characterized by rejection of people who differed from the subject in beliefs. This was clear on both the Semantic and Behavioral Differential scales. Those high on this factor considered a stimulus person who was against civil rights legislation "good." They considered most interracial issues more important than did the less-prejudiced subjects of the previous factor. We called them *belief prejudiced,* since they paid so much attention to belief about civil rights and considered most issues having to do with civil rights important. We showed that these people were also opposed to socialized medicine, disarmament, federal enforcement of the Supreme Court school desegregation decision, freedom marches, sit-ins, and so on.

Analyses of the responses of the two types of subjects on the various scales showed major differences in the way the race prejudiced and belief prejudiced reacted to the stimulus persons. Specifically, the race prejudiced showed formal social rejection, subordination, friendship rejection, and social distance much more on the basis of race than on the basis of belief. They did not show any significant effects in the way they *evaluated* the stimulus person. In other words, they saw Blacks and Whites as equally good, clean, and beautiful; the rejection was manifested on behavioral-intention scales. The belief prejudiced rejected the stimuli on the basis of beliefs. They rejected them on the basis of race only in intimate social relations. In contrast to the pattern of evaluation shown by the race prejudiced, the belief prejudiced also rejected evaluatively people who differed in beliefs. Davis and I ordered the responses of all the subjects on a continuum from formal to intimate. We showed that, when the response was formal, rejection on the basis of belief was much more probable, while, when the response was intimate, rejection on the basis of race was much more probable. However, these patterns had to be modified, depending on whether the subjects were belief prejudiced or race prejudiced. The race prejudiced showed a huge race effect for the intimate behaviors and had a substantial race effect for the formal behaviors, while the belief prejudiced showed a moderate belief effect for the formal behaviors that dropped considerably in the case of the intimate behaviors.

A replication of these findings by Goldstein and Davis (1972) is impressive because it shows that data collected four years after the previous study, from subjects in a different part of the country, utilizing different measures of behavioral intentions and completely different belief stimuli resulted in the identification of race rejectors and belief rejectors. Furthermore, the race rejectors showed many of the characteristics we found in the conventionally prejudiced, and the belief rejectors showed a pattern of responses similar to those of the belief prejudiced. In addition, Goldstein and Davis showed that the race rejectors perceived important others as being more disapproving of interracial contacts than did belief rejectors. Thus, the race rejectors gave a larger weight to the S component when an interracial contact was considered. Again, Goldstein and Davis showed that the characteristics of the stimulus persons, the characteristics of the response continuum, and the characteristics of the subjects making the responses must be taken into account to understand the behavioral intentions of individuals.

A similar point is made by Canon and Mathews (1971), who showed that *Englishmen* are judged by American Whites primarily in terms of the kinds of beliefs that they have, while *Blacks* are responded to primarily in terms of their race, rather than their beliefs. In short, one needs to consider the interaction between the stimulus and the response in determining how a subject is going to respond.

From these considerations it follows that the relative weights to be given to the various components of the model must take into account interactions among characteristics of the stimuli being judged, the types of persons making the judgments, and the type of responses being made. I've also pointed out that there are major cultural differences in the way subjects respond to others having particular patterns of characteristics. For example, Americans pay much more attention to race than do Greeks, while the latter pay much more attention to the religion of a stimulus person.

If there is anything that emerges from the argument that I've just completed, it is the need to be more specific about the types of stimuli, types of responses, types of individuals, and types of cultural settings to which any set of social-psychological findings is to be generalized.

LIMITATIONS AND FUTURE RESEARCH

The backbone of this book is a model of social behavior, which I used to synthesize many of the findings on interpersonal behavior reported in the social-psychological literature. While much of the argument seems reasonable, it should be clear to the reader that much more research is needed to establish the utility of the model. First, the actual tests of the model have been few and were done with particular populations, focusing on specific social behaviors. While this and related research have supported the model, much

more needs to be done. Second, it is as yet unclear how to combine information relevant to each of the model's components. Specifically, we don't know
whether the information obtained from the various elements of the S component should be combined additively, multiplicatively, or in some other
fashion. (Just-completed research by Brinberg, 1976, supports additivity.) Is
it desirable to add a motivation-to-comply term, as does Fishbein? In some
studies this seemed to help, and in other studies it seemed to hinder. I don't
know exactly why. Third, we know that in some cultures the S component is
more important than in others, but we don't know enough about the reasons
for such variations. We know that some people give more emphasis to one or
another of the components of the model, but we don't know about the socialization antecedents of these tendencies. We do know that some behaviors are controlled primarily by the S, A, or C component, but, again, we
have an imperfect understanding of the determinants.

Turning from the model to the understanding of the relationship
between two people, we find once again that our understanding is limited.
We don't know, for instance, exactly when two people will be making
isomorphic attributions, or even the best way to measure these. We don't
know whether changing people's expectations and changing their patterns of
interpersonal reinforcement are the most powerful of several possible
procedures for altering interpersonal behavior. We don't know how to combine attribution training, sensitivity training, and behavior modification to
develop the best package or course of action to bring about interpersonal
behavior change.

Beyond the limitations of the particular model, there are even more
fundamental challenges. There is a crisis in social psychology that stems
from our inability to develop general theories of social behavior that are likely to hold across time and place (Gergen, 1973). We do have many specific
theories, but they account for very little of the variance of any social
phenomenon. Thus, when we want to understand, predict, or explain social
phenomena, we are invariably faced with the fact that many different
theories may be applicable and are likely to apply jointly in some unspecified
way.

Interactions of our theoretically important variables with time, sampling of subjects, and place are not predictable from existing theories.
Alterations of our theoretical formulations, introduced by cultural and
temporal factors, threaten all but the most universal of our theoretical
statements.

There are even challenges to the whole enterprise of social-science
research. Many psychologists steeped in the philosophy of science, such as
Meehl (1970a, 1970b) argue that "a large portion of current research in the
behavior sciences, while meeting the conventionally accepted standards of
adequate design, must be viewed as methodologically unsound" (1970a, pp.
401–402). This conclusion is derived from careful consideration of the

method of comparison, which is the most important method of social science. We compare groups, such as an experimental and a control group, cultures, sexes, ages, nationalities, and so on. When we make such comparisons and try to control for the effects of nuisance variables, we run into serious methodological problems. For example, if we want to compare men and women, and we try to control for a nuisance variable, such as verbal fluency, we are likely to commit serious errors in drawing our conclusions. Such controls tend to make the samples unrepresentative and to unbalance them on many variables of which we are not aware. Meehl concludes that this approach is fundamentally unsound. Yet it is one of the basic designs used in social science. Furthermore, we test deductions from our theories, using statistical procedures. It can be shown that, if the sample used to test a theory is sufficiently large, there is a probability of .5 (an even chance) that even an idiotic theory will be supported at respectable levels of significance (Lykken, 1968; Meehl, 1970a).

The large number of interactions and the inadequacy of our research methodology suggest the impossibility of developing a broad theory that has the same role in the social sciences that a theory holds in the physical sciences. We can do two things. We can describe very well particular populations at particular points in time. And we can develop loose theoretical frameworks, such as the model I introduced in Chapter 1, that include the explanatory concepts we need to account for social phenomena. Such frameworks are ways of thinking about social phenomena, but they are not predictive systems or systems that account precisely for the complexity of social phenomena. This view is similar to Cronbach's conclusion: "Though enduring systematic theories about man in society are not likely to be achieved, systematic inquiry can realistically hope to make two contributions. One reasonable aspiration is to assess local events accurately, to improve short-run control. The other aspiration is to develop explanatory concepts, concepts that will help people use their heads" (1975, p. 126). Cronbach ends as follows: "The special task of the social scientist in each generation is to pin down the contemporary facts. Beyond that he shares with the humanistic scholar and the artist in the effort to gain insight into contemporary relationships, and to realign the culture's view of man with present realities. To know man as he is is no mean aspiration" (p. 126).

This pessimistic view probably applies to the development of broad theory concerning social behavior. It probably does *not* apply to the limited area of information processing, which we covered in Chapter 4, where the procedures that can be used (for example, Anderson's work) have much in common with the procedures used in psychophysics. But, aside from this exception, this view is probably applicable.

The model I presented in this book, and the loose connections shown among the concepts of this model and other concepts, should help us think about people and interpersonal behavior. They will, of course, not predict particular interpersonal behaviors, nor will they help us understand all of them. However, they are essential for what Cronbach calls "using our heads" about interpersonal behavior.

In short, this book must be seen as an introduction to a dilemma. We researchers know enough about the topic to know that we know too little about it. We need more people who will read this book and go on to study the basic literature, design more studies, answer some of the questions I've outlined, and throw light on some of the areas of ignorance I've just listed. More than that, as people engage in interpersonal behavior, they may find the analysis provided in this book helpful and a good basis for new insights. If this happens, the book will be helpful not only as a text on interpersonal behavior but also as a guide for future action.

REFERENCES

Abelson, R. P. Modes of resolution of belief dilemmas. *Journal of Conflict Resolution,* 1959, *3,* 343–352.

Abelson, R. P., Aronson, E., McGuire, W. J., Newcomb, T. M., Rosenberg, M. J., & Tannenbaum, P. H. *Theories of cognitive consistency: A sourcebook.* Chicago: Rand McNally, 1968.

Abelson, R. P., & Rosenberg, M. J. Symbolic psychologic: A model of attitudinal cognition. *Behavioral Science,* 1958, *3,* 1–13.

Aboud, F. E., & Taylor, D. M. Ethnic and role stereotypes: Their relative importance in person perception. *Journal of Social Psychology,* 1971, *85,* 17–27.

Aboud, F. E., & Taylor, D. M. Evaluative and information seeking consequences of discrepancy in ethnic perception. Mimeograph, Department of Psychology, McGill University, 1972.

Acock, A. C., & DeFleur, M. L. A configurational approach to contingent consistency in the attitude-behavior relationship. *American Sociological Review,* 1972, *37,* 714–726.

Adamopoulos, I., & Brinberg, D. An examination of the determinants of social behavior. Submitted for publication, 1975.

Adams, J. S. Inequity in social exchange. In L. Berkowitz (Ed.), *Advances in experimental social psychology.* New York: Academic Press, 1965.

Ajzen, I. Attribution of dispositions to an actor: Effects of perceiver decision freedom and behavioral utilities. *Journal of Personality and Social Psychology,* 1971, *18,* 144–156.

Ajzen, I., & Fishbein, M. The prediction of behavioral intentions in a choice situation. *Journal of Experimental Social Psychology,* 1969, *5,* 400–416.

Ajzen, I., & Fishbein, M. The prediction of behavior from attitudinal and normative variables. *Journal of Experimental Social Psychology,* 1970, *6,* 466–487.

Ajzen, I., & Fishbein, M. Attitudinal and normative variables as predictors of specific behaviors. *Journal of Personality and Social Psychology,* 1973, *27,* 41–57.

Allen, V. L., & Levine, J. M. Social support and conformity: The role of independent assessment of reality. *Journal of Experimental Social Psychology,* 1971, *7,* 48–58.

Allport, G. W. Traits revisited. *American Psychologist,* 1966, *21,* 1–10.

Altman, I., & Haythorn, W. W. Interpersonal exchange in isolation. *Sociometry,* 1965, *23,* 411–426.

Altman, I., & Taylor, D. A. *Social penetration.* New York: Holt, Rinehart and Winston, 1973.

Amir, Y. Contact hypothesis in ethnic relations. *Psychological Bulletin,* 1969, *71,* 319–342.

Anderson, N. H. Functional measurement and psychological judgment. *Psychological Review,* 1970, *77,* 153–170.

Anderson, N. H. *Information integration theory: A brief survey.* La Jolla, Calif.: Center for Information Processing, 1972. (a)

Anderson, N. H. Looking for configurality in clinical judgment. *Psychological Bulletin,* 1972, *78,* 93–102. (b)

Anderson, N. H. Cognitive algebra: Integration theory applied to social attribution. In L. Berkowitz (Ed.), *Advances in experimental social psychology* (Vol. 7). New York: Academic Press, 1974.

Arendt, H. *Eichman in Jerusalem.* New York: Viking Press, 1963.

Argyle, M., & Kendon, A. The experimental analysis of social performance. In L. Berkowitz (Ed.), *Advances in experimental social psychology.* (Vol. 3). New York: Academic Press, 1967.

Aronson, E., & Mettee, D. R. Dishonest behavior as a function of differential levels of induced self-esteem. *Journal of Personality and Social Psychology,* 1968, *9,* 121–127.

Asch, S. E. Forming impressions of personality. *Journal of Abnormal and Social Psychology,* 1946, *41,* 258–290.

Azrin, N. H., Hutchinson, R. R., & Hake, D. F. Extinction induced aggression. *Journal of Experimental Analysis of Behavior,* 1966, *9,* 191–204.

Azrin, N. H., Naster, B. J., & Jones, R. Reciprocity counseling: A rapid learning-based procedure for marital counseling. *Behavioral Research and Therapy,* 1973, *11,* 365–382.

Back, K. W. *Beyond words.* Baltimore, Md.: Penguin Books, 1973.

Back, K. W., Bunker, S., & Dunnagan, C. B. Barriers to communication and measurement of semantic space. *Sociometry,* 1972, *35,* 347–356.

Bales, R. F. *Interaction process analysis.* Cambridge, Mass.: Addison-Wesley, 1950.

Bandura, A. *Aggression: A social learning analysis.* Englewood Cliffs, N. J.: Prentice-Hall, 1972.

Bandura, A., & Walters, R. H. *Adolescent aggression.* New York: Ronald Press, 1959.

Bandura, A., & Walters, R. H. *Social learning and personality development.* New York: Holt, Rinehart and Winston, 1963.

Barker, R. *Ecological psychology. Concepts and methods for studying the environment of human behavior.* Stanford, Calif.: Stanford Press, 1968.

Baron, R. Social reinforcement effects as a function of social reinforcement history. *Psychological Review,* 1966, *73,* 527–539.

Batchelor, T. R., & Tesser, A. Attitude base as a moderator of the attitude similarity-attraction relationship. *Journal of Personality and Social Psychology,* 1971, *19,* 229–236.

Bem, D. J. An experimental analysis of self-persuasion. *Journal of Experimental Social Psychology,* 1965, *1,* 199–218.

Bem, D. J. Self-perception: An alternative interpretation of cognitive dissonance phenomena. *Psychological Review,* 1967, *74,* 183–200.

Bem, S. L. The measurement of psychological androgyny. *Journal of Consulting and Clinical Psychology,* 1974, *42,* 155–162.

Bem, S. L. Sex-role adaptability: One consequence of psychological androgyny. *Journal of Personality and Social Psychology,* 1975, *31,* 634–643.

Bender, I. E., & Hastorf, A. H. On measuring generalized empathic ability (social sensitivity). *Journal of Abnormal and Social Psychology,* 1953, *48,* 503–506.

Benjamin, L. S. Structural analysis of social behavior. *Psychological Review,* 1974, *81,* 392–425.

Berg, I. A., & Bass, B. M. *Conformity and deviation.* New York: Harper, 1961.

Berkowitz, L. *Aggression: A social psychological analysis.* New York: McGraw-Hill, 1962.

Berkowitz, L. The frustration-aggression hypothesis revisited. In L. Berkowitz (Ed.), *Roots of aggression.* New York: Atherton Press, 1969.

Berkowitz, L. *A survey of social psychology.* Hinsdale, Ill.: The Dryden Press, 1975.

Berkowitz, L., & Connor, W. H. Success, failure, and social responsibility. *Journal of Personality and Social Psychology,* 1966, *4,* 664–669.

Berkowitz, L., & Friedman, P. Some social class differences in helping behavior. *Journal of Personality and Social Psychology,* 1967, *5,* 217–225.

Bernstein, B. A. Critique of the concept of compensatory education. In B. Bernstein (Ed.), *Class, codes and control* (Vol. 1). London: Routledge & Kegan Paul, 1971.

Berry, J. W. Independence and conformity in subsistence level societies. *Journal of Personality and Social Psychology,* 1967, *7,* 415–418.

Berry, J. W. A functional approach to the relationship between stereotypes and familiarity. *Australian Journal of Psychology,* 1970, *22,* 29–33.

Berscheid, E., & Walster, E. H. *Interpersonal attraction.* Reading, Mass.: Addison-Wesley, 1969.

Berscheid, E., & Walster, E. Romantic attraction. In T. L. Huston (Ed.), *Foundation of interpersonal attraction.* New York: Academic Press, 1974.

Blumberg, H. H. Communication of interpersonal evaluations. *Journal of Personality and Social Psychology,* 1972, *23,* 157–162.

Blumberg, L., & Winch, R. F. Societal complexity and familial complexity: Evidence for the curvilinear hypothesis. *American Journal of Sociology,* 1972, *77,* 896–920.

Blumenthal, M. D. Predicting attitudes toward violence. *Science,* 1972, *176,* 1296–1303.

Bodalyev, A. A. The effect of the profession of actor in his perception and understanding of both himself and other people. Paper presented at the XXth International Congress of Psychology. *Abstract Guide of Congress,* Tokyo, 1972, 671.

Bogart, L. Warning: The Surgeon General has determined that TV violence is moderately dangerous to your child's mental health. *The Public Opinion Quarterly,* Winter 1972–1973, *36,* 491–521.

Bolles, R. C. Reinforcement, expectancy and learning. *Psychological Review,* 1972, *79,* 394–409.

Bowers, K. S. Situationism in psychology: An analysis and a critique. *Psychological Review,* 1973, *80,* 307–336.

Boyanowsky, E. O., & Allen, V. L. Ingroup norms and self-identity as determinants of discriminatory behavior. *Journal of Personality and Social Psychology,* 1973, *25,* 408–418.

Bridgeman, W. Student attraction and productivity as a composite function of reinforcement and expectancy conditions. *Journal of Personality and Social Psychology,* 1972, *23,* 249–258.

Brigham, J. C. Ethnic stereotypes. *Psychological Bulletin,* 1971, *76,* 15–38.

Brinberg, D. *Additive vs multiplicative determinants of social pressure in predicting family size intentions.* Unpublished master's thesis, University of Illinois, 1976.

Brislin, R., & Omstead, K. H. An examination of two models designed to predict behavior from attitudes and other variables. Mimeograph, Honolulu, Hawaii, East-West Center, 1973.

Broedling, L. A. Relationship of internal-external control to work motivation and performance in an expectancy model. *Journal of Applied Psychology*, 1975, *60*, 65–70.

Brown, R. *Social psychology*. New York: Free Press, 1965.

Brown, R., & Lenneberg, E. H. A study of language and cognition. *Journal of Abnormal and Social Psychology*, 1954, *49*, 454–462.

Bruner, E. M. Batak ethnic associations in three Indonesian cities. *Southwestern Journal of Anthropology*, 1972, *28*, 207–229.

Bruvold, W. H. Belief and behavior as determinants of attitude. *The Journal of Social Psychology*, 1973, *90*, 285–289.

Bryan, J. H., & Test, M. A. Models and helping: Naturalistic studies in aiding behavior. *Journal of Personality and Social Psychology*, 1967, *6*, 400–407.

Bryson, J. B. Factor analysis of impression formation processes. *Journal of Personality and Social Psychology*, 1974, *30*, 134–143.

Bugental, D. E. Inconsistency between verbal and nonverbal components in parental communication patterns: Its integration and effects. Paper presented at XXth International Congress of Psychology. *Abstract Guide (SS 4-1)*, 1972.

Bumpass, L. L., & Sweet, J. A. Differential in marital instability. *American Sociological Review*, 1972, *37*, 754–766.

Buss, A. H. Physical aggression in relation to different frustrations. *Journal of Abnormal and Social Psychology*, 1963, *67*, 1–7.

Byrne, D. *The attraction paradigm*. New York: Academic Press, 1971.

Byrne, D., & Clore, G. L. Effectance arousal and attraction. *Journal of Personality and Social Psychology Monograph*, 1967, *6*, No. 4, 1–18.

Byrne, D., Ervin, C. R., & Lamberth, J. Continuity between the experimental study of attraction and real-life computer dating. *Journal of Personality and Social Psychology*, 1970, *16*, 157–165.

Byrne, D., Fisher, J. D., Lamberth, J., & Mitchell, H. E. Evaluations of erotica: Facts or feelings? Mimeograph, 1972.

Byrne, D., & Griffitt, W. Interpersonal attraction. *Annual Review of Psychology*, 1973, *24*, 317–336.

Byrne, D., London, O., & Griffitt, W. The effect of topic importance and attitude similarity-dissimilarity on attraction in an intra-stranger design. *Psychonomic Science*, 1968, *11*, 303–304.

Campbell, A. Civil rights and the vote for President. *Psychology Today*, 1968, *1*, 26–70.

Campbell, D. T. Social attitudes and other acquired behavioral dispositions. In S. Koch (Ed.), *Psychology: A study of a science*. New York: McGraw-Hill, 1963.

Campbell, D. T. Stereotypes and the perception of group differences. *American Psychologist*, 1967, *22*, 817–829.

Campbell, D. T., & LeVine, R. A. Ethnocentrism and intergroup relations. In R. P. Abelson, E. Aronson, W. J. McGuire, T. M. Newcomb, M. J. Rosenberg, & P. H. Tannenbaum (Eds.), *Theories of cognitive consistency: A sourcebook*. Chicago: Rand McNally, 1968.

Canon, L. K., & Mathews, K., Jr. Ethnicity, belief, social distance and interpersonal evaluation: A methodological critique. *Sociometry*, 1971, *34*, 515–523.

Carter, L. F. Evaluating the performance of individuals as members of small groups. *Personnel Psychology*, 1954, *7*, 477–484.

Cauthen, N. R., Robinson, E. A., & Krauss, H. H. Stereotypes: A review of the literature 1926–1968. *Journal of Social Psychology*, 1971, *84*, 103–125.

Centers, R. Evaluating the loved one: The motivational congruency factor. *Journal of Personality*, 1971, *39*, 303–318.

Chaikin, A. L., & Cooper, J. Evaluation as a function of correspondence and hedonic relevance. *Journal of Experimental Social Psychology*, 1973, *9*, 257–264.

Chalmers, D. K. Meaning, impressions, and attitudes: A model of the evaluation process. *Psychological Review*, 1969, *76*, 450–460.

Chemers, M. M., Rice, R. W., Sundstrom, E., & Butler, W. M. Leader esteem for the least preferred co-worker score, training, and effectiveness: An experimental examination. *Journal of Personality and Social Psychology*, 1975, *31*, 401–409.

Chemers, M. M., & Skrzypek, G. J. An experimental test of the contingency model of leadership effectiveness. *Journal of Personality and Social Psychology*, 1972, *24*, 172–177.

Cherry, F., Byrne, D., & Mitchell, H. E. Clogs in the bogus pipeline: Demand characteristics and social desirability. Mimeograph, 1975.

Cialdini, R. B., Braver, S. L., & Lewis, S. K. Attributional bias and the easily persuaded other. *Journal of Personality and Social Psychology*, 1974, *30*, 631–637.

Cisin, I. H., Coffin, T. E., Janis, I. L., Klapper, J. T., Mendelsohn, H., Omwake, E., Pinderhughes, C. A., Pool, I., Siegel, A. E., Wallace, A. F. C., Watson, A. S., & Wiebe, G. D. *Television and growing up: The impact of televised violence.* Washington, D. C.: U. S. Government Printing Office, 1972.

Cline, V. B. Interpersonal perception. In B. M. Maher (Ed.), *Progress in experimental personality research* (Vol. 1). New York: Academic Press, 1964.

Clore, G. L., & Byrne, D. A reinforcement-affect model of attraction. In T. L. Huston (Ed.), *Foundation of interpersonal attraction.* New York: Academic Press, 1974.

Clore, G. L., & Bryne, D. The process of personality interaction. In R. B. Cattell & R. M. Dreger (Eds.), *Handbook of modern personality theory.* New York: Appleton-Century-Crofts, in press.

Cole, M., & Scribner, S. *Culture and thought.* New York: Wiley, 1974.

Collins, B. E. Four components of the Rotter Internal-External Scale: Belief in a difficult world, a just world, a predictable world, and a politically responsive world. *Journal of Personality and Social Psychology*, 1974, *29*, 381–391.

Collins, B. E., Martin, J. C., Ashmore, R. D., & Ross, L. Some dimensions of the internal-external metaphor in theories of personality. *Journal of Personality*, 1973, *41*, 471–492.

Cooper, J. B. Emotion in prejudice. *Science*, 1959, *130*, 314–318.

Crespi, I. What kinds of attitude measures are predictive of behavior? *Public Opinion Quarterly*, 1971, *35*, 327–334.

Crockett, W. H. Cognitive complexity and impression formation. In B. A. Maher (Ed.), *Progress in experimental personality research* (Vol. 2). New York: Academic Press, 1965.

Cronbach, L. Processes affecting scores on "understanding of others" and "assumed similarity." *Psychological Bulletin*, 1955, *52*, 177–193.

Cronbach, L. J. Beyond the two disciplines of scientific psychology, *American Psychologist*, 1975, *30*, 116–127.

Crook, J. H. The socio-ecology of primates. In J. H. Crook (Ed.), *Social behavior in birds and mammals.* New York: Academic Press, 1974.

Crouse, B., Karlins, M., & Schroder, H. Conceptual complexity and marital happiness. *Journal of Marriage and the Family*, 1968, *30*, 643–646.

Crow, W. J., & Hammond, K. B. The generality of accuracy and response in interpretation of interpersonal perception. *Journal of Abnormal and Social Psychology,* 1957, *54,* 384–390.

D'Andrade, R. G. Cognitive structure and judgment. Paper prepared for the Committee on Basic Research in Education Workshop on Cognitive Organization and Psychological Processes, Huntington Beach, Calif., 1970.

Darley, J. M., & Batson, C. D. From Jerusalem to Jericho: A study of situational and dispositional variables in helping behavior. *Journal of Personality and Social Psychology,* 1973, *27,* 100–108.

David, K. H. *Intercultural adjustment and applications of reinforcement theory to problems of "culture shock."* Hilo, Hawaii: Center for Cross-Cultural Training, 1972.

Davidson, A. *The prediction of family planning intentions.* Unpublished doctoral dissertation, University of Illinois, 1973.

Davidson, A. R. Cognitive differentiation and culture training. In R. Brislin, S. Bochner, & W. Lonner (Eds.), *Cross-cultural perspectives on learning.* New York: Halsted/Wiley, 1975.

Davidson, A. R., Jaccard, J. J., Triandis, H. C., Morales, M. L., & Diaz-Guerrero, R. Cross-cultural model testing: Toward a solution of the etic-emic dilemma. *International Journal of Psychology,* 1976.

Davidson, A. R., & Steiner, I. D. Reinforcement schedules and attributed freedom. *Journal of Personality and Social Psychology,* 1971, *19,* 357–366.

Dawes, R. M. Social selection based on multidimensional criteria. *Journal of Abnormal and Social Psychology,* 1964, *68,* 104–109.

DeFriese, G. H., & Ford, W. S. Verbal attitudes, overt acts and the influence of social constraint in interracial behavior. *Social Problems,* 1969, *16,* 493–505.

Deutsch, M. A theory of cooperation and competition. *Human Relations,* 1949, *2,* 129–152.

Dienstbier, R. A. A modified belief theory of prejudice emphasizing the mutual causality of racial prejudice and anticipated belief differences. *Psychological Review,* 1972, *79,* 146–160.

Dillehay, R. C., Bruvold, W. H., & Siegel, J. P. On the assessment of potability. *Journal of Applied Psychology,* 1967, *51,* 89–95.

Donnenwerth, G. V., & Foa, U. G. Effect of resource class on retaliation to injustice in interpersonal exchange. *Journal of Personality and Social Psychology,* 1974, *29,* 785–793.

Doob, L. W. *Resolving conflict in Africa.* New Haven, Conn.: Yale University Press, 1970.

Doob, L. W. Unofficial intervention in destructive social conflicts. In R. W. Brislin, S. Bochner, & W. J. Lonner (Eds.), *Cross-cultural perspectives on learning.* New York: Sage/Halsted/Wiley, 1975.

Duck, S. W., & Spencer, C. Personal constructs and friendship formation. *Journal of Personality and Social Psychology,* 1972, *23,* 40–45.

Dulany, D. E. The place of hypotheses and intentions: An analysis of verbal control in verbal conditioning. In C. W. Eriksen (Ed.), *Behavior and awareness.* Durham, N.C.: Duke University Press, 1962.

Dulany, D. E. Awareness, rules, and propositional control: A confrontation with behavior S-R theory. In D. Horton & T. Dixon (Eds.), *Verbal behavioral and S-R behavior theory.* New York: Prentice-Hall, 1968.

Dulany, D. E. Personal communication, 1974.

Dunnette, M. D. Sensitivity and openness: Why, when and toward whom? *Innovation,* June 1970.

Dustin, D. S., & Baldwin, P. M. Redundancy in impression formation. *Journal of Personality and Social Psychology,* 1966, *3,* 500–506.

Dutton, D. G., & Arrowood, A. J. Situational factors in evaluation congruency and interpersonal attraction. *Journal of Personality and Social Psychology,* 1971, *18,* 222–229.

Dweck, C. S. The role of expectations and attributions in the alleviation of learned helplessness. *Journal of Personality and Social Psychology,* 1975, *31,* 674–685.

Edwards, A. L. Four dimensions in political stereotypes. *Journal of Abnormal and Social Psychology,* 1940, *35,* 566–572.

Ehrlich, H. J. Attitudes, behavior, and the intervening variables. *The American Sociologist,* 1969, *4,* 29–34.

Ehrlich, H. J., & Lipsey, C. Affective style as a variable in person perception. *Journal of Personality,* 1969, *37,* 522–540.

Einhorn, H. J. Expert measurement and mechanical combination. *Organizational Behavior and Human Performance,* 1972, *7,* 86–106.

Einhorn, H. J., Komorita, S. S., & Rosen, B. Multidimensional models for the evaluation of political candidates. *Journal of Experimental Social Psychology,* 1972, *8,* 58–73.

Eisen, M. Characteristic self-esteem, sex and resistance to temptation. *Journal of Personality and Social Psychology,* 1972, *24,* 68–72.

Ekman,P. Differential communication of affect by head and body cues. *Journal of Personality and Social Psychology,* 1965, *2,* 726–735.

Ekman, P. Universals and cultural differences in facial expressions of emotion. In J. Cole (Ed.), *Nebraska symposium on motivation, 1971.* Lincoln: University of Nebraska Press, 1972.

Ekman, P., & Friesen, W. V. Head and body cues in the judgment of emotion: A reformulation. *Perceptual and Motor Skills,* 1967, *24,* 711–724.

Ekman, P., & Friesen, W. V. Hand movements. *The Journal of Communication,* 1972, *22,* 353–374.

Ekman, P., & Friesen, W. V. Nonverbal behavior and psychopathology. In R. J. Friedman & M. M. Katz (Eds.), *The psychology of depression: contemporary theory and research.* New York: Halsted Press, 1974.

Ekman, P., Sorenson, E. R., & Friesen, W. V. Pan-cultural elements in facial displays of emotions. *Science,* 1969, *164,* 86–88.

Ellsworth, P. C., Carlsmith, J. M., & Henson, A. The stare as a stimulus to flight in human subjects: A series of field experiments. *Journal of Personality and Social Psychology,* 1972, *21,* 302–311.

Epstein, R. Authoritarianism, displaced aggression, and social status of the target. *Journal of Personality and Social Psychology,* 1965, *2,* 585–589.

Epstein, S. The self concept revisited: Or, a theory of a theory. *American Psychologist,* 1973, *28,* 404–416.

Eriksen, B. A., & Eriksen, C. W. *Perception and personality.* Morristown, N. J.: General Learning Corp., 1972.

Erlanger, H. S. Violence by blacks and low income whites: Some new evidence in the subculture of violence thesis. Discussion paper 208–74, University of Wisconsin, Institute for Research on Poverty, 1974.

Eron, L. D., Walder, L. O. & Lefkowitz, M. M. *Learning of aggression in children.* Boston: Little, Brown, 1971.

Estes, W. K. Reinforcement in human behavior. *American Scientist,* 1972, *60,* 723–729.

Evans, G. W., & Howard, R. B. Personal Space. *Psychological Bulletin,* 1973, *80,* 334–344.

Farina, A., Chapnick, B., Chapnick, J., & Misiti, R. Political views and interpersonal behavior. *Journal of Personality and Social Psychology,* 1972, *22,* 273–278.

Feldman, J. M. Stimulus characteristics and subject prejudice as determinants of stereotypes attribution. *Journal of Personality and Social Psychology,* 1972, *21,* 333–340.

Feldman, R. E. Response to compatriot and foreigner who seek assistance. *Journal of Personality and Social Psychology,* 1968, *10,* 202–214.

Festinger, L. A theory of social comparison processes. *Human Relations,* 1954, *7,* 117–140.

Festinger, L. *A theory of cognitive dissonance.* Stanford, Calif.: Stanford University Press, 1957.

Festinger, L., Riecken, H., & Schachter, S. *When prophecy fails.* Minneapolis, Minn.: University of Minnesota Press, 1956.

Festinger, L., Schachter, S., & Back, K. W. *Social pressures in informal groups.* New York: Harper, 1950.

Fiedler, F. E. *A theory of leadership effectiveness.* New York: McGraw-Hill, 1967.

Fiedler, F. E., & Chemers, M. M. *Leader match.* Seattle, Wash.: Department of Psychology, 1974. (a)

Fiedler, F. E., & Chemers, M. M. *Leadership and effective management.* Glenview, Ill.: Scott, Foresman, 1974. (b)

Fiedler, F. E., Mitchell, T., & Triandis, H. C. The culture assimilator: An approach to cross-cultural training. *Journal of Applied Psychology,* 1971, *55,* 95–102.

Fischer, E. H. Who volunteers for companionship with mental patients? A study of attitude-belief-intention relationships. *Journal of Personality,* 1971, *39,* 552–563.

Fischer, H., & Trier, U. P. *Das Verhaltnis zwischen Deutschweizer und Westschweizer: Eine sozialpychologische untersuchung.* Bern: Hans Huber, 1962.

Fishbein, M. An investigation of the relationship between beliefs about an object and the attitude toward that object. *Human Relations,* 1963, *16,* 233–240.

Fishbein, M. A consideration of beliefs, attitudes and their relationship. In I. D. Steiner & M. Fishbein (Eds.), *Current studies in social psychology.* New York: Holt, Rinehart and Winston, 1965.

Fishbein, M. A behavior theory approach to the relations between beliefs about an object and the attitude toward the object. In M. Fishbein (Ed.), *Readings in attitude theory and measurement.* New York: Wiley, 1967. (a)

Fishbein, M. Attitude and the prediction of behavior. In M. Fishbein (Ed.), *Readings in attitude theory and measurement.* New York: Wiley, 1967. (b)

Fishbein, M. The prediction of behavior from attitudinal variables. In C. D. Mortensen & K. K. Sereno (Eds.), *Advances in communication research.* New York: Harper, 1973.

Fishbein, M., & Ajzen, I. Attribution of responsibility: A theoretical note. *Journal of Experimental Social Psychology,* 1973, *9,* 148–153.

Fishbein, M., & Ajzen, I. Attitudes towards objects as predictors of single and multiple behavioral criteria. *Psychological Review,* 1974, *81,* 59–74.

Fishbein, M., & Ajzen, I. *Belief, attitude, intention and behavior: An introduction to theory and research.* Reading, Mass.: Addison-Wesley, 1975.

Fishbein, M., & Hunter, R. Summation versus balance in attitude organization and change. *Journal of Abnormal and Social Psychology,* 1964, *69,* 505–510.

Fishkin, J., Kenniston, K., & MacKinnon, C. Moral reasoning and political ideology. *Journal of Personality and Social Psychology,* 1973, *27,* 109–119.

Fleishman, E. A., Harris, E. F., & Burtt, H. F. *Leadership and supervision in industry.* Columbus, Ohio: Ohio State University, Bureau of Educational Research, 1955.

Foa, U. G. Convergences in the analysis of the structure in interpersonal behavior. *Psychological Review,* 1961, *68,* 341–352.

Foa, U. G. Interpersonal and economic resources. *Science,* 1971, *171,* 345–351.

Foa, U. G., & Foa, E. B. *Societal structures of the mind.* Springfield, Ill.: Charles C. Thomas, 1974.

Foa, U. G., Mitchell, T. R., & Fiedler, F. E. Differentiation matching. *Behavioral Science,* 1971, *16,* 130–142.

Foa, U. G., Triandis, H. C. & Katz, E. W. Cross-cultural invariance in the differentiation and organization of family roles. *Journal of Personality and Social Psychology,* 1966, *4,* 316–327.

Foster, G. Peasant society and the image of limited good. *American Anthropologist,* 1965, *67,* 293–315.

Fraser, S. C., Kelem, R. T., Diener, E., & Beamna, A. L. The Halloween caper: The effects of deindividuation variables on stealing. Mimeographed report, University of Washington, 1972.

Freedman, J. L. Transgression, compliance and guilt. In J. Macaulay & L. Berkowitz (Eds.), *Altruism and helping behavior.* New York: Academic Press, 1970.

Freedman, J. L., & Fraser, S. C. Compliance without pressure: The foot-in-the-door technique. *Journal of Personality and Social Psychology,* 1966, *4,* 195–202.

Frideres, J. S., Warner, L. G., & Albrecht, S. L. The impact of social constraints on the relationship between attitudes and behavior. *Social Forces,* 1971, *50,* 102–112.

Friendly, M. L., & Glucksberg, S. On the description of subcultural lexicons: A multidimensional approach. *Journal of Personality and Social Psychology,* 1970, *14,* 55–65.

Gaertner, S., & Bickman, L. Effects of rage on the elicitation of helping behavior: The wrong number technique. *Journal of Personality and Social Psychology,* 1971, *20,* 218–222.

Gage, N., & Cronbach, L. Conceptual and methodological problems in interpersonal perception. *Psychological Review,* 1955, *62,* 411–422.

Gardiner, G. S. Complexity training and prejudice reduction. *Journal of Applied Social Psychology,* 1972, *2,* 326–342.

Gardner, R. C., Taylor, D. M., & Santos, E. H. Ethnic stereotypes: The role of contact. *Philippine Journal of Psychology,* 1969, *2,* 11–24.

Gardner, R. C., Wonnacott, E. J., & Taylor D. Ethnic stereotypes: A factor analytic investigation. *Canadian Journal of Psychology,* 1968, *22,* 35–44.

Geen, R. G. *Aggression.* Morristown, N.J.: General Learning Corp., 1972.

Geen, R. G., & Berkowitz, L. Some conditions facilitating the occurrence of aggression after the observation of violence. *Journal of Personality,* 1967, *35,* 666–676.

Geen, R. G., & O'Neal, E. C. Activation of cue elicited aggression by general arousal. *Journal of Personality and Social Psychology,* 1969, *11,* 289–292.

Geen, R. G., & Pigg, R. Acquisition of aggressive response and its generalization to verbal behavior. *Journal of Personality and Social Psychology,* 1970, *15,* 165–170.

Gergen, K. J. *The psychology of behavior exchange.* Reading, Mass.: Addison-Wesley, 1969.

Gergen, K. J. Social psychology as history. *Journal of Personality and Social Psychology*, 1973, *26*, 309–320.

Gergen, K. J. Palace revolution for social psychology. *Contemporary Psychology*. 1975, *20*, 127–128.

Gergen, K. J., Gergen, M., & Barton, W. H. Deviance in the dark. *Psychology Today*, Oct. 1973, 129–130.

Gibson, E. J. *Principles of perceptual learning and development*. New York: Appleton-Century-Crofts, 1969.

Goethals, G. R., & Nelson, R. E. Similarity in the influence process: The belief-value distinction. *Journal of Personality and Social Psychology*, 1973, *25*, 117–122.

Goffman, E. *Behavior in public places*. New York: Free Press, 1963.

Goldberg, G. N., Kiesler, C. A., & Collins, B. E. Visual behavior and face-to-face distance during interaction. *Sociometry*, 1969, *32*, 43–53.

Goldberg, L. R. Man versus model of man: A rationale, plus some evidence for a method of improving on clinical inferences. *Psychological Bulletin*, 1970, *73*, 422–432.

Goldstein, J. W. Insecurity and preference for persons similar to oneself. *Journal of Personality*, 1969, *37*, 253–268.

Goldstein, J. W., Gleason, T. C. & Korn, J. H. Whither the epidemic? Psychoactive drug use career patterns of college students. *Journal of Applied Social Psychology*, 1975, *5*, 16–33.

Goldstein, M., & Davis, E. E. Race and belief: A further analysis of the social determinants of behavioral intentions. *Journal of Personality and Social Psychology*, 1972, *22*, 346–355.

Gollob, H. F., & Fischer, G. W. Some relationships between social inference, cognitive balance, and change in impression. *Journal of Personality and Social Psychology*, 1973, *26*, 16–22.

Gollob, H. F., Rossman, B. B., & Abelson, R. P. Social inference as a function of the number of instances and consistency of information presented. *Journal of Personality and Social Psychology*, 1973, *27*, 19–33.

Goodstadt, B. E., & Hjelle, L. A. Power to the powerless: Locus of control and the use of power. *Journal of Personality and Social Psychology*, 1973, *27*, 190–196.

Goranson, R. E., & Berkowitz, L. Reciprocity and responsibility reactions to prior help. *Journal of Personality and Social Psychology*, 1966, *3*, 227–232.

Goranson, R. E., & King, D. Rioting and daily temperature. Analysis of the U. S. riots in 1967. Toronto: Department of Psychology, York University, 1971.

Gormley, R. A. Note on seven brand rating scales and subsequent purchase. *Journal of Market Research Society*, 1974, *16*, 242–244.

Gormly, J. Sociobehavioral and physiological responses to interpersonal disagreement. *Journal of Experimental Research Personality*, 1971, *5*, 216–222.

Gormly, J. A comparison of predictions from consistency and affect theories for arousal during interpersonal disagreement. *Journal of Personality and Social Psychology*, 1974, *30*, 658–663.

Gouldner, A. W. The norm of reciprocity: A preliminary statement. *American Sociological Review*, 1960, *25*, 161–178.

Griffitt, W., & Veitch, R. Hot and crowded: Influences of population density and temperature on interpersonal affective behavior. *Journal of Personality and Social Psychology*, 1971, *17*, 92–98.

Hakel, M. Significance of implicit personality theories in personality research and theory. *Proceedings of the 77th Convention of the American Psychological Association*, 1969, *4*, 403–404.

Hakel, M., Hollman, T. D., & Dunnette, M. D. Accuracy of interviewers, certified public accountants, and students in identifying the interests of accountants. *Journal of Applied Psychology*, 1970, *54*, 115–119.

Hall, E. T. *The silent language*. Garden City, N.Y.: Doubleday, 1959.

Hall, E. T. *The hidden dimension*. Garden City, N.Y.: Doubleday, 1966.

Halverson, C. F., Jr. Interpersonal perception: Cognitive complexity and trait implication. *Journal of Consulting and Clinical Psychology*, 1970, *34*, 86–90.

Hammond, K. R., & Summers, D. A. Cognitive control. *Psychological Review*, 1972, *79*, 58–67.

Harré, R. Some remarks on "rule" as a scientific concept. In T. Mischel (Ed.), *Understanding other persons*. Oxford, England: Blackwell, 1974.

Harré, R., & Secord, P. F. *The explanation of social behavior*. Totowa, N.J.: Rowman & Littlefield, 1972.

Harvey, O. J., Hunt, D. E., & Schroder, H. M. *Conceptual systems and personality development*. New York: Wiley, 1961.

Harvey, O. J., Reich, J. W., & Wyer, R. S. Effects of attitude direction, attitude intensity and structure of beliefs upon differentiation. *Journal of Personality and Social Psychology*, 1968, *10*, 472–478.

Haythorn, W. W. The composition of groups: A review of the literature. *Acta Psychologica*, 1968, *28*, 97–128.

Heider, E. R. Style and accuracy of verbal communications within and between social classes. *Journal of Personality and Social Psychology*, 1971, *18*, 33–47.

Heider, F. Attitudes and cognitive organization. *Journal of Psychology*, 1946, *21*, 107–112.

Heider, F. *The psychology of interpersonal relations*. New York: Wiley, 1958.

Heise, D. A systems approach to attitudes, behaviors and norms showing the futility of causal inference from attitude-behavior correlations. Mimeograph, 1973.

Helson, H. *Adaptation-level theory*. New York: Harper & Row, 1964.

Helson, H., Blake, R. R., & Mouton, J. S. Petition-signing as adjustment to situational and personal factors. *The Journal of Social Psychology*, 1958, *48*, 3–10.

Hendrick, C., Giesen, M., & Coy, S. The social ecology of free seating arrangements in a small group interaction context. *Sociometry*, 1974, *37*, 262–274.

Hendrick, C., & Taylor, S. P. Effects of belief similarity and aggression on attraction and counteraggression. *Journal of Personality and Social Psychology*, 1971, *17*, 342–349.

Heneman, H. G., & Schwab, D. P. Evaluation of research on expectancy theory predictions of employee performance. *Psychological Bulletin*, 1972, *78*, 1–9.

Himmelfarb, S. Effects of cue validity differences in weighting information. *Journal of Mathematical Psychology*, 1970, *7*, 531–539.

Hogan, R. Development of an empathy scale. *Journal of Consulting and Clinical Psychology*, 1969, *33*, 307–316.

Hogan, R. Moral conduct and moral character: A psychological perspective. *Psychological Bulletin*, 1973, *79*, 217–232.

Hollander, E. P. Conformity, status and idiosyncrasy credit. *Psychological Review*, 1958, *65*, 117–127.

Holman, P. A. Validation of an attitude scale as a device for predicting behavior. *Journal of Applied Psychology*, 1956, *40*, 347–349.

Homans, G. *Social behavior: The elementary forms*. New York: Harcourt Brace Jovanovich, 1961.

Horowitz, D. B. The relevance of individual interpersonal expectations, styles of response to provocation, and interaction factors, to interpersonal behaviors and satisfaction in marriage. *Dissertation Abstracts International,* 1970, *31,* 2255–2256.

Horowitz, I. A. Effect of choice and locus on dependence on helping behavior. *Journal of Personality and Social Psychology,* 1968, *8,* 373–376.

Howard, J. A., & Sheth, J. N. *The theory of buyer behavior.* New York: Wiley, 1969.

Hull, C. L. *Principles of behavior: An introduction to behavior theory.* New York: Appleton-Century-Crofts, 1943.

Huston, T. L. *Foundation of interpersonal attraction.* New York: Academic Press, 1974.

Inkeles, A., & Smith, D. H. *Becoming modern.* Cambridge, Mass,: Harvard Press, 1974.

Insko, C. A. *Theories of attitude change.* New York: Appleton-Century-Crofts, 1967.

Insko, C. A., & Robinson, J. E. Belief similarity versus race as determinants of reactions to Negroes by Southern white adolescents: A further test of Rokeach's theory. *Journal of Personality and Social Psychology,* 1967, *7,* 216–221.

Insko, C. A., Thompson, W. D., Stroebe, W., Shaud, K. F., Pinner, B. E., & Layton, B. D. Implied evaluation and the similarity-attraction effect. *Journal of Personality and Social Psychology,* 1973, *25,* 297–308.

Irwin, F. W. *Intentional behavior and motivation.* New York: Lippincott, 1971.

Isen, A. M. Success, failure, attention and reactions to others: The warm glow of success. *Journal of Personality and Social Psychology,* 1970, *15,* 294–301.

Isen, A. M., Horn, N., & Rosenhan, D. L. Effects of success and failure on children's generosity. *Journal of Personality and Social Psychology,* 1973, *27,* 239–247.

Isen, A. M., & Levin, P. F. The effect of feeling good on helping: Cookies and kindness. *Journal of Personality and Social Psychology,* 1972, *21,* 384–388.

Izard, C. *Face of emotion.* New York: Appleton-Century-Crofts, 1971.

Jaccard, J. J., & Davidson, A. R. Toward an understanding of family planning behaviors: An initial investigation. *Journal of Applied Social Psychology,* 1972, *2,* 228–235.

Jaccard, J. J., & Davidson, A. R. A comparison of two models of social behavior: Results of a survey sample. *Sociometry,* in press.

Jaccard, J. J., Davidson, A. R., Triandis, H. C., Morales, M. L., & Diaz-Guerrero, R. A. Cross-cultural tests of two models for the prediction of behavioral intentions. Submitted for publication, 1975.

Jacobs, L., Berscheid, E., & Walster, E. Self-esteem and attraction. *Journal of Personality and Social Psychology,* 1971, *17,* 84–91.

Jaffe, Y., Malamuth, N., Feingold, J., & Feshbach, S. Sexual arousal and behavioral aggression. *Journal of Personality and Social Psychology,* 1974, *30,* 759–864.

Janis, I. L. *Victims of groupthink: A psychological study of foreign policy decosopms and boas scpres.* Boston: Houghton Mifflin, 1972.

Jensen, A. R. *Genetics and education.* New York: Harper & Row, 1972.

Jensen, A. R. *Educability and group differences.* New York: Harper & Row, 1973.

Jessor, R. T., Graves, D., Hanson, R., & Jessor, S. *Society, personality, and deviant behavior: A study of a tri-ethnic community.* New York: Holt, Rinehart and Winston, 1968.

Jessor, R., & Jessor, S. L. The perceiver environment in behavioral science: Some conceptual issues and some illustrative data. *American Behavioral Scientist,* 1973, *16,* 801–828.

Johnson, C. D., Gormly, J., & Gormly, A. Disagreements and self-esteem: Support for the competence-reinfórcement model of attraction. *Journal of Research in Personality,* 1973, *7,* 165–172.

Johnson, D. W., & Johnson, S. The effects of attitude similarity, expectation of goal facilitation, and actual goal facilitation on interpersonal attraction. *Journal of Experimental Social Psychology,* 1972, *8,* 197–206.

Jones, E. E. Authoritarianism as a determinant of first-impression formation. *Journal of Personality,* 1954, *23,* 107–127.

Jones, E. E., & Davis, K. E. From acts to dispositions: The attribution process in person perception. In L. Berkowitz (Ed.), *Advances in experimental social psychology* (Vol. 2). New York: Academic Press, 1965.

Jones, E. E., & Goethals, G. R. Order effects in impression formation: Attribution context and the nature of the entity. In E. E. Jones, D. E. Kanouse, H. H. Kelley, R. E. Nisbett, S. Valins, & B. Weiner (Eds.), *Attribution: Perceiving the causes of behavior.* Morristown, N.J.: General Learning Corp., 1972.

Jones, E. E., & Gordon, E. M. Timing of self-disclosure and its effects on personal attraction. *Journal of Personality and Social Psychology,* 1972, *24,* 358–365.

Jones, E. E., & Harris, V. A. The attributions of attitudes. *Journal of Experimental Social Psychology,* 1967, *3,* 1–24.

Jones, E. E., & Nisbett, R. E. The actor and the observer: Divergent perceptions of the causes of behavior. In E. E. Jones, D. E. Kanouse, H. H. Kelley, R. E. Nisbett, S. Valins, & B. Weiner (Eds.), *Attribution: Perceiving the causes of behavior.* Morristown, N.J.: General Learning Corp., 1972.

Jones, E. E., Rock, L., Shaver, K. G., Goethals, G. R., & Ward, L. M. Pattern of performance and ability attributions: An unexpected primacy effect. *Journal of Personality and Social Psychology,* 1968, *10,* 317–340.

Jones, E. E., & Sigall, H. The bogus pipeline: A new paradigm for measuring affect and attitude. *Psychological Bulletin,* 1971, *76,* 349–364.

Jones, E. E., Worchel, S., Goethals, G. R., & Grumet, J. F. Prior expectancy and behavioral extremity as determinants of attitude attribution. *Journal of Experimental Social Psychology,* 1971, *7,* 59–80.

Jones, E. E., & Wortman, C. *Ingratiation: An attributional approach.* Morristown, N.J.: General Learning Corp., 1973.

Jones, S. C. Self- and interpersonal evaluations: Esteem theories versus consistency theories. *Psychological Bulletin,* 1973, *79,* 185–199.

Jorgenson, D. O., Dunnette, M. D., & Pritchard, R. D. Effects of the manipulation of a performance-reward contingency on behavior in a simulated work setting. *Journal of Applied Psychology,* 1973, *57,* 271–280.

Juster, T. Consumer buying intentions and purchase probability. *Journal of the American Statistical Association,* 1966, *61,* 568–696.

Kalven, H., & Zeisel, H. *The American jury.* Boston: Little, Brown, 1966.

Kanfer, F. H. The maintenance of behavior by self-generated stimuli and reinforcement. In A. Jacobs & L. B. Sachs (Eds.), *The psychology of private events.* New York: Academic Press, 1971.

Kanfer, F. H., Cox, L. E., Greiner, J. M., & Karoly, P. Contracts, demand characteristics and self-control. *Journal of Personality and Social Psychology,* 1974, *30,* 605–619.

Kanfer, F. H., & Grimm, L. G. Promising trends toward the future development of behavior modification: Ten related areas in need of exploration. In W. E. Craighead, A. E. Kazdin, & M. J. Mahoney (Eds.), *Behavior modification: Principles, issues, and applications.* Boston: Houghton Mifflin, 1975.

Kanfer, F. H., & Marston, A. R. Determinants of self-reinforcement in human learning. *Journal of Experimental Psychology,* 1963, *66,* 245–254.

Kanouse, D. E., & Hanson, L. R. Negativity in evaluations. In E. E. Jones, D. E. Kanouse, H. H. Kelley, R. E. Nisbett, S. Valins, & B. Weiner (Eds.), *At-*

tribution: Perceiving the causes of behavior. Morristown, N.J.: General Learning Corp., 1972.

Kaplan, M. F., & Anderson, N. H. Information integration theory and reinforcement theory as approaches to interpersonal attraction. *Journal of Personality
and Social Psychology,* 1973, *28,* 301–312.

Karoly, P., & Kanfer, F. H. Effects of prior contractual experiences on self-control
in children. *Developmental Psychology,* 1974, *10,* 459–460.

Karp, E., Jackson, J. H., & Lester, D. Ideal-self fulfillment in mate selection: A cor-
ollary to the complementarity need theory of mate selection. *Journal of Marriage and the Family,* 1970, *32,* 269–272.

Katz, D. The functional approach to the study of attitudes. *Public Opinion Quarterly,* 1960, *24,* 163–204.

Katz, D., & Braly, K. W. Racial stereotypes of 100 college students *Journal of Abnormal and Social Psychology,* 1933, *28,* 280–290.

Kelley, H. H. The warm-cold variable in first impressions of persons. *Journal of Personality ,* 1950, *18,* 431–439.

Kelley, H. H. Attribution theory in social psychology. In D. Levine (Ed.) *Nebraska
symposium on motivation.* Lincoln: University of Nebraska Press, 1972. (a)

Kelley, H. H. Attributions in social interaction. In E. E. Jones, D. E. Kanouse,
H. H. Kelley, R. E. Nisbett, S. Valins, & B. Weiner (Eds.), *Attribution:
Perceiving the causes of behavior.* Morristown, N.J.: General Learning Corp.,
1972. (b)

Kelley, H. H., & Stahelski, A. J. Social interaction basis of cooperators' and competitors' beliefs about others. *Journal of Personality and Social Psychology,*
1970, *16,* 66–91.

Kelly, G. A. *The psychology of personal constructs.* New York: W. W. Norton &
Co., 1955.

Kelman, H. D. Compliance, identification, and internalization: Three processes of
opinion change. *Journal of Conflict Resolution,* 1958, *2,* 51–60.

Kerckhoff, A. C., & Davis, K. E. Value consensus and need complementarity in
mate selection. *American Sociological Review,* 1962, *27,* 295–303.

Kiesler, C. A., Collins, B. E., & Miller, N. *Attitude change.* New York: Wiley, 1969.

Kiesler, C. A., & Goldberg, G. N. Multi-dimensional approach to the experimental
study of interpersonal attraction: Effect of a blunder on the attractiveness of a
competent other. *Psychological Reports,* 1968, *22,* 693–705.

Kirscht, J. P., & Dillehay, R. C. *Dimensions of authoritarianism.* Lexington: University of Kentucky Press, 1967.

Klineberg, O. *Social psychology.* New York: Holt, 1954.

Kluckhohn, F., & Strodtbeck, F. L. *Variations in value orientations.* Evanston, Ill.:
Row, Peterson, 1961.

Kohlberg, L. The development of children's orientations towards a moral order. I:
Sequence in the development of moral thought. *Vita Humana,* 1963, *6,* 11–33.

Kohn, M. L. *Class and conformity: A study in values.* Homewood, Ill.: Dorsey, 1969.

Komorita, S. S., & Bass, A. R. Attitude differentiation and evaluative scales on the
semantic differential. *Journal of Personality and Social Psychology,* 1967, *6,*
241–244.

Korten, F. F. The influence of culture and sex on the perception of persons. *International Journal of Psychology,* 1974, *9,* 31–44.

Kothandapani, V. Validation of feeling, belief and intention to act as three components of attitude and their contribution to prediction of contraceptive behavior. *Journal of Personality and Social Psychology,* 1971, *19,* 321–333.

Kraut, R. E. Effects of social labeling on giving to charity. *Journal of Experimental Social Psychology,* 1973, *9,* 551–562.

Kuhn, T. S. *The structure of scientific revolutions* (2nd ed.). Chicago: University of Chicago Press, 1970.

LaForge, R., & Suczek, R. The interpersonal dimension of personality. III. An interpersonal checklist. *Journal of Personality,* 1955, *24,* 94–112.

Lambert, W. W., & Lambert, W. E. *Social psychology.* Englewood Cliffs, N.J.: Prentice-Hall, 1973.

Landis, D., Triandis, H. C., & Adamopoulos, J. The prediction of teacher classroom behavior. Submitted for publication, 1975.

LaPiere, R. T. Attitudes vs actions. *Social Forces,* 1934, *13,* 230–237.

L'Armand, K., & Pepitone, A. Helping to reward another person: A cross-cultural analysis. *Journal of Personality and Social Psychology,* 1975, *31,* 189–198.

Larson, L. L., & Rowland, K. M. Leadership style and cognitive complexity. *Academy of Management Journal,* 1974, *17,* 37–45.

Latané, B. Studies in social comparison. *Journal of Experimental Social Psychology,* 1966, Supplement 1.

Latané, B., & Darley, J. M. *The unresponsive bystander: Why doesn't he help?* New York: Appleton-Century-Crofts, 1970.

Lay, C. H., & Jackson, D. N. Analysis of the generality of trait-inferential relationships. *Journal of Personality and Social Psychology,* 1969, *12,* 12–21.

Lazarus, R. S., Opton, E. M., Nomikos, M. S., & Rankin, N. O. The principle of short-circuiting of threat: Further evidence. *Journal of Personality,* 1965, *33,* 622–635.

Leary, T. *Interpersonal diagnosis of personality.* New York: Ronald Press, 1957.

Lefkowitz, M., Eron, L., Walder, L., & Huesmann, L. R. Television violence and child aggression: A follow up study. In G. A. Comstock & E. A. Rubinstein (Eds.), *Television and social behavior* (Vol. 3). Washington, D.C.: U.S. Government Printing Office, 1971.

Lerner, M. J. Evaluation of performance as a function of performer's reward and attractiveness. *Journal of Personality and Social Psychology,* 1965, *1,* 355–360.

Lerner, M. J. The desire for justice and reactions to victims. In J. Macaulay & L. Berkowitz (Eds.), *Altruism and helping behavior: Social psychological studies of antecedents and consequences.* New York: Academic Press, 1970.

Lerner, M. J., & Simmons, C. H. Observer's reaction to the "innocent victim": Compassion or rejection? *Journal of Personality and Social Psychology,* 1966, *4,* 203–210.

LeVine, R. A., & Campbell, D. T. *Ethnocentrism.* New York: Wiley, 1972.

Levinger, G., & Snoek, J. D. *Attraction in relationship: A new look at interpersonal attraction.* Morristown, N.J.: General Learning Corp., 1972.

Levy-Schoen, A. *L'image d'autrui chez l'enfant.* Paris: Presses Universitaires de France, 1964.

Lewin, K. *Principles of topological psychology.* New York: McGraw-Hill, 1936.

Lewin, K. Group decision and social change. In T. M. Newcomb & E. L. Hartley (Eds.), *Readings in social psychology.* New York: Holt, 1947.

Lieberman, M. A., Yalom, I. D., & Miles, M. B. *Encounter groups: First facts.* New York: Basic Books, 1973.

Liebert, R. M. Television and social learning: Some relationships between viewing violence and behaving aggressively. In J. P. Murray, E. A. Rubinstein, & G. A. Comstock (Eds.), *Television and social behavior* (Vol. 2). Washington, D.C.: U.S. Government Printing Office, 1971.

Lindzey, G., & Byrne, D. Measurement of social choice and interpersonal attractiveness. In G. Lindzey & E. Aronson (Eds.), *The handbook of social psychology*. Reading, Mass.: Addison-Wesley, 1968.

Linn, L. S. Verbal attitudes and overt behavior: A study of racial discrimination. *Social Forces*, 1964/1965, *43*, 353–364.

Lipetz, M. E., & Ossorio, P. G. Authoritarianism, aggression, and status. *Journal of Personality and Social Psychology*, 1967, *5*, 468–472.

Little, K. B. Personal space. *Journal of Experimental Social Psychology*, 1965, *1*, 237–247.

Locke, E. A. Personnel attitudes and motivation. *Annual Review of Psychology*, 1975, *26*, 457–480.

Locke, E. A., Cartledge, N., & Knerr, C. S. Studies of the relationship between satisfaction goal-setting and performance. *Organizational Behavior and Human Performance*, 1970, *5*, 135–158.

Lomax, A., & Berkowitz, N. The evolutionary taxonomy of culture. *Science*, 1972, *177*, 228–239.

Lombardo, J. P., Tator, G. D., & Weiss, R. F. Performance changes in human conditioning as a function of shifts in the magnitude of attitudinal reinforcement. *Psychonomic Science*, 1972, *28*, 215–218.

Lombardo, J. P., Weiss, R. F., & Buchanan, W. Reinforcing and attracting functions of yielding. *Journal of Personality and Social Psychology*, 1972, *21*, 359–368.

Lombardo, J. P., Weiss, R. F., & Stich, M. H. Effectance reduction through speaking in reply and its relation to attraction. *Journal of Personality and Social Psychology*, 1973, *28*, 325–332.

London, P. Personal communication, 1970.

Longabaugh, R. The structure of interpersonal behavior. *Sociometry*, 1966, *29*, 441–460.

Lopes, L. L. A unified integration model for "prior expectancy and behavioral extremity as determinants of attitude attribution." *Journal of Experimental Social Psychology*, 1972, *8*, 156–160.

Lorr, M., & McNair, D. M. Expansion of the interpersonal behavior circle. *Journal of Personality and Social Psychology*, 1965, *2*, 823–830.

Lorr, M., & Suziedelis, A. Modes of interpersonal behavior. *British Journal of Social and Clinical Psychology*, 1969, *8*, 124–132.

Lorr, M., Suziedelis, A., & Kinnane, J. F. Characteristic response modes to interpersonal situations. *Multivariate Behavioral Research*, 1969, *4*, 445–458.

Lott, A. J., Aponte, J. F., Lott, B. E., & McGinley, W. H. The effect of delayed reward on the development of positive attitudes toward persons. *Journal of Experimental Social Psychology*, 1969, *5*, 101–113.

Lowe, C. A., & Goldstein, J. W. Reciprocal liking and attributions of ability: Mediating effects of perceived intent and personal involvement. *Journal of Personality and Social Psychology*, 1970, *16*, 291–297.

Lykken, D. Statistical significance in psychological research. *Psychological Bulletin*, 1968, *70*, 151–159.

Macaulay, J. R. A shill for charity. In J. Macaulay & L. Berkowitz (Eds.), *Altruism and helping behavior*. New York: Academic Press, 1970.

Manis, M., Gleason, T. C., & Dawes, R. M. The evaluation of complex social stimuli. *Journal of Personality and Social Psychology*, 1966, *3*, 404–419.

Marx, G. *Protest and prejudice*. New York: Harper & Row, 1968.

Maslach, C., Tashiro, C., & Gergen, K. J. A cultural analysis of the role of reciprocity in social attraction. Paper presented at the International Congress of Psychology, Tokyo, Japan, 1972.

Mason, W. A. Sociability and social organization in monkeys and apes. In L. Berkowitz (Ed.), *Advances in experimental social psychology*. New York: Academic Press, 1964.

Matsui, T., Osawa, T., & Terai, T. Relation between supervisory motivation and consideration and structure aspects of supervisory behavior. *Journal of Applied Psychology*, 1975, *60*, 451–454.

McArthur, L. A., Kiesler, C. A., & Cook, B. P. Acting on an attitude as a function of self-percept and inequality. *Journal of Personality and Social Psychology*, 1969, *12*, 295–302.

McArthur, L. Z. *The how and what of why: Some determinants and consequences of causal attribution*. Unpublished doctoral dissertation, Yale University, 1970.

McGuire, W. J. The current status of cognitive consistency theories. In S. Feldman (Ed.), *Cognitive consistency*. New York: Academic Press, 1966.

McGuire, W. J. The nature of attitudes and attitude change. In G. Lindzey & E. Aronson (Eds.), *The handbook of social psychology*. Reading, Mass.: Addison-Wesley, 1969.

McLaughlin, B. Effects of similarity and likeableness on attraction and recall. *Journal of Personality and Social Psychology*, 1971, *20*, 65–69.

McMillen, D. L., & Austin, J. B. Effect of positive feedback on compliance following transgression. *Psychonomic Science*, 1971, *24*, 59–60.

Meehl, P. E. Theory testing in psychology and physics: A methodological paradox. *Philosophy of Science*, 1967, *34*, 103–115.

Meehl, P. E. Nuisance variables and the ex post facto design. *Minnesota Studies in the Philosphy of Science*, 1970, *4*, 373–402. (a)

Meehl, P. E. Some methodological reflections on the difficulties of psychoanalytic research. *Minnesota Studies in the Philosophy of Science*, 1970, *4*, 403–416. (b)

Mehrabian, A. Inference of attitudes from the posture, orientation, and distance of a communicator. *Journal of Consulting and Clinical Psychology*, 1968, *32*, 296–308.

Mehrabian, A. A semantic space for nonverbal behavior. *Journal of Consulting and Clinical Psychology*, 1970, *35*, 248–257.

Mehrabian, A. *Silent messages*. Belmont, Calif.: Wadsworth, 1971.

Mehrabian, A. *Nonverbal communication*. Chicago: Aldine-Atherton, 1972.

Mehrabian, A., & Ksionzky, S. Models for affiliative and conformity behavior. *Psychological Bulletin*, 1970, *74*, 110–126.

Mehrabian, A., & Ksionzky, S. Categories of social behavior. *Comparative Group Studies*, 1972, *3*, 425–436.

Mikula, G., & Egger, J. The acquisition of positive and negative attitudes while facing previously neutral persons. *Zeitschrift fur Experimentelle und Angewandte Psychologie*, 1974, *21*, 132–145.

Milgram, S. Nationality and conformity. *Scientific American*, Dec. 1961.

Milgram, S. Behavioral study of obedience. *Journal of Abnormal and Social Psychology*, 1963, *67*, 371–378.

Milgram, S. Some conditions of obedience and disobedience to authority. *Human Relations*, 1965, *18*, 57–75.

Miller, A. G. Some determinants of cognitive complexity. *Dissertation Abstracts*, 1968, *28*, 3901.

Miller, R. L., Brickman, P., & Bolen, D. Attribution versus persuasion as a means of modifying behavior. *Journal of Personality and Social Psychology,* 1975, *31,* 430–441.

Miller, W. B., Geertz, H., & Cutter, H. S. G. Aggression in boys' street corner group. *Psychiatry,* 1961, *24,* 283–296.

Mischel, W. *Personality and assessment.* New York: Wiley, 1968.

Mischel, W. Toward a cognitive social learning reconceptualization of personality. *Psychological Review,* 1973, *80,* 252–283.

Mischel, W. Processes in delay of gratification. In L. Berkowitz (Ed.), *Advances in experimental social psychology.* New York: Academic Press, 1974.

Mitchell, T. R. Leader complexity and leadership style. *Journal of Personality and Social Psychology,* 1970, *16,* 166–174.

Mitchell, T., & Biglan, A. Instrumentality theories. *Psychological Bulletin,* 1971, *76,* 432–454.

Mitchell, T., Dossett, D. L., Fiedler, F. E., & Triandis, H. C. Culture training: Validation evidence for the culture assimilator. *International Journal of Psychology,* 1972, *7,* 97–104.

Moos, R. H. Conceptualizations of human environments. *American Psychologist,* 1973, *28,* 652–665.

Moriarty, T. Crime, commitment, and the responsive bystander: Two field experiments. *Journal of Personality and Social Psychology,* 1975, *31,* 370–376.

Mulvihill, D. J. & Tumin, M. M. (Eds.), *Crimes of Violence: Vol. II Staff Report to the National Commission on the Causes and Prevention of Violence.* Washington, D.C.: U.S. Government Printing Office, 1969.

Murphy, G. *Personality.* New York: Harper, 1947.

Murstein, B. I. *Theories of attraction and love.* New York: Springer, 1971.

Nemeth, C. Effects of free versus constrained behavior on attraction between people. *Journal of Personality and Social Psychology,* 1970, *15,* 302–311.

Newcomb, T. M. An experiment designed to test the validity of a rating technique. *Journal of Educational Psychology,* 1931, *22,* 279–289.

Newcomb, T. M. An approach to the study of communicative acts. *Psychological Review,* 1953, *60,* 393–404.

Newcomb, T. M. The prediction of interpersonal attraction. *American Psychologist,* 1956, *11,* 575–586.

Newcomb, T. M. Dyadic balance as a source of clues about interpersonal attraction. In B. I. Murstein (Ed.), *Theories of attraction and love.* New York: Springer, 1971.

Nisbett, R. E., & Caputo, G. C. *Personality traits: Why other people do the things they do.* Unpublished manuscript, Yale University, 1971.

Nisbett, R. E., Caputo, C., Legant, P., & Marecek, J. Behavior as seen by the actor and as seen by the observer. *Journal of Personality and Social Psychology,* 1973, *27,* 154–164.

Nisbett, R. E., & Valins, S. Perceiving the causes of one's own behavior. In E. E. Jones, D. E. Kanouse, H. H. Kelley, R. E. Nisbett, S. Valins, & B. Weiner (Eds.), *Attribution: Perceiving the causes of behavior.* Morristown, N.J.: General Learning Corp., 1972.

Norman, R. Affective-cognitive consistency, attitudes, conformity, and behavior. *Journal of Personality and Social Psychology,* 1975, *32,* 83–91.

Norman, W. T. "To see ourselfs as others see us!" Relations among self-perceptions, peer perceptions, & expected peer-perceptions of personality attributes. *Multivariate Behavioral Research,* 1969, *4,* 417–443.

Novak, D. W., & Lerner, M. J. Rejection as a function of perceived similarity. *Journal of Personality and Social Psychology,* 1968, *9,* 147–152.

Oncken, G. *A predictive model of role behavior.* Unpublished master's thesis, University of Illinois, 1968.

Orlofsky, J. L., Marcia, J. E., & Lesser, I. M. Ego identity status and the intimacy versus isolation crisis of young adulthood. *Journal of Personality and Social Psychology,* 1973, *27,* 211–219.

Osgood, C. E. Dimensionality of the semantic space for communication via facial expressions. *Scandinavian Journal of Psychology,* 1966, *7,* 1–30.

Osgood, C. E., Suci, G. J., & Tannenbaum, P. H. *The measurement of meaning.* Urbana: University of Illinois Press, 1957.

Osgood, C. E., & Tannenbaum, P. H. The principle of congruity in the prediction of attitude change. *Psychological Review,* 1955, *62,* 42–55.

Paulus, P. B., & Murdoch, P. Anticipated evaluation and audience presence in the enhancement of dominant responses. *Journal of Experimental Social Psychology,* 1971, *7,* 280–291.

Peak, H. Attitude and motivation. In M. R. Jones (Ed.), *Nebraska symposium on motivation: 1955.* Lincoln: University of Nebraska Press, 1955.

Pelto, P. J. The differences between "tight" and "loose" societies. *Transaction,* April 1968, 37–40.

Pilder, R. J. Some effects of laboratory training on married couples. *Dissertation Abstracts International,* 1972, *32,* 6626.

Pomazal, R. J. *Attitudes, normative beliefs and altruism: Help for helping behavior.* Unpublished doctoral dissertation, University of Illinois, 1974.

Porter, L. W., & Lawler, E. E. *Managerial attitudes and performance.* Homewood, Ill.: Dorsey Press, 1968.

Post, E. L. *Emily Post's Etiquette.* New York: Funk & Wagnalls, Inc., 1965.

Postman, L. The experimental analysis of motivational factors in perception. In *Current theory and research in motivation.* Lincoln: University of Nebraska Press, 1953.

Price, R. H. Behavior setting theory and research. In R. H. Moos (Ed.), *The human context: Coping with social and physical environments.* New York: Wiley, 1975.

Pruitt, D. G. Reciprocity and credit building in a laboratory dyad. *Journal of Personality and Social Psychology,* 1968, *8,* 143–147.

Radloff, R. Social comparison and ability evaluation. *Journal of Experimental Social Psychology,* 1966, *1,* 6–26.

Reagan, D. T. Effects of a favor and liking on compliance. *Journal of Experimental Social Psychology,* 1971, *7,* 627–639.

Rodin, M. J. The informativeness of trait descriptions. *Journal of Personality and Social Psychology,* 1972, *21,* 341–344.

Rokeach, M., & Rothman, G. The principle of belief congruence and the congruity principle as models of cognitive interaction. *Psychological Review,* 1965, *72,* 128–142.

Rokeach, M., Smith, P. W., & Evans, R. I. Two kinds of prejudice or one? In M. Rokeach (Ed.), *The open and closed mind.* New York: Basic Books, 1960.

Rommetveit, R. The architecture of intersubjectivity. Lecture delivered in Ottawa, Ontario, at a conference on new paradigms in social psychology, 1974.

Rosen, B., & Jerdee, T. H. Effects of applicant's sex and difficulty of job on evaluations of candidates for managerial positions. *Journal of Applied Psychology,* 1974, *59,* 511–512.

Rosen, B., & Komorita, S. Attitudes and action: The effects of behavior intent and perceived effectiveness of acts. *Journal of Personality,* 1971, *39,* 189–203.

Rosenberg, M. J. Cognitive structure and attitudinal affect. *Journal of Abnormal and Social Psychology,* 1956, *53,* 367–372.

Rosenberg, M. J. An analysis of affective cognitive consistency. In M. J. Rosenberg & C. I. Hovland (Eds.), *Attitude organization and change.* New Haven, Conn.: Yale University Press, 1960.

Rosenberg, M. J. Psychological selectivity in self-esteem formation. In C. Sherif & M. Sherif (Eds.), *Attitude, ego-involvement and change.* New York: Wiley, 1967.

Rosenfeld, H. M. Instrumental affiliative functions of facial and gestural expressions. *Journal of Personality and Social Psychology,* 1966, *4,* 65–72.

Ross, M., Insko, C. A., & Ross, H. Self-attribution of attitude. *Journal of Personality and Social Psychology,* 1971, *17,* 292–297.

Rotter, J. B. *Social learning and clinical psychology.* Englewood Cliffs, N.J.:Prentice-Hall, 1954.

Rotter, J. B. Generalized expectancies for internal versus external control of reinforcement. *Psychological Monographs,* 1966, *80,* (1, Whole No. 609).

Runkel, P. J. Cognitive similarity in facilitating communication. *Sociometry,* 1956, *19,* 178–191.

Ryan, T. A. *Intentional behavior.* New York: Ronald Press, 1970.

Saegert, S., Swap, W., & Zajonc, R. B. Exposure, context and interpersonal attraction. *Journal of Personality and Social Psychology,* 1973, *25,* 234–242.

Sales, S. M. Economic threat as a determinant of conversion rates in authoritarian and non-authoritarian churches. *Journal of Personality and Social Psychology,* 1972, *23,* 420–428.

Sample, J., & Warland, R. Attitude and prediction of behavior. *Social Forces,* 1973, *51,* 292–304.

Sashkin, M. Leadership style and group decision effectiveness: Correlational and behavioral tests of Fiedler's contingency model. *Organizational Behavior and Human Performance,* 1972, *8,* 347–362.

Sashkin, M., Taylor, F. C., & Tripathi, R. C. An analysis of situational moderating effects on the relationships between least preferred coworker and other psychological measures. *Journal of Applied Psychology,* 1974, *59,* 731–740.

Schachter, S. *The psychology of affiliation.* Stanford, Calif.: Stanford University Press, 1959.

Schachter, S. The interaction of cognitive and physiological determinants of emotional state. In L. Berkowitz (Ed.), *Advances in experimental social psychology.* New York: Academic Press, 1964.

Schaefer, E. S. A circumplex model for maternal behavior. *Journal of Abnormal and Social Psychology,* 1959, *59,* 226–235.

Schaefer, E. S. A configurational analysis of children's reports of parental behavior. *Journal of Consulting Psychology,* 1965, *29,* 552–557.

Schaps, E. Cost, dependency and helping. *Journal of Personality and Social Psychology,* 1972, *21,* 74–78.

Schiffenbauer, A. Effect of observer's emotional state on judgments of the emotional state of others. *Journal of Personality and Social Psychology,* 1974, *30,* 31–35.

Schlosberg, H. Three dimensions of emotion. *Psychological Review,* 1954, *61,* 81–88.

Schnapper, M. Your actions speak louder . . . *Peace Corps Volunteer,* June 1969, 7–10.

Schneider, D. J. Implicit personality theory: A review. *Psychological Bulletin,* 1973, *79,* 294–409.

Schoen, R. Personal communication based on an actuarial analysis of the records in the state of California, 1975.

Schopler, J., & Compere, J. S. Effects of being kind or harsh to another on liking. *Journal of Personality and Social Psychology,* 1971, *20,* 155–159.

Schopler, J., & Matthews, M. W. The influence of the perceived causal locus of partner's dependence on the use of interpersonal power. *Journal of Personality and Social Psychology,* 1965, *2,* 609–612.

Schroder, H. M., Driver, M. J., & Streufert, S. *Human information processing.* New York: Holt, Rinehart and Winston, 1967.

Schuman, H. Social change and the validity of regional stereotypes in East Pakistan. *Sociometry,* 1966, *29,* 428–440.

Schutz, W. C. *FIRO-B. A three-dimensional theory of interpersonal behavior.* New York: Rinehart, 1958.

Schutz, W. C. *Joy.* New York: Grove Press, 1968.

Schwartz, S. H. Elicitation of moral obligation and self-sacrifice behavior: An experimental study of volunteering to be a bone marrow donor. *Journal of Personality and Social Psychology,* 1970, *15,* 283–293.

Schwartz, S. H. Normative explanation of helping behavior: A critique proposal and empirical test. *Journal of Experimental Social Psychology,* 1973, *9,* 349–364.

Schwartz, S. H., & Tessler, R. C. A test of a model for reducing measured attitude-behavior discrepancies. *Journal of Personality and Social Psychology,* 1972, *24,* 225–236.

Scott, W. A. Structure of natural cognitions. *Journal of Personality and Social Psychology,* 1969, *12,* 261–278.

Sears, R. R., Maccoby, E., & Levin, H. *Patterns of child-rearing.* Evanston, Ill.: Row, Peterson, 1957.

Seeman, M. On the meaning of alienation. *American Sociological Review,* 1959, *24,* 783–791.

Segal, M. W. Alphabet and attraction: An unobtrusive measure of the effect of propinquity in a field setting. *Journal of Personality and Social Psychology,* 1974, *30,* 654–657.

Seligman, M. E. P. On the generality of the laws of learning. *Psychological Review,* 1970, *77,* 406–418.

Sherif, C. W., Kelly, M., Rodgers, H. L., Jr., Sarup, G., & Tittler, B. I. Personal involvement, social judgment, and action. *Journal of Personality and Social Psychology,* 1973, *27,* 311–328.

Sherif, M. *The psychology of social norms.* New York: Harper, 1936.

Sherman, A. R. *Behavior modification: Theory and practice.* Monterey, Calif.: Brooks/Cole, 1973.

Short, J. F. *Gang delinquency and delinquent subcultures.* New York: Harper & Row, 1969.

Short, J., & Strodtbeck, F. L. *Group process and gang delinquency.* Chicago: University of Chicago Press, 1965.

Shotland, R. L., & Berger, W. G. Behavioral validation of several values from the Rokeach value scale as an index of honesty. *Journal of Applied Psychology,* 1970, *54,* 433–435.

Sigall, H., & Page, R. Current Stereotypes: A little fading, a little faking. *Journal of Personality and Social Psychology,* 1971, *18,* 247–255.

Skinner, B. F. *Science and human behavior.* New York: Macmillan, 1953.

Skinner, B. F. *Beyond freedom and dignity.* New York: Knopf, 1971.

Slack, B. D., & Cook, J. O. Authoritarian behavior in a conflict situation. *Journal of Personality and Social Psychology,* 1973, *25,* 130–136.

Slobodin, L. F., Collins, M. I., Crayton, J. L., Feldman, J. M., Jaccard, J. J., Rissman, K., & Weldon, D. E. *Culture assimilator for interaction with economically disadvantaged.* University of Illinois Department of Psychology Studies of the Economically Disadvantaged (H. C. Triandis, Principal Investigator), Vols. 1–5, 1972.

Snyder, M. The self-monitoring of expressive behavior. *Journal of Personality and Social Psychology,* 1974, *30,* 526–537.

Snyder, M., & Cunningham, M. R. To comply or not comply: Testing the self-perception explanation of the "foot-in-the-door" phenomenon. *Journal of Personality and Social Psychology,* 1975, *31,* 64–67.

Spence, J. T., Helmreich, R., & Stapp, J. The personal attributes questionnaire: A measure of sex role stereotypes and masculinity-femininity. *Catalog of Selected Documents in Psychology,* 1974, *4,* 43.

Staub, E. A child in distress: The effect of focusing responsibility on children on their attempts to help. *Developmental Psychology,* 1969, *2,* 152–153.

Stein, D. D., Hardyck, J. E., & Smith, M. B. Race and belief: An open and shut case. *Journal of Personality and Social Psychology,* 1965, *1,* 281–290.

Steiner, I. D. Perceived freedom. In L. Berkowitz (Ed.), *Advances in experimental social psychology* (Vol. 5). New York: Academic Press, 1970.

Steiner, I. D. The illusion of freedom is no mirage. *Psychology Today,* August 1973, 51–55.

Steiner, I. D., & Johnson, H. H. Authoritarianism and conformity. *Sociometry,* 1963, *26,* 21–34.

Stogdill, R. M., & Coons, A. E. *Leader behavior: Its description and measurement.* Research monograph No. 88, Ohio State University, 1957.

Stotland, E. Exploratory investigations of empathy. In L. Berkowitz (Ed.), *Advances in experimental social psychology* (Vol. 4). New York: Academic Press, 1969.

Streufert, S. Cognitive complexity: A review (TR No. 2). West Lafayette, Ind.: Purdue University, 1972.

Streufert, S., & Driver, M. J. Impression formation as a measure of the complexity of conceptual structure. *Educational and Psychological Measurement,* 1967, *27,* 1025–1039.

Streufert, S., & Streufert, S. C. Effects of conceptual structure, failure, and success on attribution of causality and interpersonal attitudes. *Journal of Personality and Social Psychology,* 1969, *11,* 138–147.

Tannenbaum, P. H. The congruity principle revisited: Studies in the reduction, induction and generalization of persuasion. In L. Berkowitz (Ed.), *Advances in experimental social psychology* (Vol. 3), New York: Academic Press, 1967.

Taylor, D. A. The development of interpersonal relationships: Social penetration processes. *Journal of Social Psychology,* 1968, *75,* 79–90.

Taylor, D. M., & Jaggi, V. Ethnocentrism and causal attribution in a south Indian context. *Journal of Cross-Cultural Psychology,* 1974, *5,* 162–171

Taylor, S. E., & Mattee, D. R. When similarity breeds contempt. *Journal of Personality and Social Psychology,* 1971, *20,* 75–81.

Tesser, A. Attitude similarity and intercorrelations as determinants of interpersonal attraction. *Journal of Experimental Research in Personality,* 1972, *6,* 142–153.

Tesser, A., Gatewood, R., & Driver, M. Some determinants of gratitude. *Journal of Personality and Social Psychology,* 1968, *9,* 233–236.

Thibaut, J., Friedland, N., & Walker, L. Compliance with rules: Some social determinants. *Journal of Personality and Social Psychology,* 1974, *30,* 792–801.

Thibaut, J. W., & Kelley, H. H. *The social psychology of groups.* New York: Wiley, 1959.

Thomas, D. R. Authoritarianism, child rearing, and ethnocentrism. Unpublished doctoral dissertation, University of Queensland, 1972.

Thorndike, E. L. A constant error in psychological ratings. *Journal of Applied Psychology,* 1920, *4,* 25–29.

Touhey, J. C. Comparison of two dimensions of attitude similarity on heterosexual attraction. *Journal of Personality and Social Psychology,* 1972, *23,* 8–10.

Triandis, H. C. Cognitive similarity and interpersonal communication in industry. *Journal of Applied Psychology,* 1959, *43,* 321–326.

Triandis, H. C. Some determinants of interpersonal communication. *Human Relations,* 1960, *13,* 279–287.

Triandis, H. C. A note on Rokeach's theory of prejudice. *Journal of Abnormal and Social Psychology,* 1961, *62,* 184–186.

Triandis, H. C. Factors affecting employee selection in two cultures. *Journal of Applied Psychology,* 1963, *47,* 89–96.

Triandis, H. C. Exploratory factor analyses of the behavioral component of social attitudes. *Journal of Abnormal and Social Psychology,* 1964, *68,* 420–430.

Triandis, H. C. Towards an analysis of the components of interpersonal attitudes. In C. Sherif & M. Sherif (Eds.), *Attitudes, ego involvement and change.* New York: Wiley, 1967.

Triandis, H. C. Some cross-cultural studies of cognitive consistency. In R. P. Abelson, E. Aronson, W. McGuire, T. Newcomb, M. Rosenberg, & P. Tannenbaum (Eds.), *Theories of cognitive consistency: A sourcebook.* Chicago: Rand McNally, 1968.

Triandis, H. C. *Attitude and attitude change.* New York: Wiley, 1971.

Triandis, H. C. The impact of social change on attitudes. In B. King & E. McGinnies (Eds.), *Attitudes, conflict and social change.* New York: Academic Press, 1972.

Triandis, H. C. Culture training, cognitive complexity, and interpersonal attitudes. In R. Brislin, S. Bochner, & W. Lonner (Eds.), *Cross-cultural perspectives on learning.* New York: Sage /Halsted/Wiley. 1975. (a)

Triandis, H. C. Social psychology and cultural analysis. *Journal for the Theory of Social Psychology,* 1975, *5,* 81–106. (b)

Triandis, H. C. (Ed.). *Variations in black and white perceptions of the social environment.* Champaign: University of Illinois Press, 1976.

Triandis, H. C., & Davis, E. E. Race and belief as determinants of behavior intentions. *Journal of Personality and Social Psychology,* 1965, *2,* 715–725.

Triandis, H. C., & Fishbein, M. Cognitive interaction in person perception. *Journal of Abnormal and Social Psychology,* 1963, *67,* 446–453.

Triandis, H. C., Fishbein, M., Hall, E., Shanmugam, A., & Tanaka, Y. Affect and behavioral intentions. In A. K. P. Sinha (Ed.), *Contributions to psychology.* New Delhi, India: Institute for Social and Psychological Research, 1968.

Triandis, H. C., & Lambert, W. W. A restatement and test of Schlosberg's theory of emotion with two kinds of subjects from Greece. *Journal of Abnormal and Social Psychology,* 1958, *56,* 321–332.

Triandis, H. C., McGuire, H., Saral, T., Yang, K., Loh, W., & Vassiliou, V. A cross-cultural study of role perception. In H. C. Triandis (Ed.), *The analysis of subjective culture.* New York: Wiley, 1972.

Triandis, H. C., & Triandis, L. M. Race, social class, religion, and nationality as determinants of social distance. *Journal of Abnormal and Social Psychology,* 1960, *61,* 110–118.

Triandis, H. C., & Vassiliou, V. Frequency of contact and stereotyping. *Journal of Personality and Social Psychology,* 1967, *7,* 316–328.

Triandis, H. C., & Vassiliou, V. A comparative analysis of subjective culture. In H. C. Triandis (Ed.), *The analysis of subjective culture.* New York: Wiley, 1972. (a)

Triandis, H. C., & Vassiliou, V. Interpersonal influence and employee selection in two cultures. *Journal of Applied Psychology,* 1972, *56,* 140–145. (b)

Triandis, H. C., Vassiliou, V., & Nassiakou, M. Three cross-cultural studies of subjective culture. *Journal of Personality and Social Psychology Monograph Supplement,* 1968, *8,* No. 4, 1–42.

Triandis, H. C., Vassiliou, V., & Thomanek, E. K. Social status as a determinant of social acceptance and friendship acceptance. *Sociometry,* 1966, *29,* 396–405.

Triandis, H. C., Vassiliou, V., Vassiliou, G., Tanaka, Y., & Shanmugam, A. *The analysis of subjective culture.* New York: Wiley, 1972.

Triandis, H. C., Weldon, D. E., & Feldman, J. M. Level of abstraction of disagreements as a determinant of interpersonal perception. *Journal of Cross-Cultural Psychology,* 1974, *5,* 59–79.

Tucker, L. A suggested alternative formulation in the developments by Hursch, Hammond, Hursch and Hammond, Hursch and Todd. *Psychological Review,* 1964, *71,* 528–530.

Tucker, L. R., & Messick, S. An individual differences model for multidimensional scaling. *Psychometrika,* 1963, *28,* 333–367.

Tuckman, B. W. Interpersonal probing and revealing and system of integrative complexity. *Journal of Personality and Social Psychology,* 1966, *3,* 655–664.

Turner, J. L., Foa, E., & Foa, U. G. Interpersonal reinforcers: Classification, interrelationship and some differential properties. *Journal of Personality and Social Psychology,* 1971, *19,* 168–180.

Tzeng, O. Personal communication, 1973.

Ulrich, R. E., & Azrin, N. J. Reflexive fighting in response to aversive stimulation. *Journal of Experimental Analysis of Behavior,* 1962, *5,* 511–520.

Ulrich, R. E., & Favell, J. E. Human aggression. In C. Neuringer & J. L. Michael (Eds.), *Behavior modification in clinical psychology.* New York: Appleton-Century-Crofts, 1970.

Vallins, S. Cognitive effects of false heart-rate feed-back. *Journal of Personality and Social Psychology,* 1966, *4,* 400–408.

Vannoy, J. S. Generality of cognitive complexity-simplicity as personality construct. *Journal of Personality and Social Psychology,* 1965, *2,* 385–396.

Vassiliou, V., Triandis, H. C., Vassiliou, G., & McGuire, H. Interpersonal contact and stereotyping. In H. Triandis (Ed.), *The analysis of subjective culture.* New York: Wiley, 1972.

Vassiliou, V., & Vassiliou, G. The implicative meaning of the Greek concept of *Philotio. Journal of Cross-Cultural Psychology,* 1973, *4,* 326–341.

Vroom, V. H. *Work and motivation.* New York: Wiley, 1964.

Walster, E. Assignment of responsibility for an accident. *Journal of Personality and Social Psychology,* 1966, *3,* 73–79.

Walster, E. Passionate love. In B. I. Murstein (Ed.), *Theories of attraction and love.* New York: Springer, 1971.

Walster, E., Aronson, V., Abrahams, D., & Rottmann, L. Importance of physical attractiveness in dating behavior. *Journal of Personality and Social Psychology,* 1966, *4,* 508–516.

Walster, E., Berscheid, E., & Walster, W. New directions in equity theory. *Journal of Personality and Social Psychology,* 1973, *25,* 151–176.

Walster, E., Walster, G. W., Piliavin, J., & Schmidt, L. "Playing hard to get": Understanding an elusive phenomenon. *Journal of Personality and Social Psychology,* 1973, *26,* 113–121.

Walters, R. H., & Brown, M. Studies of reinforcement of aggression. III: Transfer of response to an interpersonal situation. *Child Development,* 1963, *34,* 563–571.

Warner, L. G., & DeFleur, M. L. Attitude as an interactional concept: Social constraint and social distance as intervening variables between attitudes and action. *American Sociological Review,* 1969, *34,* 153–169.

Warr, P. Inference magnitude, range, and evaluative direction as factors affecting relative importance of cues in impression formation. *Journal of Personality and Social Psychology,* 1974, *30,* 191–197.

Warr, P. B., & Haycock, V. Scales for a British Personality Differential. *British Journal of Social and Clinical Psychology,* 1970, *9,* 328–337.

Warr, P. B., & Knapper, C. *The perception of people and events.* New York: Wiley, 1968.

Warr, P., & Smith, J. S. Combining information about people: Comparisons between six models. *Journal of Personality and Social Psychology,* 1970, *16,* 55–65.

Watson, O. M. *Proxemic behavior.* The Hague: Mouton, 1970.

Watson, R. I., Jr. Investigation into deindividuation using a cross-cultural survey technique. *Journal of Personality and Social Psychology,* 1973, *25,* 342–345.

Webster, E. C. *Decision making in the employment interview.* Montreal: Industrial Relations Center, McGill University, 1964.

Weigel, R. H., Vernon, D. T. A., & Tognacci, L. H. The specificity of the attitude as a determinant of attitude-behavior congruence. *Journal of Personality and Social Psychology,* 1974, *30,* 724–728.

Weiner, B., Frieze, I., Kukla, A., Reed, L., Rest, S., & Rosenbaum, R. M. Perceiving the causes of success and failure. In E. E. Jones, D. E. Kanouse, H. H. Kelley, R. E. Nisbett, S. Valins & B. Weiner (Eds.), *Attribution: Perceiving the causes of behavior.* Morristown, N.J.: General Learning Corp., 1972.

Weiner, B., & Kukla, A. An attributional analysis of achievement motivation. *Journal of Personality and Social Psychology,* 1970, *15,* 1–20.

Weinstein, A. G. Predicting behavior from attitudes. *The Public Opinion Quarterly,* 1972, *36,* 355–360.

Weiss, R. F. Some determinants of emitted reinforcing behavior: Listener reinforcement and birth order. *Journal of Personality and Social Psychology,* 1966, *9,* 489–492.

Weiss, R. F., Boyer, J. L., Colwick, J. T., & Moran, D. J. A delay of reinforcement gradient and correlated reinforcement in the instrumental conditioning of conversational behavior. *Journal of Experimental Psychology,* 1971, *90,* 33–38.

Weiss, R. F., Lombardo, J. P., Warren, D. R., & Kelley, K. A. Reinforcing effects of speaking in reply. *Journal of Personality and Social Psychology,* 1971, *20,* 186–199.

Weitz, S. Attitude, voice, and behavior: A repressed affect model of interracial integration. *Journal of Personality and Social Psychology,* 1972, *24,* 14–21.

Weldon, D. E., Carlston, D. E., Rissman, A. K., Slobodin, L., & Triandis, H. C. A laboratory test of effects of culture assimilator training. *Journal of Personality and Social Psychology,* 1975, *32,* 300–310.

Werner, H. *Comparative psychology of mental development.* New York: International Universities Press, 1948.

Wheeler, L. Social comparison and selective affiliation. In T. L. Huston (Ed.), *Foundations of interpersonal attraction.* New York: Academic Press, 1974.

Wheeler, L., & Wagner, C. M. The contagion of generosity. Paper presented at the meetings of the Eastern Psychological Association, Washington, D. C., 1968.

Whiting, J. W. M. Effects of climate on certain cultural practices. In W. H. Goodenough (Ed.), *Explorations in cultural anthropology.* New York: McGraw-Hill, 1964.

Whiting, J. W. M., & Whiting, B. B. *Children of six cultures: A psychocultural analysis.* Cambridge, Mass.: Harvard University Press, 1975.

Whyte, W. F. *Street corner society: The social structure of an Italian slum.* Chicago: University of Chicago Press, 1943.

Whyte, W. F. *Human relations in the restaurant business.* New York: McGraw Hill, 1948.

Whyte, W. H., Jr. *The organization man.* New York: Simon & Schuster, 1956.

Wicker, A. W. Attitudes versus actions: The relationship of verbal and overt behavioral responses to attitudinal objects. *Journal of Social Issues, 1969, 25,* 41–78.

Wicker, A. W. An examination of the "other variables" explanation of attitude-behavior inconsistency. *Journal of Personality and Social Psychology, 1971, 19,* 18–30.

Wicker, A. W. Processes which mediate behavior-environment congruence. *Behavior Science, 1972, 17,* 265–277.

Wicker, A. W., & Bushweiler, G. Perceived fairness and pleasantness of social exchange situations: Two factorial studies of inequity. *Journal of Personality and Social Psychology, 1970, 15,* 63–75.

Wiggins, J., Wiggins, N., & Conger, J. Correlates of heterosexual somatic preference. *Journal of Personality and Social Psychology, 1968, 10,* 82–89.

Wiggins, N. Individual differences in human judgment: A multivariate approach. In L. Rappaport & D. Summers (Eds.), *Human judgment and social interaction.* New York: Holt, Rinehart and Winston, 1971.

Wiggins, N., Hoffman, P. J., & Taber, T. Types of judges and cue utilization in judgments of intelligence. *Journal of Personality and Social Psychology, 1969, 12,* 52–59.

Wight, A. R. *Cross-cultural training: A draft handbook.* Estes Park, Colo.: Center for Research and Education, 1969.

Willis, J. A., & Goethals, G. R. Social responsibility and threat to behavioral freedom as determinants of altruistic behavior. *Journal of Personality, 1973, 41,* 376–384.

Willis, R. H. An equilibration theory of cognitive dynamics. Paper presented at the Canadian Psychological Association meeting in Saint Johns, Newfoundland, 1971.

Winch, R. F., Ktsanes, T., & Ktsanes, V. Empirical elaboration of the theory of complementary needs in mate selection. *Journal of Abnormal and Social Psychology, 1955, 51,* 508–513.

Wishner, J. Reanalysis of "Impressions of personality." *Psychological Review, 1960, 67,* 96–112.

Witkin, H. A. Psychological differentiation and forms of pathology. *Journal of Abnormal Psychology, 1965, 70,* 317–336.

Witkin, H. A., Dyk, R. B., Fatuson, H. F., Goodenough, D. R., & Karp, S. A. *Psychological differentiation.* New York: Wiley, 1962.

Wolpe, J. *Psychotherapy of reciprocal inhibition.* Stanford, Calif.: Stanford University Press, 1958.

Wolpe, J. *The practice of behavior therapy.* New York: Pergamon Press, 1969.

Wright, P. H., & Crawford, A. C. Agreement and friendship: A close look and some second thoughts. *Representative Research in Social Psychology.* 1971, *2*, No. 2.

Wyer, R. S., Jr. Category ratings as "subjective expected values": Implications for attitude formation and change. *Psychological Review,* 1973, *80,* 446–467.

Wyer, R. S., Jr., & Watson, S. F. Context effects in impression formation. *Journal of Personality and Social Psychology,* 1969, *12,* 22–33.

Zajonc, R. B. Social facilitation. *Science,* 1965, *149,* 269–274.

Zajonc, R. B. Attitudinal effects of mere exposure. *Journal of Personality and Social Psychology Monograph Supplement,* 1968, *9,* (2, Pt. 2), 2–27.

Zavalloni, M. Subjective culture, self-concept and social environment. *International Journal of Psychology,* 1973, *8,* 183–192.

Ziller, R. C. *The social self.* New York: Pergamon Press, 1973.

Ziller, R. C., Long, B. H., Ramana, K. V., & Reddy, W. E. Self-orientation of Indian and American adolescents. *Journal of Personality,* 1968, *36,* 315–330.

Zillman, D. Excitation transfer in communication-mediated aggressive behavior. *Journal of Experimental Social Psychology,* 1971, *7,* 419–434.

Zillman, D., Katcher, A. H., & Milavsky, B. Excitation transfer from physical exercise to subsequent aggressive behavior. *Journal of Experimental Social Psychology,* 1972, *8,* 247–259.

Zimbardo, P. G. The human choice: Individuation, reason and order versus deindividuation, impulse and chaos. In *Nebraska Symposium on Motivation,* 1969, 237–307.

AUTHOR INDEX

SUBJECT INDEX